Lecture Notes in Artificial Intelligence   5388

Edited by R. Goebel, J. Siekmann, and W. Wahlster

Subseries of Lecture Notes in Computer Science

Tom Schrijvers   Thom Frühwirth (Eds.)

Constraint Handling Rules

Current Research Topics

 Springer

Volume Editors

Tom Schrijvers
Katholieke Universiteit Leuven, Department of Computer Science
Celestijnenlaan 200A, 3001 Heverlee, Belgium
E-mail: tom.schrijvers@cs.kuleuven.be

Thom Frühwirth
Universität Ulm, Fakultät für Ingenieurwissenschaften und Informatik
89069 Ulm, Germany
E-mail: thom.fruehwirth@uni-ulm.de

Library of Congress Control Number: 2008942100

CR Subject Classification (1998): I.2.3-4, I.2, D.3.2, D.3.3, F.4.1, D.1.6

LNCS Sublibrary: SL 7 – Artificial Intelligence

ISSN   0302-9743
ISBN-10   3-540-92242-3 Springer Berlin Heidelberg New York
ISBN-13   978-3-540-92242-1 Springer Berlin Heidelberg New York

springer.com

© Springer-Verlag Berlin Heidelberg 2008
Printed in Germany

Typesetting: Camera-ready by author, data conversion by Scientific Publishing Services, Chennai, India
Printed on acid-free paper   SPIN: 12590667   06/3180   5 4 3 2 1 0

Preface

The Constraint Handling Rules (CHR) language came to life more than 15 years ago. Since then, it has become a major declarative specification and implementation language for constraint-based algorithms and applications. In recent years, the five Workshops on Constraint Handling Rules have spurred the exchange of ideas within the CHR community, which has led to increased international collaboration, new theoretical results and optimized implementations.

The aim of this volume of *Lecture Notes in Aritificial Intelligence* was to attract high-quality research papers on these recent advances in CHR. The 8 papers in this issue were selected from 11 submissions after careful reviewing and subsequent revisions. Each paper was reviewd by three reviewers. The accepted papers represent some of the research teams on CHR around the world. It is not by accident that the currently most active research group is featured here with three articles. We also would have liked to see contributions from other CHR teams, but space is limited and the reviewers took their job seriously.

After an introductory article that foreshadows an upcoming monograph on CHR, the accepted papers span a range of current research topics in the CHR community. It goes from extending the CHR language with search facilities and the related adaptive framework, and from generating rules from specifications of constraint solvers to implementing abductive probabilistic reasoning. They cover the theory that is a compositional semantics for CHR and finally describe efficient implementations of CHR in traditional mainstream programming languages and compiler optimizations in the context of the refined semantics of CHR.

We would like to thank the authors of submitted papers and the many reviewers for their contribution in making this collection of research papers possible.

October 2008

Tom Schrijvers
Thom Frühwirth

Organization

Referees

S. Abdennadher
M. Alberti
H. Betz
S. Brand
F. Chesani
H. Christiansen
L. De Koninck
G. Duck

F. Fages
M. Gabbrielli
R. Haemmerlé
M. Maher
M. C. Meo
E. Monfroy
P. Pilozzi
J. Robin

B. Sarna-Starosta
T. Schrijvers
J. Sneyers
M. Sulzmann
P. Tacchella
P. Van Weert
A. Wolf
P. Wuille

Table of Contents

Introduction

Search

Applications

Theory

Implementation

Welcome to Constraint Handling Rules

Thom Frühwirth

University of Ulm,
Germany
www.informatik.uni-ulm.de/pm/mitarbeiter/fruehwirth/

Abstract. Constraint Handling Rules (CHR) is a declarative concurrent committed-choice constraint logic programming language consisting of guarded rules that transform multisets of relations called constraints until no more change occurs. As an introduction to CHR as a general-purpose programming language we present some small programs using different programming styles and discuss their properties.

1 Introduction

Constraint Handling Rules (CHR) [Frü98, FA03, AFE05, SF05, Frü08] has not only cut its niche as a special-purpose language for writing constraint solvers, but also has been employed more and more as a general-purpose language in computational logic, reasoning and beyond. This is because CHR can embed many rule-based formalisms and implement algorithms in a declarative yet effective way.

CHR was motivated by the inference rules that are traditionally used in computer science to define logical relationships and arbitrary fixpoint computations. Like automated theorem proving, CHR uses formulae to derive new information, but only in a restricted syntax (e.g., no negation) and in a directional way (e.g., no contrapositives) that makes the difference between the art of proof search and an efficient programming language.

CHR adapts concepts from term rewriting systems (TRS) [BN98] for program analysis, for properties such as confluence [AFM99] and termination (e.g. [Frü00]). Other influences for the design of CHR were the General Abstract Model for Multiset Manipulation (GAMMA) [BCM88] and, of course, production rule systems like OPS5 [BFKM85], but also integrity constraints and event-condition-action rules found in relational databases and in deductive databases.

Implementations of CHR are abundant now. CHR does not necessarily impose itself as a new programming language, but as a language extension that blends in with the syntax of its host language, be it Prolog, Lisp, Haskell, C or Java. In the host language, CHR constraints can be posted; in the CHR rules, host language statements can be included.

The example programs here illustrate different programming styles in CHR. This paper is based on some example programs of the author's upcoming book on CHR [Frü08].

T. Schrijvers and T. Frühwirth (Eds.): Constraint Handling Rules, LNAI 5388, pp. 1–15, 2008.

2   Preliminaries

A *CHR program P* is a finite set of rules consisting of constraints. (We do not discuss declarations for CHR constraints here since they are implementation-specific.) There are three kinds of rules:

> *Simplification rule: Name* @ $H \Leftrightarrow G \mid B$
> [Name '@'] H '<=>' [G '|'] B.
> *Propagation rule:*   *Name* @ $H \Rightarrow G \mid B$
> [Name '@'] H '==>' [G '|'] B.
> *Simpagation rule:*   *Name* @ $H_1 \backslash H_2 \Leftrightarrow G \mid B$
> [Name '@'] H1 '\' H2 '==>' [G '|'] B.

Name is an optional, unique identifier of a rule, the *(multi-)head (lhs, left hand side) H* (or H_1 and H_2) is a non-empty conjunction of CHR constraints, the optional *guard G* is a conjunction of built-in constraints, and the *body (rhs, right hand side) B* is a goal. A *goal* is a conjunction of built-in and CHR constraints. If the guard is omitted from a rule, it means the same as *"true |"*.

Built-in constraints are predefined by the host language, while CHR constraints are defined by CHR rules.

Declaratively, a CHR rule logically relates head and body provided the guard is true. A simplification rule means that the head is true if and only if the body is true. A propagation rule means that the body is true if the head is true. A simpagation rule Head1 \ Head2 <=> Body is logically equivalent to the simplification rule Head1, Head2 <=> Head1, Body.

Basically, rules are applied to an initial conjunction of constraints (syntactically, a goal) until exhaustion (saturation), i.e. until no more change happens. An initial goal is called *query*. The intermediate goals of a computation are stored in the so-called *(constraint) store*. A final goal (store), to which no more rule is applicable, is called *answer (constraint)* or *result (of the computation)*.

We describe here (sequential) implementations according to the *refined operational semantics* [DSdlBH04] of CHR. Parallel or experimental implementations may apply the rules in different ways, but of course still respect the *standard abstract operational semantics* [Abd97].

A CHR constraint is both *code* and *data*. Every time a CHR constraint is posted (added, called, executed, asserted, imposed) as part of a goal, it checks itself the applicability of the rules it appears in. Such a constraint is called (currently) *active*. One tries and applies rules in the order they are written in the program, i.e. top-down and from left to right.

An active constraint is code which is evaluated like a procedure call. If, at the moment, no rule is applicable that removes it, the active constraint becomes passive data in the constraint store. It is called *(currently) passive* (delayed, suspended, spleeping, waiting).

Passive constraints may be woken (reconsidered, resumed, re-executed) to become active code if the environment (context) changes, concretely if their arguments get more constrained. This is the case if a variable occurring in the constraint gets more constrained by a built-in constraint.

There are several computational phases when a CHR rule is *tried* (for application) and finally *applied (executed, triggered)* (then it *fires*). These phases correspond to the constituents of a rule, read from left to right:

Head Matching. For each rule, one of its head constraints is matched against the active constraint. Matching succeeds if the constraint is an instance of the head, i.e., the head serves as a pattern. If matching succeeded and the rule has more than one head constraint, the constraint store is searched for *partner* constraints that match the other head constraints. Head constraints are searched from left to right, except that in simpagation rules, the constraints to be removed are tried before the head constraints to be kept (this is done for efficiency reasons). If the matching succeeds, the guard is checked. If there are several head constraints that match the active constraint, the rule is tried for each such matching. Otherwise the next rule is tried.

Guard Checking. A guard is a precondition on the applicability of a rule. The guard is basically a test that either succeeds or fails. If the guard succeeds, the rule applies, one *commits* to it and it fires. Otherwise the next rule is tried.

Body Execution. If the firing rule is a simplification rule, the matched constraints are removed from the store and the body of the rule is executed by executing the constraints in the body from left to right. Similarly for a firing simpagation rule, except that the constraints that matched the head part preceding '\' are kept. If the firing rule is a propagation rule the body of the rule is executed without removing any constraints. It is remembered that the propagation rule fired, so it will not fire again with the same constraints. When the currently active constraint has not been removed, the next rule is tried. According to rule type, we say that CHR constraints matching some constraint in the head of the rule are either *kept* or *removed* constraints.

3   Multiset Transformation

The following simple algorithms are similar to the ones found in other rule-based approaches, namely production rule systems and the GAMMA model of computation, but in CHR the programs are more concise.

The General Abstract Model for Multiset Manipulation (GAMMA) framework employs a *chemical metaphor*. States in a computation are chemical solutions where floating molecules interact freely according to reaction rules. Reactions can be performed in parallel provided they involve disjoint sets of molecules. This is referred to as *logical parallelism or declarative concurrency*. We can model molecules as CHR constraints.

These programs consist essentially of one constraint for representing *active data*. Pairs of such constraints are rewritten by a single simplification rule. Often, the rule can be written more compactly as a simpagation rule where one of the constraints (the catalyst) is kept and the other is removed and possibly replaced by an updated one. Optimizing CHR compilers will compile this to an efficient in-place update instead of removing and adding constraints.

3.1   Minimum

We compute the minimum of a multiset of numbers n_i, given as a computation of the query min(n_1), min(n_2),..., min(n_k). We interpret min(n_i) to mean that the number n_i is potentially the minimum, that it is a *candidate* for the minimum value.

```
min(N) \ min(M) <=> N=<M | true.
```

The simpagation rule takes two `min` candidates and removes the one with the larger value. It keeps going until only one, the smallest value, remains as single `min` constraint. The program illustrates the use of multi-headed rules instead of explicit loops or recursion for iteration over data. This keeps the code extremely compact and easy to analyse. The rule corresponds to the intuitive algorithm that when we are to find the minimum from a given a list of numbers, we just cross out larger numbers until one, the minimum, remains.

For example, this computation is possible (where constraints involved in a rule application are underlined)

```
min(1), min(0), min(2), min(1)
min(0), min(2), min(1)
min(0), min(1)
min(0)
```

Program Properties. We used the rule application order of the *refined semantics* of CHR implementations, where computation in a query proceeds from left to right. In the *abstract semantics*, any order of rule applications is allowed, for example also:

```
min(1), min(0), min(2), min(1)
min(1), min(0), min(1)
min(0), min(1)
min(0)
```

In the two examples above, the answer is the same. Actually, it is easy to see that the answer will always be the same, i.e. the minimum value, no matter in which order the rules are applied to which pair of constraints. We call this property *confluence*.

The rules can even be applied in *parallel* to different parts of the query.

```
min(1), min(0),      min(2), min(1)
min(0),              min(1)
min(0)
```

Obviously we arrive at the answer in less *computation steps*.

The program is obviously terminating, because the rule removes a CHR constraint and does not introduce new ones. Therefore the number of rule applications is one less than the number of `min` constraints. We can apply a rule in constant time. Given any two `min` constraints, we can always apply the rule - either in one pairing order or in the other. Therefore the complexity of this little program is linear in the number of min constraints, i.e. linear in the size of the initial goal.

We can also stop the computation at *any time* and observe the current store as intermediate answer. We can then continue by applying rules to this store without the need to recompute from scratch and no need to remember anything about how we arrived at the current store. If we stop again, we will observe another intermediate answer that is closer to the final answer than the one before. By closer we mean here that the store has less min constraints, i.e. less candidates for the final minimum. The intermediate answers more and more approximate the final answer. This property of a CHR program is called *anytime algorithm property*. Note that by this description, an anytime algorithm is also an *approximation algorithm*.

Now assume that while the program runs, we add a min constraint. It will eventually participate in the computation in that the rule will be applied to it. The answer will be correct, as if the newly added constraint had been there from the beginning but ignored for some time. This property of a CHR program is called *incrementality* or *online algorithm property*.

Guard Checking. So far we assumed that the min constraints contain given values. In that case, the guard acts as a test that compares two such values. But in general, under the *abstract standard semantics*, even though not necessarily in a given CHR implementation, the guard is made out of built-in constraints that hold if they are logically implied by the current *store*. While in current practical implementations of CHR, a guard check will give an instantion error or silently fail if unbound variables occur in it, the same guard check may succeed under the abstract semantics. For example, the query min(A), min(B), A=<B will reduce to min(A), A=<B, because we know that A=<B and that is exactly what the guard asks for. Similarily, the query min(A), min(B), A<B will reduce to min(A), A<B. Finally, the query min(A), min(A) will reduce to min(A). But the query min(A), min(B) will not proceed, because we know nothing about the relationship of the unknown values A and B.

Now consider what happens if we modify the program in that we strenghten the guard. If we replace N=<M by N<M, *multiple occurrences* (*duplicates*) of the final minimum constraint will no longer be removed. If we replace N=<M by N=M, we will just remove duplicates. Both rules taken together have the same behavior as our initial rule, provided we work with known values.

```
min(N) \ min(M) <=> N<M | true.
min(N) \ min(M) <=> N=M | true.
```

If values are only partially known, it turns out the the two rules are weaker than the single initial rule. Consider the previous examples. Most of them still work, but the query min(A), min(B), A=<B will not reduce at all, because the built-in constraint A=<B is too weak to imply one of the guards of the two rules, A<B or A=B. We say that these two programs are not *operationally equivalent*, even though logically, they are. (The logical reading of rules as formulae is their declarative semantics [Abd97].)

Variations. If we want to use this rule for minimum in a larger program, we may be faced with some pragmatical issues. We may want to compute several minima from different sources and need to dinstinguish them. It suffices to add an identifier to the `min` constraint and modify the minimum rule so that it refers only to constraints with the same identifier:

```
min(Id,N) \ min(Id,M) <=> N=<M | true.
```

In general, this technique of adding an explicit identifier to each constraint can be used to localize computations, i.e. to implement *local constraint stores*.

3.2   Prime Numbers Sieve of Erastosthenes

We implement the algorithm known as Sieve of Erastosthenes, but without any particular sifting order. Given some numbers, the rule just removes multiples of each of the numbers.

```
sift @ prime(I) \ prime(J) <=> J mod I =:= 0 | true.
```

We give the rule a conjunction of prime number candidates consisting of all numbers from 2 up to N, i.e., `prime(2),prime(3),prime(4),...prime(N)`. The candidates react with each other such that each number absorbs multiples of itself. When we give it all integers up to a given bound starting from 2, all composite numbers will be removed after exhaustive application of the rule, so that only prime numbers remain.

For example, this computation is possible

```
prime(7), prime(6), prime(5), prime(4), prime(3), prime(2)
prime(7), prime(5), prime(4), prime(3), prime(2)
prime(7), prime(5), prime(3), prime(2)
```

The `sift` rule is similar to the one for minimum in that it compares two numbers and removes one of them. But unlike minimum, the rule is not applicable to arbitrary pairs of prime number candidates.

As before, the program has the desirable properties that are typical for CHR. For example, the rule is obviously terminating, since it removes constraints without adding new ones.

Generating Numbers. To generate the prime number candidates, we may use an auxiliary CHR constraint `upto`[1]:

```
upto(1) <=> true.
upto(N) <=> N>1 | prime(N), upto(N-1).
```

To the same effect, we can use the `prime` constraint itself.

```
prime(N) ==> N>2 | prime(N-1).
```

Of course, this rule must come before the `sift` rule. Otherwise a prime number candidate may be removed before generating its predecessors.

---

[1] For readability, we use arithmetic expressions like `N-1` in arguments, while in Prolog, one may explicitly have to compute the result using `is/2`.

Both rule variants generate the prime candidates in descending order. Increasing order is preferable, because smaller prime candidates increase the chance that the `sift` rule is applicable. We can easily fix `upto` by exchanging the recursive call with the generation of the prime:

```
upto(N) <=> N>1 | upto(N-1), prime(N).
```

We cannot fix the variation using `prime` itself this way.

Primes Sieve in CHR for Java. The following code implements the three rules for primes in JCK, the first CHR implementation in Java. The syntax of CHR rules was chosen to be similar to that of the host language Java. For example, guards are not written between head and body of a rule, but as `if` expressions before the head. The rule name comes last. This illustrates that the concrete syntax of CHR is not fixed, but rather can be adapted to the host language.

```
handler primes { class java.lang.Integer; class IntUtil;

constraint prime(java.lang.Integer);
constraint upto(java.lang.Integer);

rules { variable java.lang.Integer N, M, I, J;

        {upto(1)} <=> {true} ;
        if (IntUtil.gt(N,1)) {upto(N)} <=>
                            {M=IntUtil.dec(N) && prime(N) && upto(M)};

        if (IntUtil.modNull(J,I)){prime(I) &\& prime(J)} <=>
                                                    {true} sift;

        }
}
```

A more recent implementation of CHR in Java, the K.U.Leuven JCHR system, uses the more traditional Prolog-style concrete syntax of CHR, which eases porting of code between Prolog and Java CHR systems.

```
handler primes {

    constraint upto(int);
    constraint prime(int);

rules { variable int N, I, J;

        upto(1) <=> true.
        upto(N) <=> IntUtil.gt(N,1)|prime(N), upto(intUtil.dec(N)).

        sift @ prime(I) \ prime(J) <=> intUtil.modZero(J,I) | true.
        }
}
```

4   Procedural Algorithms

We now employ a more tradional style of programming, where constraints are relations that resemble procedures as they are used in imperative programming languages. Results of a computation are not returned as constraints, but as values of variables that are bound. As we will already see with our first example of Fibonacci numbers, CHR supports different programming styles and it is easy to change between them.

4.1   Fibonacci

The n-th Fibonacci number is defined inductively as follows:

$$fib(0) = fib(1) = 1; fib(n) = fib(n{-}1) + fib(n{-}2) \text{ if } n \geq 2$$

When we implement this definition in CHR, we translate the functional notation of fib into relational notation, and the equivalence becomes a simplification rule.

Top-Down Evaluation. The CHR constraint fib(N,M) holds if the N-th Fibonacci number is M.

```
f0 @ fib(0,M) <=> M=1.
f1 @ fib(1,M) <=> M=1.
fn @ fib(N,M) <=> N>=2 | fib(N-1,M1), fib(N-2,M2), M is M1+M2.
```

The three rules are a direct translation of the definition. For example, the query fib(8,A) yields A=89, the query fib(12,233) succeeds, the query fib(11,233) fails, the query fib(N,233) delays.

As is well known, such a direct implementation has exponential time complexity because of the double recursion that recomputes the same Fibonacci numbers over and over again in different parts of the recursions.

Tabling and Memorization. We would like to store the results of Fibonacci numbers that we already have computed and look them up to avoid computing the same Fibonacci number several times. Since CHR constraints are both *operations and data*, it is easy to change the rules accordingly. We just have to turn the three simplification rules into propagation rules, so that the left hand side constraints are kept. In this way the result of the computation will be kept in the constraint store as data.

The rule for the look-up of already computed Fibonacci numbers has to come first, so that it is applied before we compute in the usual way using the expensive recursive definition.

```
mem @ fib(N,M1) \ fib(N,M2) <=> M1=M2.

f0 @ fib(0,M) ==> M=1.
f1 @ fib(1,M) ==> M=1.
fn @ fib(N,M) ==> N>=2 | fib(N-1,M1), fib(N-2,M2), M is M1+M2.
```

The rule `mem` for look-up enforces the functional dependency between input and output of the Fibonacci relation, in other words it uses the fact the `fib` defines a function. The query `fib(8,A)` now returns *all* Fibonacci numbers up to 8: `fib1(0,1)`, `fib1(1,1)`, `fib1(2,2)`, ..., `fib1(7,21)`, `fib1(8,34)`.

The effect of memorization is dramatic: while the original rules have exponential complexity, the new version has only linear complexity, because each Fibonacci number is only computed once. When executed from left to right, the second recursive call is just a lookup using the `mem` rule. Actually, the `mem` rule does more than just looking up computed results, it in effect merges two computations that must have the same result into one, even if both computations are still ongoing. To see this, consider a query `fib(N,A)` with `N>=2`, where the N-th Fibonacci number is computed for the first time. The constraint `fib(N,A)` will thus try the `mem` rule in vain and finally the recursive rule `fn` will apply. Since it is a propagation rule, the constraint `fib(N,A)` will not be removed.

If the N-th Fibonacci number is called again, say with `fib(N,B)`, then the constraint `fib(N,B)` will try the `mem` rule, and there it will first try to match the constraint to the right of \ under the refined semantics. This succeeds and the old `fib(N,A)` is found as a *partner constraint*. The rule applies, the new `fib(N,B)` will be removed and instead the variables for the result will be equated using `A=B`.

Bottom-Up Evaluation. Another way of computing the Fibonacci numbers efficiently is by using only data and compute larger numbers from smaller ones. Basically, the idea is to reverse head and body of the rules.

```
fn @ fib(N1,M1), fib(N2,M2) ==> N2=:=N1+1 | fib(N2+1,M1+M2).
```

Since reversing the rules `f0` and `f1` gives ill-formed CHR rules (they do not have a head), we added the first two Fibonacci numbers in the query, `fib(0,1)`, `fib(1,1)`. Of course, the resulting computation is infinite, and in order to observe the results, we have to add a rule in front such as:

```
fib(N,M) ==> write(fib(N,M)).
```

Note that if we are only interested in the Fibonacci numbers, we could drop the first arguments of `fib`.

The computation can be made finite by introducing an upper bound `Max`. The query `fib_upto(Max)` will produce all Fibonacci numbers up to `Max`. The constraint `fib_upto(Max)` is also used to introduce the first two Fibonacci numbers.

```
f01@ fib_upto(Max) ==> fib(0,1), fib(1,1).
fn @ fib_upto(Max), fib(N1,M1), fib(N2,M2) ==>
                    Max>N2, N2=:=N1+1 | fib(N2+1,M1+M2).
```

A version that is faster than any discussed so far can be achieved with a tiny change in the previous program: we turn the propagation rule into a simpagation rule that only keeps the (last) two Fibonacci numbers (we do not need more information to compute the next one).

```
fn @ fib_upto(Max), fib(N2,M2) \ fib(N1,M1) <=>
                    Max>N2, N2=:=N1+1 | fib(N2+1,M1+M2).
```

We have exchanged the order of the two `fib` constraints in the head so that the simpagation rule removes the smaller Fibonacci number.

Procedural Style Version. Since we now keep only the two last Fibonacci numbers, we can merge the three constraints of the head of the `fn` rule into one constraint, and the same for the three constraints that will be present after the rule has been applied (the two kept constraints from the head and the new one from the body). The resulting code is the most efficient:

```
f01@ fib_upto(Max) <=> fib(Max,1,1,1).
fn @ fib(Max,N,M1,M2) <=> Max>N | fib(Max,N+1,M2,M1+M2).
```

4.2 Newton's Method for Square Roots

Newton iteration is an approximation method for the value of polynomial expressions relying on derivates. We would like to compute the square root. As can be computed by Newton's method, the approximations for square roots are related by the formula $G_{i+1} = (G_i+X/G_i)/2$.

Since CHR programs already implement anytime, i.e. approximation algorithms, the implementation in CHR is straightforward. We assume that the answer is returned as a CHR constraint. `sqrt(X,G)` means that the square root of X is approximated by G. This rule computes the next approximation.

```
sqrt(X,G) <=> abs(G*G/X-1)>0 | sqrt(X,(G+X/G)/2).
```

The query is just `sqrt(GivenNumber,Guess)`. Both numbers must be positive, and if no guess is known, we may take 1. The guard stops its application if the approximation is exact. Since this is unlikely in practice when floating point numbers are used and also to improve efficiency by avoiding iterations, we replace 0 in the guard by a sufficiently small positive number ϵ.

Since the quality of approximation is often in the eye of the beholder, we may implement a more interesting, *demand-driven* version of the algorithm. An approximation step is performed *lazily*, only on demand, which is expressed by the constraint `improve(Expression)`.

```
improve(sqrt(X)), sqrt(X,G) <=> sqrt(X,(G+X/G)/2).
```

Of course the constraint `improve` can be extended with a counter or combined with a check for the quality of the approximation.

5 Graph-Based Algorithms

5.1 Transitive Closure

Transitive closure is an essential operation that occurs in many algorithms, e.g. for graphs, in automated reasoning and inside constraint solvers. The transitive closure R^+ of a binary relation R is the smallest transitive relation that contains

R. The relation xR^+y holds iff there exists a finite sequence of elements x_i such that $xRx_1, x_1Rx_2, \ldots, x_{n-1}Rx_n, x_nRy$ holds.

For example, if R is the parent relation, then its transitive closure R^+ is the ancestor relation. If R is the relation of cities connected by direct trains, then its transitive closure also contains cities reachable by changing trains.

We can depict the relation R as a *directed graph*, where there is a *directed edge (arc)* from node (vertex) x to node y iff xRy holds. The transitive closure then corresponds to all paths in the graph. The *length of the path* is the number of edges in the path.

We implement the relation xRy as edge constraint e(X,Y) and its transitive closure xR^+y as path constraint p(X,Y).

```
e(X,Y) ==> p(X,Y).
e(X,Y), p(Y,Z) ==> p(X,Z).
```

The implementation in CHR uses two propagation rules that compute the transitive closure *bottom-up*. In the first rule, for each edge, a corresponding path is added. The rule reads: If there is an edge from X to Y then there is also a path from X to Y. The second rule extends an existing path with an edge in front. It reads: If there is an edge from X to Y and a path from Y to Z then there is also a path from X to Z.

For example, the query e(1,2), e(2,3), e(2,4) adds the path constraints p(1,4),p(2,4),p(1,3),p(2,3),p(1,2). Query e(1,2), e(2,3), e(1,3) will compute p(1,3) *twice*, because there are two ways to go from node 1 to node 3, directly or via node 2.

Termination. The program does not terminate with a cyclic graph. Consider the query e(1,1), where infinitely many paths p(1,1) are generated by the second propagation rule. There are various compiler optimizations and options that avoid the repeated generation of the same constraint in this context, but here we are interested in a source-level solution that works in any implementation that follows the *refined semantics*.

Duplicate Removal. Termination can be restored easily by removing *duplicate* path constraints before they can be used. In other words, we would like to enforce a *set-based semantics* for path constraints. This is ensures termination, since in a given finite graph, there can only be a finite number of different paths. This *simpagation rule* removes duplicates:

```
p(X,Y) \ p(X,Y) <=> true.
```

The rule must come first in the program.

Single-Source Paths. We may specialize the transitive closure rules so that only paths that reach a given single target node are computed. We simply add the target node as a constraint:

```
target(Y), e(X,Y) ==> p(X,Y).
target(Z), e(X,Y), p(Y,Z) ==> p(X,Z).
```

However, this does not work if we want to fix the source node in the same way:

```
source(X), e(X,Y) ==> p(X,Y).
source(X), e(X,Y), p(Y,Z) ==> p(X,Z).
```

The reason is that in the second rule we need a path from Y to Z to be extended, but we only produce paths starting in X. If we exchange the edge and path constraints in the second rule so that we add an edge at the end of an existing path, then we can add a restriction to a source node as simply as before:

```
source(X), e(X,Y) ==> p(X,Y).
source(X), p(X,Y), e(Y,Z) ==> p(X,Z).
```

Shortest Path Lengths. Let us add an argument to the path constraint that holds the length of the path. When we adapt the duplicate removal rule, we keep the shorter path. This also ensures termination. The path propagated from an edge has length 1. A path of length n extended by an edge has length $n + 1$.

```
p(X,Y,N) \ p(X,Y,M) <=> N=<M | true.
e(X,Y) ==> p(X,Y,1).
e(X,Y), p(Y,Z,N) ==> p(X,Z,N+1).
```

For example, the query e(X,X) reduces to p(X,X,1). For the query e(X,Y), e(Y,Z), e(X,Z), the answer is
e(X,Y), e(Y,Z), e(X,Z), p(X,Z,1), p(Y,Z,1), p(X,Y,1).

These rules can be easily generalized to compute shortest distances: replace 1 by the additional distance D given in the edge constraint e:

```
p(X,Y,N) \ p(X,Y,M) <=> N=<M | true.
e(X,Y,D) ==> p(X,Y,D).
e(X,Y,D), p(Y,Z,N) ==> p(X,Z,N+D).
```

5.2   Ordered Merging and Sorting

We use a binary CHR constraint written in infix notation, A --> B, to represent a *directed edge (arc)* from node A to node B. We use a *chain* of such arcs to represent a sequence of values that are stored in the nodes, e.g. 0-->2, 2-->5.

Ordered Merging. We assume ordered chains with nodes in ascending order. So A-->B means that A=<B. We also say that B is the *immediate successor* of A.

The following one-rule program performs an ordered merge of two chains by zipping them together, provided they start with the same (smallest) node.

```
A --> B \ A --> C <=> A<B,B<C | B --> C.
```

Consider two arcs to which the rule applies. For example, consider the query 0-->2, 0-->5. It will result in 0-->2, 2-->5 after one rule application. Basically we add the arc B-->C to represent B<C. Thus the arc A-->C now becomes redundant due to transitivity and is removed. This rule in a sense undoes *transitive closure*. It flattens out a *branch* in a graph.

The code basically works like a zipper. In the rule, A denotes the current position where there is a branch. During computation, all nodes up to A have already been merged, now the successors of A in the two chains are examined. The arc from A to B, the smaller of the two successor nodes of A, is kept, since B must be the immediate successor of A. The second arc is replaced by an arc from B to C. If the first chain is not finished yet, the new branch will be at B now. The rule applies again and again until there is no more branch left by using up at least one chain. (The chains can have different length.)

For example, the query 0-->2, 2-->5, 0-->3, 3-->7 will produce the answer 0-->2, 2-->3, 3-->5, 5-->7. (Note that the constraints in the answer may not necessarily be sorted in that way.)

Termination and Correctness. Applying the rule will not change the number of arcs and the set of involved nodes, i.e. values. The nodes on the right of an arc will not change, too. Only a node on the left may be replaced by a larger node. Since the only rule replaces smaller node values by strictly larger ones without changing anything else and there is only a finite number of values, the program terminates. The application of the rule keeps the invariant that the two graphs are ordered chains.

We can prove correctness by contradiction: If there is an arc whose right node value is not the immediate successor of the left node value, then the chain is not ordered or disconnected. During computation the chains will share a longer and longer common prefix. If no rule is applicable, the two chains have been merged, there is only one chain, so that chain must be ordered, too.

Duplicate Removal. Note that duplicate values are ignored by the rule due to its guard, as they occur as arcs of the form A-->A. Also duplicate arcs of the form A-->B, A-->B are ignored. To remove duplicate values and duplicate arcs, we may add the two rules:

```
A --> A  <=> true.
A --> B \ A --> B <=> true.
```

The rule for duplicate arcs can be made redundant when we slightly generalize its guard of our initial merge rule:

```
A --> B \ A --> C <=> A<B, B=<C | B --> C.
```

Concretely, from A-->B, A-->B, where A<B, the sorting rules produces A-->B, B-->B. The arc B-->B will be removed by the rule for duplicate arcs.

Sorting. We can now perform an ordered merge of two chains that are in ascending order. But the merge rule also works with more than two chains. It will actually merge them simultaneously. Based on this observation, we can implement a merge sort algorithm. If we want to sort n values, we take n one length chains starting with the same smallest (dummy) value (in the example it is 0). Applied repeatedly to a left node, the merge rule will find its immediate successor. As before, the answer is a single, ordered chain of arcs.

In its generality, the code turns a certain type of ordered tree into an ordered chain. Actually, any graph of ordered arcs where all nodes can be reached from a single root node can be sorted. There are no duplicate nodes on the right of an arc, i.e., no right branches. The branches are on the left nodes of an arc, and they are removed by our sorting rule.

Our one-rule sorting program has quadratic complexity when the complier optimisation of *indexing* is used, an optimal lin-log complexity version is also possible with just one additional rule.

6   Conclusions

We have introduced CHR by presenting some small programs written in different programming styles. We also discussed the properties of these programs.

References

[Abd97]   Abdennadher, S.: Operational Semantics and Confluence of Constraint Propagation Rules. In: Smolka, G. (ed.) CP 1997. LNCS, vol. 1330. Springer, Heidelberg (1997)

[AFE05]   Abdennadher, S., Frühwirth, T., Holzbaur, C. (eds.): Special Issue on Constraint Handling Rules. Journal of Theory and Practice of Logic Programming (TPLP) (to appear, 2005)

[AFM99]   Abdennadher, S., Frühwirth, T., Meuss, H.: Confluence and Semantics of Constraint Simplification Rules. Constraints 4(2), 133–165 (1999)

[BCM88]   Banâtre, J.-P., Coutant, A., Le Metayer, D.: A Parallel Machine for Multiset Transformation and its Programming Style. Future Generation Computer Systems 4(2), 133–144 (1988)

[BFKM85]   Brownston, L., Farrell, R., Kant, E., Martin, N.: Programming Expert Systems in OPS5: An Introduction to Rule-based Programming. Addison-Wesley, Boston (1985)

[BN98]   Baader, F., Nipkow, T.: Term Rewriting and All That. Cambridge Univ. Press, Cambridge (1998)

[DSdlBH04] Duck, G.J., Stuckey, P.J., de la Banda, M.G., Holzbaur, C.: The Refined Operational Semantics of Constraint Handling Rules. In: Demoen, B., Lifschitz, V. (eds.) Proceedings of the 20th International Conference on Logic Programming (2004)

[FA03]   Frühwirth, T., Abdennadher, S.: Essentials of Constraint Programming. Springer, Heidelberg (2003)

[Frü98]   Frühwirth, T.: Theory and Practice of Constraint Handling Rules, Special Issue on Constraint Logic programming. Journal of Logic Programming 37(1-3), 95–138 (1998)

[Frü00]   Frühwirth, T.: Proving Termination of Constraint Solver Programs. In: Apt, K.R., Kakas, A.C., Monfroy, E., Rossi, F. (eds.) Compulog Net WS 1999. LNCS, vol. 1865, pp. 298–317. Springer, Heidelberg (2000)

[Frü08]   Frühwirth, T.: Constraint Handling Rules. Cambridge University Press, Cambridge (to appear, 2008)

[SF05]   Schrijvers, T., Frühwirth, T.: CHR Website (May 2005), http://www.cs.kuleuven.ac.be/~dtai/projects/CHR/

A Flexible Search Framework for CHR

Leslie De Koninck*, Tom Schrijvers**, and Bart Demoen

Department of Computer Science, K.U.Leuven, Belgium
FirstName.LastName@cs.kuleuven.be

Abstract. This paper introduces a framework for the specification of tree search strategies in CHR with disjunction (CHR$^\vee$). We support the specification of common search strategies such as depth-first, breadth-first and best-first, as well as constrained optimization by means of branch & bound search. The framework is given as an extension of CHR with rule priorities (CHR^{rp}) in which each branch of the search tree is assigned a *branch priority*. This approach leads to a uniform solution to execution control in CHR.

1 Introduction

Constraint Handling Rules (CHR) [12] is a high-level rule-based language, designed for the implementation of constraint solvers. It runs on top of a host language like Prolog [26], Java [4,33], Haskell or Curry [16], which provides a built-in constraint solver supporting at least a syntactic equality constraint, as well as the constraints *true* and *false*.

CHR aims at being a high-level language for implementing constraint solvers. Indeed, it is excellent at representing the propagation logic of constraint solvers: the notion of a constraint propagator corresponds with a CHR rule. The CHR$^\vee$ language extension [5] also presents a high-level means to express the search aspect of constraint solving. However, due to the non-deterministic operational semantics of these features, CHR is but an abstraction of constraint solving. Most constraint problems are of too big a size to be naively entrusted to a non-deterministic solving process. Rather, solving strategies must be specified to cleverly direct the solving process and prune the search space early and eagerly. An appropriate solving strategy can indeed reduce the solving cost by many orders of magnitude and make the difference between an infeasible and practical approach.

It is for this reason that most state-of-the-art constraint solvers offer the means to select and/or specify the desired solving strategy. For instance, there are 18 documented options, many of which are parameterized and/or can be combined, to influence the strategy of the enumeration predicate labeling/2

---

* Research funded by a Ph.D. grant of the Institute for the Promotion of Innovation through Science and Technology in Flanders (IWT-Vlaanderen).
** Post-Doctoral Researcher of the Fund for Scientific Research - Flanders (Belgium) (F.W.O. - Vlaanderen).

T. Schrijvers and T. Frühwirth (Eds.): Constraint Handling Rules, LNAI 5388, pp. 16–47, 2008.

in the `clp(fd)` library of SICStus Prolog [7]. The solving strategy often falls apart in two distinct aspects: propagator priorities for conjunctions and search priorities for disjunctions. Propagator priorities can be specified by means of rule priorities: these have been studied in CHR^{rp} [10]. In this paper, we add the missing piece: search priorities.

The main contributions of this paper are the following:

1. We present CHR$_\vee^{\text{brp}}$, a high-level approach for specifying the control flow in CHR$^\vee$ (Section 3). CHR$_\vee^{\text{brp}}$ extends CHR$^\vee$ with both **b**ranch and **r**ule **p**riorities.
2. We show how to express standard tree search strategies such as depth-first, breadth-first, depth-first iterative deepening and limited discrepancy search in CHR$_\vee^{\text{brp}}$ (Section 4).
3. We show how conflict-directed backjumping can be realized by extending our framework with justifications (Section 5). Our work extends [38] by not restricting the search strategy to left-to-right depth-first, and by addressing correctness and optimality.

This work is based on previous work in [9]. There are three main improvements. Firstly, whereas in [9], the search strategy is determined by choosing an appropriate definition of the **Split** transition, in this work, the search strategy is determined by the program. This allows using program dependent information for informed search, for example for a best-first search strategy. Secondly, our search framework is based on CHR^{rp} and the ω_p semantics, while in [9], it is based on the more low-level ω_r semantics of CHR. Finally, we also consider constrained optimization, a topic that hitherto has not been tackled.

2   CHR with Rule Priorities and Disjunction

In this section, we introduce both CHR^{rp}, CHR with rule priorities [10] (Section 2.2), and CHR$^\vee$, CHR with disjunctive rule bodies [5] (Section 2.3). We first review the syntax and semantics of regular CHR in Section 2.1.

2.1   Constraint Handling Rules

Syntax. A constraint $c(t_1, \ldots, t_n)$ is an atom of predicate c/n with t_i a host language value (e.g., a Herbrand term in Prolog) for $1 \le i \le n$. There are two types of constraints: built-in constraints and CHR constraints (also called user-defined constraints). The CHR constraints are solved by the CHR program whereas the built-in constraints are solved by an underlying constraint solver (e.g., the Prolog unification algorithm).

There are three types of Constraint Handling Rules: *simplification rules*, *propagation rules* and *simpagation rules*. They have the following form:

$$\begin{array}{llll} \textbf{Simplification} & r\ @ & H^r & \Longleftrightarrow g \mid B \\ \textbf{Propagation} & r\ @\ H^k & & \Longrightarrow g \mid B \\ \textbf{Simpagation} & r\ @\ H^k \setminus H^r & & \Longleftrightarrow g \mid B \end{array}$$

where r is the rule *name*, H^k and H^r are non-empty sequences of CHR constraints and are called the *heads* of the rule, the rule *guard* g is a conjunction of built-in constraints, and the rule *body* B is a multi-set of both CHR and built-in constraints. Throughout this text, in particular in the descriptions of the operational semantics, we use the simpagation rule form to denote any type of rule, where H^k is empty in case of a simplification rule, and H^r is empty in case of a propagation rule. A program P is a set of CHR rules.

The Theoretical Operational Semantics. Operationally, CHR constraints have multi-set semantics. To distinguish between different occurrences of syntactically equal constraints, CHR constraints are extended with a unique identifier. An identified CHR constraint is denoted by $c\#i$ with c a CHR constraint and i the identifier. We write $\mathsf{chr}(c\#i) = c$ and $\mathsf{id}(c\#i) = i$. The theoretical operational semantics of CHR, denoted ω_t, is given in [11] as a state transition system. A CHR execution state σ is represented as a tuple $\langle G, S, B, T \rangle_n$ where G is the goal, a multi-set of constraints that need to be solved; S is the CHR constraint store, a set of identified CHR constraints; B is the built-in constraint store, a conjunction of built-in constraints; T is the propagation history, a set of tuples denoting the rule instances that have already fired; and n is the next free identifier, used to identify new CHR constraints. The transitions of ω_t are shown in Table 1, where $\mathcal{D}$ denotes the built-in constraint theory, $\bar{\exists}_X Y$ denotes the existential closure of Y apart from the variables appearing in X, and $\uplus$ is the multi-set union operation which we also use for sets in case a disjoint union is required.

Table 1. Transitions of ω_t

1. Solve $\langle \{c\} \uplus G, S, B, T \rangle_n \overset{\omega_t}{\rightarrowtail}_P \langle G, S, c \wedge B, T \rangle_n$ where c is a built-in constraint.
2. Introduce $\langle \{c\} \uplus G, S, B, T \rangle_n \overset{\omega_t}{\rightarrowtail}_P \langle G, \{c\#n\} \cup S, B, T \rangle_{n+1}$ where c is a CHR constraint.
3. Apply $\langle G, H_1 \uplus H_2 \uplus S, B, T \rangle_n \overset{\omega_t}{\rightarrowtail}_P \langle C \uplus G, H_1 \cup S, \theta \wedge B, T \cup \{t\} \rangle_n$ where P contains a (renamed apart) rule $$r \;@\; H_1' \backslash H_2' \iff g \mid C$$ and a matching substitution θ such that $\mathsf{chr}(H_1) = \theta(H_1')$, $\mathsf{chr}(H_2) = \theta(H_2')$, $\mathcal{D} \models B \rightarrow \bar{\exists}_B(\theta \wedge g)$, and $t = \langle \mathsf{id}(H_1), \mathsf{id}(H_2), r \rangle \notin T$.

The **Solve** transition solves a built-in constraint from the goal, the **Introduce** transition inserts a new CHR constraint from the goal into the CHR constraint store, and the **Apply** transition fires a rule instance. A rule instance $\theta(r)$ instantiates a rule with CHR constraints matching the heads, using matching substitution θ. A state is called *final* if no transition applies to it.

The Refined Operational Semantics. The refined operational semantics of CHR, denoted by ω_r, is introduced in [11] as a formalization of the execution mechanism of most current CHR implementations. The ω_r semantics is based on the concept of an *active* constraint. The active constraint is a CHR constraint that is used as a starting point for finding applicable rule instances. To ensure that all rule instances are eventually tried, all new CHR constraints become active after they are asserted. CHR constraints that have been active before and whose variables are affected by a new built-in constraint, are reactivated.

The active constraint tries rules in textual order until either it finds a applicable rule instance or all rules have been tried. When a rule instance fires, its body is processed from left to right. Every new CHR constraint that is processed, is activated as soon as it is inserted into the constraint store. Every new built-in constraint is solved for, and all affected CHR constraints are activated one by one before processing the next constraint in the body. If the active constraint has not been removed, then after processing the rule body, it searches for the next applicable rule instance. Otherwise, processing resumes where it left before the constraint was activated.

Many programs rely on the execution order imposed by the ω_r semantics. In Section 2.2, we present an alternative to the ω_r semantics that offers a more high-level and flexible form of execution control.

2.2 CHR with Rule Priorities

CHR^{rp} extends CHR with user-defined rule priorities. It is introduced in [10] to support more high-level and flexible execution control than previously available in CHR by means of the low-level ω_r semantics, while retaining the expressive power needed for the implementation of general purpose algorithms.

Syntax. The syntax of CHR^{rp} is compatible with the syntax of (regular) CHR. A CHR^{rp} simpagation rule looks as follows:

$$p :: r \ @ \ H^k \setminus H^r \iff g \mid B$$

where r, H^k, H^r, g and B are as defined in Section 2.1. The rule *priority* p is an arithmetic expression for which holds that $\mathsf{vars}(p) \subseteq (\mathsf{vars}(H^k) \cup \mathsf{vars}(H^r))$, i.e., all variables in p also appear in the heads. A rule in which $\mathsf{vars}(p) = \emptyset$ is called a *static* priority rule: its priority is known at compile time and is the same for all its instances. A rule in which $\mathsf{vars}(p) \neq \emptyset$ is called a *dynamic* priority rule: its priority is only known at runtime and different instances of the same rule may fire at different priorities. We say that priority p is *higher* than priority p' if $p < p'$.

The Priority Semantics. The operational semantics of CHR^{rp} is called the *priority semantics* and is denoted by ω_p. It consists of a refinement of the ω_t semantics with a minimal amount of determinism in order to support rule priorities. The ω_p semantics uses the same state representation as the ω_t semantics. It restricts the applicability of the **Apply** transition with respect to the ω_t semantics: this transition is only applicable to states with an empty goal and it fires a rule instance of priority p in state σ only if there exists no ω_t **Apply** transition $\sigma \xrightarrow{\omega_t}_P \sigma'$ that fires a rule instance with a higher priority. The **Solve** and **Introduce** transitions are unchanged w.r.t. the ω_t semantics.

2.3 CHR with Disjunction

Constraint Handling Rules is extended with disjunctions in rule bodies in [5] (see also [2] and [3, Chapter 5]). The resulting language is denoted by $CHR^\vee$. The syntax of $CHR^\vee$ is the same as that of regular CHR, except that rule bodies are formulas built from atoms by conjunctions and disjunctions. In [9], we define a theoretical operational semantics $\omega_t^\vee$ for $CHR^\vee$, which extends the ω_t semantics of CHR. An $\omega_t^\vee$ execution state is a multi-set $\Sigma = \{\sigma_1, \ldots, \sigma_n\}$ of ω_t execution states. Each element $\sigma_i \in \Sigma$ represents an alternative solution. The following transitions are defined on $\omega_t^\vee$ executions states:

Table 2. Transitions of $\omega_t^\vee$

1. Derive $\{\sigma\} \uplus \Sigma \overset{\omega_t^\vee}{\rightarrowtail}_P \{\sigma'\} \uplus \Sigma$ if there exists a transition $\sigma \overset{\omega_t}{\rightarrowtail}_P \sigma'$.
2. Split $\{\langle\{G_1 \vee \ldots \vee G_m\} \uplus G, S, B, T\rangle_n\} \uplus \Sigma \overset{\omega_t^\vee}{\rightarrowtail}_P \{\langle G_1 \uplus G, S, B, T\rangle_n, \ldots, \langle G_m \uplus G, S, B, T\rangle_n\} \uplus \Sigma$.
3. Drop $\{\sigma\} \uplus \Sigma \overset{\omega_t^\vee}{\rightarrowtail}_P \Sigma$ if $\sigma = \langle G, S, B, T\rangle_n$ is a failed execution state, i.e., $\mathcal{D} \models \neg\bar\exists_\emptyset B$.

The **Drop** transition is new compared to our description in [9]. It removes failed alternatives from the search tree and is introduced to support pruning of the search tree, for example during conflict-directed backjumping (see Section 5). This pruning respects the declarative semantics of $CHR^\vee$ (see [3, Chapter 5]).

Example 1 (4-queens). A solver for the 4-queens problem can be written in $CHR^\vee$ as follows.

```
queens <=> row(1), row(2), row(3), row(4).
row(R) <=> queen(R,1) ∨ queen(R,2) ∨ queen(R,3) ∨ queen(R,4).

queen(_ ,C₁), queen(_ ,C₂) ==> C₁ =\= C₂.
queen(R₁,C₁), queen(R₂,C₂) ==> abs(R₁ - R₂) =\= abs(C₁ - C₂).
```

As goal we use $\{queens\}$. Here, a $queen(R,C)$ constraint means that there is a queen placed on the field with row R and column C. The first rule states that there are four rows. The second rule states that there is a queen in one of the columns for each row. The remaining two rules ensure that no two queens are in conflicting positions. The first of them makes sure that there are no two queens in the same column; the second that there are no two queens on the same diagonal. The program above can easily be adapted to solve the general n-queens problem. □

Search Trees. An $\omega_t^\vee$ derivation can be visualized as a search tree. Such a search tree consists of a set of nodes and a set of (directed) edges connecting these nodes. A node is either an *internal* node or a *leaf* node. An internal node represents a choice point and corresponds to a state in which a **Split** transition applies. The *root* node corresponds to the initial state $\langle G, \emptyset, true, \emptyset \rangle_1$ with G the initial goal. It can be considered an internal node corresponding to a choice point with only one alternative. A leaf node represents a successful or failed final ω_t execution state. An edge goes from one node, its *start* node, to another node, its *end* node, and represents the derivation that transforms one of the alternatives of its start node into its end node, i.e., it consists of a series of execution states that are linked by **Derive** transitions. For example, the derivation

$$\{\sigma_0\} \overset{\omega_t^{\vee}}{\rightarrowtail}_P \{\sigma_1, \sigma_2\} \overset{\omega_t^{\vee}}{\rightarrowtail}_P \{\sigma_3, \sigma_2\} \overset{\omega_t^{\vee}}{\rightarrowtail}_P \{\sigma_3, \sigma_4\} \overset{\omega_t^{\vee}}{\rightarrowtail}_P \{\sigma_3, \sigma_5, \sigma_6, \sigma_7\}$$

corresponds to the following search tree:

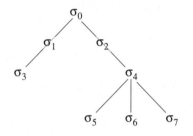

In this example case, the search tree is traversed in left-to-right, depth-first order. Note that different search trees are possible for the same goal. Consider for example the initial goal $\{(G_1 \vee G_2), (G_3 \vee G_4)\}$. For this goal, some derivations apply the **Split** transition to the subgoal $G_1 \vee G_2$ first, while others apply this transition first to $G_3 \vee G_4$.

3   A Combined Approach

In this section, we combine CHR^{rp} with CHR$^{\vee}$ into a flexible framework for defining both the search and propagation strategy to be used by the CHR constraint solver. While our previous work [9] extended the refined operational semantics of CHR with facilities for search strategy control, this work extends the more high-level priority semantics of CHR^{rp}.

First, we discuss some issues concerning search strategies and constrained optimization. A search strategy determines the order in which answers (solutions) to a problem are generated. This order is only relevant if we need a subset of all answers, in particular if we only need one. If we need all answers, then a simple sorting of these answers suffices to implement any search strategy. We assume here that search tree branches are processed independently; but see Section 5 for a discussion of conflict-directed backjumping, a search technique that does take into account results from other branches. In the case of naive optimization, implemented by computing all answers and then choosing the optimal one amongst these, the search strategy is of no importance. However, in a more intelligent form, using for example a *branch & bound* approach, a good search strategy may cause considerable pruning of the search tree.

In [9], the $\omega_r^{\vee}$ semantics states that only the first answer is derived.[1] Other answers can be retrieved on external request (e.g., from the Prolog toplevel) by discarding the first answer and continuing search using the $\omega_r^{\vee}$ **Next** transition. Similarly, under the $\omega_r^{\vee*}$ semantics presented in [38], the derivation stops as soon as the first answer is found, or the search tree is traversed completely. Retrieving the other answers is not explicitly supported, but such support can easily be added to the approach.

3.1   An Intermediate Step: CHR$_\vee^{rp}$

As an intermediate step, we introduce a simple combination of CHR^{rp} with CHR$^{\vee}$ into the combined language CHR$_\vee^{rp}$. This language supports execution control with respect to conjuncts by means of the CHR^{rp} rule priorities, but leaves the search control undetermined. The syntax of CHR$_\vee^{rp}$ is similar to that of CHR^{rp}, but also allows disjunction in the rule bodies, like in CHR$^{\vee}$. The operational semantics of CHR$_\vee^{rp}$ is almost the same as that of CHR$^{\vee}$. The only difference is that in the **Derive** transition, ω_t is replaced by ω_p. In the next subsection, we extend CHR$_\vee^{rp}$ with *branch priorities* to support the specification of search strategies. Finally, in Section 3.3, a correspondence result is given, relating CHR$_\vee^{brp}$ programs and derivations to CHR$^{\vee}$ programs and derivations.

3.2   Extending CHR$_\vee^{rp}$ with Branch Priorities

Syntax. The syntax of CHR$_\vee^{brp}$ extends the syntax of CHR$_\vee^{rp}$ with *branch priorities*. A CHR$_\vee^{brp}$ simpagation rule looks as follows:

$$(bp, rp) :: r \ @ \ H^k \setminus H^r \iff g \mid bp_1 :: B_1 \vee \ldots \vee bp_m :: B_m$$

where r, H^k, H^r and g are as defined in Section 2.1. The *rule* priority rp is as in CHR^{rp}. The *branch* priority bp is a term: there is no a priori reason to restrict the allowed terms. In the examples, we use (tuples of) (lists of) integers and variables.

The rule body consists of a set of disjuncts B_i, each of which is annotated with a branch priority bp_i ($1 \leq i \leq m$). To simplify the presentation (e.g., of the correspondence result in Section 3.3), we impose that each disjunct B_i is a conjunction of constraints. In particular, we do not support nested disjunctions. If in a rule with a single disjunct, the branch priority of this disjunct equals the one of its parent branch, then the branch priorities can be omitted, and so each CHR^{rp} rule is also a syntactically valid CHR$_\vee^{brp}$ rule.

A CHR$_\vee^{brp}$ program is a tuple $\langle \mathcal{R}, \mathcal{BP}, bp_0, \preceq \rangle$ where $\mathcal{R}$ is a set of CHR$_\vee^{brp}$ *rules*, $\mathcal{BP}$ is the *domain* of the branch priorities, $bp_0 \in \mathcal{BP}$ is the *initial branch priority*, and $\preceq$ is a *total preorder* relation over elements of $\mathcal{BP}$.[2]

---

[1] An answer (or solution) is a *successful final* ω_r execution state.

[2] We do not require that $\preceq$ is antisymmetric, i.e., $x \preceq y \wedge y \preceq x$ does not imply $x = y$.

Operational Semantics. We extend the ω_p states with a branch priority. The combination is called an *alternative* and is denoted by $bp :: \sigma$ where bp is the branch priority and σ is an ω_p execution state.[3] An alternative can be *marked*, in which case it is written as $bp :: \sigma^\star$. Marking is used to discard a solution in order to derive a next one.

The operational semantics $\omega_p^\vee$ considers (multi-)sets of alternatives. A total pre-order $\preceq$ must be defined on their branch priorities, so that an alternative with the highest priority can be determined. In practice, we most often use a total order and in the examples, we define $\preceq$ by a logical formula containing arithmetic expressions. This implies that certain parts of the branch priorities must be ground. For a set Σ of alternatives, we denote by $\mathsf{max\_bp}(\Sigma)$ the highest branch priority of any unmarked alternative in Σ, or in case Σ does not contain any unmarked alternatives, a branch priority that is smaller than any other branch priority. The transitions of $\omega_p^\vee$ are given in Table 3.

Table 3. Transitions of $\omega_p^\vee$

1a. Solve $\{bp :: \langle \{c\} \uplus G, S, B, T\rangle_n\} \uplus \Sigma \xmapsto{\omega_p^\vee}_P \{bp :: \langle G, S, c \wedge B, T\rangle_n\} \uplus \Sigma$ if $\mathsf{max\_bp}(\Sigma) \preceq bp$ and c is a built-in constraint.

1b. Introduce $\{bp :: \langle \{c\} \uplus G, S, B, T\rangle_n\} \uplus \Sigma \xmapsto{\omega_p^\vee}_P \{bp :: \langle G, \{c\#n\} \cup S, B, T\rangle_{n+1}\} \uplus \Sigma$ if $\mathsf{max\_bp}(\Sigma) \preceq bp$ and c is a CHR constraint.

1c. Apply $\{bp :: \langle \emptyset, H_1 \uplus H_2 \uplus S, B, T\rangle_n\} \uplus \Sigma \xmapsto{\omega_p^\vee}_P \{bp :: \langle C, H_1 \cup S, \theta \wedge B, T \cup \{t\}\rangle_n\} \uplus \Sigma$ if $\mathsf{max\_bp}(\Sigma) \preceq bp$ and where P contains a rule of priority rp of the form

$$(bp', rp) :: r @ H_1'\backslash H_2' \iff g \mid C$$

and a matching substitution θ exists such that $\mathsf{chr}(H_1) = \theta(H_1')$, $\mathsf{chr}(H_2) = \theta(H_2')$, $bp = \theta(bp')$, $\mathcal{D} \models B \rightarrow \bar{\exists}_B(\theta \wedge g)$, $\theta(rp)$ is a ground arithmetic expression and $t = \langle \mathsf{id}(H_1), \mathsf{id}(H_2), r\rangle \notin T$. Furthermore, no rule of priority rp' and substitution θ' exists with $\theta'(rp') < \theta(rp)$ for which the above conditions hold.

---

2. Split $\{bp :: \sigma\} \uplus \Sigma \xmapsto{\omega_p^\vee}_P \{bp_1 :: \sigma_1, \ldots, bp_m :: \sigma_m\} \uplus \Sigma$ if $\mathsf{max\_bp}(\Sigma) \preceq bp$ and where $\sigma = \langle \{bp_1 :: G_1 \vee \ldots \vee bp_m :: G_m\} \uplus G, S, B, T\rangle_n$ and $\sigma_i = \langle G_i \uplus G, S, B, T\rangle_n$ for $1 \leq i \leq m$.

---

3. Drop $\{bp :: \langle G, S, B, T\rangle_n\} \uplus \Sigma \xmapsto{\omega_t^\vee}_P \Sigma$ if $\mathsf{max\_bp}(\Sigma) \preceq bp$ and $\mathcal{D} \models \neg \bar{\exists}_\emptyset B$.

---

4. Mark $\{bp :: \sigma\} \uplus \Sigma \xmapsto{\omega_p^\vee}_P \{bp :: \sigma^\star\} \uplus \Sigma$ if $\mathsf{max\_bp}(\Sigma) \preceq bp$ and no other $\omega_p^\vee$ transition applies.

The main differences w.r.t. the $\omega_t^\vee$ semantics are the following. The **Derive** transition is split up into three transitions corresponding to the ω_p transitions in order to support matching with, and guards involving the branch priority.

---

[3] In the following, we treat states in which the goal contains a disjunction as ω_p states, but we do not call them final states, even if no ω_p transition applies to them.

These three transitions, as well as the **Split** and **Drop** transitions, only apply to the highest priority unmarked alternative. Finally, a new transition called **Mark** is introduced, whose purpose is to mark a solution (successful final state) in order to find a next solution. Given a goal G, we construct an initial $\omega_p^\vee$ state $\Sigma_0 = \{bp_0 :: \langle G, \emptyset, true, \emptyset \rangle_1\}$ where bp_0 is the initial branch priority for the program.

Noteworthy is that the branch priorities presented above, do not change the shape of the search tree. Instead, they only influence the order in which the nodes of this search tree are explored. Therefore, the search strategy used is of importance only in the following cases.

- If we require a subset of all solutions.
- If we combine the search strategy with an intelligent backtracking technique such as conflict-directed backjumping (see Section 5).
- If we need an optimal solution using a branch & bound or restart optimization approach.

In contrast, if we require all solutions and do not apply any pruning based on previously computed answers, then the search strategy is irrelevant.[4]

In general, we might be interested in retrieving solutions one at a time. This is for example supported in the Prolog context by means of the toplevel environment asking whether more solutions are needed. We define a function find_next that returns, given an $\omega_p^\vee$ state, the first answer (solution) in this state, as well as the resulting state after marking this solution, which contains the remaining answers.

$$\text{find\_next}(\Sigma) = \langle A, \Sigma_R \rangle$$

if there exists a derivation $\Sigma \overset{\omega_p^\vee}{\longmapsto}{}^*_P \Sigma_A \overset{\omega_p^\vee}{\longmapsto}_P \Sigma_R$ where the transition from Σ_A to Σ_R is a **Mark** transition and the derivation from Σ to Σ_A does not contain such a transition. In the result, $A = B \wedge \text{chr}(S)$ where $bp :: \langle \emptyset, S, B, T \rangle_n$ is the highest priority unmarked alternative in Σ_A.

Constrained Optimization. As a general approach to constrained optimization, we show how both a branch & bound, and restart optimization scheme can be implemented in $\text{CHR}_\vee^{\text{brp}}$. We consider a goal G whose *best* solution is to be returned. This best solution is such that there exists no solution that assigns a lower value to a given *cost* function F whose variables appear in G.[5] Let there be given an initial $\omega_p^\vee$ state Σ_0 based on the goal G. Under the assumption that there is a solution, we find the solution that minimizes our cost function F as find_min(Σ_0, F) where find_min is defined as

$$\text{find\_min}(\Sigma, F) = \text{let} \begin{cases} \langle A, \Sigma' \rangle = \text{find\_next}(\Sigma) \\ \Sigma'' = \text{add\_goal}(F < F(A), \Sigma') \end{cases}$$
$$\text{in if } \Sigma'' \text{ has no solution then } A$$
$$\text{else find\_min}(\Sigma'', F)$$

---

[4] This is related to the distinction between variable ordering and value ordering in case all solutions are required, see for example [30].

[5] Alternative, one can use a *utility* function that is to be maximized.

for branch & bound optimization, and for restart optimization as follows:

$$\mathsf{find\_min}(\Sigma, F) = \mathrm{let} \begin{cases} \langle A, \Sigma' \rangle = \mathsf{find\_next}(\Sigma) \\ \Sigma'' = \mathsf{add\_goal}(F < F(A), \Sigma) \end{cases}$$
$$\mathrm{in} \ \ \mathrm{if} \ \Sigma'' \ \mathrm{has \ no \ solution \ then} \ A$$
$$\mathrm{else} \ \mathsf{find\_min}(\Sigma'', F)$$

Here $\mathsf{add\_goal}(G, \Sigma)$ returns the $\omega_p^\vee$ state that results from adding the goal G to all unmarked alternatives in Σ:

$$\mathsf{add\_goal}(G, \Sigma) = \{ bp :: \sigma^\star \mid bp :: \sigma^\star \in \Sigma \} \uplus$$
$$\{ bp :: \langle G \uplus G', S, B, T \rangle_n \mid bp :: \langle G', S, B, T \rangle_n \in \Sigma \}$$

The difference between both approaches is that in branch & bound optimization, the new bound is added as a goal to all remaining alternatives, whereas in restart optimization, the new bound is added to the initial state, which is solved for again.

Dynamic Search Tree Generation. It is not always convenient or even possible to state at compile time which alternatives are to be created. In general, we may want to generate alternatives dynamically, at runtime. Let us assume we can compute, by means of a built-in constraint, a list of all alternatives to be generated, as well as a list of priorities to be used for the respective alternatives. We can then dynamically generate the alternatives by asserting a `generate_alternatives/2` constraint whose arguments are respectively the list of priorities and the list of alternatives. Let $\top \in \mathcal{BP}$ be higher than all branch priorities used for the dynamically generated alternatives. We can then define the `generate_alternatives/2` constraint by the following rules.

```
(_,1) :: generate_alternatives([P|Ps],[A|As]) <=>
                        P :: A ∨ ⊤ :: generate_alternatives(Ps,As).
(_,1) :: generate_alternatives([],[]) <=> true.
```

By using the $\top$ priority value, we ensure that all alternatives are generated before the first of them is processed.

3.3   Correspondence

In this subsection, we show that every $\omega_p^\vee$ derivation of a $\mathrm{CHR}_\vee^{\mathrm{brp}}$ program P, corresponds to an $\omega_t^\vee$ derivation of a corresponding non-deterministic $\mathrm{CHR}^\vee$ version of this program P. We first show how to create such a non-deterministic version of a $\mathrm{CHR}_\vee^{\mathrm{brp}}$ program. Next, we propose a mapping from $\omega_p^\vee$ states onto $\omega_t^\vee$ states, and finally, we give the correspondence result.

Given a $\mathrm{CHR}_\vee^{\mathrm{brp}}$ program P, we create a $\mathrm{CHR}^\vee$ program $\mathsf{nondet}(P)$ as follows. For every rule in P of the form

$$(bp, rp) :: r \ @ \ H^k \setminus H^r \iff guard \mid bp_1 :: B_1 \vee \ldots \vee bp_m :: B_m$$

nondet(P) contains a rule

$$r @ H^k \setminus H^r, \mathsf{bp}(bp) \iff guard \mid (\mathsf{bp}(bp_1), B_1) \vee \ldots \vee (\mathsf{bp}(bp_m), B_m)$$

and for every rule of the form

$$(bp, rp) :: r @ H^k \setminus H^r \iff guard \mid body$$

where $body$ does not contain a disjunction, nondet(P) contains a rule

$$r @ \mathsf{bp}(bp), H^k \setminus H^r \iff guard \mid body$$

It is easy to see that given one $\mathsf{bp}/1$ constraint in the initial goal, no state can be derived in which the CHR constraint store contains more than one such constraint. We incorporate the branch priorities of P as constraints into nondet(P) because they may appear in guards or rule bodies. In the following, we assume that no constraint identifier is used for the $\mathsf{bp}/1$ constraint and that it is ignored by the propagation history. This can be realized by a source-to-source transformation in which constraint identifiers and the propagation history are made explicit.

Now we define a mapping function map from $\omega_p^\vee$ states to $\omega_t^\vee$ states.

$$\mathsf{map}(\{bp :: \sigma\} \uplus \Sigma) = \mathsf{map}(bp :: \sigma) \uplus \mathsf{map}(\Sigma)$$

$$\mathsf{map}(bp :: \langle G, S, B, T \rangle_n) = \begin{cases} \langle G', S, B, T \rangle_n & \text{if } G \text{ consists of a disjunction} \\ \langle G, \{\mathsf{bp}(bp)\} \cup S, B, T \rangle_n & \text{otherwise} \end{cases}$$
$$\text{where } G' \text{ is found by replacing each disjunct}$$
$$bp_i :: B_i \text{ in } G \text{ by a disjunct } (\mathsf{bp}(bp_i), B_i)$$

Theorem 1 (Correspondence). *Given a* CHR$_\vee^{\mathrm{brp}}$ *program P and the corresponding* CHR$^\vee$ *program* nondet(P), *then for each transition $\Sigma \overset{\omega_p^\vee}{\rightarrowtail}_P \Sigma'$, there exists a derivation* $\mathsf{map}(\Sigma) \overset{\omega_t^\vee}{\rightarrowtail}{}^*_{\mathsf{nondet}(P)} \mathsf{map}(\Sigma')$ *and if Σ is a final $\omega_p^\vee$ state, then* $\mathsf{map}(\Sigma)$ *is a final $\omega_t^\vee$ state.*

Proof. Let there be given a transition $\Sigma \overset{\omega_p^\vee}{\rightarrowtail}_P \Sigma'$. Each $\omega_p^\vee$ transition operates on a single (highest priority, unmarked) alternative $bp :: \sigma$, and replaces this alternative with one or more new alternatives. Let $\Sigma = \{bp :: \sigma\} \uplus \Sigma_R$ and let $\Sigma' = \Sigma_N \uplus \Sigma_R$. We also have that $\mathsf{map}(\Sigma) = \mathsf{map}(bp :: \sigma) \uplus \mathsf{map}(\Sigma_R)$. Now a transition from Σ to Σ' can be one of the following:

1a. Solve. $\sigma = \langle \{c\} \uplus G, S, B, T \rangle_n$ with c a built-in constraint, and so $\mathsf{map}(bp :: \sigma) = \langle \{c\} \uplus G, \{\mathsf{bp}(bp)\} \cup S, B, T \rangle_n$. Therefore, in $\mathsf{map}(\Sigma)$, the $\omega_t^\vee$ **Derive** transition is possible since the ω_t **Solve** transition applies to $\mathsf{map}(bp :: \sigma)$. This results in the $\omega_t^\vee$ state $\{\langle G, \{\mathsf{bp}(bp)\} \cup S, c \wedge B, T \rangle_n\} \uplus \mathsf{map}(\Sigma_R)$ which is exactly $\mathsf{map}(\{bp :: \langle G, S, c \wedge B, T \rangle_n\} \uplus \Sigma_R)$.

1b. Introduce. $\sigma = \langle\{c\} \uplus G, S, B, T\rangle_n$ with c a CHR constraint, and so $\mathsf{map}(bp :: \sigma) = \langle\{c\} \uplus G, \{\mathsf{bp}(bp)\} \cup S, B, T\rangle_n$. Therefore, in $\mathsf{map}(\Sigma)$, the $\omega_t^\vee$ **Derive** transition is possible since the ω_t **Introduce** transition applies to $\mathsf{map}(bp :: \sigma)$. This results in the $\omega_t^\vee$ state $\{\langle G, \{c\#n, \mathsf{bp}(bp)\} \cup S, B, T\rangle_{n+1}\} \uplus \mathsf{map}(\Sigma_R)$ which is exactly $\mathsf{map}(\{bp :: \langle G, \{c\#n\} \cup S, c \wedge B, T\rangle_{n+1}\} \uplus \Sigma_R)$.

1c. Apply. $\sigma = \langle\emptyset, H_1 \uplus H_2 \uplus S, B, T\rangle_n$ and so $\mathsf{map}(bp :: \sigma) = \langle\emptyset, \{\mathsf{bp}(bp)\} \uplus H_1 \uplus H_2 \uplus S, B, T\rangle_n$. P contains a rule of the form

$$(bp', rp) :: r @ H_1'\backslash H_2' \iff g \mid C$$

and there exists a matching substitution θ such that $\mathsf{chr}(H_1) = \theta(H_1')$, $\mathsf{chr}(H_2) = \theta(H_2')$, $bp = \theta(bp')$, $\mathcal{D} \models B \to \bar\exists_B(\theta \wedge g)$, $\theta(rp)$ is a ground arithmetic expression and $t = \langle\mathsf{id}(H_1), \mathsf{id}(H_2), r\rangle \notin T$. Assume C consists of a disjunction, then $\mathsf{nondet}(P)$ contains a rule of the form

$$r @ H_1'\backslash H_2', \mathsf{bp}(bp') \iff g \mid C'$$

where C' is found by replacing all $\mathrm{CHR}_\vee^{\mathrm{brp}}$ disjuncts of the form $bp_i :: B_i$ by $\mathrm{CHR}^\vee$ disjuncts of the form $(\mathsf{bp}(bp_i), B_i)$. Given this rule, the ω_t **Apply** transition applies to state $\mathsf{map}(bp :: \sigma)$. In particular, we can use θ as the matching substitution. Therefore, the $\omega_t^\vee$ **Derive** transition applies to state $\mathsf{map}(\Sigma)$, resulting in the state $\{\langle C', H_1 \cup S, \theta \wedge B, T \cup \{t\}\rangle_n\} \uplus \mathsf{map}(\Sigma_R)$ where $t = \langle\mathsf{id}(H_1), \mathsf{id}(H_2), r\rangle$. This corresponds to the state $\mathsf{map}(\Sigma') = \mathsf{map}(\{bp :: \langle C, H_1 \cup S, \theta \wedge B, T \cup \{t\}\rangle_n\} \uplus \Sigma_R)$. The case that C does not contain a disjunction is similar. The difference is that the $\mathsf{bp}/1$ constraint is not removed and the rule body remains unchanged.

2. Split. $\sigma = \langle\{bp_1 :: G_1 \vee \ldots \vee bp_m :: G_m\}, S, B, T\rangle_n$ and so $\mathsf{map}(bp :: \sigma) = \langle\{(\mathsf{bp}(bp_1), G_1) \vee \ldots \vee (\mathsf{bp}(bp_m), G_m)\}, S, B, T\rangle_n$. In $\mathsf{map}(\Sigma)$, the $\omega_t^\vee$ **Split** transition applies, resulting in the state $\{\langle\{\mathsf{bp}(bp_1)\} \uplus G_1, S, B, T\rangle_n, \ldots, \langle\{\mathsf{bp}(bp_m)\} \uplus G_m, S, B, T\rangle_n\} \uplus \mathsf{map}(\Sigma_R)$. In each of the m first alternatives, the **Introduce** transition applies, introducing the $\mathsf{bp}/1$ constraint into the CHR constraint store. After these introductions, the resulting state equals $\{\langle G_1, \{\mathsf{bp}(bp_1)\} \cup S, B, T\rangle_n, \ldots, \langle G_m, \{\mathsf{bp}(bp_m)\} \cup S, B, T\rangle_n\} \uplus \mathsf{map}(\Sigma_R)$. This state equals $\mathsf{map}(\Sigma')$ since $\Sigma' = \{bp_1 :: \langle G_1, S, B, T\rangle_n, \ldots, bp_m :: \langle G_m, S, B, T\rangle_n\} \uplus \Sigma_R)$.

3. Drop. $\sigma = \langle G, S, B, T\rangle_n$ and $\mathcal{D} \models \neg\bar\exists_\emptyset B$. Since the map function does not change the built-in constraint store, the $\omega_t^\vee$ **Drop** transition applies to $\mathsf{map}(\Sigma)$ resulting in the state $\mathsf{map}(\Sigma_R)$. The result of applying the **Drop** transition to Σ is the state Σ_R and so the resulting states correspond.

4. Mark. This transition does not change the result of the map function and so $\mathsf{map}(\Sigma) = \mathsf{map}(\Sigma')$.

This proves the first part of the theorem. For the second part, consider a final $\omega_p^\vee$ state Σ. Such a state consists of a set of alternatives, each of which is marked. An alternative is marked only if no other transition applies. This means (amongst others) that the goal of such an alternative is empty and its built-in constraint store is consistent. Once an alternative is marked, it remains unchanged. Now consider the $\omega_t^{\vee}$ state $\mathsf{map}(\Sigma)$. If an $\omega_t^{\vee}$ transition applies to this state, then this must be a **Derive** transition because the map function only adds a $\mathsf{bp}/1$ constraint to the CHR constraint store of each alternative with an empty goal and so the **Split** and **Drop** transitions are not applicable. Let σ be the alternative in $\mathsf{map}(\Sigma)$ that is replaced by a **Derive** transition. Since the goal of σ is empty, the ω_t transition corresponding to the **Derive** transition must be an **Apply** transition, firing a rule of the form

$$r @ H_1'\backslash H_2', \mathsf{bp}(bp') \iff g \mid C'$$

Let $\theta(r)$ be the fired rule instance, then the CHR constraint store of state σ must contain sets of constraints H_1 and H_2 matching the heads H_1' and H_2', as well as a constraint $\mathsf{bp}(bp)$ that matches with $\mathsf{bp}(bp')$. Moreover, the built-in constraint store of σ entails the guard g in conjunction with the matching substitution θ. Now, let $bp :: \sigma'$ be the $\omega_p^{\vee}$ alternative in Σ that maps on ω_t state σ. By definition, the CHR constraint store of σ' contains the constraints in H_1 and H_2, and its built-in constraint store and propagation history are equal to the ones of σ. The $\mathrm{CHR}_{\vee}^{\mathrm{brp}}$ program P contains a rule

$$(bp', rp) :: r @ H_1'\backslash H_2' \iff g \mid C$$

for which holds that rule instance $\theta(r)$ can fire given the branch priority, CHR and built-in constraint stores and propagation history of $\omega_p^{\vee}$ alternative $bp :: \sigma'$. Potentially, $\theta(r)$ is not the highest priority applicable rule instance in $bp :: \sigma'$, but then another rule instance can fire, and so this also implies that Σ is not a final $\omega_p^{\vee}$ state. So we conclude that a non-final $\omega_t^{\vee}$ state corresponds to a non-final $\omega_p^{\vee}$ state, which proves the second part of the theorem.   □

4   Specifying Common Search Strategies

In this section, we show how different search strategies can be implemented in $\mathrm{CHR}_{\vee}^{\mathrm{brp}}$. In Section 4.1, we look at uninformed strategies such as depth-first, breadth-first and depth-first iterative deepening. It is shown that a $\mathrm{CHR}_{\vee}^{\mathrm{rp}}$ program (i.e., one without branch priorities) can be automatically translated into a $\mathrm{CHR}_{\vee}^{\mathrm{brp}}$ program that implements these search strategies. Next, in Section 4.2, we consider informed search strategies such as best-first search, A* and limited discrepancy search. Finally, in Section 4.3, we show how different strategies can be combined, with as an example a mixture of depth- and breadth-first search.

4.1   Uninformed Search Strategies

Depth-First and Breadth-First Search. In order to implement depth-first or breadth-first search, we transform each $\mathrm{CHR}_{\vee}^{\mathrm{rp}}$ rule of the form

$$rp :: H^k \backslash H^r \iff guard \mid B_1 \vee \ldots \vee B_n$$

into a $\text{CHR}_\vee^{\text{brp}}$ rule

$$(D, rp) :: H^k \setminus H^r \iff guard \mid (D+1) :: B_1 \vee \ldots \vee (D+1) :: B_n$$

The branch priorities correspond to the depth in the search tree: $\mathcal{BP} = \mathbb{N}$ and $bp_0 = 0$. We define the branch priority order $\preceq$ as follows:

- for depth-first search, $D_1 \preceq D_2 \Leftrightarrow D_1 \leq D_2$
- for breadth-first search, $D_1 \preceq D_2 \Leftrightarrow D_1 \geq D_2$

Now, the branch priorities are such that for depth-first search, the deeper alternative has a higher priority, whereas for breadth-first search, the more shallow alternative has a higher priority.

Example 2 (4-queens (ctd.)). The 4-queens solver given in Example 1 can be extended with branch and rule priorities as follows.

```
(_,1) :: queens <=> row(1), row(2), row(3), row(4).
(D,2) :: row(R) <=> (D+1) :: queen(R,1) ∨ (D+1) :: queen(R,2) ∨
                             (D+1) :: queen(R,3) ∨ (D+1) :: queen(R,4).
(_,1) :: queen(_ ,C₁), queen(_ ,C₂) ==> C₁ =\= C₂.
(_,1) :: queen(R₁,C₁), queen(R₂,C₂) ==> abs(R₁ - R₂) =\= abs(C₁ - C₂).
```

The branch priorities implement depth-first or breadth-first search, depending on the $\preceq$ order used. The rule priorities ensure that (further) labeling is done only *after* consistency checking. The derivation starts with the following initial $\text{CHR}_\vee^{\text{brp}}$ state: $\{0 :: \langle\{\text{queens}\}, \emptyset, true, \emptyset\rangle_1\}$.   □

The implementation of depth- and breadth-first search given above is still nondeterministic with respect to alternatives at equal depth. We can implement a deterministic *left-to-right* version of depth-first or breadth-first search as follows. Take as branch priorities sequences of integers ($\mathcal{BP} = \mathbb{N}^*$ and $bp_0 = \epsilon$). The length of the sequence denotes the depth in the search tree, and the ith element in the sequence denotes the number of the branch taken at level i.

The order over these priorities is defined as

$$(D, rp) :: H^k \setminus H^r \iff guard \mid (D \mathbin{+\!\!+} [1]) :: B_1 \vee \ldots \vee (D \mathbin{+\!\!+} [n]) :: B_n$$

with

$$L_1 \succeq L_2 \Leftrightarrow$$
$$\big(\text{length}(L_1) > \text{length}(L_2)\big) \vee \big(\text{length}(L_1) = \text{length}(L_2) \wedge L_1 \leq^d L_2\big)$$

for depth-first search and

$$L_1 \succeq L_2 \Leftrightarrow$$
$$\big(\text{length}(L_1) < \text{length}(L_2)\big) \vee \big(\text{length}(L_1) = \text{length}(L_2) \wedge L_1 \leq^d L_2\big)$$

for breadth-first search. Here $\leq^d$ is the lexicographic or *dictionary* order.

Depth-Limited Search and Depth-First Iterative Deepening. Depth-limited search is a variant of depth-first search in which search tree nodes are only expanded up to a given depth bound. It is an incomplete search in that it is not able to find solutions beyond this depth bound. Amongst others, depth-limited search is used in iterative deepening search. It can be implemented in $CHR_\lor^{brp}$ by using the depth-first search program given in the previous paragraph, extended with the following rule:

```
(D,1) :: limit(D) <=> false.
```

This rule ensures that any alternative at the depth limit fails. Its rule priority ensures the rule is tried before any other rule.[6] Here, the depth limit is given by an appropriate `limit/1` constraint which is to be added to the initial goal.

Depth-first iterative deepening [21] consists of iteratively running depth-limited search, increasing the depth limit in each run. Iterative deepening can be implemented by adding the following rule:

```
(_,1) :: deepen(D) <=> 1 :: limit(D) ∨ 0 :: deepen(D+1).
```

Instead of a `limit/1` constraint, the goal is extended with a `deepen(1)` constraint. Using the above approach may lead to an infinite loop in which the depth limit keeps increasing in case the search tree is finite but contains no solutions. The reason is that it is not possible to distinguish between failure because the depth limit is reached, and failure because the entire search tree has been traversed and no solutions were found. In Section 5.4 we return to this issue and show how conflict-directed backjumping can solve this problem. More precisely, it is shown that if failure is independent of the depth limit, there is no need to change it.

Iterative Broadening. Iterative broadening [15] works similar to iterative deepening, but instead of using a depth limit that is iteratively increased, the number of branches starting at any given node is limited, and this limit increases over the iterations. The domain of branch priorities $\mathcal{BP} = \{\langle D, B \rangle \mid D, B \in \mathbb{N}\}$. A node with branch priority $\langle D, B \rangle$ is at depth D in the search tree, and is the Bth alternative of its parent node. We use as initial branch priority $bp_0 = \langle 0, 1 \rangle$ and we define the $\preceq$ relation as follows:

$$\langle D_1, \_ \rangle \preceq \langle D_2, \_ \rangle \Leftrightarrow D_1 \leq D_2$$

Now, the code below implements iterative broadening.

```
(_,1) :: broaden(B) <=> B < n_max | ⟨1,1⟩ :: limit(B) ∨ ⟨0,1⟩ :: broaden(B+1).
```

```
(⟨_,B⟩,1) :: limit(L) <=> L < B | false.
```

```
(⟨D,_⟩,rp) :: r @ H^k \ H^r <=> guard | ⟨D+1,1⟩ :: B_1 ∨ ... ∨ ⟨D+1,n⟩ :: B_n.
```

---

[6] This may require increasing the rule priorities of all other rules by one.

In the above, n_{max} is an upperbound on the number of alternatives in a rule body, and is used to ensure termination. The depth-first strategy ensures that the sub-tree for a given breadth limit is completely traversed before increasing this breadth limit (by means of a broaden/1 constraint). The second component of the branch priorities of the alternatives created by the first rule, is of no importance, as long as it is less than the breadth limit. We extend the initial goal with a broaden(1) constraint to start the process.

4.2 Informed Search Strategies

Informed strategies take problem dependent heuristics into account.

Limited and Depth-Bounded Discrepancy Search. The limited discrepancy search (LDS) [19] strategy is similar to best-first search. It is designed for boolean constraint satisfaction problems in which the values of each variable are ordered according to some heuristic. The idea behind LDS is that if following the heuristic does not work, then it is probable that a solution can be found by violating the heuristic only a limited number of times. Each violation of the heuristic is called a discrepancy, and the algorithm consists of first trying those alternatives with at most one discrepancy, then the ones with at most two discrepancies and so on until a solution is found. Let there be given the following CHR_V^{rp} labeling rule:

rp :: domain(X,[V_1,V_2]) <=> (X = V_1) $\vee$ (X = V_2).

where the values in the domain are ordered according to the heuristic, i.e., V_1 is preferred over V_2. In CHR_V^{brp}, we can write this labeling rule as follows:

(D,rp) :: domain(X,[V_1,V_2]) <=> D :: (X = V_1) $\vee$ (D+1) :: (X = V_2).

The branch priority represents the number of discrepancies: $\mathcal{BP} = \mathbb{N}$. Initially, there is no discrepancy: $bp_0 = 0$. In each choice point, the discrepancy remains unchanged if we follow the heuristic, and increased by one if we deviate from this heuristic. The alternatives with fewer discrepancies are explored first: $P_1 \preceq P_2 \Leftrightarrow P_1 \geq P_2$.

Note that the description of LDS in [19] uses depth-first search combined with a limit on the number of discrepancies. Here, we use a form of best-first search where alternatives with less discrepancies are preferred. A variant of LDS in which the number of discrepancies is actually bounded, can be expressed in the same way as how we express depth-limited search, i.e., by introducing a limit/1 constraint and adding a rule

(D,1) :: limit(D-1) <=> false.

Another variant of LDS, called *depth-bounded discrepancy search* (DDS) [35] combines LDS with iterative deepening. It is best characterized as a depth-first search that only allows discrepancies below a certain depth, that is iteratively increased. As for depth-first search, the branch priority denotes the depth in the search tree ($\mathcal{BP} = \mathbb{N} \cup \{-1\}$) and we start at the root ($bp_0 = 0$). The order over these priorities is the same as for depth-first search.

The original program is transformed to:

```
(_,1) :: start <=>
                0 :: no_discrepancy ∨ -1 :: (allow_discrepancy, deepen(0)).
(_,1) :: deepen(D) <=> 0 :: limit(D) ∨ -1 :: deepen(D+1).
(D,1) :: limit(D), allow_discrepancy <=> force_discrepancy.

(D,rp) :: allow_discrepancy \ domain(X,[V₁,V₂]) <=>
                            (D+1) :: (X = V₁) ∨ (D+1) :: (X = V₂).
   rp :: force_discrepancy, domain(X,[_,V₂]) <=> no_discrepancy, X = V₂.
   rp :: no_discrepancy \ domain(X,[V₁,_]) <=> X = V₁.
```

Here, the `limit/1` constraint represents the current depth limit. Above this limit any number of discrepancies are allowed (`allow_discrepancy/0`), while below the limit no discrepancies are allowed (`no_discrepancy/0`). It gets complicated when we are at the current depth limit. Let us first focus on the iterative deepening part. The `deepen/1` constraint drives the iterative loop of installing successively increasing depth limits. The extra element $-1 \in \mathcal{BP}$ is the minimal priority, which ensures that we only install the next depth limit after the current one has been fully explored. Each successive iteration should only produce additional solutions, which have not been found in preceding iterations. Hence, all solutions should exploit the increased depth-limit and have a discrepancy at that depth. The `force_discrepancy/0` constraint makes sure this happens. By adding the `start/0` constraint to the goal, we get the process going.

Similar to the case of depth-first iterative deepening, the depth limit keeps increasing if either the problem is overconstrained, or we require all solutions. Again, using conflict-directed backjumping remedies this problem. Only if failure happens in a state in which the constraint store contains a `force_discrepancy/0` or `no_discrepancy/0` constraint (justified by a `limit/1` constraint), the depth limit is changed.

A* and Iterative Deepening A*. The A* algorithm [18] consists of using best-first search to find an optimal solution in a constrained optimization problem. Let the branch priorities be such that $p :: \sigma$ is better than $p' :: \sigma'$ for successful final states σ and σ', if and only if $p \succeq p'$; and $\{p :: \sigma\} \overset{\omega_p^\vee}{\rightarrowtail_P^*} \Sigma$ implies $p \succeq p_i$ for all $p_i :: \sigma_i \in \Sigma$. Under these conditions, the first answer found (using find_next) is also an optimal solution.

Example 3 (Shortest path distance). Consider the following program for computing the shortest path distance between two nodes in a directed graph.

```
(_,1) :: path(V,V) <=> true.
(D,2) :: neighbors(V,CU) \ path(V,W) <=> 1 :: branches(W,D,CU).

(_,1) :: branches(W,D,[C-U|CUs]) <=>
                            (D+C) :: path(U,W) ∨ 1 :: branches(W,D,CUs).
(_,1) :: branches(_,_,[]) <=> false.
```

Here, the `neighbors/2` constraints represent the edges of the graph: for each node V, there exists a `neighbors`(V, CUs) constraint with CUs a list containing a pair $C - U$ for each edge from node V to node U with cost C. The initial goal consists of a single `path/2` constraint whose arguments are the nodes for which we wish to compute the shortest path distance. The branch priorities denote the distance between the initial start node and the node represented by the first argument of the `path/2` constraint currently in the store, or, eventually in a successful final state, the distance between the initial start and end nodes. We have $\mathcal{BP} = \mathbb{N}$, $bp_0 = 0$ and $D_1 \preceq D_2 \Leftrightarrow D_1 \geq D_2$. □

Iterative deepening A* (ID-A*) is a combination of A* and depth-first iterative deepening. It consists of depth-first search in part of the search tree, only considering nodes whose cost function does not exceed a certain threshold value. If no solution is found, the threshold is increased by the minimal amount needed to include an unseen search tree node. We can easily implement a variant of ID-A* in which the threshold is increased by some fixed amount, similar to how we implement depth-first iterative deepening. However, increasing the threshold with the minimal amount needed to include the lowest cost unseen node, falls outside of the scope of our framework as it requires communication between different branches of the search tree.

4.3   Combining Search Strategies

Now we show that the $\text{CHR}_\vee^{\text{brp}}$ language is expressive enough to formulate complex search strategies. In particular, with an appropriate choice of priorities and orderings, compositions of the previous search strategies can be expressed. In this subsection, we give two examples of such strategy compositions.

Example 4. Consider we want to use breadth-first search, but only up to a certain depth, e.g. so as not to exceed available memory. Beyond the depth limit, the search should switch to a depth-first strategy.

To implement this more complex strategy, we use the same branch priorities as the ones used for depth-first and breadth-first search in Section 4.1. The following definition for the $\preceq$ relation is used

$$D_1 \preceq D_2 \Leftrightarrow (D_2 \leq T \wedge D_2 \leq D_1) \vee (T \leq D_1 \leq D_2)$$

where T is the depth threshold which is given by the user. In words, beyond the threshold, the deeper alternative is preferred, whereas below the threshold, the more shallow alternative is preferred. An alternative whose depth is below the threshold is preferred over one whose depth is beyond the threshold. □

In the second example, we show how to traverse the states resulting from some **Split** transitions in a depth-first order, and others in a breadth-first order.

Example 5. Let us assume a $\text{CHR}_\vee^{\text{rp}}$ program containing the following two binary labeling rules:

```
1 :: label_df @ df_domain(X,[V1,V2]) <=> X = V1 ∨ X = V2.
1 :: label_bf @ bf_domain(X,[V1,V2]) <=> X = V1 ∨ X = V2.
```

Furthermore assume we want the labeling by rule `label_df` to proceed in depth-first, and the labeling by rule `label_bf` in breadth-first order. We define a *depth-first subtree* as part of the search tree in which all internal nodes correspond to depth-first splits. A *breadth-first* subtree is similarly defined. Comparing alternatives within a depth-first or breadth-first subtree is straightforward. For alternatives across such subtrees, we proceed as follows.

Let there be two alternatives A_1 and A_2, let $N^1 = [N_1^1, \ldots, N_{n_1}^1]$ be the sequence of nodes on the unique path from the root of the search tree, to (but excluding) alternative A_1, and let $N^2 = [N_1^2, \ldots, N_{n_2}^2]$ be the sequence of nodes on the path from the root to alternative A_2. Let $i_1 \in \{1, \ldots, n_1 + 1\}$ be the first index for which holds that node N_{i_1} corresponds to a breadth-first (depth-first) split or $n_1 + 1$ if no such index exists. In particular, the nodes in the subsequence $[N_1^1, \ldots, N_{i_1-1}^1]$ all correspond to depth-first (breadth-first) splits. Let $i_2 \in \{1, \ldots, n_2 + 2\}$ be similarly defined. If $i_1 > i_2$ ($i_1 < i_2$) then alternative A_1 has priority over alternative A_2 and if $i_1 < i_2$ ($i_1 > i_2$) then the opposite holds. Finally, if $i_1 = i_2$, we compare the depths of the first depth-first (breadth-first) splits in sequences $[N_{i_1}^1, \ldots, N_{n_1}^1]$ and $[N_{i_2}^2, \ldots, N_{n_2}^2]$ and so on until either the depths are different or there are no more nodes to consider, in which case both alternatives have an equal priority.

Figure 1 shows an example search tree including its depth-first and breadth-first subtrees. Node 2 (as well as all alternatives on the edge from Node 1 to Node 2) has priority over Node 1 as both are part of the same depth-first subtree and Node 2 is deeper than Node 1. Node 1 has priority over Nodes 3 and 4, even though the latter are deeper in the global search tree. The reasoning is as follows. The depth of the first breadth-first split in the path from the root node to respectively Nodes 1, 3 and 4 all equals 2 (for Node 1, there is no such split). In the remaining subpaths (for Node 1, this path is empty), the depth of the first

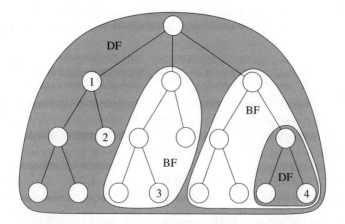

Fig. 1. Search tree for mixed depth-and-breadth-first search

depth-first split equals 1 for Node 1, 3 for Node 3 and 2 for Node 4. Therefore, Node 1 has priority over Nodes 3 and 4. Furthermore, Node 4 has priority over Node 3. Finally, by transitivity, Node 2 also has priority over Nodes 3 and 4.

In $CHR_\lor^{brp}$, we can model the above described preference relation using the following rules.

```
(P,1) :: label_df @ df_domain(X,[V₁,V₂]) <=>
         df_child_priority(P) :: X = V₁ ∨ df_child_priority(P) :: X = V₂.
(P,1) :: label_bf @ bf_domain(X,[V₁,V₂]) <=>
         bf_child_priority(P) :: X = V₁ ∨ bf_child_priority(P) :: X = V₂.
```

where the functions `df_child_priority` and `bf_child_priority` are implemented as follows:[7]

```
df_child_priority(Parent) = Child :-
       (   length(Parent) mod 2 = 0
       ->  Child = Parent ++ [2]
       ;   append(Context,[Depth],Parent),
           Child = Context ++ [Depth + 1]
       ).


bf_child_priority(Parent) = Child :-
       (   length(Parent) mod 2 = 1
       ->  Child = Parent ++ [2]
       ;   append(Context,[Depth],Parent),
           Child = Context ++ [Depth + 1]
       ).
```

The initial branch priority is set to ϵ. We define the order relation $\succeq$ as follows:

$$L_1 \succeq L_2 \Leftrightarrow L_1 \succeq^d L_2$$

where

$$[H_1|T_1] \succeq^d \epsilon$$
$$[H_1|T_1] \succeq^d [H_2|T_2] \Leftrightarrow H_1 > H_2 \lor (H_1 = H_2 \land T_1 \succeq^b T_2)$$

and

$$\epsilon \succeq^b [H_2|T_2]$$
$$[H_1|T_1] \succeq^b [H_2|T_2] \Leftrightarrow H_1 < H_2 \lor (H_1 = H_2 \land T_1 \succeq^d T_2)$$

The branch priority of an alternative is a list of depths of the first depth-first or breadth-first split in consecutive subpaths from the root to the alternative as defined earlier.[8] For example, in Figure 1, the branch priority equals [2] for Node 1, [3] for Node 2, [2, 3] for Node 3, and [2, 2, 2] for Node 4. It is assumed

---

[7] We use Mercury syntax here [31], wich supports a functional notation for predicates; $p(\bar{X}, X_n) :-$ *body* is equivalent to $p(\bar{X}) = X_n :-$ *body*.

[8] The list is implicitly assumed to end with an infinite sequence ones = [1|ones].

that the root node is a depth-first node; if necessary, a dummy depth-first split can be created to ensure this is true. One can now verify that

$$[3] \succeq [2] \succeq [2, 2, 2] \succeq [2, 3] \qquad \qquad \square$$

5   Look Back Schemes: Conflict-Directed Backjumping

In [38], Wolf et al. use *justifications* and *conflict sets* to define an *extended and refined operational semantics* $\omega_r^{\vee*}$, which supports *look back* schemes like conflict-directed backjumping (CBJ) [24] and dynamic backtracking [14] as opposed to standard chronological backtracking. In this section, we show how their approach can be combined with our framework. More precisely, we propose an extended version of the $\omega_p^{\vee}$ semantics that supports conflict-directed backjumping, and discuss the correctness and optimality of this extension. We note that the benefits of CBJ are limited when strong constraint propagation and a good variable ordering heuristic is used (see for example [8]). We have chosen not to support dynamic backtracking, as it requires changing the shape of the search tree, which may conflict with the execution order imposed by the rule priorities. Moreover, for efficiency it requires an adaptive version of CHR [37].

5.1   Justifications and Labels

Justifications are introduced in the CHR context in [37] and used for the purpose of finding *no-goods* in conflict-directed backjumping in [38]. In that context, justifications consist of the *choices* that caused a given constraint to hold. The ω_p semantics can easily be extended to support justifications by annotating each constraint in the goal, CHR constraint store, and built-in constraint store with a justification. A constraint c with justification J is denoted by c^J and we write $\mathsf{just}(c^J) = J$. The transitions of the extended ω_p semantics are given as part of the extended priority semantics of $\mathrm{CHR}_\vee^{\mathrm{brp}}$ in the next subsection.

In case of depth-first search, conflicts can be uniquely described using only the search tree levels at which the conflicting choices were made. This is the approach taken in [38]. For more general search strategies, we need a more precise specification of the choices involved in a conflict. Therefore, we introduce a labeling scheme for search tree nodes that allows us to distinguish between such nodes, and to decide whether a given node is a descendant of another. In general, we can use as labels the branch priorities used in the (deterministic) left-to-right versions of depth- and breadth-first search proposed in Section 4.1.

5.2   The Extended Priority Semantics of $\mathrm{CHR}_\vee^{\mathrm{brp}}$

In analogy with [38], we extend the $\omega_p^{\vee}$ semantics into the $\omega_p^{\vee*}$ semantics, whose states are tuples $\langle K, S \rangle$ where K is the *conflict set*, a set of *no-goods*, i.e., justifications of failures; and S is a set of (marked and unmarked) ω_p states extended with a branch priority and branch label: $S = \{bp_1 :: bl_1 @ \sigma_1, \ldots, bp_n :: bl_n @ \sigma_n\}$.

By slight abuse of notation, we use bl to refer to just the label, or to the labeled alternative $bp :: bl @ \sigma$, depending on the context.

While in case of depth-first search, backjumping consists of skipping a series of alternatives, in general, it requires pruning of the search tree. This is because the alternatives that are skipped with depth-first search are exactly the (remaining) children of the deepest conflict, while in general, these children may be scheduled for later resolution when using a different search strategy and hence they cannot be skipped.

Table 4. Transitions of $\omega_p^{\vee \star}$

1a. Solve $\langle K, \{bp :: bl @ \langle \{c^J\} \uplus G, S, B, T\rangle_n\} \uplus \Sigma\rangle \xrightarrow{\omega_p^{\vee \star}}_P \langle K, \{bp :: bl @ \langle G, S, c^J \wedge B, T\rangle_n\} \uplus \Sigma\rangle$ if $\mathsf{max\_bp}(\Sigma) \preceq bp$ and c is a built-in constraint.

1b. Introduce $\langle K, \{bp :: bl @ \langle \{c^J\} \uplus G, S, B, T\rangle_n\} \uplus \Sigma\rangle \xrightarrow{\omega_p^{\vee \star}}_P \langle K, \{bp :: bl @ \langle G, \{c^J \#n\} \cup S, B, T\rangle_{n+1}\} \uplus \Sigma\rangle$ if $\mathsf{max\_bp}(\Sigma) \preceq bp$ and c is a CHR constraint.

1c. Apply $\langle K, \{bp :: bl @ \langle \emptyset, H_1 \uplus H_2 \uplus S, B, T\rangle_n\} \uplus \Sigma\rangle \xrightarrow{\omega_p^{\vee \star}}_P \langle K, \{bp :: bl @ \langle C^J, H_1 \cup S, \theta \wedge B, T \cup \{t\}\rangle_n\} \uplus \Sigma\rangle$ if $\mathsf{max\_bp}(\Sigma) \preceq bp$ and where P contains a rule of priority rp of the form

$$(bp', rp) :: r @ H_1' \backslash H_2' \iff g \mid C$$

and a matching substitution θ exists such that $\mathsf{chr}(H_1) = \theta(H_1')$, $\mathsf{chr}(H_2) = \theta(H_2')$, $bp = \theta(bp')$, $\mathcal{D} \models B \to \bar{\exists}_B(\theta \wedge g)$, $\theta(rp)$ is a ground arithmetic expression and $t = \langle \mathsf{id}(H_1), \mathsf{id}(H_2), r\rangle \notin T$. Furthermore, no rule of priority rp' and substitution θ' exists with $\theta'(rp') < \theta(rp)$ for which the above conditions hold. The justification $J = \mathsf{just}(H_1) \cup \mathsf{just}(H_2) \cup \mathsf{just}(E)$ where E is a minimal subset of B for which holds that $\mathcal{D} \models E \to \bar{\exists}_E(\theta \wedge g)$.

---

2. Split $\langle K, \{bp :: bl @ \sigma\} \uplus \Sigma\rangle \xrightarrow{\omega_p^{\vee \star}}_P \langle K, \{bp_1 :: bl_1 @ \sigma_1, \ldots, bp_m :: bl_m @ \sigma_m\} \uplus \Sigma\rangle$ where $\sigma = \langle ((bp_1 :: G_1 \vee \ldots \vee bp_m :: G_m)^J \wedge G, S, B, T\rangle_n$, $\mathsf{max\_bp}(\Sigma) \preceq bp$, and $\sigma_i = \langle G_i^{J \cup \{bl_i\}} \wedge G, S, B, T\rangle_n$ for $1 \leq i \leq m$.

3a. Backtrack $\langle K, \{bp :: bl @ \langle G, S, B, T\rangle_n\} \uplus \Sigma\rangle \xrightarrow{\omega_p^{\vee \star}}_P \langle K \cup \{J\}, \Sigma\rangle$ if $\mathsf{max\_bp}(\Sigma) \preceq bp$, $\mathcal{D} \models \neg\bar{\exists}_\emptyset B$, and there exists at least one alternative in Σ that is a descendant of the parent of bl. Here, J is the justification of the inconsistency of B.

3b. Backjump $\langle K, \{bp :: bl @ \sigma\} \uplus \Sigma\rangle \xrightarrow{\omega_p^{\vee \star}}_P \langle K \setminus K', \{bp :: bl' @ \langle \emptyset, \emptyset, \mathsf{false}^J, \emptyset\rangle_1\} \uplus \Sigma'\rangle$ if $\mathsf{max\_bp}(\Sigma) \preceq bp$, σ is a failed ω_p state, and there exists no other alternative in Σ that is a descendant of the parent of bl. Let K' be the justifications in K that involve bl or one of its siblings. A new no-good J is created by merging these justifications, removing the labels of bl and its siblings. Now let bl' be the deepest alternative in J. We find Σ' by removing from Σ all descendants of bl'.

---

4. Mark $\langle K, \{bp :: bl @ \sigma\} \uplus \Sigma\rangle \xrightarrow{\omega_p^{\vee \star}}_P \langle K, \{bp :: bl @ \sigma^\star\} \uplus \Sigma\rangle$ if $\mathsf{max\_bp}(\Sigma) \preceq bp$ and no other $\omega_p^{\vee \star}$ transition applies.

The transitions of the extended priority semantics of $CHR_\vee^{brp}$ are given in Table 4. The **Backjump** transition implements what corresponds to a multi-step backjump in [38]. It works by constructing a new failed alternative as a child of the node to which is jumped back. If this alternative is the only remaining child of its parent, then the next applicable transition will again be a **Backjump** transition. Otherwise, a **Backtrack** transition will follow, which just removes the failed alternative. The latter is treated as a special case in [38], by the single-step backjump transition.

Example 6 (6-queens). Consider the 6-queens problem where we are labeling the last row and all previously rows have their queens set as in the figure below.

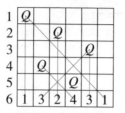

We see that all positions in the last row are conflicting with some previously set queen. For each position, we have given the *first* row which contains a conflicting queen. Note that some positions conflict with more than one queen: for example for the second column, these are the queens in rows 3 and 4. Because the fifth row participates in none of the conflicts, we can jump back to the queen in the fourth row and move her, instead of considering alternative places for the queen in the fifth row.

In $CHR_\vee^{brp}$, we can use the following solver for the 6-queens problem:

```
    1   :: queens <=> row(1), ..., row(6).
(D,7)   :: row(R) <=> (D+1) :: queen(R,1) ∨ ... ∨ (D+1) :: queen(R,6).
   R₁   :: queen(R₁,C₁), queen(_ ,C₂) ==> C₁ =\= C₂.
   R₁   :: queen(R₁,C₁), queen(R₂,C₂) ==> abs(R₁ - R₂) =\= abs(C₁ - C₂).
```

This solver differs from the one in Example 2 in that conflicts with queens in early rows are preferred above those with queens in later rows. This preference is imposed by using the row number of the conflicting queen as rule priority.[9] It ensures that we jump back as far as possible.

In the remainder of this example, we use a simplified notation for $\omega_p^{\vee^*}$ states. More precisely, we represent an alternative of the form $bp :: bl @ \langle G, S, B, T \rangle_n$ as $bp :: chr(S) \cup B$, i.e., we do not show the branch label (which is assumed to be equal to the branch priority), goal, propagation history or next free identifier, and we represent CHR constraints without their identifier. We assume a depth-first strategy which implies that it is sufficient to use the depth in the search tree as branch labels. Now using our simplified representation, the $\omega_p^{\vee^*}$ state right before labeling the last row looks as follows:

$$\langle K, \{(5 :: Q_5 \cup \{row(6)^\emptyset\})\} \cup \Sigma \rangle$$

---

[9] A conflict between the queens in rows i and j ($i < j$) can be detected by a rule instance of priority i, and a symmetric one of priority j. Only the first one fires.

where $Q_4 = \{\text{queen}(1,1)^{\{1\}}, \text{queen}(2,3)^{\{2\}}, \text{queen}(3,5)^{\{3\}}, \text{queen}(4,2)^{\{4\}}\}$, $Q_5 = Q_4 \cup \{\text{queen}(5,4)^{\{5\}}\}$ and $\Sigma = \{(5 :: Q_4 \cup \{\text{queen}(5,5)^{\{5\}}, \text{row}(6)^{\emptyset}\}), (5 :: Q_4 \cup \{\text{queen}(5,6)^{\{5\}}, \text{row}(6)^{\emptyset}\})\} \cup \Sigma'$. The contents of K and Σ' is not relevant to our presentation. The labeling rule replaces this $\omega_p^{\vee^*}$ state by

$$\langle K, \{(6 :: Q_5 \cup \{\text{queen}(6,1)^{\{6\}}\}), \ldots, (6 :: Q_5 \cup \{\text{queen}(6,6)^{\{6\}}\})\} \cup \Sigma \rangle$$

Now each of the queens on row 6 conflicts with a queen in an earlier row. These conflicts lead to failures that are justified by the conflicting constraints' labels. After having dealt with columns 1 to 5, the resulting $\omega_p^{\vee^*}$ state is

$$\langle K \cup \{\{1,6\}, \{3,6\}, \{2,6\}, \{4,6\}, \{3,6\}\}, \{(6 :: Q_5 \cup \{\text{queen}(6,6)^{\{6\}}\})\} \cup \Sigma \rangle$$

So far, we have only used **Backtrack** transitions to deal with failures. The last alternative position on the sixth row again leads to failure, this time with justification $\{1,6\}$. Now, the **Backjump** transition applies, which forms a new justification by merging the ones involving the sixth row. This new justification equals $\{1,2,3,4\}$. The **Backjump** transition removes all (two) remaining alternatives on the fifth row and creates a new failed alternative, resulting in the state

$$\langle K, \{(6 :: \text{false}^{\{1,2,3,4\}})\} \cup \Sigma' \rangle$$

after which (in this case) a **Backtrack** transition follows and the next alternative on row 4 is tried:

$$\langle K \cup \{\{1,2,3,4\}\}, \Sigma' \rangle \qquad \qquad \square$$

5.3   Correctness and Optimality Issues

We now discuss three issues concerning the correctness and optimality of conflict-directed backjumping in $\text{CHR}^{\vee}$ (and $\text{CHR}_{\vee}^{(b)\text{rp}}$). Firstly, for correctness, we need to impose restrictions on the programs for which we can use conflict-directed backjumping. In particular, we require that a program is confluent with respect to the $\omega_t^{\vee}$ semantics. The following theorem states the correctness of the $\omega_p^{\vee^*}$ semantics.

Theorem 2. *For a given program P whose non-deterministic version* $\text{nondet}(P)$ *is confluent with respect to the $\omega_t^{\vee}$ semantics, it holds that $\Sigma_0 \overset{\omega_p^{\vee^*}}{\rightarrowtail}{}^*_P \Sigma_n$ with Σ_n a final $\omega_p^{\vee^*}$ state, if and only if $\Sigma_0 \overset{\omega_p^{\vee}}{\rightarrowtail}{}^*_P \Sigma_n$.*

Proof (sketch). The main proof obligation consists of showing that the **Backjump** transition is correct, i.e., that it does not discard any solutions. We show that this is true given that the existence of a failing $\omega_t^{\vee}$ derivation for a state $\text{map}(\Sigma)$ in the non-deterministic version $\text{nondet}(P)$ of a program P, implies that all such derivations fail.

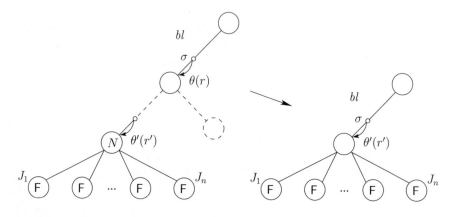

Fig. 2. Construction of a failing derivation, justifying a backjump

Consider a node N, all of whose children have failed, where the failures are justified by justifications $J_1, \ldots, J_n$. A justification J_i $(1 \leq i \leq n)$ is a set of branch labels. After the last child of N fails, a **Backjump** transition applies under $\omega_p^{\vee^*}$. This transition consists of merging the justifications $J_1, \ldots, J_n$ into a new justification J by uniting the respective sets of branch labels, discarding the labels of children of N.

Let bl be the branch label of the deepest alternative in J. The branch labeled bl ends in a node, i.e., a state in which a **Split** transition applies (see Section 2.3), which is preceded by an **Apply** transition, firing some rule instance $\theta(r)$. Let $bp :: bl @ \sigma$ be the alternative right before $\theta(r)$ fired. In this alternative and under the $\omega_t^{\vee}$ semantics, we can also fire the rule instance that lead to the creation of node N, say $\theta'(r')$, in state $\mathsf{map}(bp :: \sigma)$ using program $\mathsf{nondet}(P)$ (see Section 3.3). The reasoning is that none of the children of N depend on constraints derived after state σ as their branch labels would otherwise have been part of the justification J.

Now there exists a failing derivation $D = \{\mathsf{map}(bp :: \sigma)\} \overset{\omega_t^{\vee}}{\underset{\mathsf{nondet}(P)}{\rightarrowtail}}^* \emptyset$ which consists of first firing rule instance $\theta'(r')$ and then repeating the derivations that lead to the failure of each of the children of node N. If we have that the existence of a failing derivation such as D, implies that all derivations starting in the same state also fail, then we also have that all children of the ending node of branch bl fail under the $\omega_p^{\vee^*}$ semantics, and so we can safely discard them as is done in the **Backjump** transition. We call the above property *conflict preservation*. It is a notion weaker than confluence in the sense that all solutions should only be the same in case one of them is a failure. In practice we can use the notion of *confluence*, for which a decidable test exists in case of a terminating program [1],[10] to decide whether or not we can apply conflict-directed backjumping to a

---

[10] This test is defined for the ω_t semantics, but can easily be extended towards the $\omega_t^{\vee}$ semantics.

program. Figure 2 shows how the failing $\omega_t^\vee$ derivation D can be constructed, starting in state $\mathsf{map}(bp :: \sigma)$, and justifying the backjump.   □

The following example shows how solutions can be missed in case a program is not confluent.

Example 7. Consider the $\mathrm{CHR}_\vee^{\mathrm{rp}}$ program below, with initial goal $\{g\}$.

```
1 :: a, e <=> false.
1 :: a, f <=> false.
1 :: a, d <=> true.

2 :: g ==> a ∨ b.
3 :: g ==> c ∨ d.
4 :: g ==> e ∨ f.
```

We have left out branch priorities as they are not needed for the example. Assume a first labeling step chooses a, then c is chosen, and finally both e and f fail due to a and hence regardless of the second choice point (in which c was chosen). However, we cannot jump back to the first choice, because if we choose d in the second choice point, the a constraint is 'consumed' and both e and f are consistent. The problem is that the program is not confluent w.r.t. the $\omega_t^\vee$ semantics. For example, if the constraint store in a given state consists of the CHR constraints a, e and d, then the result can be either a failed state, or a state in which the constraint store contains the constraint e.   □

A second issue is concerned with optimality. In general, when it is detected that a constraint is in conflict with some other constraints, there might be other sets of conflicting constraints as well. In the conflict-directed backjumping algorithm, it is assumed that testing for conflicts follows the order in which the variables are instantiated. In general, we prefer conflicts with constraints that appear closer to the root of the search tree.

In the 6-queens program of Example 6, we dealt with this issue by giving conflicts with earlier queens a higher (rule) priority. This approach easily extends towards other finite domain constraint solvers that do not apply look-ahead schemes. However, in general, a conflict may involve multiple CHR and built-in constraints, each of which has its own justification. Therefore, it might not always be clear which rule instance is preferred. We could for example minimize the depth of the deepest choice, the number of choices, or the sum of the depths of the choices involved in a conflict. Some strategies maximize the depth of the first backjump, while others maximize for example the total number of nodes skipped.

A final issue is that choice points should preferably be created only after all constraint propagation and consistency checking is completed. Otherwise, it is possible that a failure is independent of the last choice made. By assigning a low rule priority to labeling rules, we reach consistency before further labeling.

5.4 Iterative Deepening Revisited

In Section 4.1 the iterative deepening strategy is implemented. However, as noted, there is a problem with termination. In iterative deepening, the depth limit should only increase if the search tree contains an unexplored subtree. So, when a depth-limited search fails, we are interested in why it fails. This type of information is not available in the $\omega_p^\vee$ semantics, but it is available in the $\omega_p^{\vee^*}$ semantics by means of the conflict set.

When a failure occurs because the depth limit is reached, this failure is due to the following rule:

```
(D,1) :: limit(D-1) <=> false.
```

The justification for the failure hence contains the justification of the `limit/1` constraint. If however no failure occurs because the depth limit is reached, then the justification for the failure does not contain the one of the `limit/1` constraint and therefore, the second alternative of the rule that generated this constraint, namely

```
(_,1) :: deepen(D) <=> 1 :: limit(D) ∨ 0 :: deepen(D+1).
```

will be pruned by the **Backjump** transition.

Noteworthy is that the above approach only works if branch priorities are annotated with justifications themselves, and these justifications are taken into account when constraints rely on the branch priority. To simplify the presentation, we have ignored this in our description of the $\omega_p^{\vee^*}$ semantics in Section 5.2. We note that a constraint, asserted after firing some rule instance $\theta(r)$, should contain the justification of the branch priority only if either the firing of $\theta(r)$ depends on the branch priority, or the branch priority is used in the arguments of the constraint. If we do not take into account the justifications of the branch priority, then it may happen that a backjump is made to change the depth limit if all children of some node fail due to this depth limit, without taking into account that other nodes may be below the depth limit.

6 Related Work

Adding different search strategies to declarative languages, and in particular Constraint (Logic) Programming languages, has been done before. For a more thorough overview, see for example [13,28]. In [29] it is shown how search tree states can be encapsulated in the multi-paradigm language Oz. The encapsulation is implemented using a variable scoping mechanism and local versions of the constraint store, and allows the implementation of different search strategies. A generalization of this work is presented for the functional logic programming language Curry in [17]. An important aspect there is that the encapsulated search tree states are evaluated lazily.

Much related to our work is the OPL modeling language [32] in which search strategies consist of three parts: the *exploration strategy*, the *limit strategy* and the *selection strategy*. The exploration strategy consists of an evaluation function that assigns a score to search tree nodes, much like our branch priorities, combined with a procedure to decide when to switch to another node. The limit strategy imposes bounds on the time and space used for searching. Finally, the selection strategy determines which solutions are returned and can be used for instance to implement constrained optimization.

Constraint Logic Programming systems such as ECL^iPS^e [34] or SICStus Prolog's clp(fd) [7] are usually limited by Prolog's built-in depth-first search mechanism.[11] However, using language features such as the findall/3 predicate or blackboard primitives, other strategies can be implemented. For example, in Ciao Prolog [20], breadth-first and depth-first iterative deepening search are supported using a source transformation. In [6], the blackboard primitives of SICStus Prolog are used to implement intelligent backtracking in Prolog.

In all of the above mentioned work, the search strategy is stated independently of the program logic and therefore treats all search in a uniform way. Our approach supports both uniform and rule specific strategies, thereby allowing the use of different search strategies for different parts of the program.

Related Work in the CHR Context. In the context of $CHR^\vee$, Menezes et al. propose in [22] a $CHR^\vee$ implementation for Java in which the search tree is made explicit and manipulated at runtime to improve efficiency. In particular, when a rule firing is independent of the choice made in a previous choice point, the result of this rule firing is valid for all alternatives in that choice point, and so by reordering the nodes in the search tree, some redundant work is avoided. In a sense, this reasoning takes into account *justifications* of constraints, i.e., those constraints that caused the derivation of any given constraint.

Justifications are introduced in CHR in the context of adaptive CHR [37], which extends CHR by supporting the incremental adaption of CHR derivations in the context of both constraint insertions and deletions. In [36], justifications, in particular for the built-in constraint *false*, are used to implement intelligent search algorithms such as *conflict-directed backjumping* and *dynamic backtracking*. A new operational semantics for $CHR^\vee$, called the *extended and refined operational semantics* $\omega_r^{\vee*}$, which formally combines the concept of justifications with $CHR^\vee$, is given in [38]. The semantics in fact implements conflict-directed backjumping. We extend the work in [38] by also supporting search strategies different from left-to-right depth-first in combination with conflict-directed backjumping, and by discussing optimality and correctness issues.

In [25], it is proposed to transform the disjuncts in $CHR^\vee$ into special purpose constraints which can be dealt with by an external search component. An example of such an external search component is the Java Abstract Search Engine (JASE), which is part of the Java Constraint Kit (JACK) [4], a CHR implementation for Java. Since Java does not offer native search in contrast with Prolog, Java-based CHR implementations need to implement their own search support.

---

[11] Search strategies in these systems mostly consist of different ways of *shaping* the search tree, with the *exploration* strategy being fixed to left-to-right depth-first.

In practice, this often means more flexibility compared to the built-in search in Prolog. In particular, Prolog only supports a limited way of movement between nodes of the search tree, whereas in JASE, one can jump from one search tree node to another by means of trailing, copying or recomputation, as well as combinations of these methods.

7   Conclusion

To conclude, we summarize our contributions. In Section 3 we combined and extended two language extensions of CHR, namely CHR^{rp} and $CHR^{\vee}$, into a flexible framework for execution control in CHR. In this framework, called $CHR_{\vee}^{brp}$, the propagation strategy is determined by means of *rule priorities*, whereas the search strategy is determined by means of *branch priorities*. In Section 4, we have shown how various tree search strategies can be expressed in our framework. These strategies include *uninformed* search strategies such as depth-first, breadth-first and depth-first iterative deepening (Section 4.1), *informed* strategies such as limited discrepancy search (Section 4.2), as well as combinations of different strategies (Section 4.3). Finally, in Section 5, we have adapted the work of [38] which proposes a combination of conflict-directed backjumping (CBJ) with $CHR^{\vee}$, to our framework, by adding support for search strategies different from left-to-right depth-first. Moreover, we have established correctness and optimality conditions for this combination of CBJ with $CHR_{\vee}^{brp}$.

Future Work. A first topic for future work is the (efficient) implementation of our search framework in CHR systems. In particular, it is worth considering adding such search support to systems that currently do not offer search facilities like the K.U.Leuven JCHR [33] and CCHR [39] systems. Some issues that an optimized implementation should deal with are the use of specialized priority queues for e.g. depth-first and breadth-first search, and the choice between copying, trailing and recomputation (as well as combinations of these) for the task of jumping between search tree nodes (see also [27]).

It would also be interesting to have a high-level way to combine different search strategies. The approach we have taken in Section 4.3 is rather ad hoc, and in general it remains unclear what the priority domain, order relation, and priority assignments should look like.

Finally, we have already shown how information from successes (e.g., branch & bound in Section 3.2) and failures (e.g., conflict-directed backjumping in Section 5) in other branches of the search tree can be used to speed up the constraint solving process. It would be interesting to see how similar approaches can be used, for example to implement iterative deepening A^* or the dynamic variable ordering technique proposed in [23]. The latter consists of changing the variable to be labeled next after a backjump, taking into account the reason for the backjump.

References

1. Abdennadher, S.: Operational semantics and confluence of constraint propagation rules. In: Smolka, G. (ed.) CP 1997. LNCS, vol. 1330, pp. 252–266. Springer, Heidelberg (1997)
2. Abdennadher, S.: A language for experimenting with declarative paradigms. In: 2nd Workshop on Rule-Based Constraint Reasoning and Programming (2000)
3. Abdennadher, S.: Rule Based Constraint Programming: Theory and Practice. Habilitation, Institut für Informatik, Ludwig-Maximilians-Universität München (2001)
4. Abdennadher, S., Krämer, E., Saft, M., Schmauss, M.: JACK: A Java constraint kit. Electronic Notes in Theoretical Computer Science, vol. 64 (2002)
5. Abdennadher, S., Schütz, H.: CHR$^\vee$: A flexible query language. In: Andreasen, T., Christiansen, H., Larsen, H.L. (eds.) FQAS 1998. LNCS, vol. 1495, pp. 1–14. Springer, Heidelberg (1998)
6. Bruynooghe, M.: Enhancing a search algorithm to perform intelligent backtracking. Theory and Practice of Logic Programming 4(3), 371–380 (2004)
7. Carlsson, M., Ottosson, G., Carlson, B.: An open-ended finite domain constraint solver. In: Glaser, H., Hartel, P.H., Kuchen, H. (eds.) PLILP 1997. LNCS, vol. 1292, pp. 191–206. Springer, Heidelberg (1997)
8. Chen, X., van Beek, P.: Conflict directed backjumping revisited. Journal of Artificial Intelligence Research 14, 53–81 (2001)
9. De Koninck, L., Schrijvers, T., Demoen, B.: Search strategies in CHR (Prolog). In: Schrijvers, T., Frühwirth, T. (eds.) 3rd Workshop on Constraint Handling Rules, Report CW 452, pp. 109–123. Dept. of Computer Science, K.U.Leuven (2006)
10. De Koninck, L., Schrijvers, T., Demoen, B.: User-definable rule priorities for CHR. In: Leuschel, M., Podelski, A. (eds.) 9th International ACM SIGPLAN Conference on Principles and Practice of Declarative Programming. ACM Press, New York (2007)
11. Duck, G.J., Stuckey, P.J., García de la Banda, M., Holzbaur, C.: The refined operational semantics of Constraint Handling Rules. In: Demoen, B., Lifschitz, V. (eds.) ICLP 2004. LNCS, vol. 3132, pp. 90–104. Springer, Heidelberg (2004)
12. Frühwirth, T.: Theory and practice of Constraint Handling Rules. Journal of Logic Programming 37(1-3), 95–138 (1998)
13. Frühwirth, T., Michel, L., Schulte, C.: Constraints in procedural and concurrent languages. In: Rossi, F., van Beek, P., Walsh, T. (eds.) Handbook of Constraint Programming. Foundations of Artificial Intelligence, ch. 13, pp. 453–494. Elsevier Science Publishers, Amsterdam (2006)
14. Ginsberg, M.L.: Dynamic backtracking. Journal of Artificial Intelligence Research 1, 25–46 (1993)
15. Ginsberg, M.L., Harvey, W.D.: Iterative broadening. Artificial Intelligence 55(2), 367–383 (1992)
16. Hanus, M.: Adding Constraint Handling Rules to Curry. In: Fink, M., Tompits, H., Woltran, S. (eds.) 20th Workshop on Logic Programming, INFSYS Research Report 1843-06-02, pp. 81–90. TU Wien (2006)
17. Hanus, M., Steiner, F.: Controlling search in declarative programs. In: Palamidessi, C., Glaser, H., Meinke, K. (eds.) ALP 1998 and PLILP 1998. LNCS, vol. 1490, pp. 374–390. Springer, Heidelberg (1998)
18. Hart, P.E., Nilsson, N.J., Raphael, B.: A formal basis for the heuristic determination of minimum cost paths. IEEE Transactions on Systems Science and Cybernetics 4(2), 100–107 (1968)

19. Harvey, W.D., Ginsberg, M.L.: Limited discrepancy search. In: 14th International Joint Conference on Artificial Intelligence, vol. 1, pp. 607–615. Morgan Kaufmann, San Francisco (1995)

20. Hermenegildo, M.V., Bueno, F., Cabeza, D., Carro, M., García de la Banda, M.J., López-García, P., Puebla, G.: The CIAO multi-dialect compiler and system: An experimentation workbench for future (C)LP systems. In: Lucio, P., Martelli, M., Navarro, M. (eds.) 1996 Joint Conference on Declarative Programming, APPIA-GULP-PRODE, pp. 105–110 (1996)

21. Korf, R.E.: Depth-first iterative-deepening: An optimal admissible tree search. Artificial Intelligence 27(1), 97–109 (1985)

22. Menezes, L., Vitorino, J., Aurelio, M.: A high performance $CHR^\vee$ execution engine. In: Schrijvers, T., Frühwirth, T. (eds.) 2nd Workshop on Constraint Handling Rules, Report CW 421, pp. 35–45. Dept. of Computer Science, K.U.Leuven (2005)

23. Müller, H.: Static and dynamic variable sorting strategies for backtracking-based search algorithms. In: Wolf, A., Frühwirth, T.W., Meister, M. (eds.) 19th Workshop on (Constraint) Logic Programming. Ulmer Informatik-Berichte, vol. 2005-01, pp. 99–110 (2005)

24. Prosser, P.: Hybrid algorithms for the constraint satisfaction problem. Computational Intelligence 9, 268–299 (1993)

25. Robin, J., Vitorino, J., Wolf, A.: Constraint programming architectures: Review and a new proposal. Journal of Universal Computer Science 13(6), 701–720 (2007)

26. Schrijvers, T., Demoen, B.: The K.U.Leuven CHR system: implementation and application. In: Frühwirth, T., Meister, M. (eds.) First Workshop on Constraint Handling Rules: Selected Contributions. Ulmer Informatik-Berichte, vol. 2004-01, pp. 1–5. Universität Ulm (2004)

27. Schulte, C.: Comparing trailing and copying for constraint programming. In: De Schreye, D. (ed.) 1999 International Conference on Logic Programming, pp. 275–289. MIT Press, Cambridge (1999)

28. Schulte, C., Carlsson, M.: Finite domain constraint programming systems. In: Rossi, F., van Beek, P., Walsh, T. (eds.) Handbook of Constraint Programming, Foundations of Artificial Intelligence, ch. 14, pp. 495–526. Elsevier Science Publishers, Amsterdam (2006)

29. Schulte, C., Smolka, G., Würtz, J.: Encapsulated search and constraint programming in Oz. In: Borning, A. (ed.) PPCP 1994. LNCS, vol. 874, pp. 134–150. Springer, Heidelberg (1994)

30. Smith, B.M., Sturdy, P.: Value ordering for finding all solutions. In: Kaelbling, L.P., Saffiotti, A. (eds.) 19th International Joint Conference on Artificial Intelligence, pp. 311–316. Professional Book Center (2005)

31. Somogyi, Z., Henderson, F., Conway, T.: The execution algorithm of Mercury, an efficient purely declarative logic programming language. Journal of Logic Programming 29(1-3), 17–64 (1996)

32. van Hentenryck, P., Perron, L., Puget, J.-F.: Search and strategies in OPL. Transactions on Computational Logic 1(2), 285–320 (2000)

33. Van Weert, P., Schrijvers, T., Demoen, B.: K.U.Leuven JCHR: A user-friendly, flexible and efficient CHR system for Java. In: Schrijvers, T., Frühwirth, T. (eds.) 2nd Workshop on Constraint Handling Rules, Report CW 421, pp. 47–62. Dept. of Computer Science, K.U.Leuven (2005)

34. Wallace, M., Novello, S., Schimpf, J.: ECL^iPS^e: A platform for constraint logic programming. ICL Systems Journal 12(1), 159–200 (1997)

35. Walsh, T.: Depth-bounded discrepancy search. In: 15th International Joint Conference on Artificial Intelligence, vol. 2, pp. 1388–1395. Morgan Kaufmann, San Francisco (1997)
36. Wolf, A.: Intelligent search strategies based on adaptive Constraint Handling Rules. Theory and Practice of Logic Programming 5(4-5), 567–594 (2005)
37. Wolf, A., Gruenhagen, T., Geske, U.: On the incremental adaptation of CHR derivations. Applied Artificial Intelligence 14(4), 389–416 (2000)
38. Wolf, A., Robin, J., Vitorino, J.: Adaptive CHR meets CHR$^\vee$: An extended refined operational semantics for CHR$^\vee$ based on justifications. In: Schrijvers, T., Frühwirth, T. (eds.) Constraint Handling Rules. LNCS (LNAI), vol. 5388, pp. 48–69. Springer, Heidelberg (2008)
39. Wuille, P., Schrijvers, T., Demoen, B.: CCHR: The fastest CHR implementation. In: In Khalil Djelloul, C., Duck, G.J., Sulzmann, M. (eds.) 4th Workshop on Constraint Handling Rules, pp. 123–137. U.Porto (2007)

Adaptive CHR Meets CHR$^\vee$

An Extended Refined Operational Semantics for CHR$^\vee$ Based on Justifications

Armin Wolf[1], Jacques Robin[2], and Jairson Vitorino[2]

[1] Fraunhofer FIRST, Kekuléstr. 7, D-12489 Berlin, Germany
armin.wolf@first.fraunhofer.de
[2] Centro de Informática, Universidade Federal de Pernambuco,
Caixa Postal CDU 7851, Receife, PE, Brazil
{jacques.robin,jairson}@gmail.com

Abstract. Adaptive constraint processing with Constraint Handling Rules (CHR) allows the application of intelligent search strategies to solve Constraint Satisfaction Problems (CSP), but these search algorithms have to be implemented in the host language of adaptive CHR which is currently Java. On the other hand, CHR$^\vee$ enables to explicitly formulate search in CHR, using disjunctive bodies to model choices. However, a naive implementation for handling disjunctions, in particular chronological backtracking (as implemented in Prolog), might cause "thrashing" due to an inappropriate order of decisions. In order to avoid this, a first combination of adaptive CHR and CHR$^\vee$ is presented to offer a more efficient embedded search mechanism to handle disjunctions. Therefore, the refined operational semantics of CHR is extended for disjunctions and adaptation.

1 Introduction

Constraint Handling Rules (CHR) [4,5] define a rule-based formalism which is primarily designed to specify constraint solvers on a rather abstract, declarative level. Secondly, it is also an executable, Turing-complete, committed choice, high-level programming language [8,14] that allows elegant and efficient formulations of algorithms, e.g. optimal union-find [13].

There are several extensions of the 'original' CHR: probabilistic CHR for probabilistic reasoning [3], adaptive CHR [18] that allows adaptation of CHR reasoning in dynamic environments and – last but not least – CHR$^\vee$ [1] handling disjunctions of constraints.

With respect to constraint solving, adaptive CHR and CHR$^\vee$ offer helpful features concerning search. In general (systematic) search is the most appropriate method to determine solutions of constraint problems because most of these problems, e.g. various scheduling problems, are NP-complete [6].[1] On the one

---

[1] Alternatively, guessing is another but less appropriate method: e.g. the existence of a solution is not decidable.

T. Schrijvers and T. Frühwirth (Eds.): Constraint Handling Rules, LNAI 5388, pp. 48–69, 2008.

hand, adaptive CHR justifies *all* derived constraints – especially false – enabling the implementation of intelligent search algorithms [17] like *dynamic backtracking* [7] or *conflict directed backjumping* [11]. Currently, these search algorithms have to be implemented in Java, the host language of adaptive CHR [16]. Therefore, the programmer has to be familiar with both languages: CHR which is logic- and rule-based and Java which is object-oriented and imperative. On the other hand, CHR$^\vee$ allows the formulation of disjunctive choices within CHR and thus the explicit formulation of search in CHR. The chosen decisions span a (virtual) decision/search tree concerning CHR$^\vee$'s operational semantics in [1]: There, the introduced **Split** computation step branches CHR$^\vee$ derivations, i.e. *"The step leads to branching in the computation in the same way as we had it for SLD resolutions. So we will again get a tree rather than a chain of states."* This means that search in CHR$^\vee$ does not require any knowledge about the host language. However, any naive implementation of the CHR$^\vee$ operational semantics may cause trees of exponential size due to the combinatorial explosion of the choices. While chronological backtracking, systematic depth-first search (as in Prolog) is efficient in space, it is in general not efficient in time. So the idea arises to combine both extensions of CHR retaining the declarative formulation of search within CHR itself from CHR$^\vee$ and using intelligent strategies enabled by adaptive CHR while performing search.

The paper is organized as follows: Initially, we introduce CHR as well as its extension CHR$^\vee$ by examples. Then we present a refined operational semantics for CHR$^\vee$. This operational semantics is further extended using the mechanism developed for adaptive CHR to realize conflict-directed backjumping. Its advantages with respect to efficiency are shown by a detailed example. Additionally some theoretical results are provided showing that the further extended operational semantics is sound with respect to the refined operational semantics of CHR$^\vee$. Finally a conclusion is drawn and the next steps of future work are outlined.

2   Adaptive CHR and CHR$^\vee$ by Example

Figure 1 shows CHR that handle graph-coloring problems with at most three colors where any two nodes connected by a common edge must have different colors. Some constraints represent the edges between the nodes of a graph while others define the domains of these nodes, i.e. their possible colors. The CHR constraint edge(A, B) means that there is an undirected edge between the nodes A and B. The CHR constraint neq(A, B) means that the nodes A and B must have different colors. The CHR constraint indomain(A, L) means that the node A may be colored with one of the values in the list L.[2]

In general, there are three kinds of rules: simplifications, propagations and simpagations. Simplifications and propagations are special cases of simpagations. The general form of a *simpagation rule* is (cf. [2]):

$$r \ @ \ H_1 \backslash H_2 \Longleftrightarrow G \mid B$$

---

[2] The lists of colors are represented explicitly to be independent of some Prolog-specific built-ins like `member/2`.

```
symmetry @ edge(X,Y)₁ <=> neq(X,Y), neq(Y,X).
notEqual @ neq(X,X)₂ <=> false.
ground1stOf3 @ indomain(X,[X,B,C])₃ <=> true.
ground2ndOf3 @ indomain(X,[A,X,C])₄ <=> true.
ground3rdOf3 @ indomain(X,[A,B,X])₅ <=> true.
ground1stOf2 @ indomain(X,[X,B])₆  <=> true.
ground2ndOf2 @ indomain(X,[A,X])₇  <=> true.

prune1stOf3 @ neq(X,Y)₉  \ indomain(X,[Y,B,C])₈ <=> indomain(X,[B,C]).
prune2ndOf3 @ neq(X,Y)₁₁ \ indomain(X,[A,Y,C])₁₀ <=> indomain(X,[A,C]).
prune3rdOf3 @ neq(X,Y)₁₃ \ indomain(X,[A,B,Y])₁₂ <=> indomain(X,[A,B]).
prune1stOf2 @ neq(X,Y)₁₅ \ indomain(X,[Y,B])₁₄  <=> X=B.
prune2ndOf2 @ neq(X,Y)₁₇ \ indomain(X,[A,Y])₁₆  <=> X=A.
```

Fig. 1. A CHR program for graph-coloring problems with at most 3 colors

where r is the rule's optional *name*. If the rule's name is omitted, then the delimiter '@' is omitted, too. H_1 as well as H_2 are possibly empty sequences of CHR constraints: the *head* constraints. Either H_1 or H_2 might be empty but not both. If one is empty, then the delimiter '\' is omitted. If H_1 is empty, then the rule is a *simplification rule*. If H_2 is empty, then the rule is a *propagation rule*. In order to discriminate these both rule types, the symbol '$\Longleftrightarrow$' is replaced by '$\Longrightarrow$' in case of propagations. G is a possibly empty conjunction of built-in constraints: the *guard* constraints. In case of an empty guard the delimiter '|' is omitted or the guard is made explicit to be true. B is a possibly empty sequence of CHR or built-in constraints: the *body* constraints. An empty sequence of body constraints is considered as true, too. Finally, a sequence of CHR is called a CHR *program*. For its operational semantics (cf. [2]) the head constraints in the rules are uniquely numbered top-down, *right-to-left* with the integers $1, 2, \ldots$, etc.[3]

Example 1. In Fig. 1 only special instances of two out of three kinds of rules are presented: *simplification* rules, e.g. like ground1stOf3 and *simpagation* rules, e.g. like prune2ndOf2. The intended semantics of the first rule is that if a node X is colored by the first value in its domain then the domain information is redundant because the node's color is determined. Operationally, this means that such domain constraints are removed from the constraint store, e.g. the constraint indomain(red, [red, green, blue]) is removed. The intended meaning of the second rule is that if there is an edge from node X to node Y and the node Y is labeled with the second color in the domain of node X, then X must be labeled with the first color in its domain because it must have a different color, i.e. the domain constraint is replaced by a simple equation.

Adaptive CHR annotates each constraint with a *justification*, i.e. a finite set of integral identifiers. Any application of a CHR unites the justifications of all involved constraints, i.e. of the head constraints and the built-in constraints

---

[3] This order prefers simplification over propagation (cf. [2]).

necessary for *head matching* and *guard entailment*. Then, the body constraints are justified (i.e. annotated) by these unions (cf. [18] for the details). – The following example illustrates how these unions are computed:

Example 2. The CHR program

```
cleanup @ gcd(0)          <=> true.
reduce  @ gcd(N) \ gcd(M) <=> 0<N, N=<M, L is M mod N | gcd(L).
```

computes the greatest common divisor of some positive integer numbers $n_1, \ldots, n_k$ if they are represented by CHR constraints $gcd(n_1), \ldots, gcd(n_k)$. The program will terminate with exactly one CHR constraint $gcd(m)$ containing the result m. It is worth noticing that the assignment (". is .") is considered as a built-in constraint in the guard. It is entailed if the left-hand-side is a *free local* variable, i.e. neither occurring in the head constraints nor being constrained otherwise, and if the right-hand-side is an *evaluable* arithmetic term, i.e. all variables are bound to numbers.

Now, let the *justified* CHR constraints $gcd(X)^{\{1\}}, gcd(Y)^{\{2\}}$ and the built-in constraints $(X = 5)^{\{3\}}, (Y = 15)^{\{4\}}$ be given. Here $\{1\}, \{2\}$ are the justifications of the CHR constraints and $\{3\}, \{4\}$ are the justifications of the syntactical equations.

It holds that the CHR constraints are matching the head constraints of the rule `reduce` in the given order. So *head matching* is determined by the union $\{1\} \cup \{2\} = \{1, 2\}$. In detail, head matching results in the *justified* equations $(N = X)^{\{1\}}, (M = Y)^{\{2\}}$. Considering guard entailment, the first inequality $0 < N$ is entailed because $(N = X)^{\{1\}}$ and $(X = 5)^{\{3\}}$ hold. Furthermore, this entailment ist justified by the union of their justifications, namely $\{1\} \cup \{3\} = \{1, 3\}$. Analogously, the entailment of $N \leq M$ is justified by $\{1, 2, 3, 4\}$ and the assignment L `is` $15 \mod 5$ is justified by $\{1, 2, 3, 4\}$ resulting in the *justified* equation $(L = 0)^{\{1,2,3,4\}}$. Finally, the derived CHR constraint $gcd(L)$ is justified by the union of all head matching and guard entailment justifications, i.e. it holds $gcd(L)^{\{1,2,3,4\}}$ or even $gcd(0)^{\{1,2,3,4\}}$ if the local variable L is eliminated by projection (cf. [15]).

In particular justification of inconsistencies is illustrated by the following example:

Example 3 (continuation of Example 1). Let two *justified* constraints be given: $neq(P, blue)^{\{1\}}$ and $indomain(P, [green, blue])^{\{3,5\}}$ *justified* by $\{1\}$ and $\{3, 5\}$ respectively. Then the application of the rule `prune2ndOf2` to these both constraints replaces them by the equation $(P = green)^{\{1,3,5\}}$ justified by the union $\{1\} \cup \{3, 5\}$. Now if there are additional constraints $neq(P, Q)^{\{2\}}$ and $(Q = green)^{\{4\}}$ then the rule `notEqual` applies yielding an inconsistency, i.e. $false^{\{1,2,3,4,5\}}$, justified by the union $\{2\} \cup \{1, 3, 5\} \cup \{4\}$.

In CHR$^\vee$ the body C of a rule $r \,@\, H_1 \backslash H_2 \Longleftrightarrow G \mid C$ is a possibly empty sequence of subsequences of CHR or built-in constraints: a *choice* of (conjunctions of) constraints separated by the delimiter ';'. Thus any CHR program is a $CHR^\vee$ program, too.[4]

Example 4. The CHR program introduced in Fig. 1 extended by the $CHR^\vee$ rules

```
label3 @ label(X)₁₉,indomain(X,[A,B,C])₁₈ <=> X=A; X=B; X=C.
label2 @ label(X)₂₁,indomain(X,[A,B])₂₀   <=> X=A; X=B.
```

is a $CHR^\vee$ program that allows to solve graph-coloring problems. It replaces for any variable X (representing a node) "declared" to be labeled via the constraint label(X) its domain constraint by a disjunction that equals this variable with the colors in the domain. For instance, the CHR constraints label(N), indomain(N, [red, green, blue]) will be replaced by the disjunction of equations $N = $ red; $N = $ green; $N = $ blue. Then these *alternatives* for the variable's labeling are tried in separate branches of the derivation tree (cf. Sect. 3).

The label/1 constraint and its according rules are introduced last in the program in order to trigger the search process after the propagation/simplification of all other constraints, i.e. after all other rules are tried. Furthermore, this approach supports the selection of the "next" variable to be labeled and thus variable ordering heuristics like the *first-fail* principle, i.e. choose a not yet labeled variable with smallest domain.

3   The Refined Operational Semantics $\omega_r^\vee$ of $CHR^\vee$

In this section a refined tree-based operational semantics of $CHR^\vee$ is given *without* determining the order how this tree has to be traversed. A more sophisticated semantics using a depth-first or breadth-first strategy is presented in [9,10]. Based on the refined operational semantics ω_r of CHR [2] the following notions are adopted:

An *identified* CHR constraint $c\#i$ is a CHR constraint c associated with some unique integer i. This number serves to differentiate among clones of the same constraint. The defined functions chr and id on identified CHR constraint with $chr(c\#i) = c$ and $id(c\#i) = i$ are extended to sequences and sets canonically, e.g. $chr(c\#i, d\#j) = c, d$ and $id(\{c\#i, d\#j\}) = \{i, j\}$.

An *occurrenced* identified CHR constraint $c\#i : j$ indicates that only matches with the j-th occurrence of constraint c should be considered when the constraint is active. For instance, an active edge$(P, Q)\#i : 1$ is matched against the head of the symmetry rule in Fig. 1.

A *choice* $(a_1; \ldots; a_n)$ is a tuple of sequences $a_1, \ldots, a_n$ of constraints, e.g. $a_i = c_{i_1}, \ldots, c_{i_k}$.[5]

---

[4] Here, for simplicity and without loss of generality, it is assumed that the body constraints are in *disjunctive normal form*.

[5] Only finite sequences are considered using the notation $e_1, \ldots, e_k$ and $U \circ V$ for the concatenation of two sequences U and V. Any single entity e is considered as a sequence, too. It is the topmost entity in $e \circ V$. The empty sequence is represented by λ.

An *execution state* is a tuple $\sigma = \langle A, S, B, T \rangle_m$ in $\omega_r^\vee$. Additionally in CHR$^\vee$ there might be *alternative execution states* $[\sigma_1 \mid \ldots \mid \sigma_n]$ $(n > 0)$. Further, the *execution stack* A is a sequence of constraints, *choices*, *identified* CHR constraints, and of *occurrenced* identified CHR constraints. In the stack A only the top-most entity is *active*.

The *CHR constraint store* S is a set of *identified* CHR constraints containing *candidates* that can be *matched* with rules in a CHR$^\vee$ program.

The *built-in constraint store* B is an internal representation of all built-in constraints passed to the underlying built-in solver, i.e. "*... an abstract logical conjunction of constraints.*" [2]

The *propagation history* T is a set of tuples containing the identifiers of identified CHR constraints which fired a rule and the rule's uniquely defined name.[6] – The maintenance of the propagation history avoids multiple identical applications of a propagation rule to the same sequence of CHR constraints and prevents trivial non-termination. Finally the integral number m is the next integer that has not yet been used to identify a CHR constraint.

The *initial states* in $\omega_r^\vee$ are the same as in ω_r: $\langle A, \emptyset, \mathsf{true}, \emptyset \rangle_1$ having empty constraint stores and histories, and where the constraints to be handled, i.e. the *goals*, are in the execution stack. Here, each *goal* is either a constraint c or a choice $(a_1; \ldots; a_n)$. Just as in ω_r, execution proceeds by exhaustively applying transitions to an initial state until the built-in store of the resulting state is *inconsistent*, i.e. the built-in constraint store is equivalent to false or no further transitions are applicable. These states are called *final states*.

We assume that the transitions Solve, Activate, Reactivate, Drop, Simplify, Propagate and Default in ω_r are based on a CHR program where all rules are uniquely named. Now, if $\sigma \rightarrowtail \sigma'$ holds for two states σ and σ' in ω_r, it also holds in $\omega_r^\vee$. Vice-versa, if $\sigma \rightarrowtail \sigma'$ holds for those transitions and two states σ and σ' in $\omega_r^\vee$, then it holds in ω_r, too.

For handling choices in the execution stack there is an additional transition splitting choices into separate branches, i.e. $\sigma \rightarrowtail [\sigma_1' \mid \ldots \mid \sigma_k']$ for some states $\sigma, \sigma_1', \ldots, \sigma_k'$. So these transitions define *derivation trees* accordingly:

- each initial state is the *root node* of a derivation tree, i.e. the unique state at the root level 0 of such a tree.
- any state σ' is a *node* of a derivation tree at level $l + 1$ if there is a (predecessor) state/node σ at level l in this tree and there is either a transition $\sigma \rightarrowtail \sigma'$ or $\sigma \rightarrowtail [\sigma_1' \mid \ldots \mid \sigma' \mid \ldots \mid \sigma_k']$

It is worth noticing that derivation trees are not necessarily finite and that the leaves of finite branches are final states and final states are only leaves.

Split: If there is no inconsistency and the next goal is a choice, then the derivation is split into several branches: one branch for each alternative (conjunction of) constraint(s) to be handled in a subsequent state:

---

[6] In the following we assume that each rule has such a name.

$$\langle (a_1; \ldots; a_n) \circ A, S, B, T \rangle_m \rightarrowtail [\langle a_1 \circ A, S, B, T \rangle_m \mid \ldots \mid \langle a_n \circ A, S, B, T \rangle_m]$$

if the built-in store is consistent, i.e. $B \neq \mathsf{false}$.

Now, let $[\sigma_1 \mid \ldots \mid \sigma_n]$ be the states at some level l in the derivation tree and $\sigma_{i_j} \rightarrowtail \sigma'_{i_j}$ hold for a subsequence $\sigma_{i_1}, \ldots \sigma_{i_k}$ of $\sigma_1, \ldots, \sigma_n$ in $\omega_r^\vee$, especially if $\sigma'_{i_j} = [\theta_1 \mid \ldots \mid \theta_q]$ is the result of a split. Further, let σ_p be final for each $p \in \{1, \ldots, n\} \setminus \{i_1, \ldots i_k\}$. Then, $[\sigma_1 \mid \ldots \mid \sigma_n] \rightarrowtail [\sigma'_{i_1} \mid \ldots \mid \sigma'_{i_k}]$ holds in $\omega_r^\vee$ defining the next level $l+1$ in the derivation tree (cf. [1] for the '.$\mid \ldots \mid$.' notation).[7]

Example 5 (continuation of Example 4). Take the CHR program in Fig. 1 extended by the CHR$^\vee$ rules `label2` and `label3` presented in Example 4. Then let the goal be $A_0 = (\mathsf{edge}(X_1, X_2) \circ A_1)$ with

$$A_1 = (\mathsf{edge}(X_2, X_3), \ldots, \mathsf{edge}(X_{n-1}, X_n), \mathsf{edge}(U, V), \mathsf{edge}(V, W), \mathsf{edge}(W, U),$$
$$\mathsf{indomain}(X_1, [\mathsf{red}, \mathsf{green}, \mathsf{blue}]), \ldots, \mathsf{indomain}(X_n, [\mathsf{red}, \mathsf{green}, \mathsf{blue}]),$$
$$\mathsf{indomain}(U, [\mathsf{red}, \mathsf{green}]), \mathsf{indomain}(V, [\mathsf{red}, \mathsf{green}]), \mathsf{indomain}(W, [\mathsf{red}, \mathsf{green}]),$$
$$\mathsf{label}(X_1), \ldots, \mathsf{label}(X_n), \mathsf{label}(U), \mathsf{label}(V), \mathsf{label}(W)) \ .$$

So the initial state roots in a single branch where the `edge/2` constraints are replaced by `neq/2` constraints:

$$\langle \mathsf{edge}(X_1, X_2) \circ A_1, \emptyset, \mathsf{true}, \emptyset \rangle_1$$
$$\rightarrowtail_{\mathsf{Activate}} \langle \mathsf{edge}(X_1, X_2)\#1 : 1 \circ A_1, \{\mathsf{edge}(X_1, X_2)\#1\}, \mathsf{true}, \emptyset \rangle_2$$
$$\rightarrowtail_{\mathsf{Simplify}} \langle \mathsf{neq}(X_1, X_2) \circ \mathsf{neq}(X_2, X_1) \circ A_1, \emptyset, \mathsf{true}, \emptyset \rangle_2 \quad \rightarrowtail \ldots$$

Then the `label/1` constraints will span a derivation tree that will initially have 3 siblings – one for each possible color of X_1. Each of these siblings will be the root of a binary subtree that will represent all possible combinations of the remaining colors of $X_2, \ldots, X_n, U, V$, and W, e.g. in the subtree where $X_1 = \mathsf{blue}$ holds, these remaining colors are `red` and `green`. Obviously all leaves of these subtrees will be inconsistent states because all bindings of the variables U, V and W with the available colors `red` and `green` will result in an inconsistency because there must be at least 3 different colors for these variables to be labeled with pairwise different values – however, there are only two.

Due to the unfortunate circumstances that the variables U, V, and W are labeled last, the detection of the inconsistency of the coloring problem requires the consideration of the whole derivation tree of size $O(2^n)$. So the necessary computation effort is at least $O(2^n)$, too.

Soundness and Completeness: The operational semantics of CHR$^\vee$ presented in [1] is a canonical extension of the of the *theoretical* operational semantics ω_t defined in [2]. Furthermore, the Split transition presented here is a canonical adaptation of the Split transition given in [1]. So it follows that Theorem 1 (Correspondence) in [2] still holds for the extended theoretical operational semantics $\omega_t^\vee$ and the extended operational semantics $\omega_r^\vee$.

---

[7] Nested brackets, i.e. '[$\ldots \mid$[$\ldots$]$\mid \ldots$]', are flattened, i.e. inner brackets are omitted.

4   The Extended and Refined Operational Semantics $\omega_r^{\vee*}$

In this section we propose an extended operational semantics of CHR$^\vee$ that realizes *conflict-directed backjumping* (CBJ). Computation on this semantics only derives one final state. However, this state is only inconsistent if there is no consistent final state in the whole (virtual) derivation tree. We focus on CBJ because we discovered that it performs very well in collaboration with a Boolean CHR solver (cf. [17]) on SAT problems, i.e. an important problem class of high practical relevance. Examinations showed that CBJ compared to chronological backtracking reduces the runtime in general one to two orders of magnitude even if the overhead for maintaining the justifications of adaptive CHR is considered.

Based on the previously defined operational semantics $\omega_r^\vee$ an *extended execution state* is a tuple (l, W, K, σ) where $l \in \mathbb{N}$ is a *level indicator* within the (virtual) derivation tree spanned by the CHR$^\vee$ rules, W is a sequence of *choices*, K is a *conflict set*, i.e. an integer set, containing the identifiers of decisions that causes an inconsistency at the current level. The tuple $\sigma = \langle A, S, B, T \rangle_m$ is an execution state in $\omega_r^\vee$. A *choice* $l : (a_1; \ldots; a_n)^J$ consists of a sequence $a_1, \ldots, a_n$ of sequences of constraints, e.g. $a_i = c_{i_1}, \ldots, c_{i_k}$ at a *level* indicated by an integer value l, annotated by a *justification* J, i.e. a set of integral identifiers. Further, any (sequence of) constraint(s) c may be annotated by a justification, too: c^J. By convention, if a justification is missing, it is assumed to be the empty set. In detail, *identified* CHR constraints as well as *occurrenced* identified CHR constraints are justified, too. Thus, an *identified* CHR constraint $c^J \#i$ is a CHR constraint c annotated by a *justification* J and associated with some unique identifier i. Further, it holds $chr(c^J \#i) = c$ and $id(c^J \#i) = i$ for the already defined functions. These functions are also extended to sequences and sets canonically, e.g. $chr(c^J \#i, d^I \#j) = c, d$ and $id(\{c^J \#i, d^I \#j\}) = \{i, j\}$.

An *occurrenced* identified CHR constraint $c^J \#i : j$ is accordingly defined.

The built-in constraint store B contains an abstract justified logical conjunction of constraints resulting from an underlying solver. In the case of an inconsistency the built-in store becomes false^F. Then the justification F contains identifiers of constraints chosen from choices that are responsible for this inconsistency.

The *initial states* are of the form $(0, \lambda, \emptyset, \langle A, \emptyset, \mathsf{true}, \emptyset \rangle_1)$ having empty sequences of choices, conflict sets, constraint stores and histories. The constraints to be handled, i.e. the *goals*, are in the execution stack. Again, *goals* are either constraints $c^\emptyset$ or choices $(a_1; \ldots; a_n)^\emptyset$. Here it is assumed that they are always justified by the empty set – in general any justifications are possible.[8]

Similar but not identical to ω_r, execution proceeds by exhaustively applying transitions to an initial state until the built-in store of the resulting state is either *inconsistent*, i.e. the built-in constraint store is equivalent to false *and* neither Backtrack nor Backjump transitions (defined later in this section) are applicable, or no other transition is applicable. These states are called *final states*.[9]

---

[8] However, the identifiers have to be disjoint to the level indicators.

[9] So inconsistent states are not necessarily final states.

We assume that the transitions Solve, Activate, Reactivate, Drop, Simplify, Propagate and Default in ω_r are based on a CHR program where all rules are named and that the annotated justifications are maintained as in [18]. Now, if (and only if) $\sigma \rightarrowtail \sigma'$ holds for these transitions, we have the analogous extended transitions:

$$(l, W, K, \sigma) \rightarrowtail (l, W, K, \sigma') \ ,$$

where any annotated justifications of the constraints or choices are passed without consideration, except within the Simplify and Propagate transitions. Here the union of the justifications of all constraints necessary for these transitions justifies the body constraints and the equations in the required substitutions. Therefore, we define the function $just$ that unites the justifications of sets and conjunctions of justified constraints, i.e. $just(c_1^{J_1} \wedge \ldots \wedge c_n^{J_n}) = J_1 \cup \ldots \cup J_n$ and $just(\{c_1^{J_1}, \ldots, c_n^{J_n}\}) = J_1 \cup \ldots \cup J_n$. In detail, the transitions Simplify and Propagate work as follows:

Simplify: Perform the derivation step

$$(l, W, K, \langle (c^I \# i : j \circ A, \{c^I \# i\} \uplus H_1 \uplus H_2 \uplus H_3 \uplus S, B, T \rangle_m)$$
$$\rightarrowtail (l, W, K, \langle C^J \circ A, H_1 \uplus S, \theta^J \wedge B, T \rangle_m)$$

if $B \neq \mathsf{false}^F$ for any justification F and the jth occurrence of the CHR predicate of c in a new rule variant in P is $r @ H_1' \setminus H_2', d_j, H_3' \Longleftrightarrow G \mid C$ and there exists a matching substitution θ such that $c = \theta(d_j)$, $chr(H_1) = \theta(H_1')$, $chr(H_2) = \theta(H_2')$, $chr(H_3) = \theta(H_3')$, and $B = E \wedge B'$ such that $\mathcal{D} \models E \longrightarrow \bar{\exists}_E(\theta \wedge G)$ holds. Concerning the justifications, $J = I \cup just(H_1) \cup just(H_2) \cup just(H_3) \cup just(E)$ holds, where E is an appropriate (e.g. minimal) sub-conjunction of the built-in store B entailing head matching and the guard conditions (as required).

So if there is no inconsistency and the active constraint occurs in the currently considered position in the heads to be removed of a rule variant in a CHR program P and there is a matching substitution for all kept and removed heads that is entailed by the built-in store as well as the rule's guard, then the rule is applied. The added body constraints as well as the syntactical equations in the substitution are justified by all constraints that are necessary to apply this rule.

It is worth noticing that there is neither the necessity to consider the history T nor to extend it because the considered constraint $c^I \# i$ is "consumed".

Propagate: Perform the derivation step

$$(l, W, K, \langle (c^I \# i : j \circ A, \{c^I \# i\} \uplus H_1 \uplus H_2 \uplus H_3 \uplus S, B, T \rangle_m)$$
$$\rightarrowtail (l, W, K, \langle C^J \circ c^I \# i : j \circ A, \{c^I \# i\} \uplus H_1 \uplus H_2 \uplus S, \theta^J \wedge B, T' \rangle_m)$$

under almost the same preconditions as Simplify, i.e. if $B \neq \mathsf{false}^F$ for any justification F and the jth occurrence of the CHR predicate of c in a new rule variant in P is $r @ H_1', d_j, H_2' \setminus H_3' \Longleftrightarrow G \mid C$ and there exists a matching substitution θ such that $c = \theta(d_j)$, $chr(H_1) = \theta(H_1')$, $chr(H_2) = \theta(H_2')$, $chr(H_3) = \theta(H_3')$, and

$B = E \wedge B'$ such that $\mathcal{D} \models E \longrightarrow \bar{\exists}_E(\theta \wedge G)$ holds. Additionally it must hold that the tuple $(id(H_1) \circ i \circ id(H_2) \circ id(H_3) \circ r) \notin T$, i.e. it is not in the propagation history T.

Concerning the justifications, it holds $J = I \cup just(H_1) \cup just(H_2) \cup just(H_3) \cup just(E)$, where E is an appropriate (e.g. minimal) sub-conjunction of the built-in store B entailing head matching and the guard conditions (as required). In order to avoid re-application of the same rule to the same CHR constraints, the propagation history T is extended by the tuple of their identifiers: $T' = T \cup \{(id(H_1) \circ i \circ id(H_2) \circ id(H_3) \circ r)\}$.

So if there is no inconsistency and the active constraint occurs in the currently considered position in the heads to be kept of a rule variant in a CHR program P and there is a matching substitution for all kept and removed heads that is entailed by the built-in store as well as the rule's guard, then the rule is applied. The added body constraints as well as the syntactical equations in the substitution are justified by all constraints that are necessary to apply this rule.

Additionally there are the following transitions to handle choices:

Choose: Perform the derivation step

$$(l, W, K, \langle (a_1; \ldots; a_n)^J \circ A, S, B, T \rangle_m)$$
$$\rightarrowtail (l+1, l : (a_2; \ldots; a_n)^J \circ W, K, \langle a_1^{J \cup \{l\}} \circ A, S, B, T \rangle_m)$$

if $B \neq \mathsf{false}^F$ for any justification F. So if there is no inconsistency and the next goal is a choice, then the first alternative constraint is chosen and its justification is extended by the level indicator. This justified constraint replaces the whole alternative in the goal. The remaining alternatives are stored under the level indicator for any presumable backtracking or backjumping in the future. Finally this indicator is increased.

Backtrack: Perform the derivation step

$$(l+1, l : (a_i; \ldots; a_n)^J \circ W, K, \langle A, S, \mathsf{false}^F, T \rangle_m)$$
$$\rightarrowtail (l+1, l : (a_{i+1}; \ldots; a_n)^J \circ W, K \cup (F \setminus \{l\}), \langle a_i^{J \cup \{l\}} \circ A', S', B', T' \rangle_m)$$

if $(l+1, l : (a_i; \ldots; a_n)^J \circ W, K, \langle a_{i-1}^{J \cup \{l\}} \circ A', S', B', T' \rangle_m$ is the most recent consistent state (with $B' \neq \mathsf{false}^{F'}$ for any justification F') of that kind in the derivation performed so far.[10]

In the special case where only one alternative is left and $(l+1, l : (a_n)^J \circ W, K, \langle a_{n-1}^{J \cup \{l\}} \circ A, S'', B', T' \rangle_m$ is the most recent state of that kind in the derivation performed so far, it holds:

$$(l+1, l : (a_n)^J \circ W, K, \langle A, S, \mathsf{false}^F, T \rangle_n)$$
$$\rightarrowtail (l+1, l : () \circ W, K \cup (F \setminus \{l\}), \langle a_n^{J \cup \{l\}} \circ A', S', B', T' \rangle_m)$$

---

[10] This state is computable via adaptation(cf. [16]).

In both cases, the conflict set K is extended by the identifiers of previously chosen constraints that are responsible for the occurred inconsistency.

So if any chosen alternative constraint results directly in an inconsistency, i.e. no other **Choose** transition is applicable[11] and there are remaining alternatives, then the consequences of the chosen constraint are discarded and the next alternative constraint is chosen.

Single-Step-Backjump: Perform the derivation step

$$(l+1, l : () \circ \cdots \circ h : (a_i; \ldots; a_n)^J \circ W, K, \langle A, S, \mathsf{false}^F, T \rangle_m)$$
$$\rightarrowtail (h+1, h : (a_{i+1}; \ldots; a_n)^J \circ W, (K \cup (F \setminus \{l\})) \setminus \{h\},$$
$$\langle a_i^{J \cup \{h\}} \circ A', S', B', T' \rangle_m)$$

if $K \cup (F \setminus \{l\}) \neq \emptyset$, $h = \max(K \cup (F \setminus \{l\}))$ hold, and $(h+1, h : (a_i; \ldots; a_n)^J \circ W, K', \langle a_{i-1}^{J \cup \{h\}} \circ A', S', B', T' \rangle_m)$ is the most recent consistent state (with $B' \neq \mathsf{false}^{F'}$ for any justification F') of that kind in the derivation performed so far.

The conflict set K is extended by the identifiers of previously chosen (conjunctions of) constraints that are responsible for the currently occurred inconsistency because some previous choices at levels $> l$ are already inconsistent: for each alternative $b_1 \ldots, b_m$ at level l inconsistencies were already derived: $\neg(A_1 \wedge b_1), \ldots, \neg(A_m \wedge b_m)$ for some conjunctions of constraints $A_1, \ldots, A_m$ at levels $> l$. Thus $\neg(A_1 \wedge b_1) \wedge \ldots \wedge \neg(A_m \wedge b_m) \wedge (b_1 \vee \ldots \vee b_m)$ implies $\neg(A_1 \wedge \ldots \wedge A_m)$. – Otherwise, if $K \cup (F \setminus \{l\}) = \emptyset$ holds, no further transition is applicable, i.e. there is no consistent final state.

This means that if all chosen alternative constraints result directly in inconsistencies, i.e. no further **Choose** transition was applied, processing "jumps back". It returns to the most recently performed **Choose** transition that is involved in one of these inconsistencies, i.e. its level indicator is the maximum of the actual conflict set. This conflict set is the union of the justifications of the inconsistencies resulting from all alternatives at level l. If there are remaining alternatives at the maximum level $h < l$, then the already chosen is replaced by the next. Otherwise, if the actual conflict set is empty, any alternative will result in an inconsistency, i.e. this transition is not applicable.

Multi-Step-Backjump: Perform the derivation step

$$(l+1, l : () \circ \cdots \circ h : () \circ W, K, \langle A, S, \mathsf{false}^F, T \rangle_m)$$
$$\rightarrowtail (h+1, h : () \circ W, (K \cup (F \setminus \{l\})) \setminus \{h\}, \langle A', S', \mathsf{false}^{F \setminus \{l\}}, T' \rangle_m)$$

if $K \cup (F \setminus \{l\}) \neq \emptyset$, $h = \max(K \cup (F \setminus \{l\}))$ hold and $(h+1, h : () \circ W, K', \langle a^{J \cup \{h\}} \circ A', S', B', T' \rangle_m)$ is the most recent consistent state (with $B' \neq \mathsf{false}^{F'}$ for any justification F') of that kind in the derivation performed so far. Again, the conflict set K is extended by the identifiers of previously chosen (conjunctions of)

---

[11] Otherwise the level indicator would be greater than $l + 1$.

constraints that are responsible for the occurred inconsistency except the identifier of the current level because there another alternative is chosen. Additionally the justification of false is adapted, too, i.e. identifiers greater than the resulting level h are removed because the accompanying decisions are discarded. Otherwise, if $K \cup (F \setminus \{l\}) = \emptyset$ holds, no further transition is applicable.

This means that if all necessary preconditions for a Single-Step-Backjump transition hold, except that no remaining alternatives are left at level h, it will "jump back" to level $h' < h$ with remaining alternatives. Otherwise, if there are no remaining alternatives, nothing is performed.

Example 6 (Continuation of Example 5). For $n = 2$ the initial state is $\sigma_0 = (0, \lambda, \emptyset, \langle A_0, \emptyset, \text{true}, \emptyset \rangle_1)$ with the initial goals

$$A_0 = (\text{edge}(X_1, X_2)^0, \text{edge}(U, V)^0, \text{edge}(V, W)^0, \text{edge}(W, U)^0,$$
$$\text{indomain}(X_1, [\text{red, green, blue}])^0, \text{indomain}(X_2, [\text{red, green, blue}])^0,$$
$$\text{indomain}(U, [\text{red, green}])^0, \text{indomain}(V, [\text{red, green}])^0, \text{indomain}(W, [\text{red, green}])^0,$$
$$\text{label}(X_1)^0, \text{label}(X_2)^0, \text{label}(U)^0, \text{label}(V)^0, \text{label}(W)^0) \ .$$

These goals model a graph coloring problem that consists of an arc between X_1 and X_2 and a separate subgraph that connects U, V, W with each other. After processing the CHR program in Fig. 1 on the edge/2 and indomain/2 constraints of the initial goals it holds $\sigma_0 \rightarrowtail \cdots \rightarrowtail (0, \lambda, \emptyset, \langle A_a, S_a, \text{true}, \emptyset \rangle_{18}) = \sigma_a$, where

$$A_a = (\text{label}(X_1)^0, \text{label}(X_2)^0, \text{label}(U)^0, \text{label}(V)^0, \text{label}(W)^0)$$
$$S_a = \{\text{neq}(X_1, X_2)^0 \#2, \text{neq}(X_2, X_1)^0 \#3, \text{neq}(U, V)^0 \#5, \text{neq}(V, U)^0 \#6,$$
$$\text{neq}(V, W)^0 \#8, \text{neq}(W, V)^0 \#9, \text{neq}(W, U)^0 \#11, \text{neq}(U, W)^0 \#12,$$
$$\text{indomain}(X_1, [\text{red, green, blue}])^0 \#13, \text{indomain}(X_2, [\text{red, green, blue}])^0 \#14,$$
$$\text{indomain}(U, [\text{red, green}])^0 \#15, \text{indomain}(V, [\text{red, green}])^0 \#16,$$
$$\text{indomain}(W, [\text{red, green}])^0\} \#17\} \ .$$

Continued constraint processing labels variable X_1 with color red in two steps: First, the indomain/2 constraint formulated on X_1 is replaced by a choice due to a Simplify transition. Second, the first alternative is chosen due to a Choose transition storing the remaining two alternatives at root level 0. The chosen alternative $X_1 = \text{red}$ that holds at level 1 is justified by the set $\{0\}$ because this decision is made at root level:

$$\sigma_a \rightarrowtail_{\text{Activate}} (0, \lambda, \emptyset, \langle (\text{label}(X_1)^0 \#18 : 1, \text{label}(X_2)^0, \text{label}(U)^0, \text{label}(V)^0, \text{label}(W)^0)$$
$$\{\text{label}(X_1)^0 \#18\} \cup S_a, \text{true}, \emptyset \rangle_{19})$$
$$\rightarrowtail_{\text{Default}}^{\times 18} (0, \lambda, \emptyset, \langle (\text{label}(X_1)^0 \#18 : 19, \text{label}(X_2)^0, \text{label}(U)^0, \text{label}(V)^0, \text{label}(W)^0),$$
$$\{\text{label}(X_1)^0 \#18\} \cup S_a, \text{true}, \emptyset \rangle_{19})$$
$$\rightarrowtail_{\text{Simplify}} (0, \lambda, \emptyset, \langle ((X_1 = \text{red}; X_1 = \text{green}; X_1 = \text{blue})^0,$$
$$\text{label}(X_2)^0, \text{label}(U)^0, \text{label}(V)^0, \text{label}(W)^0),$$
$$S_a \setminus \{\text{indomain}(X_1, [\text{red, green, blue}])^0 \#13\}, \text{true}, \emptyset \rangle_{19})$$
$$\rightarrowtail_{\text{Choose}} (1, (0 : (X_1 = \text{green}; X_1 = \text{blue})^0), \emptyset, \langle ((X_1 = \text{red})^{\{0\}},$$

$$\mathsf{label}(X_2)^\emptyset, \mathsf{label}(U)^\emptyset, \mathsf{label}(V)^\emptyset, \mathsf{label}(W)^\emptyset),$$

$$S_a \setminus \{\mathsf{indomain}(X_1, [\mathsf{red}, \mathsf{green}, \mathsf{blue}])^\emptyset \#13\}, \mathsf{true}, \emptyset\rangle_{19})$$

$$\rightarrowtail_{\mathsf{Solve}} (1, (0 : (X_1 = \mathsf{green}; X_1 = \mathsf{blue})^\emptyset), \emptyset, \langle(\mathsf{neq}(X_2, X_1)^\emptyset \#3,$$

$$\mathsf{label}(X_2)^\emptyset, \mathsf{label}(U)^\emptyset, \mathsf{label}(V)^\emptyset, \mathsf{label}(W)^\emptyset),$$

$$S_a \setminus \{\mathsf{indomain}(X_1, [\mathsf{red}, \mathsf{green}, \mathsf{blue}])^\emptyset \#13\},$$

$$((X_1 = \mathsf{red})^{\{0\}}), \emptyset\rangle_{19}) = \sigma_a'.$$

To keep the derivation in this example simple, only the "inactive" constraint $\mathsf{neq}(X_2, X_1)^\emptyset \#3$ was re-introduced in the last Solve transition.

Now, this constraint removes the color red from the domain of X_2 after its re-activation. A Simplify transition replaces the $\mathsf{indomain/2}$ constraint in the CHR constraint store by a new one on top of the execution stack that is justified by the set $\{0\}$ because the transition is justified by the active neq constraint and the equality $X_1 = \mathsf{red}$:

$$\sigma_a' \rightarrowtail_{\mathsf{Reactivate}} (1, (0 : (X_1 = \mathsf{green}; X_1 = \mathsf{blue})^\emptyset), \emptyset, \langle(\mathsf{neq}(X_2, X_1)^\emptyset \#3 : 1,$$

$$\mathsf{label}(X_2)^\emptyset, \mathsf{label}(U)^\emptyset, \mathsf{label}(V)^\emptyset, \mathsf{label}(W)^\emptyset),$$

$$S_a \setminus \{\mathsf{indomain}(X_1, [\mathsf{red}, \mathsf{green}, \mathsf{blue}])^\emptyset \#13\}, ((X_1 = \mathsf{red})^{\{0\}}), \emptyset\rangle_{19})$$

$$\rightarrowtail_{\mathsf{Default}}^{\times 8} (1, (0 : (X_1 = \mathsf{green}; X_1 = \mathsf{blue})^\emptyset), \emptyset, \langle(\mathsf{neq}(X_2, X_1)^\emptyset \#3 : 9,$$

$$\mathsf{label}(X_2)^\emptyset, \mathsf{label}(U)^\emptyset, \mathsf{label}(V)^\emptyset, \mathsf{label}(W)^\emptyset),$$

$$S_a \setminus \{\mathsf{indomain}(X_1, [\mathsf{red}, \mathsf{green}, \mathsf{blue}])^\emptyset \#13\}, ((X_1 = \mathsf{red})^{\{0\}}), \emptyset\rangle_{19})$$

$$\rightarrowtail_{\mathsf{Simplify}} (1, (0 : (X_1 = \mathsf{green}; X_1 = \mathsf{blue})^\emptyset), \emptyset,$$

$$\langle(\mathsf{indomain}(X_2, [\mathsf{green}, \mathsf{blue}])^{\{0\}},$$

$$\mathsf{label}(X_2)^\emptyset, \mathsf{label}(U)^\emptyset, \mathsf{label}(V)^\emptyset, \mathsf{label}(W)^\emptyset),$$

$$S_a \setminus \{\mathsf{indomain}(X_1, [\mathsf{red}, \mathsf{green}, \mathsf{blue}])^\emptyset \#13,$$

$$\mathsf{indomain}(X_2, [\mathsf{red}, \mathsf{green}, \mathsf{blue}])^\emptyset \#14\},$$

$$((X_1 = \mathsf{red})^{\{0\}}), \emptyset\rangle_{19}) = \sigma_b .$$

For the sake of simplicity let

$$S_b = S_a \setminus \{\mathsf{indomain}(X_1, [\mathsf{red}, \mathsf{green}, \mathsf{blue}])^\emptyset \#13, \mathsf{indomain}(X_2, [\mathsf{red}, \mathsf{green}, \mathsf{blue}])^\emptyset \#14\} .$$

Then, the new $\mathsf{indomain/2}$ constraint is inserted into the CHR constraint store:

$$\sigma_b \rightarrowtail_{\mathsf{Activate}} (1, (0 : (X_1 = \mathsf{green}; X_1 = \mathsf{blue})^\emptyset), \emptyset,$$

$$\langle(\mathsf{indomain}(X_2, [\mathsf{green}, \mathsf{blue}])^{\{0\}} \#19 : 1,$$

$$\mathsf{label}(X_2)^\emptyset, \mathsf{label}(U)^\emptyset, \mathsf{label}(V)^\emptyset, \mathsf{label}(W)^\emptyset),$$

$$\{\mathsf{indomain}(X_2, [\mathsf{green}, \mathsf{blue}])^{\{0\}} \#19\} \cup S_b, ((X_1 = \mathsf{red})^{\{0\}}), \emptyset\rangle_{20})$$

$$\rightarrowtail_{\mathsf{Default}}^{\times 21} (1, (0 : (X_1 = \mathsf{green}; X_1 = \mathsf{blue})^\emptyset), \emptyset,$$

$$\langle(\mathsf{indomain}(X_2, [\mathsf{green}, \mathsf{blue}])^{\{0\}} \#19 : 22,$$

$$\mathsf{label}(X_2)^\emptyset, \mathsf{label}(U)^\emptyset, \mathsf{label}(V)^\emptyset, \mathsf{label}(W)^\emptyset),$$

$$\{\mathsf{indomain}(X_2, [\mathsf{green}, \mathsf{blue}])^{\{0\}} \#19\} \cup S_b, ((X_1 = \mathsf{red})^{\{0\}}), \emptyset\rangle_{20})$$

$\rightarrowtail_{\text{Drop}}$ $(1, (0 : (X_1 = \text{green}; X_1 = \text{blue})^\emptyset), \emptyset,$

$\langle (\text{label}(X_2)^\emptyset, \text{label}(U)^\emptyset, \text{label}(V)^\emptyset, \text{label}(W)^\emptyset),$

$\{\text{indomain}(X_2, [\text{green}, \text{blue}])^{\{0\}} \# 19\} \cup S_b, ((X_1 = \text{red})^{\{0\}}), \emptyset\rangle_{20}) = \sigma_c$.

Further, the next `label/1` constraint is activated. It labels variable X_2 with color green in a similar manner as before X_1. However, this decision depends on the labeling of X_1:

$\sigma_c \rightarrowtail_{\text{Activate}} (1, (0 : (X_1 = \text{green}; X_1 = \text{blue})^\emptyset), \emptyset,$

$\langle (\text{label}(X_2)^\emptyset \# 20 : 1, \text{label}(U)^\emptyset, \text{label}(V)^\emptyset, \text{label}(W)^\emptyset),$

$\{\text{label}(X_2)^\emptyset \# 20, \text{indomain}(X_2, [\text{green}, \text{blue}])^{\{0\}} \# 19\} \cup S_b,$

$((X_1 = \text{red})^{\{0\}}), \emptyset\rangle_{21})$

$\rightarrowtail_{\text{Default}}^{\times 20} (1, (0 : (X_1 = \text{green}; X_1 = \text{blue})^\emptyset), \emptyset,$

$\langle (\text{label}(X_2)^\emptyset \# 20 : 21, \text{label}(U)^\emptyset, \text{label}(V)^\emptyset, \text{label}(W)^\emptyset),$

$\{\text{label}(X_2)^\emptyset \# 20, \text{indomain}(X_2, [\text{green}, \text{blue}])^{\{0\}} \# 19\} \cup S_b,$

$((X_1 = \text{red})^{\{0\}}), \emptyset\rangle_{21})$

$\rightarrowtail_{\text{Simplify}} (1, (0 : (X_1 = \text{green}; X_1 = \text{blue})^\emptyset), \emptyset,$

$\langle ((X_2 = \text{green}; X_2 = \text{blue})^{\{0\}},$

$\text{label}(U)^\emptyset, \text{label}(V)^\emptyset, \text{label}(W)^\emptyset), S_b, ((X_1 = \text{red})^{\{0\}}), \emptyset\rangle_{21})$

$\rightarrowtail_{\text{Choose}} (2, (1 : (X_2 = \text{blue})^{\{0\}}, 0 : (X_1 = \text{green}; X_1 = \text{blue})^\emptyset), \emptyset,$

$\langle ((X_2 = \text{green})^{\{0,1\}},$

$\text{label}(U)^\emptyset, \text{label}(V)^\emptyset, \text{label}(W)^\emptyset), S_b, ((X_1 = \text{red})^{\{0\}}), \emptyset\rangle_{21})$

$\rightarrowtail_{\text{Solve}} (2, (1 : (X_2 = \text{blue})^{\{0\}}, 0 : (X_1 = \text{green}; X_1 = \text{blue})^\emptyset), \emptyset,$

$\langle (\text{label}(U)^\emptyset, \text{label}(V)^\emptyset, \text{label}(W)^\emptyset),$

$S_b, ((X_1 = \text{red})^{\{0\}} \wedge (X_2 = \text{green})^{\{0,1\}}), \emptyset\rangle_{21}) = \sigma_d$.

For the sake of simplicity, we have not reactivated the constraints containing X_2, i.e. neither $\text{neq}(X_1, X_2)$ nor $\text{neq}(X_2, X_1)$, because they will not trigger any of the rules in the considered CHR program.

Continuing the derivation process, the variable U is labeled in a similar manner as X_1 and X_2 before. In contrast to the labeling of X_2 the labeling of U is independent from X_1 and X_2 due to the graph's topology.

$\sigma_d \rightarrowtail_{\text{Activate}} (2, (1 : (X_2 = \text{blue})^{\{0\}}, 0 : (X_1 = \text{green}; X_1 = \text{blue})^\emptyset), \emptyset,$

$\langle (\text{label}(U)^\emptyset \# 21 : 1, \text{label}(V)^\emptyset, \text{label}(W)^\emptyset), \{\text{label}(U)^\emptyset \# 21\} \cup S_b,$

$((X_1 = \text{red})^{\{0\}} \wedge (X_2 = \text{green})^{\{0,1\}}), \emptyset\rangle_{22})$

$\rightarrowtail_{\text{Default}}^{\times 20} (2, (1 : (X_2 = \text{blue})^{\{0\}}, 0 : (X_1 = \text{green}; X_1 = \text{blue})^\emptyset), \emptyset,$

$\langle (\text{label}(U)^\emptyset \# 21 : 21, \text{label}(V)^\emptyset, \text{label}(W)^\emptyset), \{\text{label}(U)^\emptyset \# 21\} \cup S_b,$

$((X_1 = \text{red})^{\{0\}} \wedge (X_2 = \text{green})^{\{0,1\}}), \emptyset\rangle_{22})$

$\rightarrowtail_{\text{Simplify}} (2, (1 : (X_2 = \text{blue})^{\{0\}}, 0 : (X_1 = \text{green}; X_1 = \text{blue})^\emptyset), \emptyset,$

$\langle ((U = \text{green}; U = \text{blue})^\emptyset, \text{label}(V)^\emptyset, \text{label}(W)^\emptyset),$

$$S_b \setminus \{\text{indomain}(U, [\text{green}, \text{blue}])^\emptyset \#15\},$$
$$((X_1 = \text{red})^{\{0\}} \wedge (X_2 = \text{green})^{\{0,1\}}), \emptyset)_{22})$$
$$\rightarrowtail_{\text{Choose}} (3, (2 : (U = \text{blue})^\emptyset, 1 : (X_2 = \text{blue})^{\{0\}}, 0 : (X_1 = \text{green}; X_1 = \text{blue})^\emptyset), \emptyset,$$
$$\langle ((U = \text{green})^{\{2\}}, \text{label}(V)^\emptyset, \text{label}(W)^\emptyset),$$
$$S_b \setminus \{\text{indomain}(U, [\text{green}, \text{blue}])^\emptyset \#15\},$$
$$((X_1 = \text{red})^{\{0\}} \wedge (X_2 = \text{green})^{\{0,1\}}), \emptyset)_{22})$$
$$\rightarrowtail_{\text{Solve}} (3, (2 : (U = \text{blue})^\emptyset, 1 : (X_2 = \text{blue})^{\{0\}}, 0 : (X_1 = \text{green}; X_1 = \text{blue})^\emptyset), \emptyset,$$
$$\langle (\text{neq}(V, U)^\emptyset \#6, \text{neq}(W, U)^\emptyset \#11, \text{label}(V)^\emptyset, \text{label}(W)^\emptyset),$$
$$S_b \setminus \{\text{indomain}(U, [\text{green}, \text{blue}])^\emptyset \#15\},$$
$$((X_1 = \text{red})^{\{0\}} \wedge (X_2 = \text{green})^{\{0,1\}} \wedge (U = \text{green})^{\{2\}}), \emptyset)_{22}) = \sigma_e .$$

The chosen value of variable U reactivates the two constraints $\text{neq}(V, U)^\emptyset \#6$ and $\text{neq}(W, U)^\emptyset \#11$. Reactivation of the first determines the value of V. Thus, for $S_c = S_b \setminus \{\text{indomain}(U, [\text{green}, \text{blue}])^\emptyset \#15\}$, it holds:

$$\sigma_e \rightarrowtail_{\text{Reactivate}} (3, (2 : (U = \text{blue})^\emptyset, 1 : (X_2 = \text{blue})^{\{0\}}, 0 : (X_1 = \text{green}; X_1 = \text{blue})^\emptyset), \emptyset,$$
$$\langle (\text{neq}(V, U)^\emptyset \#6 : 1, \text{neq}(W, V)^\emptyset \#9, \text{label}(V)^\emptyset, \ldots), S_c,$$
$$((X_1 = \text{red})^{\{0\}} \wedge (X_2 = \text{green})^{\{0,1\}} \wedge (U = \text{green})^{\{2\}}), \emptyset)_{22})$$
$$\rightarrowtail_{\text{Default}}^{\times 14} (3, (2 : (U = \text{blue})^\emptyset, 1 : (X_2 = \text{blue})^{\{0\}}, 0 : (X_1 = \text{green}; X_1 = \text{blue})^\emptyset), \emptyset,$$
$$\langle (\text{neq}(V, U)^\emptyset \#6 : 15, \text{neq}(W, V)^\emptyset \#9, \text{label}(V)^\emptyset, \ldots), S_c,$$
$$((X_1 = \text{red})^{\{0\}} \wedge (X_2 = \text{green})^{\{0,1\}} \wedge (U = \text{green})^{\{2\}}), \emptyset)_{22})$$
$$\rightarrowtail_{\text{Simplify}} (3, (2 : (U = \text{blue})^\emptyset, 1 : (X_2 = \text{blue})^{\{0\}}, 0 : (X_1 = \text{green}; X_1 = \text{blue})^\emptyset), \emptyset,$$
$$\langle ((V = \text{blue})^{\{2\}}, \text{neq}(W, V)^\emptyset \#9, \text{label}(V)^\emptyset, \ldots),$$
$$S_c \setminus \{\text{indomain}(V, [\text{green}, \text{blue}])^\emptyset \#16\},$$
$$((X_1 = \text{red})^{\{0\}} \wedge (X_2 = \text{green})^{\{0,1\}} \wedge (U = \text{green})^{\{2\}}), \emptyset)_{22})$$
$$\rightarrowtail_{\text{Solve}} (3, (2 : (U = \text{blue})^\emptyset, 1 : (X_2 = \text{blue})^{\{0\}}, 0 : (X_1 = \text{green}; X_1 = \text{blue})^\emptyset), \emptyset,$$
$$\langle (\text{neq}(W, V)^\emptyset \#9, \text{label}(V)^\emptyset, \ldots), S_c \setminus \{\text{indomain}(V, [\text{green}, \text{blue}])^\emptyset \#16\},$$
$$((X_1 = \text{red})^{\{0\}} \wedge (X_2 = \text{green})^{\{0,1\}} \wedge (U = \text{green})^{\{2\}}$$
$$\wedge (V = \text{blue})^{\{2\}}), \emptyset)_{22}) = \sigma_f .$$

Again, for the sake of simplicity, it is assumed that the constraint $\text{neq}(W, V)^\emptyset \#9$ will be the first to be reconsidered. Its reactivation results in analogous transitions as before. This means that the constraint $\text{neq}(W, V)^\emptyset \#9$ will be reactivated again. Then the built-in store becomes inconsistent, i.e. for $S_d = S_c \setminus \{\text{indomain}(V, [\text{green}, \text{blue}])^\emptyset \#16\}$ it holds:

$$\sigma_f \rightarrowtail_{\text{Reactivate}} \cdots$$
$$\rightarrowtail_{\text{Solve}} (3, (2 : (U = \text{blue})^\emptyset, 1 : (X_2 = \text{blue})^{\{0\}}, 0 : (X_1 = \text{green}; X_1 = \text{blue})^\emptyset), \emptyset,$$
$$\langle (\text{neq}(W, V)^\emptyset \#9, \text{label}(V)^\emptyset, \ldots), S_d \setminus \{\text{indomain}(W, [\text{green}, \text{blue}])^\emptyset \#17\},$$
$$((X_1 = \text{red})^{\{0\}} \wedge (X_2 = \text{green})^{\{0,1\}} \wedge (U = \text{green})^{\{2\}}$$
$$\wedge (V = \text{blue})^{\{2\}} \wedge W = \text{blue})^{\{2\}}), \emptyset)_{22})$$

$\rightarrowtail_{\text{Reactivate}}$ $(3, (2 : (U = \text{blue})^\emptyset, 1 : (X_2 = \text{blue})^{\{0\}}, 0 : (X_1 = \text{green}; X_1 = \text{blue})^\emptyset), \emptyset,$
$\qquad \langle(\text{neq}(W, V)^\emptyset \#9 : 1, \text{label}(V)^\emptyset, \ldots),$
$\qquad S_d \setminus \{\text{indomain}(W, [\text{green}, \text{blue}])^\emptyset \#17\},$
$\qquad ((X_1 = \text{red})^{\{0\}} \wedge (X_2 = \text{green})^{\{0,1\}} \wedge (U = \text{green})^{\{2\}}$
$\qquad \wedge (V = \text{blue})^{\{2\}} \wedge W = \text{blue})^{\{2\}}), \emptyset\rangle_{22})$

$\rightarrowtail_{\text{Default}}$ $(3, (2 : (U = \text{blue})^\emptyset, 1 : (X_2 = \text{blue})^{\{0\}}, 0 : (X_1 = \text{green}; X_1 = \text{blue})^\emptyset), \emptyset,$
$\qquad \langle(\text{neq}(W, V)^\emptyset \#9 : 2, \text{label}(V)^\emptyset, \ldots),$
$\qquad S_d \setminus \{\text{indomain}(W, [\text{green}, \text{blue}])^\emptyset \#17\},$
$\qquad ((X_1 = \text{red})^{\{0\}} \wedge (X_2 = \text{green})^{\{0,1\}} \wedge (U = \text{green})^{\{2\}}$
$\qquad \wedge (V = \text{blue})^{\{2\}} \wedge W = \text{blue})^{\{2\}}), \emptyset\rangle_{22})$

$\rightarrowtail_{\text{Simplify}}$ $(3, (2 : (U = \text{blue})^\emptyset, 1 : (X_2 = \text{blue})^{\{0\}}, 0 : (X_1 = \text{green}; X_1 = \text{blue})^\emptyset), \emptyset,$
$\qquad \langle(\text{false}^{\{2\}}, \text{label}(V)^\emptyset, \ldots),$
$\qquad S_d \setminus \{\text{indomain}(W, [\text{green}, \text{blue}])^\emptyset \#17, \text{neq}(W, V)^\emptyset \#9\},$
$\qquad ((X_1 = \text{red})^{\{0\}} \wedge (X_2 = \text{green})^{\{0,1\}} \wedge (U = \text{green})^{\{2\}}$
$\qquad \wedge (V = \text{blue})^{\{2\}} \wedge W = \text{blue})^{\{2\}}), \emptyset\rangle_{22})$

$\rightarrowtail_{\text{Solve}}$ $(3, (2 : (U = \text{blue})^\emptyset, 1 : (X_2 = \text{blue})^{\{0\}}, 0 : (X_1 = \text{green}; X_1 = \text{blue})^\emptyset), \emptyset,$
$\qquad \langle(\text{label}(V)^\emptyset, \ldots), S_d \setminus \{\text{indomain}(W, [\text{green}, \text{blue}])^\emptyset \#17, \text{neq}(W, V)^\emptyset \#9\},$
$\qquad (\text{false}^{\{2\}}), \emptyset\rangle_{22}) = \sigma_h$.

The detected inconsistency triggers a Backtrack transition solely justified by the last decision. Thus the conflict set is not changed. The next chosen labeling leads to another inconsistency. Again, it is solely justified by this last alternative:

$\sigma_h \rightarrowtail_{\text{Backtrack}}$ $(3, (2 : (), 1 : (X_2 = \text{blue})^{\{0\}}, 0 : (X_1 = \text{green}; X_1 = \text{blue})^\emptyset), \emptyset,$
$\qquad \langle((U = \text{blue})^{\{2\}}, \text{label}(V)^\emptyset, \ldots), S_b \setminus \{\text{indomain}(U, [\text{green}, \text{blue}])^\emptyset \#15\},$
$\qquad ((X_1 = \text{red})^{\{0\}} \wedge (X_2 = \text{green})^{\{0,1\}}), \emptyset\rangle_{22})$

$\rightarrowtail_{\text{Activate}}$ $\cdots$

$\rightarrowtail_{\text{Solve}}$ $(3, (2 : (), 1 : (X_2 = \text{blue})^{\{0\}}, 0 : (X_1 = \text{green}; X_1 = \text{blue})^\emptyset), \emptyset,$
$\qquad \langle(\text{label}(V)^\emptyset, \ldots), S_d \setminus \{\text{indomain}(W, [\text{green}, \text{blue}])^\emptyset \#17, \text{neq}(W, V)^\emptyset \#9\},$
$\qquad (\text{false}^{\{2\}}), \emptyset\rangle_{22}) = \sigma_i$.

In state σ_i there is no alternative left for the choice processed at level 2, i.e. $2 : ()$ holds. So backjumping will be considered. However, any backjump to another alternative labeling of X_2 or X_1 is not performed because the conflict set is empty. This shows that the assignments to the variables X_1 and X_2 are not involved in the inconsistency that consists in the subgraph of U, V, W that must be colored with at least 3 different colors. Consequently CHR processing stops without superfluous consideration of other – exponentially many – derivations as in Example 5 when using the semantics $\omega_r^\vee$.

5   Relationships between the Presented CHR$^\vee$ Semantics

In this section the soundness of the extended and refined operational semantics $\omega_r^{\vee^*}$ is shown with respect to the refined operational semantics $\omega_r^\vee$. Due to the correspondence of the latter semantics with the theoretical operational semantics $\omega_t^\vee$ the extended and refined operational semantics $\omega_r^{\vee^*}$ is also sound with respect to $\omega_t^\vee$. Before proving this important property the following necessary lemma will be proved:

Lemma 1. *Let an $\omega_r^{\vee^*}$ derivation*

$$(0, \lambda, \emptyset, \langle A_0, \emptyset, \text{true}, \emptyset \rangle_1)$$
$$\rightarrowtail \cdots \rightarrowtail (l+1, l : (a_i; \ldots; a_n)^J \circ W, K, \sigma)$$

for a level indicator l, an index $1 < i \leq n+1$, a choice $(a_i; \ldots; a_n)$, a justification J, a sequence of choices W, a conflict set K and a execution state σ be given.[12] Furthermore, the derivation's last state, i.e. σ, be consistent.

Then there are a conflict set $K^\star$, some constraints $a_1, \ldots, a_{i-1}$, an activation stack $A^\star$, a CHR constraint store $S^\star$, a built-in constraint store $B^\star$, a propagation history $T^\star$, an index $m^\star$ and a derivation step within this derivation

$$(l, W, K^\star, \langle (a_1; \ldots; a_n)^J \circ A^\star, S^\star, B^\star, T^\star \rangle_{m^\star})$$
$$\rightarrowtail (l+1, l : (a_2; \ldots; a_n)^J \circ W, K^\star, \langle a_1^{J \cup \{l\}} \circ A^\star, S^\star, B^\star, T^\star \rangle_{m^\star})$$

which is based on a Choose *transition.*

Proof. The proposition is proved by induction over the length of the derivation. Obviously there is at least one derivation step such that the given derivation has a positive length, i.e. $d > 0$.

Induction base, i.e. $d = 1$: Analyzing all defined transitions this derivation step can only match the pattern of a Choose transition. By its definition there is an execution stack A such that $A_0 = (a_1; \ldots; a_n)^J \circ A$ and

$$(0, \lambda, \emptyset, \langle A_0, \emptyset, \text{true}, \emptyset \rangle_1) \rightarrowtail (1, 1 : (a_2; \ldots; a_n)^J, \emptyset, \langle a_1^{J \cup \{l\}} \circ A, \emptyset, \text{true}, \emptyset \rangle_1)$$

hold. Obviously the proposition to be proven holds, too.

Induction step, i.e. $d \rightsquigarrow d+1$: It is assumed that the length of the given $\omega_r^{\vee^*}$ derivation is $d+1$ with $d \geq 1$, i.e. it has the structure

$$(0, \lambda, \emptyset, \langle A_0, \emptyset, \text{true}, \emptyset \rangle_1) \rightarrowtail \cdots \rightarrowtail$$
$$(l', W', K', \sigma') \rightarrowtail (l+1, l : (a_i; \ldots; a_n)^J \circ W, K, \sigma)$$

Analyzing all defined transitions the last derivation step can match the patterns of all transitions except Multi-Step-Backjump because σ is consistent.

---

[12] It is assumed that choice $(a_i; \ldots; a_n)$ might be also empty, i.e. (), indicated by $i = n+1$.

If the last derivation step is either a Solve, Activate, Reactivate, Simplify, PropagateDrop or Default transition then by definition it holds

$$(l', W', K', \sigma') = (l+1, l : (a_i; \ldots; a_n)^J \circ W, K, \sigma')$$

By induction hypothesis there are a conflict set $K^\star$, some constraints $a_1, \ldots, a_{i-1}$, an activation stack $A^\star$, a CHR constraint store $S^\star$, a built-in constraint store $B^\star$, a propagation history $T^\star$, a number $m^\star$ and a derivation step within this derivation

$$(l, W, K^\star, \langle (a_1; \ldots; a_n)^J \circ A^\star, S^\star, B^\star, T^\star \rangle_{m^\star})$$
$$\rightarrowtail (l+1, l : (a_2; \ldots; a_n)^J \circ W, K^\star, \langle a_1^{J \cup \{l\}} \circ A^\star, S^\star, B^\star, T^\star \rangle_{m^\star})$$

which is based on a Choose transition.

If the last derivation step is a Choose transition, then the state to be proven holds obviously (cf. induction base). In remaining two cases either a Backtrack or a Single-Step-Backjump transition is applied. So by definition of these transitions there are a conflict set K'', two constraint a_{i-2}, a_{i-1}, an execution stack A, a CHR constraint store S, a built-in constraint store B, a propagation history T, a number m and an intermediate state

$$(l+1, l : (a_{i-1}; \ldots; a_n)^J \circ W, K'', \langle a_{i-2}^{J \cup \{l\}} \circ A, S, B, T \rangle_m)$$

in the derivation of length d. By induction hypothesis it follow that there are a conflict set $K^\star$, some constraints $a_1, \ldots, a_{i-3}$, an activation stack $A^\star$, a CHR constraint store $S^\star$, a built-in constraint store $B^\star$, a propagation history $T^\star$, a number $m^\star$ and a derivation step within this derivation

$$(l, W, K^\star, \langle (a_1; \ldots; a_n)^J \circ A^\star, S^\star, B^\star, T^\star \rangle_{m^\star})$$
$$\rightarrowtail (l+1, l : (a_2; \ldots; a_n)^J \circ W, K^\star, \langle a_1^{J \cup \{l\}} \circ A^\star, S^\star, B^\star, T^\star \rangle_{m^\star})$$

which is based on a Choose transition. Summarizing, the proposition to be proven holds in all possible cases.   □

Now the soundness of $\omega_r^{\vee^\star}$ with respect to $\omega_r^\vee$ will be proven on the basis of this lemma. In detail it is shown that for each derivation in $\omega_r^{\vee^\star}$ resulting in a consistent state there is a corresponding path in the virtual derivation tree in $\omega_r^\vee$ to an $\omega_r^\vee$ state "wrapped" by this $\omega_r^{\vee^\star}$ state:

Theorem 1 (Soundness of $\omega_r^{\vee^\star}$ with respect to $\omega_r^\vee$). *Let an $\omega_r^{\vee^\star}$ derivation*

$$(0, \lambda, \emptyset, \langle A_0, \emptyset, \text{true}, \emptyset \rangle_1) \rightarrowtail \cdots \rightarrowtail (l, W, K, \sigma)$$

be given where (l, W, K, σ), in particular σ, is a consistent state. If the annotated justifications in σ are omitted, then there is an $\omega_r^\vee$ derivation

$$\langle A_0, \emptyset, \text{true}, \emptyset \rangle_1 \rightarrowtail \cdots \rightarrowtail [\ldots \mid \sigma \mid \ldots] \ .$$

Proof. The proposition will be proved by induction over the length d of the given $\omega_r^{\vee^*}$ derivation.

Induction base, i.e. $d = 0$: Obviously the proposition holds if the length of the $\omega_r^{\vee^*}$ derivation is zero, i.e. the initial execution stack A_0 is empty.

Induction step, i.e. $d \rightsquigarrow d + 1$: It is assumed that the length of the given $\omega_r^{\vee^*}$ derivation is $d + 1$ with $d \geq 0$, i.e. it has the structure

$$(0, \lambda, \emptyset, \langle A_0, \emptyset, \mathsf{true}, \emptyset \rangle_1) \rightarrowtail \cdots \rightarrowtail (l', W', K', \sigma') \rightarrowtail (l, W, K, \sigma)$$

where (l, W, K, σ), especially σ, is a consistent state.

Now let the derivation step $(l', W', K', \sigma') \rightarrowtail (l, W, K, \sigma)$ be based on one of the transitions Solve, Activate, Reactivate, Drop, Simplify, Propagate, or Default. Then (l', W', K', σ') is a consistent state and there is an $\omega_r^{\vee}$ derivation

$$\langle A_0, \emptyset, \mathsf{true}, \emptyset \rangle_1 \rightarrowtail \cdots \rightarrowtail [\ldots \mid \sigma' \mid \ldots]$$

by induction hypothesis. Furthermore, by definition of $\omega_r^{\vee^*}$ it holds that

$$\langle A_0, \emptyset, \mathsf{true}, \emptyset \rangle_1 \rightarrowtail \cdots \rightarrowtail [\ldots \mid \sigma' \mid \ldots] \rightarrowtail [\ldots \mid \sigma \mid \ldots] \ ,$$

i.e. the proposition to be proven is valid in those cases.

Now let the derivation step $(l', W', K', \sigma') \rightarrowtail (l, W, K, \sigma)$ be based on a Choose transition. Then there are a choice $(a_1; \ldots; a_n)$, a justification J, an execution stack A, a CHR constraint store S, a built-in constraint store B, a propagation history T and a counter m such that

$$\sigma' = \langle (a_1; \ldots; a_n)^J \circ A, S, B, T \rangle_m$$
$$\sigma = \langle a_1^{J \cup \{l\}} \circ A, S, B, T \rangle_m$$

hold. Then by induction hypothesis there is an $\omega_r^{\vee}$ derivation

$$\langle A, \emptyset, \mathsf{true}, \emptyset \rangle_1 \rightarrowtail \cdots \rightarrowtail [\ldots \mid \sigma' \mid \ldots]$$

Omitting the annotated justifications in σ' and σ, a Split transition is applicable to σ'. This results in $\sigma' \rightarrowtail [\sigma \mid \ldots \mid \langle a_n \circ A, S, B, T \rangle_m]$ in $\omega_r^{\vee}$ proving the asserted proposition in this case.

Now let the derivation step $(l', W', K', \sigma') \rightarrowtail (l, W, K, \sigma)$ be based on a Backtrack transition. Then there are a level indicator l'', a choice $(a_i; \ldots; a_n)$, justifications J, F, a sequence of choices W'', a conflict set K', execution stacks A, A', CHR constraint stores S, S', a built-in constraint store B', a propagation history T and a number m such that

$$(l', W', K', \sigma') = (l'' + 1, l'' : (a_i; \ldots; a_n)^J \circ W'', K', \langle A, S, \mathsf{false}^F, T \rangle_m)$$

$$(l, W, K, \sigma) = (l'' + 1, l'' : (a_{i+1}; \ldots; a_n)^J \circ W'', K, \langle a_i^{J \cup \{l''\}} \circ A', S', B', T' \rangle_m)$$

hold by definition of a Backtrack transition. Thus, concerning Lemma 1, there are a conflict set $K^\star$ and some constraints $a_1, \ldots, a_{i-1}$ and a derivation step in the given derivation

$$(l'', W'', K^\star, \langle (a_1; \ldots; a_n)^J \circ A', S', B', T' \rangle_m)$$
$$\rightarrowtail (l'' + 1, l'' : (a_2; \ldots; a_n)^J \circ W'', K^\star, \langle a_1^{J \cup \{l''\}} \circ A', S', B', T' \rangle_m)$$

based on a **Choose** transition. It follows by induction hypothesis that there is an $\omega_r^\vee$ derivation

$$\langle A_0, \emptyset, \mathsf{true}, \emptyset \rangle_1 \rightarrowtail \cdots \rightarrowtail [\ldots \mid \langle (a_1; \ldots; a_n) \circ A', S', B', T' \rangle_m \mid \ldots]$$

where a **Split** transition is applicable to $\langle (a_1; \ldots; a_n) \circ A', S', B', T' \rangle_m$. This results in the derivation

$$\langle A_0, \emptyset, \mathsf{true}, \emptyset \rangle_1 \rightarrowtail \cdots \rightarrowtail [\ldots \mid \langle (a_1; \ldots; a_n) \circ A', S', B', T' \rangle_m \mid \ldots]$$
$$\rightarrowtail [\ldots \mid \langle a_i^{J \cup \{l''\}} \circ A', S', B', T' \rangle_m \mid \ldots] \ ,$$

i.e. the proposition to be proven holds in this case.

Finally let the derivation step $(l', W', K', \sigma') \rightarrowtail (l, W, K, \sigma)$ be based on a **Single-Step-Backjump** transition. Then there are level indicators l'', h, a choice $(a_{i+1}; \ldots; a_n)$, a constraint a_i, justifications J, F, a sequence of choices W'', a conflict set K', execution stacks A, A', CHR constraint stores S, S', a built-in constraint store B', a propagation history T and a number m such that

$$(l', W', K', \sigma')$$
$$= (l'' + 1, l'' : () \circ \cdots \circ h : (a_i; \ldots; a_n)^J \circ W'', K', \langle A, S, \mathsf{false}^F, T \rangle_m)$$
$$(l, W, K, \sigma)$$
$$= (h + 1, h : (a_{i+1}; \ldots; a_n)^J \circ W'', K, \langle a_i^{J \cup \{h\}} \circ A', S', B', T' \rangle_m)$$

hold by definition of a **Single-Step-Backjump** transition. Thus, concerning Lemma 1, there are a conflict set $K^\star$ and some constraints $a_1, \ldots, a_{i-1}$ and a derivation step in the given derivation

$$(h, W'', K^\star, \langle (a_1; \ldots; a_n)^J \circ A', S', B', T' \rangle_m)$$
$$\rightarrowtail (h + 1, h : (a_2; \ldots; a_n)^J \circ W'', K^\star, \langle a_1^{J \cup \{h\}} \circ A', S', B', T' \rangle_m)$$

based on a **Choose** transition. So by induction hypothesis there is an $\omega_r^\vee$ derivation

$$\langle A_0, \emptyset, \mathsf{true}, \emptyset \rangle_1 \rightarrowtail \cdots \rightarrowtail [\ldots \mid \langle (a_1; \ldots; a_n) \circ A', S', B', T' \rangle_m \mid \ldots]$$

where a **Split** transition is applicable to $\langle (a_1; \ldots; a_n) \circ A', S', B', T' \rangle_m$. This results in

$$\langle A_0, \emptyset, \mathsf{true}, \emptyset \rangle_1 \rightarrowtail \cdots \rightarrowtail [\ldots \mid \langle (a_1; \ldots; a_n) \circ A', S', B', T' \rangle_m \mid \ldots]$$
$$\rightarrowtail [\ldots \mid \langle a_i^{J \cup \{l''\}} \circ A', S', B', T' \rangle_m \mid \ldots] \ ,$$

i.e. the asserted proposition holds in this case. Further, it holds in all cases under the considered assumption that the last state is consistent because any derivation step based on a **Multi-Step-Backjump** transition results in an inconsistent state. $\qquad\square$

Theorem 1 especially shows that for each derivation in $\omega_r^{\vee^\star}$ resulting in a consistent final state it holds that this final state "wraps" a consistent final state in $\omega_r^\vee$, i.e. a solution of the considered constraint problem modeled as the goal A_0.

6　Conclusion and Future Work

The main result of this article is a combination of the flexibility allowed by providing disjunctions in CHR with the efficiency of a procedure to handle disjunctive bodies based on justifications. We extended the refined operational semantics of CHR presented in [2] to accommodate several new transitions that makes use of the mechanism for adaptive CHR to embed conflict-directed backjumping for handling choices in $CHR^\vee$. We presented a detailed example on graph-coloring to demonstrate empirically the advantages of this approach. Furthermore, this case-study is amended with an important theoretical result: the soundness of the extended and refined operational semantics $\omega_r^{\vee*}$.

Ongoing theoretical work is on the formulation and proof of an additional proposition that show that the presented operational semantics correspond to each other, especially showing that the extended and refined operational semantics $\omega_r^{\vee*}$ is also complete with respect to $\omega_r^\vee$ [10].

The next practical step will be an implementation realizing the new transitions of the presented operational semantics. We will conduct this as a sub-task of the on-going project ROARS [12] which aims to build the first model-driven $CHR^\vee$ compiler integrating adaptive CHR and handling of disjunctions.

Acknowledgment

Many thanks to the anonymous reviewers for their constructive comments.

References

1. Abdennadher, S., Schütz, H.: $CHR^\vee$: A flexible query language. In: Andreasen, T., Christiansen, H., Larsen, H.L. (eds.) FQAS 1998. LNCS (LNAI), vol. 1495, pp. 1–14. Springer, Heidelberg (1998)
2. Duck, G.J., García de la Banda, M., Stuckey, P.J., Holzbaur, C.: The refined operational semantics of constraint handling rules. In: Demoen, B., Lifschitz, V. (eds.) ICLP 2004. LNCS, vol. 3132, pp. 90–104. Springer, Heidelberg (2004)
3. Frühwirth, T., Di Pierro, A., Wiklicky, H.: Probabilistic constraint handling rules. Electronic Notes in Theoretical Computer Science 76, 1–16 (2002)
4. Frühwirth, T.: Constraint Handling Rules. In: Podelski, A. (ed.) Constraint Programming: Basics and Trends. LNCS, vol. 910, pp. 90–107. Springer, Heidelberg (1995)
5. Frühwirth, T.: Theory and practice of Constraint Handling Rules. The Journal of Logic Programming 37, 95–138 (1998)
6. Garey, M.R., Johnson, D.S.: Computers and Intractability: A Guide to the Theory of NP-Completeness. Series of Books in the Mathematical Sciences. W. H. Freeman & Co., New York (1979)
7. Ginsberg, M.L.: Dynamic backtracking. Journal of Artificial Intelligence Research 1, 25–46 (1993)
8. Holzbaur, C., Frühwirth, T.: A Prolog Constraint Handling Rules compiler and runtime system. Applied Artificial Intelligence 14(4), 369–388 (2000)

9. De Koninck, L., Schrijvers, T., Demoen, B.: Flexible search strategies in Prolog CHR. Report CW 447, Department of Computer Science, K. U. Leuven (May 2006); Also presented at the Workshop on CHR (2006)
10. De Koninck, L., Schrijvers, T., Demoen, B.: A Flexible Search Framework for CHR. In: Schrijvers, T., Frühwirth, T. (eds.) Constraint Handling Rules. LNCS (LNAI), vol. 5388, pp. 16–47. Springer, Heidelberg (2008)
11. Prosser, P.: Hybrid algorithms for the constraint satisfaction problem. Computational Intelligence 9(3), 268–299 (1991); also available as technical report AISL-46-91, Stratchclyde (1991)
12. The ROARS project (last visited February 25, 2008), http://www.cin.ufpe.br/~jr/mysite/RoarsProject.html
13. Schrijvers, T., Frühwirth, T.: Optimal union-find in constraint handling rules. Theory and Practice of Logic Programming 6(1–2), 213–224 (2006)
14. Sneyers, J., Schrijvers, T., Demoen, B.: The computational power and complexity of constraint handling rules. In: Schrijvers, T., Frühwirth, T. (eds.) Proceedings of CHR 2005, Second Workshop on Constraint Handling Rules, number CW 421 in CW Reports, pp. 3–17. Katholieke Universiteit Leuven, Department of Computer Science (2005) (last visited August 26, 2008), http://www.cs.kuleuven.be/publicaties/rapporten/cw/CW421.abs.html
15. Wolf, A.: Projection in adaptive constraint solving based on chrs. In: Apt, K.R., Kakas, A.C., Monfroy, E., Rossi, F. (eds.) Proceedings of the ERCIM/COMPULOG Workshop on Constraints, Department of Computer Science, University of Cyprus, Nicosia, Cyprus (October 1999)
16. Wolf, A.: Adaptive constraint handling with CHR in Java. In: Walsh, T. (ed.) CP 2001. LNCS, vol. 2239, pp. 256–270. Springer, Heidelberg (2001)
17. Wolf, A.: Intelligent search strategies based on adaptive constraint handling rules. Theory and Practice of Logic Programming 5(4–5), 567–594 (2005)
18. Wolf, A., Gruenhagen, T., Geske, U.: On incremental adaptation of CHR derivations. Applied Artificial Intelligence 14(4), 389–416 (2000)

Constructing Rule-Based Solvers for Intentionally-Defined Constraints

Ingi Sobhi[1], Slim Abdennadher[1], and Hariolf Betz[2]

[1] Faculty of Media Engineering and Technology, German University in Cairo, Egypt
{Slim.Abdennadher,Ingi.Sobhi}@guc.edu.eg
[2] Faculty of Engineering and Computer Science, University of Ulm, Germany
Hariolf.Betz@uni-ulm.de

Abstract. Developing constraint solvers which are key requisites of constraint programming languages is time consuming and difficult. In this paper, we propose a generic algorithm that symbolically constructs rule-based solvers from the intensional definition of the constraint. Unlike the well-established "generate and test" approach, our symbolic construction approach is capable of generating recursive rules from a recursive constraint definition. Combining the two approaches gives better filtering capabilities than either of the approaches acting alone.

1 Introduction

"Constraint Programming represents one of the closest approaches computer science has yet made to the Holy Grail of programming: the user states the problem, the computer solves it." [E. Freuder]

The validity of this statement for a Constraint Logic Programming (CLP) language is contingent on the existence of constraint solvers. These associate constraints with filtering algorithms that remove variable values which cannot belong to any solution of the problem.

Constraint Handling Rules (CHR) is a multi-headed guarded and concurrent constraint logic programming language. To incorporate constraint solvers in CHR, a scheme was proposed in [1] to automatically derive the solvers given the intentional definition of the constraints. The scheme is based on a generate and test approach where rule candidates are enumerated and tested for validity against the constraint definition. Although the approach performs an extensive search for valid rules, given a recursive constraint definition it is unable to generate recursive rules.

To overcome this, we propose a scheme where valid rules are symbolically constructed from the clauses of a CLP program defining the constraint. The idea behind the construction stems from the observation that if in a non-overlapping CLP program the execution of a clause leads to a solution, the execution of all other clauses will not. Thus our constructed CHR rules simplify the constraint to the body of a clause only if all other clauses do not hold. Moreover, we combine the two schemes to achieve better filtering.

T. Schrijvers and T. Frühwirth (Eds.): Constraint Handling Rules, LNAI 5388, pp. 70–84, 2008.
© Springer-Verlag Berlin Heidelberg 2008

Example 1 (Motivation). Consider the lexicographic order constraint [2,3,4]. Given two sequences L_1 and L_2 of variables of the same length, then *lex* holds if L_1 is lexicographically smaller than or equal to L_2. The following CLP program defines the $lex(L_1, L_2)$ constraint:

$$lex([], [])$$
$$lex([X_1|T_1], [X_2|T_2]) \leftarrow X_1 < X_2$$
$$lex([X_3|T_3], [X_4|T_4]) \leftarrow X_3 = X_4 \wedge lex(T_3, T_4)$$

The generate and test approach [1] generates rules that reason about the first elements of the two lists such as:

$$lex(L_1, L_2) \Rightarrow L_1 = [X_1|T_1] \wedge L_2 = [X_2|T_2] \mid X_1 \leq X_2 \tag{1}$$

The symbolic construction approach proposed in this paper generates the following solver:

$$lex(L_1, L_2) \Leftrightarrow L_1 = [] \vee L_2 = [] \mid L_1 = [] \wedge L_2 = [] \tag{2}$$
$$lex(L_1, L_2) \Leftrightarrow L_1 = [X_1|T_1] \wedge L_2 = [X_2|T_2] \wedge X_1 \neq X_2 \mid X_1 < X_2 \tag{3}$$
$$lex(L_1, L_2) \Leftrightarrow L_1 = [X_1|T_1] \wedge L_2 = [X_2|T_2] \wedge X_1 \geq X_2 \mid X_1 = X_2 \wedge lex(T_1, T_2) \tag{4}$$

Given the query $\langle lex([A_1, A_2, A_3], [B_1, B_2, B_3]) \rangle$ where the domains of the variables are defined as follows:

$$A_1 = \{1, 3, 4\}, \ A_2 = \{2, 3, 4\}, \ A_3 = \{1, 2\}$$
$$B_1 = \{1\}, \quad B_2 = \{2\}, \quad B_3 = \{0, 1, 2\}$$

The generate and test approach enforces the constraint $A_1 \leq B_1$, which removes the values $\{3, 4\}$ from the domain of A_1. The solution becomes:

$$A_1 = \{1\}, \ A_2 = \{2, 3, 4\}, \ A_3 = \{1, 2\},$$
$$B_1 = \{1\}, \quad B_2 = \{2\}, \quad B_3 = \{0, 1, 2\},$$
$$lex([A_1, A_2, A_3], [B_1, B_2, B_3])$$

For the symbolic construction approach since $A_1 \geq B_1$, rule (4) is executed enforcing equality on the values of A_1 and B_1 before calling *lex* recursively on the remaining list elements. Since $A_2 \geq B_2$ rule (4) is applied again, whereas for A_3 and B_3 no rule is applicable. The solution becomes:

$$A_1 = \{1\}, \ A_2 = \{2\}, \ A_3 = \{1, 2\},$$
$$B_1 = \{1\}, \ B_2 = \{2\}, \ B_3 = \{0, 1, 2\},$$
$$lex([A_3], [B_3])$$

Combining both approaches prunes the domains of the variables further since rule (1) is applicable to $lex([A_3], [B_3])$ and filters the domain of B_3. The combined solution becomes:

$$A_1 = \{1\}, \ A_2 = \{2\}, \ A_3 = \{1, 2\},$$
$$B_1 = \{1\}, \ B_2 = \{2\}, \ B_3 = \{1, 2\},$$
$$A_3 \leq B_3, lex([A_3], [B_3])$$

We will proceed with the *lex* constraint in all examples of this paper.

The paper is a revised and extended version of [5] and is organized as follows. In section 3, we present the symbolic construction approach and prove soundness and termination of the constructed solvers. In section 4, we apply post-processing methods to improve the run-time complexity of the solvers. Finally, section 5 combines the symbolic construction approach with the "generate and test" approach to achieve better filtering.

2   Preliminaries

2.1   Intentional Definition

Let p be a constraint. A CLP program P defines p if p occurs with the same arity in the head of all the clauses and all true instances of p are accounted for (closed world assumption). The program P is of the usual form:

$$p(\bar{t}_1) \leftarrow C_1, p(\bar{t}_2) \leftarrow C_2, \ldots, p(\bar{t}_n) \leftarrow C_n$$

where $\bar{t}_i$ stands for a sequence of terms and C_i is a conjunction of built-in and user-defined constraints. Built-in constraints are those defined by a constraint theory and for which solvers are available. These solvers are assumed to be well-behaved (terminating and confluent), closed under negation, and achieve arc-consistency. User-defined constraints are those for which solvers are needed. The symbolic construction approach requires that there are no variables in C_i that are not in $\bar{t}_i$ and that all clauses are non-overlapping (i.e. in a computation at most one clause can lead to a solution).

Definition 1. *The logical reading of P denoted by P^* is given by its* Clark completion *[6]:*

$$\forall \bar{x} \; (p(\bar{x}) \leftrightarrow \bigvee_{i=1}^{n} \exists \bar{y}_i \; (\bar{x}=\bar{t}_i \wedge C_i))$$

where $\bar{x}$ is a sequence of distinct fresh variables and $\bar{y}_i$ is the sequence of variables in $\bar{t}_i$. The expression $\bar{x}=\bar{t}_i$ stands for the conjunction of equations between respective elements of the sequences $\bar{x}$ and $\bar{t}_i$.

Example 2 (Clark Completion). The Clark completion of the CLP program defining *lex* is:

$\forall L_1, L_2 \; lex(L_1, L_2) \leftrightarrow$
$\qquad (L_1=[] \wedge L_2=[]) \vee$
$\qquad \exists X_1, X_2, T_1, T_2 \; (L_1=[X_1|T_1] \wedge L_2=[X_2|T_2] \wedge X_1<X_2) \vee$
$\qquad \exists X_3, X_4, T_3, T_4 \; (L_1=[X_3|T_3] \wedge L_2=[X_4|T_4] \wedge X_3=X_4 \wedge lex(T_3, T_4))$

2.2   Constraint Solver

CHR [7] specifies how new constraints interact with the constraint store and is thus especially suited for writing constraint solvers. It has two main rule types:

$$\text{Simplification Rule:} \quad H \Leftrightarrow G \mid B$$
$$\text{Propagation Rule:} \quad H \Rightarrow G \mid B$$

where the *head* H are user-defined constraints, the *guard* G are built-in constraints and the *body* constraints B are both.

Definition 2. *The* logical meaning *of a simplification rule is a logical equivalence provided the guard holds:*

$$\forall \bar{x} \forall \bar{y} \ (G \rightarrow (H \leftrightarrow \exists \bar{z} \ B))$$

where $\bar{x}$ is the set of variables occurring in H, the variables $\bar{y}$ are the set occurring in G but not in H and $\bar{z}$ are the variables occurring in B only. Similarly, the logical meaning of a propagation rule is an implication provided the guard holds.

Prompted with a query, applicable rules are executed until a fixpoint is reached where no more rules can be applied or a contradiction occurs. A rule is applicable provided that constraints from the query match the head and imply the guard. Execution of a simplification rule rewrites constraints that match the head by the body while execution of a propagation rule adds the body constraints to the constraint store.

2.3   Generate and Test Approach

In this section, we summarize the generate and test approach presented in [1]. Given a CLP program defining the constraint as well as the syntactic form of the candidate rules defined by the following sets:

- $Base_{lhs}$ contains constraints that must appear in the head of all rules,
- $Cand_{lhs}$ contains constraints to be used in conjunction with $Base_{lhs}$ to form the head, and
- $Cand_{rhs}$ contains constraints that may appear in the body.

The generate and test approach generates valid rules as follows. Candidate propagation rules of the form $H \Rightarrow B$ are enumerated, and subjected to a validity test based on the observation that a rule is valid if the execution of the goal $H \wedge \neg(B)$ finitely fails with respect to the CLP program.

Example 3 (Generate and Test Approach). Given the syntactic form of candidate rules for *lex* as:

$Base_{lhs} = \{lex(L_1, L_2)\}$
$Cand_{lhs} = \{L_1 = [], L_2 = [], L_1 = [X_1|T_1], L_2 = [X_2|T_2], X_1 \leq X_2, X_1 > X_2, X_1 < X_2, \ldots\}$
$Cand_{rhs} = Cand_{lhs}$

The generate and test approach generates (among others) the following rule for *lex*:

$$lex([X_1|T_1], [X_2|T_2]) \Rightarrow X_1 \leq X_2$$

The rule is generated since executing the goal $\langle lex([X_1|T_1],[X_2|T_2]), X_1 > X_2 \rangle$ fails as demonstrated by the following derivation tree:

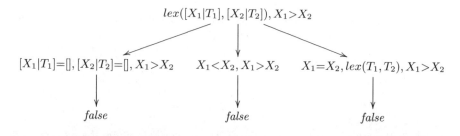

3 Symbolic Construction Approach

The symbolic construction approach (Fig. 1) constructs a solver for a constraint by symbolically transforming the Clark completion of the CLP program defining the constraint to semantically valid rules. The idea of the transformation stems from the observation that in a non-overlapping CLP program if the execution of one clause leads to a solution then the execution of all other clauses will not. Thus to construct a rule that simplifies the constraint to the body of one clause, the negation of the bodies of all other clauses is added to the guard. This ensures that the rule is applicable only when all other clauses are not valid and hence maintains consistency with the constraint definition.

---

begin
        p: left hand side of the Clark completion
        $Disjuncts$: set of disjuncts of right hand side of the Clark completion
        $Rules=\{\}$: resultant rule set

        for each D **in** $Disjuncts$ **do**
            $Other=Disjuncts\backslash\{D\}$
            $Rules=Rules \cup \{p \Leftrightarrow \neg Other \mid D\}$
        end for
end

Fig. 1. Symbolic Construction Algorithm

3.1 Guard Determination

More formally, given the definition of a constraint $p(\bar{x})$:

$$\forall \bar{x} \left(p(\bar{x}) \leftrightarrow \bigvee_{i=1}^{n} \exists \bar{y}_i \left(\bar{x} = \bar{t}_i \wedge C_i \right) \right)$$

The symbolic construction algorithm constructs rules of the form:

$$p(\bar{x}) \Leftrightarrow \neg \bigvee_{j=1, j \neq i}^{n} \exists \bar{y}_j \left(\bar{x} = \bar{t}_j \wedge C_j\right) \mid \bar{x} = \bar{t}_i \wedge C_i \quad \text{for each } i \in \{1, \ldots, n\}$$

where $\bar{x} = \bar{t}_j$ stands for the conjunction of equations between respective elements of the sequences $\bar{x}$ and $\bar{t}_j$. According to the soundness proof (given in the next section), this is equivalent to:

$$p(\bar{x}) \Leftrightarrow \bigwedge_{j=1, j \neq i}^{n} \forall \bar{y}_j \left(\bar{x} \neq \bar{t}_j\right) \vee \exists \bar{y}_j \left(\bar{x} = \bar{t}_j \wedge \neg C_j\right) \mid \bar{x} = \bar{t}_i \wedge C_i$$

where $\bar{x} \neq \bar{t}_j$ stands for the disjunction of negated equations between respective elements of the sequences $\bar{x}$ and $\bar{t}_j$ and $\neg C_j$ is a disjunction of negated constraints. The symbolic construction approach distinguishes between the two cases for negated constraints: Negated built-ins are replaced by the corresponding positive constraints since built-ins are closed under negation. Negated user-defined constraints are discarded and constructing an entailment checker that determines if a user-defined constraint does not hold is left for future work. Thus, the general form of the rules is:

$$p(\bar{x}) \Leftrightarrow \bigwedge_{j=1, j \neq i}^{n} \bigvee_{k=1}^{|x|+m_j} E_j^k \mid \bar{x} = \bar{t}_i \wedge C_i$$

where

$$E_j^k = \forall \bar{y}_j^k \left(x^k \neq t_j^k\right) \qquad \text{for } k \in \{1, \ldots, |x|\},$$

$$E_j^{|x|+k} = \exists \bar{y}_j \left(\bar{x} = \bar{t}_j \wedge \neg c_j^k\right) \qquad \text{for } k \in \{1, \ldots, m_j\},$$

the $\bar{y}_j^k$ is the sequence of variables in the term t_j^k and m_j is the number of built-in constraints in C_j.

Example 4 (Symbolic Construction Approach). The *lex* constraint has three disjuncts namely:

$D_1:$ $L_1 = [] \wedge L_2 = []$

$D_2:$ $\exists X_1, X_2, T_1, T_2 \ (L_1 = [X_1 | T_1] \wedge L_2 = [X_2 | T_2] \wedge X_1 < X_2)$

$D_3:$ $\exists X_3, X_4, T_3, T_4 \ (L_1 = [X_3 | T_3] \wedge L_2 = [X_4 | T_4] \wedge X_3 = X_4 \wedge lex(T_3, T_4))$

To construct a rule that simplifies *lex* to the first disjunct, the negation of the other two disjuncts is added to the guard:

$$\neg(\exists X_1, X_2, T_1, T_2 \ (L_1 = [X_1 | T_1] \wedge L_2 = [X_2 | T_2] \wedge X_1 < X_2) \ \vee$$
$$\exists X_3, X_4, T_3, T_4 \ (L_1 = [X_3 | T_3] \wedge L_2 = [X_4 | T_4] \wedge X_3 = X_4 \wedge lex(T_3, T_4)))$$

This is equivalent to:

$$(\forall X_1, T_1(L_1 \neq [X_1|T_1]) \ \lor \ \forall X_2, T_2(L_2 \neq [X_2|T_2]) \ \lor$$
$$\exists X_1, X_2, T_1, T_2(L_1 = [X_1|T_1] \land L_2 = [X_2|T_2] \land X_1 \geq X_2)) \ \land$$
$$(\forall X_3, T_3(L_1 \neq [X_3|T_3]) \ \lor \ \forall X_4, T_4(L_2 \neq [X_4|T_4]) \ \lor$$
$$\exists X_3, X_4, T_3, T_4(L_1 = [X_3|T_3] \land L_2 = [X_4|T_4] \land X_3 \neq X_4))$$

where negated built-ins are replaced by the corresponding positive constraints and negated user-defined constraints discarded.

Since the arguments of *lex* are (ordered) lists, the constraint $\forall X, T \ L \neq [X|T]$ can be simplified to $L = []$. The expression becomes:

$$(L_1 = [] \ \lor \ L_2 = [] \ \lor \ (L_1 = [X_1|T_1] \land L_2 = [X_2|T_2] \land X_1 \geq X_2)) \ \land$$
$$(L_1 = [] \ \lor \ L_2 = [] \ \lor \ (L_1 = [X_3|T_3] \land L_2 = [X_4|T_4] \land X_3 \neq X_4))$$

Thus the constructed rule is:

$$lex(L_1, L_2) \Leftrightarrow$$
$$(L_1 = [] \ \lor \ L_2 = [] \ \lor \ (L_1 = [X_1|T_1] \land L_2 = [X_2|T_2] \land X_1 \geq X_2)) \ \land$$
$$(L_1 = [] \ \lor \ L_2 = [] \ \lor \ (L_1 = [X_3|T_3] \land L_2 = [X_4|T_4] \land X_3 \neq X_4))$$
$$| \ L_1 = [] \land L_2 = []$$

3.2   The Solver Properties

In this section we prove soundness and termination as well as discuss completeness of the constructed solvers.

Soundness. A simplification rule $H \Leftrightarrow G \mid B$ is *valid* w.r.t. a CLP program P and the constraint theory CT iff $P^* \cup CT \models \forall \bar{x} \ (\exists \bar{y} \ G \rightarrow (H \leftrightarrow \exists \bar{z} \ B))$.

Theorem 1 (Soundness). *The symbolic construction algorithm constructs valid simplification rules w.r.t. the CLP program and the constraint theory.*

Proof (Soundness). Consider Clark's completion of the CLP program defining a constraint p:

$$\forall \bar{x} \left(p(\bar{x}) \leftrightarrow \left(\bigvee_{i=1}^{n} \exists \bar{y}_i \ (\bar{x} = \bar{t}_i \land C_i) \right) \right)$$

For every $i \in \{1, \ldots, n\}$, we therefore have:

$$\forall \bar{x} \left(\left(\neg \bigvee_{j=1, j \neq i}^{n} \exists \bar{y}_j \ (\bar{x} = \bar{t}_j \land C_j) \right) \rightarrow (p(\bar{x}) \leftrightarrow \exists \bar{y}_i \ (\bar{x} = \bar{t}_i \land C_i)) \right)$$

and consequently:

$$\forall \bar{x} \left(\left(\bigwedge_{j=1, j \neq i}^{n} \neg \exists \bar{y}_j \ (\bar{x} = \bar{t}_j \land C_j) \right) \rightarrow (p(\bar{x}) \leftrightarrow \exists \bar{y}_i \ (\bar{x} = \bar{t}_i \land C_i)) \right)$$

which is the logical reading of a CHR rule:

$$p(\bar{x}) \Leftrightarrow G \mid \bar{x} = \bar{t}_i \wedge C_i$$

where G is equivalent to:

$$\bigwedge_{j=1, j \neq i}^{n} \neg \exists \bar{y}_j \, (\bar{x} = \bar{t}_j \wedge C_j)$$

Recall that $\bar{y}_j$ denotes the variables in $\bar{t}_j$ and that $\bar{y}_j$ is disjoint from $\bar{x}$. Therefore, for every $j \in \{1, \ldots, n\}$ and every valuation of $\bar{x}$ such that $\bar{x} = \bar{t}_j$ is satisfiable, there exists a sequence of terms $\bar{u}_j$ such that:

$$(\bar{x} = \bar{t}_j) \Leftrightarrow (\bar{y}_j = \bar{u}_j)$$

This observation guarantees the existence of a function u_j for each $j \in \{1, \ldots, n\}$ that maps from sequences of terms to sequences of terms such that:

$$(\exists \bar{y}_j \; \bar{x} = \bar{t}_j) \Rightarrow ((\bar{x} = \bar{t}_j) \Leftrightarrow (\bar{y}_j = u_j(\bar{x})))$$

and consequently:

$$(\bar{x} = \bar{t}_j) \Rightarrow (\bar{y}_j = u_j(\bar{x}))$$

Using function u_j, we have that:

$$\neg \exists \bar{y}_j \; (\bar{x} = \bar{t}_j \wedge C_j)$$

is equivalent to:

$$\neg \exists \bar{y}_j \; (\bar{x} = \bar{t}_j \wedge \bar{y}_j = u_j(\bar{x}) \wedge C_j)$$

From there, the substitution property of equality gives us:

$$\neg \exists \bar{y}_j \; (\bar{x} = \bar{t}_j \wedge C_j[\bar{y}_j / u_j(\bar{x})])$$

We move the negation to the inside of the formula and get:

$$\forall \bar{y}_j \; (\bar{x} \neq \bar{t}_j \vee \neg C_j[\bar{y}_j / u_j(\bar{x})])$$

As the variables $\bar{y}_j$ do not appear in the formula $\neg C_j[\bar{y}_j / u_j(\bar{x})]$, we can move it outside of the universal quantification:

$$\forall \bar{y}_j \; (\bar{x} \neq \bar{t}_j) \vee \neg C_j[\bar{y}_j / u_j(\bar{x})]$$

Applying $(A \vee B) \Leftrightarrow (A \vee (\neg A \wedge B))$ gives us:

$$\forall \bar{y}_j \; (\bar{x} \neq \bar{t}_j) \vee (\exists \bar{y}_j \; (\bar{x} = \bar{t}_j) \wedge \neg C_j[\bar{y}_j / u_j(\bar{x})])$$

As the variables $\bar{y}_j$ do not appear in the formula $\neg C_j[\bar{y}_j / u_j(\bar{x})]$, we can move it into the scope of their existential quantification:

$$\forall \bar{y}_j \; (\bar{x} \neq \bar{t}_j) \vee \exists y_j \; (\bar{x} = \bar{t}_j \wedge \neg C_j[\bar{y}_j / u_j(\bar{x})])$$

According to the definition of the function u_j, $\bar{x}=\bar{t}_j$ implies $\bar{y}_j=u_j(\bar{x})$:

$$\forall \bar{y}_j \ (\bar{x}\neq\bar{t}_j) \vee \exists y_j \ (\bar{x}=\bar{t}_j \wedge \bar{y}_j=u_j(\bar{x}) \wedge \neg C_j[\bar{y}_j/u_j(\bar{x})])$$

We apply the substitution property of equality again to get:

$$\forall \bar{y}_j \ (\bar{x}\neq\bar{t}_j) \vee \exists y_j \ (\bar{x}=\bar{t}_j \wedge \bar{y}_j=u_j(\bar{x}) \wedge \neg C_j)$$

As $(\bar{x}=\bar{t}_j) \Rightarrow (\bar{y}_j=u_j(\bar{x}))$, this is equivalent to:

$$\forall \bar{y}_j \ (\bar{x}\neq\bar{t}_j) \vee \exists y_j \ (\bar{x}=\bar{t}_j \wedge \neg C_j)$$

Therefore, the guard G of the generated CHR rule is equivalent to:

$$\left(\bigwedge_{j=1, j\neq i}^{n} (\forall \bar{y}_j \ (\bar{x}\neq\bar{t}_j) \vee \exists y_j \ (\bar{x}=\bar{t}_j \wedge \neg C_j)) \right)$$

Termination. In [8] proving the termination of CHR solvers is based on polynomial interpretations where the rank of a term or an atom is defined by a linear positive combination of the rankings of its arguments. The basic idea is to prove that the rank of the head of a rule is strictly larger than that of its body. Moreover, built-in solvers are assumed to be well-behaved (terminating and confluent) and thus the rank of built-in constraints is defined as 0.

Theorem 2 (Termination). *For constraints defined by a CLP program where the rank of the head of every clause is strictly larger than that of its body, the symbolic construction approach constructs terminating solvers.*

Proof (Termination). If for each clause of the CLP program, the rank of the head of the clause is strictly larger than that of its body, then the constructed solver terminates. The head and body of a constructed rule are the same as the clause and only built-in constraints which are defined as 0 are added to the guard. Thus the head of a constructed rule is strictly larger than that of its body and the solver terminates.

Completeness. The constructed solvers can not guarantee propagation completeness for non-trivial constraints since negated user-defined constraints are ignored.

4   Solver Optimization

To improve the runtime efficiency of the solvers and readability of the rules, redundant guard entailment checks are removed. This is achieved by expanding the guard expressions to disjunctive normal form and splitting each disjunct into a new rule. Then, we apply the redundant rules removal algorithm of [9] on the complete rule set. After redundant rules are removed, guards originating from the same rule are recombined to avoid loss of completeness.

4.1 Guard Splitting

The symbolic construction approach constructs rules of the form:

$$p(\bar{x}) \Leftrightarrow \bigwedge_{j=1, j \neq i}^{n} \bigvee_{k=1}^{|x|+m_j} E_j^k \mid \bar{x} = \bar{t}_i \wedge C_i$$

where

$$E_j^k = \forall \bar{y}_j^k \left(x^k \neq t_j^k \right) \qquad \text{for } k \in \{1, \ldots, |x|\},$$

$$E_j^{|x|+k} = \exists \bar{y}_j \left(\bar{x} = \bar{t}_j \wedge \neg c_j^k \right) \qquad \text{for } k \in \{1, \ldots, m_j\},$$

the $\bar{y}_j^k$ is the sequence of variables in the term t_j^k and m_j is the number of built-in constraints in C_j.

To split the guard into rules (Fig. 2), we distribute the conjunction over the disjunction and get a formula in disjunctive normal form where the number of disjuncts is $\Pi_{j=1, j \neq i}^{n} |x| + m_j$. Then each disjunct is simplified to an equivalent conjunction of constraints by the available built-in solver and superfluous disjuncts removed. These include multiple occurrences of a disjunct (irrespective of the order of constraints within the disjunct) and *false*. Each simplified disjunct is split into a new rule.

---

begin
    $Rules_{in}$: initial rule set
    $Rules_{out} = \{\}$: resultant rule set

    while $Rules_{in} \neq \{\}$ **do**
        Remove from $Rules_{in}$ an element denoted R
        R is of the form $p \Leftrightarrow E \mid D$
        G is the cartesian product of the $n-1$ conjuncts of the guard E

        while $G \neq \{\}$ **do**
            Remove from G an element denoted G_e
            G_{simp}: the result of executing G_e by the built-in solver
            if $G_{simp} \neq false$ **then**
                $Rules_{out} = Rules_{out} \cup \{p \Leftrightarrow G_{simp} \mid D\}$
            end if
        end while
    end while
end

Fig. 2. Guard Splitting

Example 5 (Guard Splitting). Consider the previously constructed rule of *lex*:

$lex(L_1, L_2) \Leftrightarrow$

$$(L_1=[] \lor L_2=[] \lor (L_1=[X_1|T_1] \land L_2=[X_2|T_2] \land X_1 \geq X_2)) \land$$
$$(L_1=[] \lor L_2=[] \lor (L_1=[X_3|T_3] \land L_2=[X_4|T_4] \land X_3 \neq X_4))$$
$$| L_1=[] \land L_2=[]$$

Transforming the guard expression to disjunctive normal form, we get:

$(L_1=[] \land L_1=[]) \lor$
$(L_1=[] \land L_2=[]) \lor$
$(L_1=[] \land L_1=[X_3|T_3] \land L_2=[X_4|T_4] \land X_3 \neq X_4) \lor$
$(L_2=[] \land L_1=[]) \lor$
$(L_2=[] \land L_2=[]) \lor$
$(L_2=[] \land L_1=[X_3|T_3] \land L_2=[X_4|T_4] \land X_3 \neq X_4) \lor$
$(L_1=[X_1|T_1] \land L_2=[X_2|T_2] \land X_1 \geq X_2 \land L_1=[]) \lor$
$(L_1=[X_1|T_1] \land L_2=[X_2|T_2] \land X_1 \geq X_2 \land L_2=[]) \lor$
$(L_1=[X_1|T_1] \land L_2=[X_2|T_2] \land X_1 \geq X_2 \land L_1=[X_3|T_3] \land L_2=[X_4|T_4] \land X_3 \neq X_4)$

To simplify the resultant expression, each disjunct is executed by the built-in constraints solver and superfluous disjuncts removed. We assume that for the conjunction of constraints, the built-in solver:

– Removes identical occurrences of constraints
– Simplifies constraints (e.g. $L=[] \land L=[X|T] \Leftrightarrow false$ and $X \geq Y \land X \neq Y \Leftrightarrow X > Y$)
– Propagates new constraints (e.g. $L_1=[X_1|T_1] \land L_2=[X_2|T_2] \land L_1=[X_3|T_3] \land L_2=[X_4|T_4] \Rightarrow X_1=X_3 \land T_1=T_3 \land X_2=X_4 \land T_2=T_4$)

The expression simplifies to:

$$(L_1=[]) \lor (L_1=[] \land L_2=[]) \lor (L_2=[]) \lor (L_1=[X_1|T_1] \land L_2=[X_2|T_2] \land X_1 > X_2)$$

which splits into the following rules:

$lex(L_1, L_2) \Leftrightarrow L_1=[] \mid L_1=[] \land L_2=[]$
$lex(L_1, L_2) \Leftrightarrow L_1=[] \land L_2=[] \mid L_1=[] \land L_2=[]$
$lex(L_1, L_2) \Leftrightarrow L_2=[] \mid L_1=[] \land L_2=[]$
$lex(L_1, L_2) \Leftrightarrow L_1=[X_1|T_1] \land L_2=[X_2|T_2] \land X_1 > X_2 \mid L_1=[] \land L_2=[]$

4.2   Redundant Rules Removal

To remove redundant rules, the algorithm of [9] is used. The idea of the algorithm is based on operational equivalence of programs. The algorithm (Fig. 3) basically checks if the computation step due to a rule can be performed by the remainder

begin

  $Rules_{in}$: the initial rule set

  $Rules_{out}$: the resultant rule set without redundancy

  $Rules_{out}=Rules_{in}$

  while $Rules_{in}\neq\{\}$ **do**

    Remove from $Rules_{in}$ an element denoted R

    lhs: the head and guard of the rule R

    S_1: the result of executing lhs in $Rules_{out}$

    $Rules_{remaining}=Rules_{out}\backslash\{R\}$

    S_2: the result of executing lhs in $Rules_{remaining}$

    if S_1 is identical to S_2 **then**

      $Rules_{out}=Rules_{remaining}$

    end if

  end while

end

Fig. 3. Redundancy Removal Algorithm

of the program. It determines this by executing the head and guard in both the program and the program without the rule in it. If the results are identical upto renaming of variables and logical equivalence of built-in constraints), then the rule is obviously redundant and can be removed.

Example 6 (Redundant Rules Removal). Consider the following two rules of *lex*:

$$lex(L_1, L_2) \Leftrightarrow L_1=[] \mid L_1=[] \wedge L_2=[]$$
$$lex(L_1, L_2) \Leftrightarrow L_1=[] \wedge L_2=[] \mid L_1=[] \wedge L_2=[]$$

The second rule is redundant since its operation is covered by the first rule. Removing the second rule from the rule set and querying the remaining set with its head and guard $\langle A=[] \wedge B=[] \wedge lex(A, B)\rangle$, the first rule is applied and gives the same result $\langle A=[] \wedge B=[]\rangle$ as the second rule.

After redundant rules are removed, guards originating from the same rule are recombined to avoid loss of completeness. Further guard optimization techniques have been addressed in [10].

5   Combined Approach

To improve the filtering capabilities of our constructed solvers, we propose extending our solvers with rules generated by the orthogonal approach "generate and test" of [1]. To reduce the search space of the generate and test method, the symbolic construction algorithm is run first and the constructed rules eliminated from the enumeration tree of the generate and test. Moreover, the algorithm of [9] is used to remove the redundant rules of the combined solver. In general, the combined solvers are more expressive than the solvers of either approaches.

Example 7 (Combined Approach). The combined solver for *lex* is given below. The first three rules represent the solver obtained from the symbolic construction approach and the last rule is added by the generate and test.

$$lex(L_1, L_2) \Leftrightarrow L_1=[] \vee L_2=[] \mid L_1=[] \wedge L_2=[] \tag{1}$$

$$lex(L_1, L_2) \Leftrightarrow L_1=[X_3|T_3] \wedge L_2=[X_4|T_4] \wedge X_3 \neq X_4 \mid$$
$$L_1=[X_1|T_1] \wedge L_2=[X_2|T_2] \wedge X_1 < X_2 \tag{2}$$

$$lex(L_1, L_2) \Leftrightarrow L_1=[X_1|T_1] \wedge L_2=[X_2|T_2] \wedge X_1 \geq X_2 \mid$$
$$L_1=[X_3|T_3] \wedge L_2=[X_4|T_4] \wedge X_3=X_4 \wedge lex(T_3, T_4) \tag{3}$$

$$lex([X_1|T_1], [X_2|T_2]) \Rightarrow X_1 \leq X_2 \tag{4}$$

The solver is sound. All rules are logical consequences of the constraint definition.

The solver terminates. The interesting case for termination is the recursive rule (3). The ranking function for $lex(L_1, L_2)$ is defined as the positive combination of the rank of its arguments:

$$rank(lex(L_1, L_2)) = length(L_1) + length(L_2)$$

The length of a list is expressed in the ranking function scheme as:

$$length([]) = 0$$
$$length([H|T]) = 1 + length(T)$$

All other constraints in the rule are built-ins and are ranked as 0. The rule terminates since the rank of the head and guard is greater than that of its body:

$$rank(lex([X_1|T_1], [X_2|T_2])) > rank(lex(T_1, T_2))$$

The solver is not propagation complete. In [4] the below complete *lex* solver was presented:

$$lex([], []) \Leftrightarrow true \tag{5}$$

$$lex([X_1|T_1], [X_2|T_2]) \Leftrightarrow X_1 < X_2 \mid true \tag{6}$$

$$lex([X_1|T_1], [X_2|T_2]) \Leftrightarrow X_1 = X_2 \mid lex(T_1, T_2) \tag{7}$$

$$lex([X_1|T_1], [X_2|T_2]) \Rightarrow X_1 \leq X_2 \tag{8}$$

$$lex([X_1, U|T_1], [X_2, V|T_2]) \Leftrightarrow U > V \mid X_1 < X_2 \tag{9}$$

$$lex([X_1, U|T_1], [X_2, V|T_2]) \Leftrightarrow U \geq V \wedge T_1=[\_|\_] \mid$$
$$lex([X_1, U], [X_2, V]) \wedge lex([X_1|T_1], [X_2|T_2]) \tag{10}$$

The solver consists of three pairs of rules: the first two correspond to base cases of the recursion, the middle two perform forward reasoning, and the last two perform backward reasoning. By comparison we find that the backward reasoning rules are not subsumed by our combined *lex* solver rendering the solver incomplete.

Consider the query $\langle lex([A_1, A_2, A_3, A_4], [B_1, B_2, B_3, B_4]) \rangle$ where the domains of the variables are defined as follows:

$$A_1 = \{1, 3, 4\}, A_2 = \{1, 2, 3, 4, 5\}, A_3 = \{1, 2\}, A_4 = \{3, 4, 5\}$$
$$B_1 = \{1\}, B_2 = \{0, 1, 2, 3, 4\}, B_3 = \{0, 1\}, B_4 = \{0, 1, 2\}$$

In the case of the combined solver for *lex*, rule (3) is fired since $A_1 \geq B_1$ enforcing equality on the values of A_1 and B_1 before calling *lex* recursively on the remaining list elements. The relation between A_2 and B_2 satisfies none of the guards, thus rule (4) is fired which enforces $A_2 \leq B_2$. The solution becomes:

$$A_1 = \{1\}, A_2 = \{1, 2, 3, 4\}, A_3 = \{1, 2\}, A_4 = \{3, 4, 5\},$$
$$B_1 = \{1\}, B_2 = \{1, 2, 3, 4\}, B_3 = \{0, 1\}, B_4 = \{0, 1, 2\},$$
$$A_2 \leq B_2, lex([A_2, A_3, A_4], [B_2, B_3, B_4])$$

In the case of the *lex* solver of [4], rules (8), (7), (10), and (9) are applied in that order and further constrain the domains of the variables to:

$$A_1 = \{1\}, A_2 = \{1, 2, 3\}, A_3 = \{1, 2\}, A_4 = \{3, 4, 5\},$$
$$B_1 = \{1\}, B_2 = \{2, 3, 4\}, B_3 = \{0, 1\}, B_4 = \{0, 1, 2\},$$
$$A_2 < B_2, lex([A_2, A_3], [B_2, B_3])$$

6   Conclusion

In this paper we have presented an algorithm that automatically constructs rule-based solvers from the constraint definition. The algorithm is an orthogonal approach to the general direction of the work done in the field as it is based on symbolic construction rather than a generate and test method. Contrary to other approaches, given a recursive constraint definition the algorithm is able to generate recursive rules which allow reasoning over arguments of arbitrary length.

The constructed solvers are a good basis for constraint reasoning and can be extended manually or with rules generated using other approaches. We have proposed extending our rules with those generated by the algorithm in [1]. In general, the solvers generated using the combined approach are more expressive than those generated by either of the two approaches acting alone.

An interesting direction for future work to improve the expressiveness of the generated solvers is to incorporate negated user-defined constraints in the symbolic construction approach.

Acknowledgments. We would like to thank Thom Frühwirth, Frank Raiser, Jon Sneyers and the anonymous reviewers for valuable comments on a preliminary version of this paper.

References

1. Abdennadher, S., Rigotti, C.: Automatic Generation of CHR Constraint Solvers. Journal of Theory and Practice of Logic Programming (TPLP) 5(4-5), 403–418 (2005)
2. Carlsson, M., Beldiceanu, N.: Revisiting the Lexicographic Ordering Constraint. Technical Report T2002-17, Swedish Institute of Computer Science (2002)
3. Frisch, A., Hnich, B., Kzltan, Z., Miguel, I., Walsh, T.: Global Constraints for Lexicographic Orderings. In: Van Hentenryck, P. (ed.) CP 2002. LNCS, vol. 2470, pp. 93–108. Springer, Heidelberg (2002)
4. Frühwirth, T.: Complete Propagation Rules for Lexicograhic Order Constraints over Arbitary Domains. In: Hnich, B., Carlsson, M., Fages, F., Rossi, F. (eds.) CSCLP 2005. LNCS, vol. 3978, pp. 14–28. Springer, Heidelberg (2006)
5. Abdennadher, S., Sobhi, I.: Generation of Rule-based Constraint Solvers: Combined Approach. In: King, A. (ed.) LOPSTR 2007. LNCS, vol. 4915, pp. 106–120. Springer, Heidelberg (2008)
6. Clark, K.: Negation as Failure. In: Logic and Databases, pp. 293–322. Plenum Press, New York (1978)
7. Frühwirth, T.: Theory and Practice of Constraint Handling Rules, Special Issue on Constraint Logic Programming. Journal of Logic Programming 37(1-3), 95–138 (1998)
8. Frühwirth, T.: Proving Termination of Constraint Solver Programs. In: Apt, K.R., Kakas, A.C., Monfroy, E., Rossi, F. (eds.) Compulog Net WS 1999. LNCS, vol. 1865, pp. 298–317. Springer, Heidelberg (2000)
9. Abdennadher, S., Frühwirth, T.: Integration and Optimization of Rule-based Constraint Solvers. In: Bruynooghe, M. (ed.) LOPSTR 2004. LNCS, vol. 3018, pp. 198–213. Springer, Heidelberg (2004)
10. Sneyers, J., Schrijvers, T., Demoen, B.: Guard and Continuation Optimization for Occurrence Representations of CHR. In: Gabbrielli, M., Gupta, G. (eds.) ICLP 2005. LNCS, vol. 3668, pp. 83–97. Springer, Heidelberg (2005)

Implementing
Probabilistic Abductive Logic Programming
with Constraint Handling Rules

Henning Christiansen

Research group PLIS: Programming, Logic and Intelligent Systems
Department of Communication, Business and Information Technologies
Roskilde University, P.O. Box 260, DK-4000 Roskilde, Denmark
henning@ruc.dk

Abstract. A class of Probabilistic Abductive Logic Programs (PALPs) is introduced and an implementation is developed in CHR for solving abductive problems, providing minimal explanations with their probabilities. Both all-explanations and most-probable-explanations versions are given.

Compared with other probabilistic versions of abductive logic programming, the approach is characterized by higher generality and a flexible and adaptable architecture which incorporates integrity constraints and interaction with external constraint solvers.

A PALP is transformed in a systematic way into a CHR program which serves as a query interpreter, and the resulting CHR code describes in a highly concise way, the strategies applied in the search for explanations.

1 Introduction

Logic programs provide a very flexible and general representation scheme for knowledge about complex and interrelated phenomena. Deductive reasoning, i.e., reasoning about what is known, in logic programs may be done within the Prolog programming language, and various extensions for synthetic reasoning such as abduction and induction have been developed. Abductive reasoning means to search for missing world facts, which can explain observations of the state of affairs. Diagnosis in medicine and fault finding in mechanical or virtual systems are some of the obvious applications.

In general, abductive reasoning based on logic programs tends to provide too many and often strange explanations, and integrity constraints, which are formalized conditions which must hold in the possible worlds expressed by different explanations, can be applied for ruling out some of those. Another important issue is that explanations should be minimal, in the sense that they do not contain information which is not necessary in order to explain the observation.

Finally, adding probabilities to a knowledge representation formalism provides a way to prioritize among different explanations, giving a measurement of which

T. Schrijvers and T. Frühwirth (Eds.): Constraint Handling Rules, LNAI 5388, pp. 85–118, 2008.

one is better (i.e., more probable) than others. Probabilities may furthermore be applied to optimize the search for explanations, always going in the most probable direction, so that investigation of less probable alternatives is suppressed or postponed.

While a lot of research has been made, and several systems developed, in logic programming based settings, far less work has been done in combining with probabilities. We suggest here an implementation of abduction in probabilistic logic programs in Constraint Handling Rules (CHR) which serves two purposes. Firstly, it overcomes certain limitations of earlier work and provides a very flexible architecture, which points forward to different extensions such as interaction with a non-monotonically evolving world. Secondly, it demonstrates CHR's suitability as a metalanguage for implementing advanced reasoning patterns, which is a direction we have pursued also in earlier work.

In fact, the major part of the CHR rules that we present expose in a clear and abstract way, the strategies used in the search for minimal, probabilistic explanations. In this way, CHR is experienced as a unique metaprogramming language for an overall methodology, which is to apply CHR's constraint store as a pool of pending computational processes, which collectively maintains the meaning of the observation posted as a query to the system, and where each process gradually moves towards an explanation, perhaps splitting into other processes along the way. These processes can be run either exhaustively in the arbitrary order provided by the underlying CHR system, or using an explicit scheduling policy such as best-first.

In addition to provide working implementations, our work may also be useful in a pedagogical context (teaching students *what* is and *how* to make probabilistic abduction), and finally it may provide executable specifications for detailed and very efficient implementations in low-level language such as C. In the present paper, we present implementations in terms of concrete and executable code, with only very few details left out. Notice that in some cases, we have given priority to brevity of the code rather than ultimate efficiency.

Overview

Section 2 introduces the language of Probabilistic Abductive Logic Programs (PALPs) with its logic and probabilistic semantics. PALP programs include declarations of abducibles with prior probabilities, integrity constraints, calls to external predicates, but no negation. External predicates can be a defined in Prolog or be constraints for which a solver is given, by additional CHR rules or otherwise.

In section 3, we provide specifications of auxiliary predicates used in our subsequent implementations, which define, so to speak, an abstract datatype for explanations. We consider two alternative implementations (details in appendix B), a straightforward and efficient one which aborts in case of nonground abducibles, and another one with full generality.

Our implementation of PALPs is given as a systematic transformation of a given program into a CHR program which, then, serves as a query interpreter. Section 4 explains this transformation for a propositional subset of PALPs in order to outline the basic principles; two implementations are given, an all-solutions and a best-first version. Section 5 adds the remaining details to provide implementations for the full PALP language.

We do not specify in detail the semantics used for CHR in our proofs, but assume a semantics "as usual", given by [24]; in our proofs, we argue in a semi-formal style in terms of an operational semantics for CHR which in most cases considers it as a nondeterministic rewriting system, and occasionally we need to refer to CHR's sequential search for rules to apply and its left-to-right execution of rule bodies (cf. [22]).

Section 6 indicates further extensions and optimizations, firstly inspired by Dijkstra's shortest path algorithm [21] which is relevant in cases where the residual query in each branch is a single atom, and secondly, by using simplification techniques [18, 33] to speed up integrity checking. Finally, we consider the addition of a limited form of negation and we can argue that a logically more satisfactory version of negation is difficult to handle probabilistically.

Section 7 provides two fully developed example PALP programs, including diagnosis and finding most the probable path in a network. Both are implemented in CHR using best-first search, and the second one shows also the Dijkstra optimization indicated above.

The final section 8 provides for a summary, an overview of related work, and perspectives for applications and extensions of the present work.

2   Probabilistic Abductive Logic Programs

2.1   Syntax and Logic Meaning

Definition 1. *A probabilistic abductive logic program* (PALP) *is character-ized by*

- *a set of predicate symbols, each with a fixed arity, distinguished into four disjoint classes,* abducibles, program defined, external *and* $\perp$,
- *for each abducible predicate* a/n, *a probability declaration of form*
    abducible($a(\_1, \ldots, \_n)$, p), *with* $0 < p < 1$.
- *a set of clauses of form,* $A_0 : -A_1, \ldots, A_n$, *of which the following kinds are possible,*
    - *ordinary clauses where* A_0 *is an atom of a program defined predicate and none of* $A_1, \ldots, A_n$, $n \geq 0$, *are* $\perp$,
    - *integrity constraints in which* $A_0 = \perp$ *and* $A_1, \ldots, A_n$, $n \geq 1$, *are abducible atoms.*

As usual, an arbitrary and infinite collection of function symbols, including constants, are assumed and atoms defined in the standard way.   □

Notice that $\perp$ is a distinguished predicate rather that a representation of falsity. The relationship $\models$ refers to the usual, completion-based semantics for logic programs [31, 37]; for external predicates, we assume a semantics independently of the actual program, and without specifying further, an priori defined truth value for $\models e$ is given for any ground external atom e. In practice, external predicates can be Prolog built-ins or defined by additional Prolog clauses, or constraints given either by a Prolog library or by additional CHR rules. We need to require that any call to an external predicate always succeeds at most once; for simplicity, we leave out externals defined as constraints from our formal considerations, but indicate in the text how they should be treated. The difference is basically that satisfiability of a constraint depends on the current execution state, which makes statements about correctness more complicated but adds no conceptual difficulties.

When no ambiguity arises, a clause is usually an ordinary clause, and integrity constraints will be referred to as such. In the context of a PALP Π, a formula is called *basic*, if it can be rewritten into an equivalent form using the equivalences defined by the clauses of Π, consisting of conjunctions, disjunctions, negations and a finite number of ground abducible atoms and $\bot$. In the following we refer to different terms or formulas being *separated* meaning that they have no variables in common.

The notation $[\![F_1, \ldots, F_n]\!]$, F_i being formulas, is taken as a shorthand for $\exists (F_1 \wedge \cdots \wedge F_n) \wedge \neg \bot$. Notice the following trivial properties,

$$[\![A \wedge B]\!] \equiv [\![A]\!] \wedge [\![B]\!] \quad \text{for separated formulas } A \text{ and } B \tag{1}$$

$$[\![A \vee B]\!] \equiv [\![A]\!] \vee [\![B]\!] \quad \text{for arbitrary formulas } A \text{ and } B. \tag{2}$$

Example 1. Consider the following PALP.

```
abducible(some(_),0.1).
some_nat:- some(N), nat(N).
nat(0).                                                    (3)
nat(s(N)):- nat(N).
loop(N):- some(N), loop(s(N)).
```

Here formulas some_nat and loop(0) are not basic; nat(s(s(0))) is basic. It is well-known that natural numbers can be represented by zero and a successor function, and that addition and multiplication can be implemented by a logic program. For subsequent examples, we assume the program above extended with for arithmetic and a predicate sequence/1 with the following properties; the actual and lengthy definition is left out and n is used as a convenient writing of s^n(0).

```
sequence(1)  ↔  some(1)
sequence(2)  ↔  some(2), some(3)
sequence(3)  ↔  some(4), some(5), some(6)
⋮                                                          (4)
```
$$\texttt{sequence}(n) \ \leftrightarrow \ \texttt{some}(\tfrac{(n-1) \times n}{2} + 1), \ \ldots, \ \texttt{some}(\tfrac{n \times (n+1)}{2})$$
```
⋮
```

□

Definition 2. *A* query *or* goal *is a conjunction of non-$\bot$ atoms; a finite set (or conjunction) of ground abducible atoms is called a* state; *a finite set of (not necessarily ground) abducible atoms is called a* state term. *In the context of a PALP Π, we say that state or state term S is* inconsistent *whenever $\Pi \cup \forall S \models \bot$ and otherwise* consistent. *For two separated state terms S_1, S_2, we say that S_1* subsumes S_2 *and that S_1 is* more general than S_2, *whenever*

$$\models \exists S_1 \leftarrow \exists S_2. \tag{5}$$

Whenever S_1 subsumes S_2 and vice-versa, we say that they are equivalent; *if S_1 subsumes S_2 and they are not equivalent, we say that S_1* strictly subsumes S_2; *if neither S_1 subsumes S_2 nor the reverse, we say that they are* incompatible.

Given a PALP Π and a query Q, an explanation *for Q is a state term E such that*

$$\Pi \cup \exists E \models [\![Q]\!] \tag{6}$$

An explanation E for Q is minimal *if it is not a subsumed by any other explanation for Q. A finite set of minimal and pairwise separated explanations $\mathbf{E} = \{E_1, \ldots E_n\}$ for Q is* complete *whenever*

$$\Pi \models [\![Q]\!] \leftrightarrow \exists E_1 \vee \cdots \vee \exists E_n. \tag{7}$$

$\square$

In practice, an answer for a query to an abductive logic program may include, in addition to the explanation as defined above, also a variable substitution and a set of normalized constraints of any external constraint solver applied. These details, which are straightforward to add, are left out for simplicity.

In non-probabilistic abduction, a preference is often given to explanations with as few literals as possible, but this is not relevant as we introduce a more precise measurement for explanations, namely their probabilities.

Example 2. Explanation $\{a(X)\}$ subsumes $\{a(1)\}$ as well as $\{a(1), a(2)\}$.

Explanation $\{a(X), a(1)\}$ is equivalent to $\{a(1)\}$. However, explanations are built in an incremental way during the execution of a program (as explained later in this paper), in which variables may be quantified and bound at different levels. In the example, $\{a(X), a(1)\}$ as a partial explanation may be affected by X=2 and lead to final explanation $\{a(2), a(1)\}$. In order words, the replacement of one explanation by a smaller, equivalent one is only relevant for a final explanation to a query. $\square$

Example 3. Consider again the PALP of example 1 above. The query some_ nat(N) has minimal explanations $\{some(0)\}$, $\{some(1)\}$, $\ldots$; loop(N) has no explanations; sequence(N) has explanations $\{some(1)\}$, $\{some(2), some(3)\}$, $\{some(4), some(5), some(6)\}$, $\ldots$. $\square$

Lemma 1. *Whenever E is an explanation for Q in a program Π and X a set of abducible atoms, $E \cup X$ is an explanation for Q iff $E \cup X$ is consistent. Any explanation E for Q has a subset which is a minimal explanation for Q.*

Proof. Trivial. $\square$

Lemma 2. *The complete set of minimal explanations $\{E_1, \ldots, E_n\}$ for Q in a PALP Π is unique qua equivalence on individual explanations. When, furthermore, E is an arbitrary explanation for Q, it holds for some i, $1 \leq i \leq n$, that E_i subsumes E.*

Proof. See appendix A. ☐

Lemma 3. *Let Q be a query to a PALP Π and $E_1, \ldots, E_n$ consistent and pairwise separated state terms where E_i does not subsume E_j for any $i \neq j$. Whenever*

$$\Pi \models \llbracket Q \rrbracket \leftrightarrow \exists E_1 \vee \cdots \vee \exists E_n. \tag{8}$$

it holds that $E_1, \ldots, E_n$ comprise a complete set of explanations for Q.

Proof. See appendix A. ☐

Example 4. Consider the following PALP, which we call Π_0.

```
abducible(a, 0.5).
abducible(b, 0.5).
abducible(c, 0.5).
p:- a, q.                                    (9)
q:- b.
q:- c.
⊥:- a,b.
```

We notice that $\{a, c\}$ is a minimal explanation for p, and $\{\{a, c\}\}$ is complete. Other the other hand, we have that $\Pi_0 \cup \{a, b\} \models p$, but it is not an explanation as $\Pi_0 \cup \{a, b\} \models \bot$ and thus $\Pi_0 \cup \{a, b\} \not\models \llbracket p \rrbracket$. ☐

2.2 Probability Distributions for PALPs

A probabilistic model for a PALP Π is given by considering any ground abducible literal[1] A as a random variable with two outcomes, *true* with probability p and *false* with probability $1 - p$, where p is the probability declared in Π for A. Any two such random variables are considered independent. We consider the outcome of the probabilistic experiment of giving values to all those variables as the state of those that come out as true. The joint distribution for a given PALP is defined formally as follows.

Definition 3. *For given PALP Π, the probability distribution P_Π is defined as follows.*

- $P_\Pi(true) = 1$
- *Whenever* abducible$(A, p) \in \Pi$, *let $P_\Pi(a) = p$ for any ground instance a of A.*

---

[1] Notice that this may indicate an infinity of random variables, when an abducible declarations contain variables. However, for any query to a well-behaved program, only a finite number of these are actually accessed, and the infinitely many remaining ones can be ignored.

- *Whenever $\Pi \models A \leftrightarrow B$, let $P_\Pi(A) = P_\Pi(B)$.*
- *Whenever $P_\Pi(A) = p$, let $P_\Pi(\neg A) = 1 - p$.*
- *Whenever a and b are two distinct ground abducibles, let $P_\Pi(a \wedge b) = P_\Pi(a) \times P_\Pi(b)$ and $P_\Pi(a \vee b) = P_\Pi(a) + P_\Pi(b) - P_\Pi(a \wedge B)$.*
- *Whenever A has an infinite set of ground explanations $E_1, E_2, \ldots$, let $P_\Pi(A) = \lim_{n \to \infty} P_\Pi(E1 \vee \cdots \vee E_n)$.* □

We observe, for the last case of the definition, that we need only consider minimal explanations, and that this part may overlap, but is not in conflict, with the other cases. Notice the following properties of the probability distribution. Whenever the program Π is clear from context, we may write P instead of P_Π.

Proposition 1. *Let Π be a PALP and P_Π its probability distribution.*

- *Whenever A is a nonground abducible atom, $P_\Pi(\forall A) = 0$ and $P_\Pi(\exists A) = 1$.*
- *For any basic formula F over Π, $P(F) = 1$ iff $\Pi \models F$.*
- *For any formula F over Π, $P(F) = 0$ iff $\Pi \not\models F$.*
- *For any formula F over Π, $P(F) > 0$ iff $\Pi \cup S \models F$ for some state S.* □

The restriction to basic terms is essential in the second case. For example, when $a/1$ is an abducible predicate, we have that $P_\Pi(\exists x\, a(x)) = 1$ but not necessarily $\Pi \models \exists x\, a(x)$. To see this, assume $\emptyset$ is a model Π, but $\emptyset$ is not a model of $\exists x\, a(x)$. Notice that the exclusion of probabilities 0 and 1 for abducibles is essential for the proposition.

Example 5. Consider the PALP of example 1. Here we get the following examples of probabilities for non-basic formulas.

$$P(\exists n\, \mathtt{some\_nat}(n)) = 1$$
$$P(\exists n\, \mathtt{loop}(n)) = 0$$
$$P(\exists n\, \mathtt{sequence}(n)) = p$$
$$\text{where } 0.1 < p < 0.1 + (0.1)^2 + (0.1)^3 + \cdots = 0.1111 \cdots$$

The last example indicates that the limit construction may give a sum different from one or zero. This conclusion is based on formula (17) below. □

As is customary in formulas of probability theory, comma is used interchangeably with $\wedge$. Whenever F is a formula with free variables, we let $P(F)$ be a shorthand for $P(\exists F)$.

It is crucial for defining a probability distribution with reasonable properties, that $\bot$ is defined as a special predicate rather that falsity; using falsity would mean that a set of integrity constraints implied a complicated set of dependencies among the random variables (i.e., they were no longer independent).

Example 6. Consider again the program of example 4. We notice that $P(\bot) = P(a, b) = P(a) \times P(b) = 0.25$ and thus $P(\neg \bot) = 0.75$. This means the only 75% of all states are relevant for the search for explanations for, say, p.

The probability $P(\mathtt{p})$ is an uninteresting number as it counts also contributions from inconsistent states. The probability $P([\![\mathtt{p}]\!]) = 0.125$ measures p among all states, and gives here a lower figure than $P([\![\mathtt{p}]\!] | \neg \bot) = 0.167$ which measures among consistent states only. □

In the example, we indicated that $P(\llbracket Q \rrbracket | \neg \perp)$ for some query Q may be more appropriate than $P(\llbracket Q \rrbracket)$ to characterize Q, but we should be aware that $P(\llbracket Q \rrbracket)$ is sufficient for comparing the relative order of probabilities, as the two measures are proportional:

$$P(\llbracket Q \rrbracket | \neg \perp) = \frac{P(\llbracket Q \rrbracket, \neg \perp)}{P(\neg \perp)} = \frac{P(\llbracket Q \rrbracket)}{P(\neg \perp)}. \tag{10}$$

Notice that the introduction of integrity constraints in probability distribution has an interesting effect on observed probabilities of abducibles.

Example 7. We consider the program of examples 4 and 6. While $P(a) = 0.5$ according to its declaration, we have the following since state $\{a, b\}$ is inconsistent.

$$P(\llbracket a \rrbracket | \neg \perp) = \frac{P(\llbracket a \rrbracket)}{P(\neg \perp)} = \frac{P(a \wedge \neg b)}{P(a \wedge \neg b) + P(\neg a \wedge b) + P(\neg a \wedge \neg b)} \tag{11}$$

$$= \frac{0.25}{0.25 + 0.25 + 0.25} = 1/3. \tag{12}$$

In other words, the restriction to consistent states modifies the probability abducibles. An integrity constraint such as $\perp :\text{-} a, b$ does not conflict with the basic assumption of a and b being independent. However, $\llbracket a \rrbracket$ and $\llbracket b \rrbracket$ becomes dependent. □

The following observations may help to simplify the notation.

$$P(\llbracket F \rrbracket) = 0 \qquad \text{whenever} \quad \Pi \cup F \models \perp \tag{13}$$
$$P(F) = P(\llbracket F \rrbracket) \quad \text{whenever} \quad \Pi \cup F \not\models \perp \tag{14}$$

Especially when F is a set of abducibles $\{a_1, ..., a_n\}$, we can write $\llbracket a_1, ..., a_n \rrbracket$ in a probabilistic formula to give it same weight as F when consistent (as are, e.g., explanations) and 0 otherwise. We notice the following trivial properties.

$$P(\llbracket A \wedge B \rrbracket) = P(\llbracket A \rrbracket \wedge \llbracket B \rrbracket) \quad \text{for separated formulas } A \text{ and } B \tag{15}$$
$$P(\llbracket A \vee B \rrbracket) = P(\llbracket A \rrbracket \vee \llbracket B \rrbracket) \quad \text{for arbitrary formulas } A \text{ and } B. \tag{16}$$

Notice especially, when $E_1, \ldots, E_n$ are separated state terms that we have the following.

$$
\begin{aligned}
P(E_1 \vee \ldots \vee E_n) = {} & P(E_1) + \cdots + P(E_n) \\
& - \sum_{1 \le i_1 < i_2 \le n} P(E_{i_1}, E_{i_2}) \\
& + \sum_{1 \le i_1 < j_2 < j_3 \le n} P(E_{i_1}, E_{i_2}, E_{i_3}) \\
& \quad \vdots \\
& + (-1)^{k+1} \sum_{1 \le i_1 < \cdots < i_k \le n} P(E_{i_1}, \ldots, E_{i_k}) \\
& \quad \vdots \\
& + (-1)^{n+1} P(E_1, \ldots E_n)
\end{aligned}
\tag{17}
$$

$$P(\llbracket E_1 \vee \ldots \vee E_n \rrbracket) = P(\llbracket E_1 \rrbracket) + \cdots + P(\llbracket E_n \rrbracket)$$
$$- \sum_{1 \leq i_1 < i_2 \leq n} P(\llbracket E_{i_1}, E_{i_2} \rrbracket)$$
$$+ \sum_{1 \leq i_1 < j_2 < j_3 \leq n} P(\llbracket E_{i_1}, E_{i_2}, E_{i_3} \rrbracket)$$
$$\vdots \tag{18}$$
$$+ (-1)^{k+1} \sum_{1 \leq i_1 < \cdots < i_k \leq n} P(\llbracket E_{i_1}, \ldots, E_{i_k} \rrbracket)$$
$$\vdots$$
$$+ (-1)^{n+1} P(\llbracket E_1, \ldots E_n \rrbracket)$$

When using (18), we need for each summand $P(\llbracket E_{i_1}, \ldots, E_{i_k} \rrbracket)$, to check if the state comprised by $E_{i_1}, \ldots, E_{i_k}$ together with the integrity constraints can prove $\perp$ in which case the result is 0; otherwise, duplicates are removed and probabilities for the abducibles are multiplied.

The following propositions and observation indicate relationships between probabilities and subsumption.

Proposition 2. *Let S_1 and S_2 be state terms. Whenever S_1 subsumes S_2 it holds that $P(S_1) \geq P(S_2)$.*

When, furthermore, S_1 and S_2 are ground and subsumption is strict, it holds that $P(S_1) > P(S_2)$. □

Proposition 3. *Let S_1 and S_2 be ground state terms with $P(S_1) \geq P(S_2)$; then either S_1 subsumes S_2 or they are incompatible.*

When $P(S_1) > P(S_2)$, either S_1 strictly subsumes S_2 or they are incompatible. □

The first part of proposition 3 does not hold for nonground state terms. For example, if $a(-)$ and b are abducible, we have with $S_1 = \{a(\_), b\}$ and $S_2 = \{b\}$ that $P(S_1) = P(S_2) = P(b)$, but S_1 does not subsume S_2.

3 Specifications of Auxiliary Predicates

The different query interpreters use a common collection of auxiliary predicates specified as follows; alternative implementations are shown appendix B.

We do not need to specify a representation for explanations here but we assume there is a notion of a *reduced form* of representations; we anticipate representations as lists of abducible literals, and the reduced form meaning no such literals entailed by others. From a logical point of view, the reduced form is not interesting, but is useful for efficiency and when presenting final explanations to the user. We assume a context which includes a PALP so that we can refer to the notion of consistency and a probability distribution P.

subsumes$(E_1, E_2) \equiv E_1$ subsumes E_2, i.e., $\models \exists E_2 \rightarrow \exists E_1$, when E_1, E_2 are consistent and separate state terms.

entailed$(A, E) \equiv \models \forall(E \rightarrow A)$ when A is an abducible atom and E a consistent state term.

`extend`$(A,E,P(E),E',P(E')) \equiv \models \forall(E' \leftrightarrow A \wedge E)$ when A is an abducible atom and E, E' consistent state terms so that `entailed`(A,E) does not hold.

`normalize_final`$(E_1,E_2) \equiv E_2$ is a normalized explanation such that E_1 and E_2 are equivalent.

Notice the different usages of quantifiers. For `entailed/2` and `extend/5`, the presence of common variables in the arguments is significant, and variables may be bound later in the computation, whereas `subsumes/2` concerns different final explanations arising in different branches of computation; compare with example 2.

The `normalize_final/2` predicate is logically redundant but is used to provide an intuitively more pleasing appearance of final explanations. We can illustrate the purpose, referring to example 2, above. Here it was argued that $\{\text{a(X)}, \text{a(1)}\}$ is equivalent to $\{\text{a(1)}\}$ and also that it is incorrect to replace $\{\text{a(X)}, \text{a(1)}\}$ by the smaller one during the execution as X might be bound to some value. However, in the case $\{\text{a(X)}, \text{a(1)}\}$ is recognized as an explanation for the initial query, the situation is different; there is no partial query left to manipulate X, so we can now replace it by the smaller and logically equivalent $\{\text{a(1)}\}$. We leave the predicate out in the detailed descriptions of the interpreters below as this is anyhow trivial to add and has no influence on the correctness statements.

The following predicate is used whenever an explanation may be affected by unifications, which may be a consequence of applying a rule of the given PALP or executing a call to an external predicate.

`recalculate`$(E,E_1,P(E_1)) \equiv \forall(E \leftrightarrow E_1)$, E_1 is in reduced form, when E and E_1 are consistent state terms.

We have introduced this predicate since it can be implemented quite efficiently by multiplying probabilities for the abducibles in E_1. It very seldom pays off to analyze the detailed effect of a unification in order to reuse the previous probability.

Finally, we need the following renaming predicates in order to create alternative variants of a query when the execution splits in different branches for alternative clauses of the given PALP.

`rename`$(T_1,T_2) \equiv T_2$ is a variant of T_1 with new variables that are not used anywhere else.

Be aware that these predicates, as specified only works when external predicates exclude constraints of delayed calls. To include constraints, subsumption needs to be defined as $\Sigma \cup \Delta \models \exists E_2 \rightarrow \exists E_1$ where is Σ refers to the current execution state and Δ gives the semantics of the underlying constraint solver. The other predicates above that refer to $\models$ should be extended in similar ways, and `rename` must also add constraints to the state whenever variables in the input argument are covered by constraints. More details and examples are discussed in section 5.3 below.

As shown in the appendix, the implementation of subsumption and entailment can be greatly simplified if it can be guaranteed that the explanations always are ground. In that case, explanations can be represented as lists sorted by Prolog's term ordering (denoted @<) and subsumption test becomes an efficient sublist test for sorted lists (see appendix B). It is possible to define syntactic restrictions to ensure that abducibles always are ground so that the efficient implementation can be used, but our ground version uses runtime checks instead.

Lists of nonground abducibles have, furthermore, also the complication that a unification induced by a rule application or external predicate can destroy the sortedness of a list as well as making elements equal (more generally, making some elements subsumed by others).

4 Query Interpreters for Propositional Programs

We consider firstly a propositional version of probabilistic abductive logic programs (PPALPs), i.e., all predicates have arity 0. For simplicity we assume also that PPALPs contain no recursion, and that any non-abducible predicate appears as the head of at least one clause; furthermore, we exclude integrity constraints and external predicates, which means that there are no loops and failures to worry about.

Example 8. The following is a PPALP which introduces abducibles a, b, c, d, each with probability 0.5, and three clauses.

```
abducible(a, 0.5).
abducible(b, 0.5).
abducible(c, 0.5).
abducible(d, 0.5).                                    (19)
g:- a,b.
g:- c.
g:- c,d.
```

A set of minimal explanations for g with probabilities is given by $P(a, b) = 0.25$, $P(c) = 0.5$. Using (17), we get $P(g) = 0.5^2 + 0.5 - 0.5^3 = 0.625$.   □

4.1 Transforming PPALPs into All-Explanations Query Interpreters in CHR

Here we explain how any given PPALP Π can be transformed into a CHR program Γ_Π, which serves as a query interpreter. Such an interpreter takes a query Q to Π as input and returns a final constraint store, which contains a complete set of minimal explanation for Q in Π with their probabilities. The best-first interpreters and interpreters for more general classes of programs described later are all adaptation of what we show for PPALPs here.

We demonstrate the principles for compiling PPALPs into CHR for the program of example 8.

To find explanations for a goal such as g, we call the top-level predicate explain([g]) which is defined as follows.

$$explain(G) :- explain(G, [], 1). \tag{20}$$

The predicate $explain(Q, E, p)$ is a CHR constraint governed by the rules given below; its meaning is that the query Q is what remains to be proven in order to find an explanation for the initial query; E is the partial explanation used so far in order to get from the initial query to Q, and p is the probability of E; Q is represented as a list of atomic goals. We do not need to consider the actual representation of explanations as the auxiliary predicates specified in section 3 provide an abstract datatype for them; the only assumption is that the empty explanation is represented as [].

The following CHR rule interprets a query whose first subgoal is an abducible, adds it to the accumulating explanation if necessary (and adjusts the probability accordingly) and emits a recursive call for the remaining part of the query.

$$
\begin{aligned}
&\texttt{explain([A|G], E, P) <=> abducible(A,PA) |}\\
&\quad\texttt{(entailed(A,E) -> explain(G, E, P)}\\
&\quad\texttt{;}\\
&\quad\texttt{extend(A,E,P,E1,P1), explain(G, E1, P1)).}
\end{aligned}
\tag{21}
$$

Each collection of clauses defining a given predicate in the PPALP is transformed into one CHR rule which produces new calls to explain/3 for each clause. For our example program there is one such CHR rule.

$$
\begin{aligned}
&\texttt{explain([g|G], E, P) <=>}\\
&\quad\texttt{explain([a,b|G],E,P),}\\
&\quad\texttt{explain([c|G],E,P),}\\
&\quad\texttt{explain([c,d|G],E,P).}
\end{aligned}
\tag{22}
$$

These clauses are sufficient to produce a complete set of explanations, represented as a final constraint store consisting of constraints $explain([], E, P(E))$ where E is an explanation for the initial query.

In order to remove non-minimal explanations, the following CHR rule is added as a first one to the interpreter program.[2]

$$
\begin{aligned}
&\texttt{explain([],E1,\_) \textbackslash\ explain(\_,E2,\_) <=>}\\
&\quad\texttt{subsumes(E1,E2) | true.}
\end{aligned}
\tag{23}
$$

Notice that it may discard a branch early as soon as it can be seen that the possible explanations generated along that branch are deemed non-minimal.

To interpret the query g in the original PPALP, we can now pose the query explain([g]) to the CHR program described above, which, in accordance with our expectations, yields the following final constraint store.

$$
\begin{aligned}
&\texttt{explain([],[c],0.5),}\\
&\texttt{explain([],[a,b],0.25)}
\end{aligned}
\tag{24}
$$

---

[2] Logically, rule (23) can be placed anywhere in the CHR program, but having it as the first rule makes it more effective in discarding irrelevant branches as early as possible.

Notice that the constraint `explain([d],[c],0.5)` has appeared in the constraint store during the execution, but discarded by rule (23) and thus never executed until the end.

Lemma 4. *Let Π be a PPALP, Q a query, and Γ the transformation of Π into a CHR program as described above in this section. Any constraint store which arises in the execution of* `explain(Q,[],1)` *in Γ is of the form*

$$\texttt{explain}(Q_1,E_1,p_1),\ldots,\ \texttt{explain}(Q_n,E_n,p_n) \tag{25}$$

where

$$\Pi \models Q \leftrightarrow ((Q_1 \wedge E_1) \vee \cdots \vee (Q_n \wedge E_n)) \tag{26}$$

and for all i, $1 \le i \le n$, $\Pi \models (Q_i \wedge E_i) \to Q$ and $P(E_i) = p_i$.

Proof. See appendix A.   □

Theorem 1. *Assume the setting of lemma 4. Whenever* `explain(Q)` *is posed as a query to Γ, the final constraint store is of the form*

$$\texttt{explain}([],E_1,p_1),\ldots,\ \texttt{explain}([],E_n,p_n) \tag{27}$$

where $E_1,\ldots,E_n$ comprise a complete set of minimal explanations for Q in Π, and all i, $1 \le i \le n$, $P(E_i) = p_i$.

Proof. See appendix A.   □

4.2   Conditional Probabilities

For a typical abductive problem, the probability of a given explanation may be very small and not very informative to the user. It may be more interesting to have the interpreter produce instead the conditional probability of each explanation E given the observation Q (i.e., the initial query), which is given as follows.

$$P(E|[\![Q]\!]) = \frac{P(E,[\![Q]\!])}{P([\![Q]\!])} = \frac{P(E)}{P([\![Q]\!])} \tag{28}$$

Probabilities $P(E)$ are those calculated by the CHR program shown above, and $P([\![Q]\!])$ can be calculated from the final constraint store based on formula (17) (or (18) when we generalize to PALPs). In the example, we get $P(\texttt{g}) = 0.625$ and thus, with the hinted extensions to the program, the following final constraint store.

$$\begin{aligned}&\texttt{explain\_conditional([],[c],0.8),}\\&\texttt{explain\_conditional([],[a,b],0.4)}\end{aligned} \tag{29}$$

Notice that the sum of these probabilities is > 1, which comes from the fact that both minimal explanations subsumes the non-minimal `[a,b,c]`, which has conditional probability $0.5^3/0.625 = 0.2$.

Whenever an abdicible a appears in more that one explanation, it may be interesting to calculate the probability of a given the observation.

$$P([\![a]\!] | [\![Q]\!]) = \frac{P([\![a]\!], [\![Q]\!])}{P([\![Q]\!])} = \frac{P([\![a, Q]\!])}{P([\![Q]\!])} \tag{30}$$

This can be found by first calculating $P([\![Q]\!])$ as above and then $P([\![a, Q]\!])$. However, with a bit of programming, it is be possible to obtain the value of $P([\![a, Q]\!])$ from the final constraint store used for finding $P([\![Q]\!])$, by summing up probabilities for the explanations that include a (or, in the general case, entail a).

4.3   Best-First Query Interpreters for PPALPs

For complex abductive problems it can be too cumbersome to calculate all possible minimal explanations, and instead we may want to calculate a minimal explanation with highest probability.

We can change the query interpreters shown so far, so they consider the constraint store as a priority queue of calls to explain/3, ordered by their current probabilities. During the process, we select the one with highest probability, allows it to make one step, and put back the derived calls; this continues until an explanation is found.

To implement this, we may replace explain/3 by two other constraints queue_explain/3 and step_explain/3. Whenever queue_explain/3 is called, it means to enter a call into the queue; selecting a queue_explain($q,e,P(e)$) for execution is done by promoting it to another constraint step_explain($q,e,$ $P(e)$), which then makes one step for the first subgoal of q similarly to what we have seen above.

There will be at most one step_explain/3 constraint in the store at a time, and it is selected either by an explicit call (when it is known by context that a particular constraint can be selected) or by an explicit search process. Searching the currently most probable partial explanation is done by posting a constraint select_best/0 implemented by the following rules; max_prob/1 is an auxiliary constraint used in the guard to check that the queue_explain/3 constraint in focus actually is the best one.

```
queue_explain(G,E,P)#W, select_best <=> max_prob(P) |
    step_explain(G,E,P)
    pragma passive(W).
max_prob(P0), queue_explain(_,_,P1)#W <=> P0 < P1 | fail
    pragma passive(W).
max_prob(_) <=> true.
```
(31)

This is clearly not the most efficient way to implement a priority queue, but has been chosen here for the brevity of the code. See [30, 42] for more detailed studies of priority queues in CHR. Notice, that while constraints in the guard of a CHR rule may lead to dubious semantics, the call to max_prob in (31) makes sense as it does not change the constraint store or bind variables; it is handled sensibly by most CHR implementations.

We can extend this interpreter so it can generate more explanations in order of decreasing probabilities when requested by the user. This requires that we store solutions already printed out so that (partial) explanations subsumed by any of those can be discarded; to this end, we introduce an additional constraint printed_explain/3 in order to avoid interference with the search for the currently best among non-printed, partial explanation.

We show the entire query interpreter which is a straightforward adaptation of the one shown in section 4.1; it encodes the same sample PPALP program as above (example 8).

```
explain(G):- step_explain([G],[],1).

printed_explain([],E1,_) \ queue_explain(_,E2,_) <=>
    subsumes(E1,E2) | true.

queue_explain(G,E,P)#W, select_best <=> max_prob(P) |
    step_explain(G,E,P)
    pragma passive(W).
```
(32)

```
step_explain([],E,P) <=>
    printed_explain([],E,P),
    write('Most probably solution: '), write(E),
    write(', P='), write(P),nl,
    ( user_wants_more -> select_best ; true ).

step_explain( [g|G], E, P) <=>
    queue_explain([a,b|G],E,P),
    queue_explain([c,d|G],E,P),
    step_explain([c|G],E,P). % select an arbitrary one

step_explain( [A|G], E, P) <=> abducible(A,PA) |
    (entailed(A,E) -> explain(G, E, P)
```
(33)
```
    ;
    extend(A,E,P,E1,P1), explain(G, E1, P1) ).

user_wants_more:-
    Ask user; if answer is y, succeed, otherwise fail.
```

The following shows part of the dialogue for the execution of the query q to the sample program.

```
| ?- explain(g).
Most probably solution: [c], P=0.5
Another and less probable explanation? y
Most probably solution: [a,b], P=0.25
```
(34)

Correctness of the best-first query interpreter can be stated and proved similarly to theorem 1 above. In fact a CHR derivation made by the best-first query interpreter corresponds to one possible derivation performed by the all-explanations query interpreter (given a nondeterministic operational semantics for CHR).

For any solution found by the query interpreter, it is possible to provide an estimate[3] of the probability of the observation (in the example: g) and thus of the conditional probabilities considered in section 4.2 above. Assume that the query interpreter at a given stage of executing a query Q prints a minimal explanation E_k and that it has already printed $E_1, \ldots, E_{k-1}$, and let $E_{k+1}, \ldots, E_n$ be the remaining partial explanations in the store. Then we have

$$P(E_1, \ldots, E_k) \leq P(Q) \leq P(E_1, \ldots, E_n) \tag{35}$$

The probabilities defining the upper and lower limits can be calculated from the current constraint store based on formula (17).

5   Programs with Variables, Unification, Integrity Constraints and External Predicates

We now generalize the construction above to handle general PALPs, including parameterized abducibles, integrity constraints, and possibly external predicates.

The query interpreters for PPALPs of section 4.1 are straightforward to extend to handle variables. Whenever a non-abducible subgoal g with continuation c is rewritten into alternatives corresponding to clauses of the PALP, we produce a variant with new variables g', c' for each alternative; if g' unifies with the head of a clause, this alternative is continued, otherwise this branch is discarded (and thus avoiding failure in the overall process).

As already mentioned, the auxiliary predicates specified in section 3 are provided in two versions, an efficient one which aborts in case of nonground abducibles, and a more general and less efficient one which handles nonground abducibles in a correct way; both are given in appendix B.

5.1   Variables in Queries and Abducibles

Bindings made to variables an a query during its execution should be reported to the user. We may extend the interpreters with an extra argument for this, but we can also access the values by introducing a special abducible predicate for the purpose.

```
abducible(value_of(_,_),1).                                    (36)
```

Stating now a query to a correct query interpreter (such as those introduced below) in the following way,

```
query([value_of('X',X), q(X)]),                                (37)
```

---

[3] This is inspired by [34]; our formula is a bit different from that of [34] since the basic assumptions are different.

any explanation will be of the form $\{$value_of('X',v)$\} \cup E_v$, where v is the value (if any; otherwise it is returned as a variable) bound to variable X in the construction of explanation E_v.

Notice that we defined abducibles earlier to have probabilities strictly less that 1 in order to have proposition 1. However, as value_of atoms are expected to be posted in the top-level query only and will remain fixed (but possibly affected by unifications) throughout the execution and with probability 1, it does not itself affect the probabilities of the explanations. The intuition that variable bindings add additional commitments is reflected in the subsumbtion hierarchy.

Example 9. Let $E_1 = \{$value_of('X',X),a(X)$\}$ and $E_2 = \{$value_of('X',1), a(1)$\}$ where a is an abducible predicate declared with probability 0.5. Then E_1 subsumes E_2 and $P(E_1) = 1 > 0.5 = P(E_2)$. □

5.2 Unification and Failure

We illustrate the general principle by an example. Assume the predicate p/1 is defined by the following clauses.

```
p(X):- q(X,Y), r(Y).
p(X):- a(X).                                    (38)
p(1).
```

These clauses are compiled into the CHR rule (39) below; notice for a variable in the head of a clause, that we can propagate this variable into the body rather than performing an explicit unification; when all arguments in the head are variables, the unification is deemed to succeed, so a test for failure can be omitted. The last line shows handling of failure which in this case may arise when the variable Xr3 has a ground value different from 1. Notice for the last alternative, that renaming is suppressed since no further usages are made of the variables in the original query. The pattern (*test -> continue* ; true) means that a possible failure of *test* is absorbed, and the branch *continue* vanishes rather that provoking a failure in the execution of the CHR rules (that would make the entire process fail); this technique is also used in [12, 25]. Recalculation of the probability in the last alternative is needed as the unification might have unified some variable in the explanation with a value, thus possibly lowering the probability.

```
explain( [p(X)|G], E, P) <=>
    rename([p(X)|G]+E, [p(Xr1)|Gr1]+E1),
    explain([q(Xr1,Y),r(Y)|Gr1], E1, P),
    rename([p(X)|G]+E, [p(Xr2)|Gr2]+E2),       (39)
    explain([a(Xr2)|Gr2], E2, P),
    (X=1 ->
      recalculate(E,Er,Pr), explain(G, Er, Pr)
    ; true).
```

With the version of the auxiliaries that assumes always ground explanations (and aborts otherwise), the explanations need not be passed through the renaming and the call to recalculate/3 can be left out.

The rule for accessing abducibles (21) is unchanged.

An aside Remark on Splitting by Unification of Abducible: Aiming at explanations that are minimal in the number of abducible atoms, the majority of non-probabilistic abduction methods [20, 28] tries to unify a new abducible with existing ones if possible. However, in order not to sacrifice completeness, two brances of computation are initiated in each such case. For example if $a(s)$ is added to a partial explanation $\{a(t), \cdots\}$, one branch may continue after unifying s and t, with $\{a(t), \cdots\}$, and another one with $\{a(s), a(t), \cdots\}$ with the additional constraint that s and t must remain different. Our notion of minimality is based on subsumption and we avoid this splitting into two brances, and even we produce minimal explanations.

We have, in fact, two objections to the splitting approach; first of all conceptually since the unification of the two abducibles above indicates a commitment which is not grounded for in the knowledge base (see a detailed argument in [13]), and secondly, it may result in an exponential explosion in the number of brances that needs to be investigated.

5.3   External Predicates

External predicates are exported to the underlying Prolog+CHR system by the following rule; when placed following rules (39,21), there is no need to include a test that the predicate of the first subgoal (X below) actually is external. Possible failure of the external predicates is handled as described above, section 5.2.

```
explain([X|G], E, P) <=> true |
   (call(X) ->
      recalculate(E,Er,Pr), explain(G,Er,Pr)
   ; true).
```
(40)

All other parts of the query interpreters are unchanged, i.e., rules (20,21,23).

In case of external predicates that use constraints or delays, we need to have the renaming of the current query produce new versions of constraints and other delayed calls pending on the variables in the query. Implementing a generalized renaming predicate that takes care of delayed call is quite straightforward provided that facilities are available for getting access to the delayed calls pending on specific variables.

Example 10. SICStus Prolog [43] includes a delaying predicate for non-equality, dif/2. Consider the case when there is a delayed call dif(X,7) for the variable X occurring in a query [p(X),...]. When this query is renamed into, say [p(X1),...], we need also produce the new variant dif(X1,7) of the delayed call in order to provide a correct semantics.

The SICStus built-in predicate frozen(X,C) will assign to C a representation of all calls delayed on variable X, including C=prolog:dif(X,7) in the example above. The delayed calls can now have their variables renamed simultaneously with the query, and the resulting variant calls, say dif(X1,7), can be entered into the program state simply by calling them. In this way the semantics is preserved in the copied query.   □

Example 11. The `clpr` and `clpq` libraries of SICStus Prolog [9, 43] provide constraint solvers over real, resp., rational numbers, which can be used as external predicates in PALP. It provides a predicate `projecting_assert` by means of which a clause capturing the constraints on indicated variables can be created dynamically. Such a clause can be used in a straightforward way to produce the desired variants of constraints. We illustrate its use by an example; the curly brackets indicate the syntax for calling the constraint solver. Executing

$$\{X=Y+Z\}, \ \texttt{projecting\_assert(aux(p(X,Y,Z)))}. \tag{41}$$

creates a clause equivalent with the following,

$$\texttt{aux(p(X,Y,Z)):- } \{X=Y+Z\}. \tag{42}$$

Calling this predicate with new arguments can set up the relevant constraints. The renaming predicate in appendix B is defined in the following standard way,

$$\texttt{rename(X,Y):- assert(aux(X)),retract(aux(Y))}. \tag{43}$$

and we can modify it for `clpr` and `clpq` as follows.

```
rename(X,Y):-
    assert(aux(X)),retract(aux(Y)),
    projecting_assert(aux(X)),
    aux(Y), retract((aux(_):- _)).
```
$$\tag{44}$$

No more adjustments are needed to incorporate these constraint solvers.   □

We have not developed extended definitions (nor implementations) of subsumption and entailment that takes external constraints into account. For example, explanations including constraints $\{a(X),\{X>7\}\}$ and $\{a(X)\}$ are considered equally good; intuitively, the last one should be preferred by a best first interpreter.

5.4 Correctness of the All-Explanations Query Interpreter for a PALP

To sum up, the PALPs interpreters are similar to those given for PPALPs in section 4 except that rules of form (39) replaces those of form (22), and that (40) is added.

Lemma 5. *Let Π be a PALP, Q a query, and Γ the transformation of Π into a CHR program, including auxiliary definitions, as described above in sections 5.2–5.3. Any constraint store which arises in the execution of* `explain(Q,[],1)` *in Γ is of the form*

$$\texttt{explain}(Q_1,E_1,p_1),\ldots, \texttt{explain}(Q_n,E_n,p_n) \tag{45}$$

where $Q_1 + E_1, \ldots, Q_n + E_n$ are pairwise separate, and

$$\Pi \models [\![Q]\!] \leftrightarrow [\![Q_1, E_1]\!] \vee \cdots \vee [\![Q_n, E_n]\!] \tag{46}$$

and for all i, $1 \le i \le n$, $\Pi \models [\![Q_i, E_i]\!] \rightarrow [\![Q]\!]$ and $P(E_i) = p_i$.

Proof. See appendix A. □

Theorem 2. *Assume the setting of lemma 5. Whenever* `explain(Q)` *is posed as a query to Γ, and the derivation terminates without error messages, the final constraint store is of the form*

$$\texttt{explain([]}, E_1, p_1), \ldots, \texttt{explain([]}, E_n, p_n) \tag{47}$$

where $E_1, \ldots, E_n$ comprise a complete set of explanations for Q in Π, and for all i, $1 \le i \le n$, $P(E_i) = p_i$.

Proof. See appendix A. □

Whether the interpreter terminates depends on the program, and since PALP is a Turing complete language, termination is undecidable, and we can refer to general termination proof methods that are based on sufficient conditions.

5.5   Other Variants of the PALP Query Interpreter

The principles for calculation of conditional probabilities and for best-first search described for the propositional case in sections 4.2 and 4.3 can be incorporated into the general PALP query interpreter described here with no problems, so we omit the details.

Any query which terminates correctly for a given PALP in the all-explanations version will also terminate correctly with the best-first version. Some programs may terminate with best-first, giving a best solution, but loop with all-solutions. This may happen when the program has a loop in a branch with lower probability, or if it has an infinite number of explanations.

There is a small blemish in the best-first interpreter as it may emit non-minimal explanations containing non-ground abducibles. This comes from the fact that the search is controlled by probabilities, which means that

$$\texttt{queue\_explain([], [a(\_),b], 0.5)} \tag{48}$$

may be selected before

$$\texttt{queue\_explain([\textit{Rest}], [b], 0.5)}; \tag{49}$$

and it may be the case the *Rest* succeeds later without referring to other abducibles (see also proposition 3 with remarks, above).

The remedy is to hold back final explanations with non-ground abducibles, as in (48), until there are no subsuming explanations with the same probability as in (49). In the example, this means that (48) must wait until (49) has transformed into c = queue_explain([],[b],0.5). Then c would be selected and printed out before (48), and (48) then immediately eliminated by the subsumption removal rule (2nd rule of (32) above).

Another efficient, but admittedly *ad-hoc* approach, is to fake a probability of 0.999 to non-ground abducibles instead of the correct value 1. This may work correctly in all but extreme cases.

6   Optimizations and Extensions

The architecture of the query interpreters described above provide a flexibility to plug in different optimizations and extensions, of which we consider some examples here.

6.1   Optimization *à la* Dijkstra's Shortest Path Algorithm

We suggest here an optimization of the best-first query interpreters inspired by Dijkstra's shortest path algorithm [21]. Whenever we have two or more processes with the same remaining subgoal (e.g., for finding a path from the same intermediate node to the terminal node in the shortest path example), we keep only the best one; in CHR:

$$
\begin{aligned}
&\texttt{queue\_explain([G],E1,P1) \textbackslash\ queue\_explain([G],E2,P2) <=>}\\
&\texttt{prority\_less\_than(P2,P1) | true.}
\end{aligned}
\qquad (50)
$$

This will suppress the partial execution of some branches which are deemed not to become best in the end.

Notice that we indicated the rest query by a pattern that matches only queries with a single atom, which means that the rule is quickly bypassed for any query with two or more atoms. We could in principle have used a variable that matches any query, but this would lead to slower tests for matching of the two queries (and which likely fails in most cases).

If, furthermore, an analysis of the PALP under consideration tells which predicate(s) that may appear in singleton queries, we can make the pattern even more specific. An example of this optimization is given in section 7.2 below.

6.2   Optimizing Integrity Checks by Simpification

We mention also the possibility of applying simplified integrity constraints in specialized rules for each abducibles predicate. Simplification was suggested by [33] for database integrity checking; an unfolding of the theoretical foundations and a powerful method is given by [18]. The overall idea is to assume the database (here the current explanation) be consistent before an update, and based on that knowledge, to construct for each possible update a specialized check that considers only the part of the database which may interfere with the update. A typical speed up by this technique is an order of magnitude or more, when compared with a full check.

Integrity checking in our interpreters shown so far are hidden in the `extend` and `recalculate` auxiliary predicates, which do not take the actual update into account. Consider, as an example, the integrity constraint

$$\perp :- \ a(X), \ b(X). \tag{51}$$

Without any special indexing techniques, this needs quadratic time measured in the size of the explanation E being checked, e.g., by a combination of two calls to `member`, `member(a(X),E)`, `member(b(X),E)`. If we know that explanation E is consistent, we can obtain by simplification for update `a(Y)` the linear check `member(b(Y),E)`.

We may now replace the generic rule for handling abducibles by specialized ones for each abducible predicate, e.g., as follows.

```
explain([a(X)|G],E,P) <=>
    (member(b(X),E) -> true    % vanish
    ;
    insert(a(X),E,E1), P1 is P*0.9,
    explain(Q,E1,P1)).
```
(52)

This principle can be further extended with specialized treatment for PALP clauses with more that one abducible in the body.

6.3   A Note on Negation

A limited form of explicit negation of abducibles can be implemented through integrity constraints. When `a/1` is an abducible predicate, we may let `not_a/1` stand for the negation of `a/1` and define the intended semantics by the integrity constraint $\perp :- \ a(X), \ not\_a(X)$.

While this may be practical for many applications, we lack support for the other axiom for negation, namely $a(X) \lor not\_a(X)$. We cannot handle this currently, as integrity checking becomes considerably more complicated. The extra axiom will imply that arbitrary logic programs can be encoded in the integrity constraints; the check, then, amounts to testing satisfiability of such programs, for which we have no straightforward embedding in CHR. See section 8.2 below which gives a suggestion for a more satisfactory treatment of negation.

We notice that the approach of [35], described in more detail in section 8.1 below, to probabilistic abduction includes negation with support of both axioms, but excludes integrity constraints and require any negated call to an abducible or defined predicate to be ground.

7   Program Examples

7.1   A Standard Diagnosis Case

We consider a power supply network which has one power plant `pp`, a number of directed wires w_i and connecting nodes n_i, which may lead electricity to a collection of villages v_i. The overall structure is as follows.

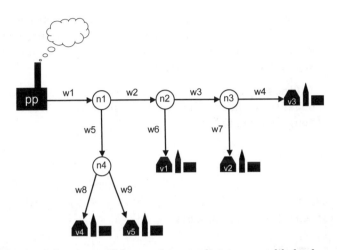

Probabilistic abduction will be used to predict to most likely damages in the network given observations about which villages have electricity and which have not. As abducibles, we use `up/1` and `down/1` which apply to the power plant and the wires (for simplicity, the connecting nodes are assumed always to work). The network structure is represented by the following facts.

$$
\begin{array}{lll}
\texttt{edge(w1, pp, n1).} & \texttt{edge(w4, n3, v3).} & \texttt{edge(w7, n3, v2).} \\
\texttt{edge(w2, n1, n2).} & \texttt{edge(w5, n1, n4).} & \texttt{edge(w8, n4, v4).} \\
\texttt{edge(w3, n2, n3).} & \texttt{edge(w6, n2, v1).} & \texttt{edge(w9, n4, v5).}
\end{array}
\tag{53}
$$

The fact that a given point in the network has electricity, is described as follows.

$$
\begin{array}{l}
\texttt{haspower(pp):- up(pp).} \\
\texttt{haspower(N2):- edge(W,N1,N2), up(W), haspower(N1).}
\end{array}
\tag{54}
$$

As no negation is supported, the program includes also clauses that simulate the negation of `haspower`.

$$
\begin{array}{l}
\texttt{hasnopower(pp):- down(pp).} \\
\texttt{hasnopower(N2):- edge(W,\_,N2), down(W).} \\
\texttt{hasnopower(N2):- edge(\_,N1,N2), hasnopower(N1).}
\end{array}
\tag{55}
$$

To express that `up/1` and `down/1` are each other's negation, we introduce an integrity constraint, and define probabilities that sum to one.

$$
\begin{array}{l}
\texttt{abducible(up(\_), 0.9).} \\
\texttt{abducible(down(\_), 0.1).} \\
\texttt{\(\bot\):- up(X), down(X).}
\end{array}
\tag{56}
$$

The predicate definitions are compiled in CHR as explained above; we show here the one for the `haspower` predicate.

```
step_explain( [haspower(N)|G], E, P) <=>
  rename([haspower(N)|G], [haspower(Nr1)|Gr1]),
  (Nr1=pp -> queue_explain([up(pp)|Gr1], E, P) ; true),      (57)
  queue_explain([edge(W2,N12,N),up(W2),haspower(N12)|G],E,P),
  select_best.
```

The implementation of the **extend** auxiliary (which is used when a new abducible is encountered) includes the checking of the integrity constraint. The following excerpt of a screen dialogue shows how the observation that no village have electricity is explained by the interpreter.

```
| ?- explain([hasnopower(v1), hasnopower(v2),
    hasnopower(v3), hasnopower(v4), hasnopower(v5)]).
Best solution: [down(w1)]
Prob=0.1
Another solution? y
Best solution: [down(pp)]
Prob=0.1
Another solution? y
Best solution: [down(w2),down(w5)]
Prob=0.01
Another solution? y
Best solution: [down(w3),down(w5),down(w6)]
Prob=0.001
Another solution? y
Best solution: [down(w2),down(w8),down(w9)]
Prob=0.001
Another solution?
⋮
```

(58)

It appears that the two intuitively most reasonable hypotheses, namely that the power plant or the single wire connecting it with the rest of the network is down, are generated as the first ones with highest probability. Then follow combinations with lower and lower probability of different wires being down. The original output indicated insignificant rounding errors in the calculated probabilities which have been retouched away above.

7.2   Most Probable Path with Dijkstra Optimization

Here we illustrate both the optimization described in section 6.1 above for a best-first interpreter and an extended syntax for declaration of abducibles. We consider the problem of finding most probable paths through a network such as the following.

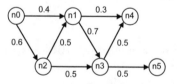

The figures for the outgoing edge of a node indicate the probability for choosing a particular edge from that node. We could in principle declare one nullary abducible predicate for each edge, but to facilitate writing the PALP, we use one common predicate select(n,m) describing the event that the indicated edge is chosen. We declare it as follows, extending the syntax of definition 1 above.

```
abducible(select(n0,n1), 0.4).
abducible(select(n0,n2), 0.6).                    (59)
etc.
```

I.e., we have several declarations for the same abducible predicate, specifying different probabilities for different arguments. The intuitively correct semantics is preserved provided that no two declared abducible atoms can unify. The implementation needs one single adjustment so that the call to an abducible predicate, say select(n0,X), launches a new branch for each possible choice of declaration with which it unifies; this is done analogously to the way that defined predicates are handled (section 5.2, above). The path program can be implemented as follows, using the "generic" abducible predicate.

```
path(N1,N3):- select(N1,N2), path(N2,N3).         (60)
path(N,N).
```

We may add integrity constraints of the form $\perp$:- select(n,x), select(n,y), for all cases of $n \rightarrow x$ and $n \rightarrow y$ being different differet edges going out from n, but due the best-first search, they are in fact not necessary.

This program is translated into a best-first query interpreter in CHR as decribed above, and we add the following rule in order to prune any initial path segment, which is less optimal than another such segment ending in the same node.

```
queue_explain([path(N,M)],_,P1)
    \ queue_explain([path(N,M)],E,P2)             (61)
<=> P2 < P1 | true.
```

The query

```
?- explain(path(n0,n4)).                          (62)
```

provides one answer, namely

```
[select(n0,n2),select(n2,n3),select(n3,n4)], Prob=0.15.    (63)
```

No more answers are produced as rule (61) has removed all segments that could lead to less optimal paths through the graph. A test print indicates that the following constraints have been deleted by this rule.

```
queue_explain(path(n1,n4),[select(n0,n2),select(n2,n1)],0.3)
queue_explain(path(n3,n4),[select(n0,n1),select(n1,n3)],0.28) (64)
queue_explain(path(n4,n4),[select(n0,n1),select(n1,n4)],0.12)
```

8   Conclusion

We have defined a class of Probabilistic Abductive Logic Programs and described implementations in terms of a systematic transformation into CHR rules. This framework differs from other approaches to probabilistic logic programming (that we are aware of) by having both interaction with external constraint solvers and integrity constraints. We support no general negation in abductive logic programs, as is done in several methods for non-probabilistic abduction, and we have argued that (at least our approach to) the probabilistic semantics is difficult to adapt to negation; we have, however, indicated how a simplified version of explicit negation can be implemented with integrity constraints.

8.1   Related Work

Abduction in logic programming without probabilities has attracted a lot of attention, and several algorithms, including metainterpreters written in Prolog have been made; see [20, 28] for overview and references. We may emphasize an early work by Console *et al* [19] from 1991, that explained abductive reasoning in terms of deductive reasoning in the completion of the abductive logic program. This principle was extended into an abstract procedure for abduction by Fung and Kowalski in 1997 [27], which inspired several implemented systems. Ignoring the probabilistic part of our own interpreters, they show similarity with the principle of [19] in the sense that we map abductive programs into CHR, which is a purely deductive paradigm; as shown in lemmas 4, 5, the execution state represents at any time the semantics given by the initial query and any transformation made by a CHR rules can be explained from and respects the program completion.

Abduction without probabilities has been approached using CHR, initially by [1] translating abductive logic programs into the dialect called $CHR^\vee$ [2] that features disjunctions in rule bodies. In that approach, abducibles are represented directly as CHR constraints and integrity constraints as CHR rules, and predicate definitions are translated into $CHR^\vee$ with a disjunct for each clause. In later work [16], this principle has been modified by representing the clauses of an abductive logic program directly as their Prolog equivalents, leading to a very efficient implementation of abduction with no interpretational overhead; [13] provides an overview of this direction and extends with methods for interaction with arbitrary external constraint solvers, similarly to what we have explained in the present paper in a probabilistic version. These implementations could in principles be adapted to top-down (but not best-first) abduction, simply by calculating the probability for each generated answer when printing it out. However, integrity constraints would here need to be limited to the sort we use in the present paper, as an instance of the more general pattern such as a,b ==> c indicates a probabilistic dependency, which our semantics is not prepared for; an analogous phenomenon was discussed in 6.3 in relation to negation.

In [16], it is also shown how so-called assumptions can be implemented in a similar way with CHR; assumptions are like abducibles, but with explicit creation, application (perhaps being consumed) and scope rules; [11, 15, 16, 17] show linguistic applications of logical grammars (as DCGs or bottom-up parsing with CHR) extended with abduction using CHR. A notion of Global Abduction [40, 41], allowing a sort of destructive non-monotonic updates and interaction between different processes (or agents) have been implemented in CHR by [12] using the constraint store as a process pool, as in the present paper.

In [10], a reversal implementation of the proof predicate demo(p,q), meaning that query q succeeds in program p, is described and implemented using CHR for the primitive operations within the metainterpreter that defines the proof predicate. Reversibility means that it can fill in missing parts of the program argument in order to make specified queries provable, and thus it can also perform abduction, although no notion of minimality is supported.

Recent approaches to abductive logic programming, e.g., [4, 23, 29], have studied the interaction with externally defined constraint solvers, but implementations tend to be specialized to specific constraint solvers. SCIFF [4] is an approach to abductive logic programming which includes negation, integrity constraints, external constraints solvers, and other specialized facilities; the existence of an implementation made with CHR is indicated in [3], but no details are given which allow for a comparison.

Probabilistic versions of abductive logic programming have not been studied nearly to the same extent. We can refer to the work by D. Poole [34] considering probabilistic abduction for a class of Probabilistic Horn Abduction Theories; this is later [35] generalized into Independent Choice Logic. Abducible predicates are grouped by so-called *disjoint declarations* of the form disjoint([a_1:p_1, ..., a_n:p_n]). The intension is that common instances of a_i, a_j, $i \neq j$ cannot coexist in the same explanation, corresponding to integrity constraints $\bot$:-a_i,a_j for all $i \neq j$; other integrity constraints are not possible. Probabilities are given by $P(a_i') = p_i$ for a ground instance a_i' of a_i, and it holds that $p_1 + \cdots + p_n = 1$. The framework does not assign probabilities to non-ground abducibles. A metainterpreter written in Prolog is described in [34], which works best-first using a probability ranked priority queue analogous to what we have described (however, with a more complicated way of attaching probabilities to items in the queue). In [35], the appoach is extended for negation as failure of ground goals G, presupposing that the set of all minimal explanations $\{E_i\}_{i \in I}$ is finite and each of those finite and always ground. In such a case, explanations for the negation of G can be found by regrouping of negated elements of the E_i explanations; this excludes best-first search as the interpreter needs to keep track of all explanations.

The PRISM system [38] is a powerful reasoning system, which is based on logic programming extended with multivalued random variables that work slightly differently from abducible predicates as descibed in the present paper, but it is straightforward to rewrite an abductive logic program into a PRISM program. PRISM has no support for integrity constraints or interface to external constraint solvers. PRISM includes a variety of top-level predicates which can generate abductive explanations, including finding the best ones using a generalized viterbi algorithm. Another central feature of PRISM is its machine learning capabilities, which means that in can learn probabilities from training data.

Reasoning in Bayesian networks can also be considered an instance of probabilistic abduction, but we will refrain from giving detailed references, since the knowledge representations are different. Bayesian networks are easily embedded in abductive logic programming and can be simulated in our system as well as [34, 38]. One of the advantages of Bayesian networks is that there exist very efficient implementations which can find approximative solution for huge networks.

Logic programs with associated probability distribution have been used elsewhere, including for inductive logic programming, but the issue of abduction does not seem to have been addressed; e.g., [32, 36].

Probabilistic Constraint Handling Rules are introduced by [26]; probabilities are assigned to each rule of a program for it to apply and it is defined by a an operational semantics and implemented by a transformation into CHR; [30] describes user-defined priorities for CHR.

There is an inherent similarity between answer set programming (ASP) and abductive reasoning with integrity, which has been noted by many authors; [6] describes an extension of ASP with probabilities which, thus, is capable of doing probabilistic abductive reasoning (no implementation is reported, though). However, this framework excludes programs that exhibit the property illustrated in example 7, that the probability of abducibles considering consistent states only is different from the probability defined by the programmer; this means that many probabilistic abductive programs with integrity constraints are not covered. By nature, ASP programs can only produce ground abductive explanations.

8.2   Perspectives and Future Work

Obvious applications of our framework seem to be diagnosis and stochastic language processing. Relatively efficient methods exist for stochastic context-free grammars already, but we may approach property grammars [7, 8] which are a formalism based entirely on constraint satisfaction rather than tree structure; by nature, these grammars have a very high degree of ambiguity so a probabiistic approach using best-first search may be relevant.

Probabilistic extensions of Global Abduction (see related work section above) or similar frameworks may be relevant to apply for applications monitoring and interacting with the real world. It seems also possible to extend the probabilistic best-first search strategy to take into account changing probabilities, e.g., produced by a learning agent or an agent monitoring specific subsystems by means of, say, a Bayesian network.

The present approach can be immediately generalized for arbitrary monotonic priority functions, e.g., represent some object function to be optimized or adjusted probabilities; in computational linguistics in may be relevant to use adjusted probabilities for partial explanations according to the length of the text segment they represent. See [14] for an initial publication on this approach; it is also relevant to compare with [30] that considers CHR with rule priorities.

In order to extend the approach with negation and maintain a relatively good efficiency, the principle of compiling a logic program into another one that expresses its negation is under consideration; see [5, 39] for such methods. The example of section 7.1 showed a trivial and manually produced example of such a translation.

Finally, we mention that our implementation principle, transforming PALPs systematically into CHR, can be embedded in a compiler, so that PALPs can be written in Prolog source files and compiled automatically into CHR. Prolog's metaprogramming facilities including the so-called term expansion facilities, see, e.g., [43], make the implementation of such a compiler a minor task; [11, 16] explain systems based on CHR implemented in this way.

Acknowledgement. This work is supported by the CONTROL project, funded by Danish Natural Science Research Council.

References

1. Abdennadher, S., Christiansen, H.: An experimental CLP platform for integrity constraints and abduction. In: Proceedings of FQAS 2000, Flexible Query Answering Systems: Advances in Soft Computing series, pp. 141–152. Physica-Verlag, Springer (2000)
2. Abdennadher, S., Schütz, H.: CHR$^\vee$: A flexible query language. In: Andreasen, T., Christiansen, H., Larsen, H.L. (eds.) FQAS 1998. LNCS, vol. 1495, pp. 1–14. Springer, Heidelberg (1998)
3. Alberti, M., Chesani, F., Gavanelli, M., Lamma, E.: The CHR-based implementation of a system for generation and confirmation of hypotheses. In: Wolf, A., Frühwirth, T.W., Meister, M. (eds.) W(C)LP. Ulmer Informatik-Berichte, vol. 2005-01, pp. 111–122. Universität Ulm, Germany (2005)
4. Alberti, M., Chesani, F., Gavanelli, M., Lamma, E., Mello, P., Torroni, P.: Verifiable agent interaction in abductive logic programming: the SCIFF framework. ACM Transactions on Computational Logic 9(4) (to appear, 2008)
5. Alferes, J.J., Pereira, L.M., Swift, T.: Abduction in well-founded semantics and generalized stable models via tabled dual programs. Theory and Practice of Logic Programming 4(4), 383–428 (2004)
6. Baral, C., Gelfond, M., Rushton, J.N.: Probabilistic reasoning with answer sets. In: Lifschitz, V., Niemelä, I. (eds.) LPNMR 2004. LNCS, vol. 2923, pp. 21–33. Springer, Heidelberg (2003)
7. Blache, P.: Property grammars: A fully constraint-based theory. In: Christiansen, H., Skadhauge, P.R., Villadsen, J. (eds.) CSLP 2005. LNCS, vol. 3438, pp. 1–16. Springer, Heidelberg (2005)
8. Blache, P., Balfourier, J.-M.: Property grammars: a flexible constraint-based approach to parsing. In: IWPT. Tsinghua University Press (2001)
9. Holzbaur, C.: OFAI clp(q,r) Manual, Edition 1.3.3. Technical Report TR-95-09, Austrian Research Institute for Artificial Intelligence, Vienna (1995)
10. Christiansen, H.: Automated reasoning with a constraint-based metainterpreter. Journal of Logic Programming 37(1-3), 213–254 (1998)
11. Christiansen, H.: CHR Grammars. Int'l. Journal on Theory and Practice of Logic Programming 5(4-5), 467–501 (2005)

12. Christiansen, H.: On the implementation of global abduction. In: Inoue, K., Satoh, K., Toni, F. (eds.) CLIMA 2006. LNCS, vol. 4371, pp. 226–245. Springer, Heidelberg (2007)
13. Christiansen, H.: Executable specifications for hypotheses-based reasoning with Prolog and Constraint Handling Rules. Journal of Applied Logic (to appear, 2008)
14. Christiansen, H.: Prioritized abduction with CHR. In: Schrijvers, T., Raiser, F., Frühwirth, T. (eds.) CHR 2008, The 5th Workshop on Constraint Handling Rules (proceedings). RISC-Linz Report Series No. 08-10, pp. 159–173 (2008)
15. Christiansen, H., Dahl, V.: Logic grammars for diagnosis and repair. International Journal on Artificial Intelligence Tools 12(3), 227–248 (2003)
16. Christiansen, H., Dahl, V.: HYPROLOG: A new logic programming language with assumptions and abduction. In: Gabbrielli, M., Gupta, G. (eds.) ICLP 2005. LNCS, vol. 3668, pp. 159–173. Springer, Heidelberg (2005)
17. Christiansen, H., Dahl, V.: Meaning in Context. In: Dey, A.K., Kokinov, B., Leake, D.B., Turner, R. (eds.) CONTEXT 2005. LNCS, vol. 3554, pp. 97–111. Springer, Heidelberg (2005)
18. Christiansen, H., Martinenghi, D.: On simplification of database integrity constraints. Fundamenta Informatica 71(4), 371–417 (2006)
19. Console, L., Dupré, D.T., Torasso, P.: On the relationship between abduction and deduction. Journal of Logic and Computation 1(5), 661–690 (1991)
20. Denecker, M., Kakas, A.C.: Abduction in logic programming. In: Kakas, A.C., Sadri, F. (eds.) Computational Logic: Logic Programming and Beyond. LNCS, vol. 2407, pp. 402–436. Springer, Heidelberg (2002)
21. Dijkstra, E.W.: A note on two problems in connexion with graphs. Numerische Mathematik 1(4), 269–271 (1959)
22. Duck, G.J., Stuckey, P.J., García de la Banda, M.J., Holzbaur, C.: The refined operational semantics of Constraint Handling Rules. In: Demoen, B., Lifschitz, V. (eds.) ICLP 2004. LNCS, vol. 3132, pp. 90–104. Springer, Heidelberg (2004)
23. Endriss, U., Mancarella, P., Sadri, F., Terreni, G., Toni, F.: The ciff proof procedure for abductive logic programming with constraints. In: Alferes, J.J., Leite, J.A. (eds.) JELIA 2004. LNCS, vol. 3229, pp. 31–43. Springer, Heidelberg (2004)
24. Frühwirth, T.: Theory and practice of constraint handling rules, special issue on constraint logic programming. Journal of Logic Programming 37(1–3), 95–138 (1998)
25. Frühwirth, T.W., Holzbaur, C.: Source-to-source transformation for a class of expressive rules. In: Buccafurri, F. (ed.) APPIA-GULP-PRODE, pp. 386–397 (2003)
26. Frühwirth, T.W., Di Pierro, A., Wiklicky, H.: Probabilistic constraint handling rules. Electronic Notes in Theoretical Computer Science 76 (2002)
27. Fung, T.H., Kowalski, R.A.: The iff proof procedure for abductive logic programming. Journal of Logic Programmming 33(2), 151–165 (1997)
28. Kakas, A.C., Kowalski, R.A., Toni, F.: The role of abduction in logic programming. In: Gabbay, D.M., Hogger, C.J., Robinson, J.A. (eds.) Handbook of Logic in Artificial Intelligence and Logic Programming, vol. 5, pp. 235–324. Oxford University Press, Oxford (1998)
29. Kakas, A.C., Michael, A., Mourlas, C.: ACLP: Abductive Constraint Logic Programming. Journal of Logic Programming 44, 129–177 (2000)
30. De Koninck, L., Schrijvers, T., Demoen, B.: User-definable rule priorities for chr. In: Leuschel, M., Podelski, A. (eds.) PPDP, pp. 25–36. ACM, New York (2007)
31. Lloyd, J.W.: Foundations of logic programming; Second, extended edition. Springer, Heidelberg (1987)

32. Muggleton, S.: Stochastic logic programs. In: de Raedt, L. (ed.) Advances in Inductive Logic Programming, pp. 254–264. IOS Press, Amsterdam (1996)
33. Nicolas, J.-M.: Logic for improving integrity checking in relational data bases. Acta Informatica 18, 227–253 (1982)
34. Poole, D.: Logic programming, abduction and probability - a top-down anytime algorithm for estimating prior and posterior probabilities. New Generation Computing 11(3), 377–400 (1993)
35. Poole, D.: Abducing through negation as failure: stable models within the independent choice logic. Journal of Logic Programming 44(1-3), 5–35 (2000)
36. Reitzler, S.: Probabilistic Constraint Logic Programming. PhD thesis, 1998. Appearing as AIMS, Arbeitspapiere des Instituts für Maschinelle Sprachverarbeitung, Lehrstuhl für Theoretische Computerlinguistic, Universität Stuttgart, Vol. 5(1) (1999)
37. Robinson, J.A.: A machine-oriented logic based on the resolution principle. J. ACM 12(1), 23–41 (1965)
38. Sato, T., Kameya, Y.: Prism: A language for symbolic-statistical modeling. In: IJCAI, pp. 1330–1339 (1997)
39. Sato, T., Tamaki, H.: First order compiler: A deterministic logic program synthesis algorithm. Journal of Symbolic Computation 8(6), 605–627 (1989)
40. Satoh, K.: "All's well that ends well" - a proposal of global abduction. In: Delgrande, J.P., Schaub, T. (eds.) NMR, pp. 360–367 (2004)
41. Satoh, K.: An application of global abduction to an information agent which modifies a plan upon failure - preliminary report. In: Leite, J.A., Torroni, P. (eds.) CLIMA 2004. LNCS, vol. 3487, pp. 213–229. Springer, Heidelberg (2005)
42. Sneyers, J., Schrijvers, T., Demoen, B.: Dijkstra's algorithm with Fibonacci heaps: An executable description in CHR. In: Fink, M., Tompits, H., Woltran, S. (eds.) WLP. INFSYS Research Report, vol. 1843-06-02, pp. 182–191. Technische Universität Wien, Austria (2006)
43. Swedish Institute of Computer Science. SICStus Prolog user's manual, Version 4.0.2. Most recent version (2007), http://www.sics.se/isl

A   Proofs for Important Properties

Proof (lemma 2). Let $\{E_1, \ldots, E_n\}$ be a complete set of minimal explanation for Q in a PALP Π and E an arbitrary explanation for Q. Since $\Pi \cup \exists E \models [\![Q]\!]$ and $\Pi \models [\![Q]\!] \leftrightarrow \exists E_1 \vee \cdots \vee \exists E_n$, both by definition, we have that $\Pi \models \exists E \to \exists E_1 \vee \cdots \vee \exists E_n$ and thus $\models \exists E \to \exists E_1 \vee \cdots \vee \exists E_n$. Since $E, E_1, \ldots, E_2$ are conjunctions of atoms, this means that $\models \exists E \to \exists E_i$ for some E_i, $1 \leq i \leq n$ which the same as E_i subsumes E.

From this part of the lemma, the uniqueness of complete sets of minimal explanations follows immediately.   □

Proof (lemma 3). It is sufficient to show that every E_i is a minimal explanation. Clearly E_i is an explanation, and according to lemma 1 there is a minimal explanation E_i' with $E_i' \subseteq E_i$. As in the proof of lemma 2, we find that $\models E_i' \to E_1 \vee \cdots \vee E_n$: By assumption we cannot have $\models E_i' \to E_j$ for $i \neq j$, which means that $\models E_i' \to E_i$. In other words $E_i \subseteq E_i'$ and thus $E_i = E_i'$.   □

Proof (lemma 4). The initial constraint store $\{\texttt{explain}(Q,\texttt{[]},\texttt{1})\}$ satisfies the property. It is straightforward to verify that each of the CHR rules (21,22,23) preserves the property, so it follows by induction that it holds for any subsequent constraint store. ◻

Proof (theorem 1). Termination is guaranteed as a PPALP has no recursion, and since each step performed by CHR rules (21,22) introduces new $\texttt{explain/3}$ constraints, each of which represents a step in an SLD derivation in $\Pi \cup A$ where A is the set of all abducibles.

From lemma 4 and the fact that rule (23) removes any $\texttt{explain}(\_,E_i,\_)$ constraint for which there is another $\texttt{explain}(\texttt{[]},E_j,\_)$ with $E_j \subseteq E_i$, $i \neq j$, it can be seen the final constraint store is of the form

$$\texttt{explain}(\texttt{[]},E_1,p_1),\ldots,\ \texttt{explain}(\texttt{[]},E_n,p_n) \tag{65}$$

where $E_j \not\subseteq E_i$ for all $i \neq j$. The theorem follows now from lemmas 3 and 4. ◻

Proof (lemma 5). As in the proof of lemma 4, we notice that the initial constraint store satisfies the property and that each possible derivation step preserves the property. It should be noticed that rules (39,21,40) in some cases suppress constraints $\texttt{explain}(Q,E,p)$ for which $\Pi \not\models [\![Q,E]\!]$. ◻

Proof (theorem 2). The arguments are identical to those in the proof of theorem 1 except that we refer to lemma 5 instead of lemma 4. ◻

B   Implementations of Auxiliary Predicates

We describe here the two alternative implementations for the auxiliary predicates specified in section 3, an effficient one for ground abducibles, and another one at more general one that can handle nonground abducibles.

B.1   For Ground Abducibles

Here we represent explanations as lists of ground abducibles sorted by Prolog's built on term ordering denoted @<.

```
subsumes(S1,S2):- fastsubset(S2).

fastsubset([],_).
fastsubset([X|Xs],[Y|Ys]):-
  X==Y -> fastsubset(Xs,Ys)
  ;  X @> Y -> fastsubset([X|Xs],Ys).

entailed(A,S):- fastmember(A,S).

fastmember(X,[Y|Ys]):-
  X==Y -> true
  ; X @> Y -> fastmember(X,Ys).
```

```
extend(A,S,P,S1,P1):-
  extend1(A,S,S1),
  \+ inconsistent(S1),
  abducible(A,PA), P1 is P*PA.

extend1(X,[],[X]).
extend1(X,[Y|Ys],[X,Y|Ys]):- X@<Y, !.
extend1(X,[Y|Ys],[Y|Ys1]):- extend1(X,Ys,Ys1).

% recalculate/3 not used here

% normalize/2 not relevant here

rename(X,Y):- assert(aux(X)), retract(aux(Y)).
```

Inconsistency is defined specifically for the PALP at hand. Assume, as an example, that it contains the following integrity constraints.

$$\begin{aligned}
&\bot\text{:- a, b.}\\
&\bot\text{:- c(X), b(X).}
\end{aligned} \tag{66}$$

Then the predicate is defined as follows.

```
inconsistent(E):- subset([a,b],E).
inconsistent(E):- subset([c(X),b(X)],E).
```

$$\tag{67}$$

```
subset([],_).
subset([X|Xs],S):- member(X,S), subset(Xs,S).
```

B.2   For Nonground Abducibles

Sideeffects in terms of unifications can occur which will destroy the term ordering within a list of nonground abducibles, so we use non-sorted lists instead. We show here a version which does not take into account possible delayed called or external constraints pending on the variables of the explanations and abducibles that are operated on. This is a bit tricky to add but involves no conceptual difficulties.

```
subsumes(S1,S2):-
  rename(S1,S1copy),
  rename(S2,S2sko), numbervars(S2sko,0,_),
  subset(S1copy,S2sko).

entailed(A,S):- \+ hard_member(B,S).

extend(A,S,P,[A|S],P1):-
  \+ inconsistent([A|S]),
  (ground(A) -> P=P1 ; abducible(A,PA), P1 is P*PA).
```

```
recalculate(E,E1,P1):-
    remove_dups(E,E1),
    prob(E1,P1).

remove_dups([],[]).

remove_dups([A|As], L):-
    hard_member(A,As) -> remove_dups(As, L)
    ; remove_dups(As, L1), L=[A|L1].

hard_member(A,[B|Bs]):-
    A==B -> true ; hard_member(A,Bs).

prob([],1).
prob([A|As],P):-
    \+ ground(A) -> prob(As,P)
    ; abducible(A,PA), prob(As,PAs), P is PA*PAs.

% rename/2, as above

% inconsistent/2, as above

% subset/2 as above
```

The predicate normalize_final($E1, E2$) is in its present version defined in a way so it tries out all possible subsets, and selects as E_2 a smallest one which is equivalent to E_1.

A Compositional Semantics for CHR
with Propagation Rules

Maurizio Gabbrielli[1], Maria Chiara Meo[2], and Paolo Tacchella[1]

[1] Dipartimento di Scienze dell'Informazione, Università di Bologna,
Mura A.Zamboni 7, 40127 Bologna, Italy
{gabbri,Paolo.Tacchella}@cs.unibo.it
[2] Dipartimento di Scienze, Università di Chieti-Pescara
Viale Pindaro 42, 65127 Pescara, Italy
cmeo@unich.it

Abstract. Constraint Handling Rules (CHR) is a committed-choice declarative language which has originally been designed for writing constraint solvers and which is nowadays a general purpose language.

In [7,11] a trace based, compositional semantics for CHR has been defined. Such a compositional model uses as reference operational semantics the original "naive" one [9] which, due to the propagation rule, admits trivial non-termination. In this paper we extend the work of [7,11] by considering a more refined operational semantics which avoids trivial non-termination.

1   Introduction

Constraint Handling Rules (CHR) is a declarative, committed-choice language which was originally specifically designed for writing constraint solvers [9] and which is nowadays a general purpose language. A CHR program consists of a set of guarded (simplification, propagation and simpagation) rules which allows to transform multisets of atomic formulas (constraints) into simpler ones. In this way it is rather easy to define solvers for some specific user-defined predicates and to introduce them in some existing host language, which is typically Prolog [17] even though several other languages support CHR implementations, including HAL [12], Haskell [18], Java [2], Curry [13] and C [20].

According to the original CHR semantics of [9] propagation rules can introduce trivial infinite computations. In fact, since a propagation rule does not remove any constraint from the goal, once such a rule can fire it can fire infinitely many times. In order to avoid this problem more refined semantics have been defined [1,8] which consider the history of computation.

All these semantics, as well some other versions defined elsewhere, are not compositional w.r.t. the conjunctions of atoms in a goal. This was probably due to the fact that the presence of multiple heads complicates considerably the semantics of the language. Nevertheless, compositionality is a very desirable feature for semantics, as it permits us to manage partially defined components and it can be the basis for defining incremental and modular tools for software analysis and verification. For these reasons in [7,11] a fix-point, and-compositional semantics for CHR was defined, which allows one to retrieve the semantics of a conjunctive query from the semantics of its components. This

T. Schrijvers and T. Frühwirth (Eds.): Constraint Handling Rules, LNAI 5388, pp. 119–160, 2008.

was obtained by considering as reference semantics the "naive" one of [9] and by using semantic structures based on traces, similar to those used in the compositional models of data-flow languages [16], imperative concurrent languages [5] and concurrent constraint languages [4]. However, due to the presence of multiple heads in CHR, the traces in [7,11] were more complicated than those used for the other languages, since they contained also assumptions on the constraints which can appear in the heads of the rules.

In this paper we extend the work of [7,11] by considering as reference semantics the theoretical one ω_t, defined in [1], rather than the one introduced in [9]. As previously mentioned, the semantics of [9] admits trivial non termination which is avoided in the semantics ω_t by using a, so called, token store. This allows one to memorize the history of applied propagation rules and therefore to avoid the same rule being applied more than once to the same sequence of constraints in a derivation. The need to represent the information contained in the token store further complicates the semantic model, since when composing two traces representing two parallel processes (or, in logical terms, a conjunctions of two atoms) we must ensure that the same propagation rule is not applied twice to the same constraint. The resulting compositional semantics is therefore technically involved, even though the underlying idea is simple. The semantics defined in this paper is proven correct w.r.t. data sufficient answers, an input/ouput characterization of CHR programs.

The remaining part of this paper is organized as follows. The next section introduces some preliminaries about CHR. Section 3 contains the definition of the semantics, while Section 4 presents the compositionality and correctness results. Section 5 concludes by discussing directions for future works. The proofs of some technical lemmata are deferred to the Appendix, in order to improve the readability of the paper.

2   Preliminaries

In this section we first introduce some preliminary notions and some notations. Then we define the CHR syntax and the theoretical operational semantics ω_t. Even though we try to provide a self-contained exposition, some familiarity with constraint logic languages and first order logic would be useful (see for example [15]). CHR uses two kinds of constraints: the built-in and the CHR ones, also known as user-defined.

Built-in constraints are defined by

$$c ::= a \mid c \wedge c \mid \exists_x c$$

where a is an atomic built-in constraint[1]. These constraints are handled by an existing solver and we assume given a first order theory CT which describes their meaning. We also assume that built-in constraints contain $=$ which is described, as usual, by the Clark's Equality Theory.

A user-defined constraint is a conjunction of atomic user-defined constraints which are defined by program rules. We use c, d to denote built-in constraints, g, h, k to denote

---

[1] We could consider more generally speaking first order formulas as built-in constraints, as far as the results presented here are concerned.

CHR constraints and a, b to denote both built-in and user-defined constraints, which we will call generically constraints. The capital versions of these notations are used to denote sets and multisets of constraints, while the symbol $\uplus$ represents the multiset union and $\mathcal{U}$ is the set of user-defined constraints. We also denote by false any inconsistent constraint and by true the empty built-in constraint multiset.

We will often use "," rather than $\wedge$ to denote conjunction and we will frequently consider a conjunction of atomic constraints as a multiset (in particular this is the case when considering the syntax of CHR). The notation $\exists_{-V}\phi$, where V is a set of variables, denotes the existential closure of a formula ϕ with the exception of the variables V which remain unquantified. $Fv(\phi)$ denotes the free variables appearing in ϕ. $[n, m]$ with $n, m \in \mathbb{N}$ represents the set of all the natural numbers between n and m (n and m are included). We also denote the concatenation of sequences by $\cdot$, and the set difference operator by $\backslash$.

We can now define the CHR syntax as follows.

Definition 1 (Syntax). *[8,9] A CHR simplification rule has the form $r@H \Leftrightarrow C \mid B$, a CHR propagation rule has the form $r@H \Rightarrow C \mid B$, a CHR simpagation rule has the form $r@H_1 \backslash H_2 \Leftrightarrow C \mid B$ where r is a unique identifier of a rule, H, H_1 and H_2 are sequences of user-defined constraints with H and $(H_1 \cdot H_2)$ different from the empty sequence, C is a possibly empty multiset of built-in constraints and B is a possibly empty multiset of (built-in and user-defined) constraints. H (or $H_1 \backslash H_2$) is called head, C is called guard and B is called body of the rule.*

In the remainder of the paper, we will omit the guard when it is the true constraint.

Intuitively, a *simplification* rule rewrites a conjunction of constraints in simpler ones, while a *propagation* rule adds redundant constraints that are useful for the computation, without removing anything. A *simpagation* rule allows to remove the constraints in H_2 and not those in H_1. Hence such a rule permits to simulate both a simplification and propagation rule, depending on the fact that either H_1 or H_2 is empty, respectively. For this reason all our semantic definitions will be given by considering only simpagation rules. A *CHR program* is a finite set of CHR simplification, propagation and simpagation rules. A *CHR goal* is a multiset of both user-defined and built-in constraints. *Goals* is the set of all goals.

Example 1. The following CHR program [9] encodes the "less than or equal to" constraint:

$$
\begin{array}{lll}
rfl @ & X =< Y \Leftrightarrow X = Y \mid \text{true} & \text{reflexivity} \\
asx @ & X =< Y, Y =< X \Leftrightarrow X = Y & \text{antisymmetry} \\
trs @ & X =< Y, Y =< Z \Rightarrow X =< Z & \text{transitivity} \\
idp @ & X =< Y \backslash X =< Y \Leftrightarrow \text{true} & \text{idempotence}
\end{array}
$$

We describe now the operational semantics ω_t for CHR, introduced in [1], by using a transition system $Tx_t = (Conf_t, \longrightarrow_{\omega_t})$. Configurations in $Conf_t$ are tuples of the form $\langle G, S, c, T \rangle_n$ with the following meaning: G, the goal, is a multiset of constraints to be evaluated. The CHR constraint store S is the multiset of identified CHR constraints that can be matched with rules in the program P: An identified CHR constraint $g\#i$ is a CHR constraint g associated with some unique integer i which allows to distinguish different copies of the same constraint. We will also use the functions $chr(g\#i)=g$ and $id(g\#i)=i$, possibly extended to sets and sequences of identified CHR constraints

Table 1. The standard transition system Tx_t for CHR

Solve$_{\omega_t}$

$$\frac{CT \models c \wedge d \leftrightarrow d' \text{ and c is a built-in constraint}}{\langle \{c\} \uplus G, S, d, T \rangle_n \longrightarrow_{\omega_t} \langle G, S, d', T \rangle_n}$$

Introduce$_{\omega_t}$

$$\frac{h \text{ is a user-defined constraint}}{\langle \{h\} \uplus G, S, c, T \rangle_n \longrightarrow_{\omega_t} \langle G, \{h \# n\} \cup S, c, T \rangle_{n+1}}$$

Apply$_{\omega_t}$

$$\frac{r@H_1' \setminus H_2' \Leftrightarrow C \mid B \in P \quad CT \models c \rightarrow \exists_x((chr(H_1, H_2) = (H_1', H_2')) \wedge C)}{\langle G, \{H_1\} \cup \{H_2\} \cup S, c, T \rangle_n \longrightarrow_{\omega_t} \langle B \uplus G, \{H_1\} \cup S, (chr(H_1, H_2) = (H_1', H_2')) \wedge c, T' \rangle_n}$$

where $x = Fv(H_1', H_2')$, $r@id(H_1, H_2) \notin T$ and $T' = T \cup \{r@id(H_1, H_2)\}$

---

in the obvious way. The built-in constraint store c contains any built-in constraint that has been passed to the underlying solver. We model it in terms of conjunction. The set T is the *propagation history*, also called *token store*, and it contains tokens of the form $r@i_1, \ldots, i_l$, where r is the name of the applied rule and $i_1, \ldots, i_l$ is the sequence of identifiers associated with constraints to which the head of the rule is applied. Such a propagation history is used to prevent trivial non-termination arising from propagation rules. In fact, without tokens (as in the naive operational semantics in [9]) the repeated application of the same propagation rule to the same constraints can generate a (trivial) infinite computation. On the other hand, by using tokens one can ensure that a propagation rule is used at most once to reduce a goal, thus avoiding trivial infinite computations. Finally, the counter n represents the next free integer which can be used to number a CHR constraint.

Given a goal G, the *initial configuration* has the form $\langle G, \emptyset, \text{true}, \emptyset \rangle_1$ and consists of a goal G, an empty CHR constraint, an empty built-in constraint and an empty set of tokens. A *final configuration* has either the form $\langle G, S, \text{false}, T \rangle_n$ when it is *failed*, i.e. when it contains an inconsistent built-in constraint store, or it has the form $\langle \emptyset, S, c, T \rangle_n$ when it represents a successful computation (terminated because there are no more applicable rules).

Given a program P, the transition relation $\longrightarrow_{\omega_t} \subseteq Conf_t \times Conf_t$ is the least relation satisfying the rules in Table 1 (for the sake of simplicity, we omit indexing the relation with the name of the program). The **Solve**$_{\omega_t}$ transition allows us to update the constraint store by taking into account a built-in constraint contained in the goal. Without loss of generality we will assume that $Fv(d') \subseteq Fv(d) \cup Fv(c)$. The **Introduce**$_{\omega_t}$ transition is used to move a user-defined constraint from the goal to the CHR constraint store, where it can be handled by applying CHR rules. The **Apply**$_{\omega_t}$ transition rewrites user-defined constraints in the CHR store by using the rules of program. It assumes that all the variables appearing in a program clause are renamed with fresh ones in order to avoid variable names clashes. The **Apply**$_{\omega_t}$ transition can fire if the current store (c) is strong enough to entail the guard of the rule (C), once the parameter passing has been performed (this is expressed by the equation $chr(H_1, H_2) = (H_1', H_2')$). Note that, due to the existential quantification over the variables x appearing in H_1', H_2', in such a parameter passing the information flow is from the actual parameters (in H_1, H_2) to the formal parameters (in H_1', H_2'), that is, it is required that the constraints H_1, H_2 which have to be rewritten are an instance of the head H_1', H_2'. The transition adds the body B to the current goal, the equation $chr(H_1, H_2) = (H_1', H_2')$ to the built-in constraint store and it removes the constraints H_2. Apply$_{\omega_t}$ can fire a propagation rule (H_2 empty) if the token that it would add to T is not yet present in T.

Given a goal G, the operational semantics that we consider observes the final stores of computations, terminating with an empty goal and an empty user-defined constraint. Following the terminology of [9] we call these observables data sufficient answers.

Definition 2 (Data sufficient answers). *Let P be a program and let G be a goal. The set $\mathcal{S}A_P(G)$ of data sufficient answers for the query G in the program P is defined as follows:*

$$\mathcal{S}A_P(G) = \{\exists_{-Fv(G)}d \mid \langle G, \emptyset, \text{true}, \emptyset\rangle_1 \longrightarrow^*_{\omega_t} \langle \emptyset, \emptyset, d, T\rangle_n\}$$
$$\cup$$
$$\{\text{false} \mid \langle G, \emptyset, \text{true}, \emptyset\rangle_1 \longrightarrow^*_{\omega_t} \langle G', K, d, T\rangle_n \text{ and}$$
$$CT \models d \leftrightarrow \text{false}\}.$$

A different notion of answer [9] is obtained by considering computations terminating with a user-defined constraint which does not need to be empty:

Definition 3 (Qualified answers). *Let P be a program and let G be a goal. The set $\mathcal{Q}A_P(G)$ of qualified answers for the query G in the program P is defined as follows:*

$$\mathcal{Q}A_P(G) = \{\exists_{-Fv(G)}(chr(K) \wedge d) \mid \langle G, \emptyset, \text{true}, \emptyset\rangle_1 \longrightarrow^*_{\omega_t} \langle \emptyset, K, d, T\rangle_n \not\longmapsto_{\omega_t}\}$$
$$\cup$$
$$\{\text{false} \mid \langle G, \emptyset, \text{true}, \emptyset\rangle_1 \longrightarrow^*_{\omega_t} \langle G', K, d, T\rangle_n \text{ and}$$
$$CT \models d \leftrightarrow \text{false}\}.$$

Note that both previous notions of observables characterize an input/output behavior, since the input constraint is implicitly considered in the goal.

3   A Compositional Trace Semantics

Given a program P, we say that a semantics $\mathcal{S}_P$ is and-compositional if $\mathcal{S}_P(A, B) = \mathcal{C}(\mathcal{S}_P(A), \mathcal{S}_P(B))$ for a suitable composition operator $\mathcal{C}$ which does not depend on the program P. Due to the presence of the commit operator and of multiple heads, the semantics which associates to a CHR program P the data sufficient answers $\mathcal{S}A_P$ is not and-compositional. In fact, goals which have the same input/output behavior in terms of data sufficient answers, can behave differently when composed with other goals. While the problem with the commit (and the guard mechanism) is common to other concurrent languages, the case of multiple heads is specific of CHR, hence we illustrate this point with an example.

Consider the program P consisting of the single rule

$$r@g, h \Leftrightarrow \text{true} | c$$

where c is a built-in constraint. According to Definition 2 we have $\mathcal{S}A_P(g) = \mathcal{S}A_P(h) = \emptyset$, while $\mathcal{S}A_P(g, h) = \{\exists_{-Fv(g,h)}c\} \neq \emptyset = \mathcal{S}A_P(h, h)$. An analogous example can be made to show that the semantics $\mathcal{Q}A$ is not and-compositional.

In order to solve the problem exemplified above, following [7,11] we define our semantics in terms of sequences (or traces) of tuples, where essentially each tuple describes the input/output behaviour of a process (goal) at a time instant, that is, each tuple describes the output produced by the process under the assumption that the external environment (i.e. the other parallel processes, or conjunctive goals) provides a given input. This assumption on the input is needed both for enabling guards and for enabling the firing of a rule by providing the "missing" parts of the heads. While the first type of assumption is common to all concurrent languages which use some guard mechanism, the assumption of the heads is specific of CHR. For example, when considering the program P above, we should be able to state that the goal g produces the constraint c, provided that the external environment (i.e. a conjunctive goal) contains the user-defined constraint h. When composing (by using a suitable notion of composition) such a semantics with the one of a goal which contains h, we can verify that the "assumption" h is satisfied and therefore obtain the correct semantics for g, h. In order to model correctly the interaction of different processes we have to use sequences, analogously to what happens with other concurrent paradigms.

Our compositional model is obtained in terms of a standard fix-point construction by using a new transition system $Tx = (Conf, \longrightarrow_P)$ that introduces the assumptions mentioned above and is used to generate the sequences. Configurations in $Conf$ are triples of the form $\langle \tilde{G}, c, T \rangle_n$ where $\tilde{G}$ is a set of built-in and identified CHR constraints (the goal), c is a conjunction of built-in constraints (the store), T is a set of tokens and n is an integer greater or equal to the biggest identifier used either to number a CHR constraint in $\tilde{G}$ or a token in T. Given a program P, the transition relation $\longrightarrow_P \subseteq Conf \times Conf \times \wp(\mathcal{U})$ is the minimal relation satisfying the rules in Table 2 (where $\wp(A)$ denotes the powerset of A). Note that we modify the notion of configuration used before by merging the goal store with the CHR store, since we do not need to distinguish between them. Consequently, the **Introduce** rule is now useless and we can eliminate it. On the other hand, we need the information on the new assumptions, which is added as a label to the transitions.

We need some further notations: given a goal G, we denote by $\tilde{G}$ one of the possible identified versions of G. Moreover, assuming that G contains m CHR-constraints, we define a function $I_n^{n+m}(G)$ which identifies each CHR constraint in G by associating to it a unique integer in $[n + 1, m + n]$, according to the lexicographical order. The identifier association is applied both to the initial goal store, at the beginning of the derivation and to the body of a rule during the computational steps. If $m = 0$ we assume that $I_n^n(G) = G$.

Let us now briefly consider the rules in Table 2. **Solve'** is essentially the same rule as the one defined in Table 1, while the **Apply'** rule is modified to consider assumptions: when reducing a goal G by using a rule having head H, the set of assumptions $K = H \setminus G$ (with $H \neq K$) is used to label the transition. Note that since we apply the function I_n^{n+k} to the assumption K, each atom in K is associated with an identifier in $[n + 1, n + k]$. As before, we assume that program rules use fresh variables to avoid

Table 2. The transition system Tx for the compositional semantics

---

Solve'

$$CT \models c \wedge d \leftrightarrow d' \text{ and } c \text{ is a built-in constraint}$$
$$\overline{\langle \{c\} \uplus \tilde{G}, d, T\rangle_n \longrightarrow_P^{\emptyset} \langle \tilde{G}, d', T\rangle_n}$$

Apply'

$$\frac{r@H'_1 \setminus H'_2 \Leftrightarrow C \mid B \in P \quad CT \models c \rightarrow \exists_x((chr(\tilde{H}_1, \tilde{H}_2) = (H'_1, H'_2)) \wedge C)}{\langle \tilde{G} \cup \tilde{G}', c, T\rangle_n \longrightarrow_P^K \langle I_{n+k}^{n+k+m}(B) \cup \{\tilde{H}_1\} \cup \tilde{G}', (chr(\tilde{H}_1, \tilde{H}_2) = (H'_1, H'_2)) \wedge c, T'\rangle_{n+k+m}}$$

where $x = Fv(H'_1, H'_2)$, $G \neq \emptyset$,
k and m are the number of CHR constraints in K and in B respectively,
$\{\tilde{G}\} \cup \{I_n^{n+k}(K)\} = \{\tilde{H}_1\} \cup \{\tilde{H}_2\}$, $r@id(\tilde{H}_1, \tilde{H}_2) \notin T$ and
if $\tilde{H}_1 = \emptyset$ then $T' = T$ else $T' = T \cup \{r@id(\tilde{H}_1, \tilde{H}_2)\}$

---

variable name captures. Given a goal G with m CHR-constraints an *initial configuration* has the form $\langle I_0^m(G), \texttt{true}, \emptyset\rangle_m$, where $I_0^m(G)$ is the identified version of the goal. A *final configuration* has either the form $\langle \tilde{G}, \texttt{false}, T\rangle_n$ (if it has *failed*) or has the form $\langle \emptyset, c, T\rangle_n$ (if it is successful).

The following example shows a derivation obtained by using the new transition system.

Example 2. Given the goal $(C = 7, A =< B, C =< A, B =< C, B =< C)$ and the program of Example 1, by using the transition system of Table 2 we obtain the following derivation where the last step is not a final one

$$\langle\{C{=}7, A{=} < B\#1, C{=} < A\#2, B{=} < C\#3, B{=} < C\#4\}, \texttt{true}, \emptyset\rangle_4 \rightarrow^{\emptyset} \qquad Solve'$$
$$\langle\{A{=} < B\#1, C{=} < A\#2, B{=} < C\#3, B{=} < C\#4\}, C{=}7, \emptyset\rangle_4 \rightarrow^{\emptyset} \qquad trs@1,3$$
$$\langle\{A{=} < C\#5, A{=} < B\#1, C{=} < A\#2, B{=} < C\#3, B{=} < C\#4\}, C{=}7, \{trs@1,3\}\rangle_5 \rightarrow^{\emptyset} \quad asx@5,2$$
$$\langle\{A{=}C, A{=} < B\#1, B{=} < C\#3, B{=} < C\#4\}, C{=}7, \{trs@1,3\}\rangle_5 \rightarrow^{\emptyset} \qquad Solve'$$
$$\langle\{A{=} < B\#1, B{=} < C\#3, B{=} < C\#4\}, (A{=}C \wedge C{=}7), \{trs@1,3\}\rangle_5 \rightarrow^{\emptyset} \quad asx@1,3$$
$$\langle\{B{=}C, B{=} < C\#4\}, (A{=}C \wedge C{=}7), \{trs@1,3\}\rangle_5 \rightarrow^{\emptyset} \qquad Solve'$$
$$\langle\{B{=} < C\#4\}, (B{=}C \wedge A{=}C \wedge C{=}7), \{trs@1,3\}\rangle_5$$

The semantic domain of our compositional semantics is based on sequences which represent derivations obtained by the transition system in Table 2. More precisely, we first consider "concrete" sequences, consisting of tuples of the form

$$\langle \tilde{G}, c, T, m, I_m^{m+k}(K), \tilde{G}', d, T', m'\rangle.$$

Such a tuple represents exactly a derivation step $\langle \tilde{G}, c, T\rangle_m \longrightarrow_P^K \langle \tilde{G}', d, T'\rangle_{m'}$ where k is the number of CHR atoms in K. The sequences we are about to define are terminated by tuples of the form $\langle \tilde{G}, c, T, n, \emptyset, \tilde{G}, c, T, n\rangle$ (with either $c = \texttt{false}$ or $\tilde{G}$ is a set of identified CHR constraints), which represent a terminating step (see the precise definition below). Since a sequence represents a derivation, we also assume that if

$$\ldots \langle \tilde{G}_i, c_i, T_i, m_i, \tilde{K}_i, \tilde{G}'_i, d_i, T'_i, m'_i\rangle$$
$$\langle \tilde{G}_{i+1}, c_{i+1}, T_{i+1}, m_{i+1}, \tilde{K}_{i+1}, \tilde{G}'_{i+1}, d_{i+1}, T'_{i+1}, m'_{i+1}\rangle \ldots$$

appears in a sequence, then $\tilde{G}'_i = \tilde{G}_{i+1}$, $T'_i = T_{i+1}$ and $m'_i \leq m_{i+1}$ hold.

On the other hand, the input store c_{i+1} can be different from the output store d_i produced by previous steps. In fact, in order to obtain a compositional semantics we need to perform all the possible assumptions on the constraint c_{i+1} produced by the external environment. However, we can assume that $CT \models c_{i+1} \rightarrow d_i$ holds, i.e. the assumption made on the external environment cannot be weaker than the constraint store produced by the previous step. This reflects the monotonic nature of computations, where information can be added to the constraint store but cannot be deleted from it. Note that a sequence containing a gap between the input store (at step $i + 1$) c_{i+1} and the output store (at step i) d_i does not correspond to a real computation. In order to have a real computation in fact such a gap has to be filled by a constraint d (produced by another process) such that $d \wedge d_i$ is equivalent to c_{i+1}. This concept will be made more precise later when we will introduce the notion of connected sequence.

Finally, note that assumptions on user-defined constraints (label K) are made only for the atoms which are needed to "complete" the current goal in order to apply a clause. In other words, no assumption can be made in order to apply clauses whose heads do not share any predicate with the current goal.

Example 3. The following is the representation of the derivation of Example 2 in terms of concrete sequences:

$$\langle \{C = 7, A =< B\#1, C =< A\#2, B =< C\#3, B =< C\#4\}, \texttt{true}, \emptyset, 4, \emptyset$$
$$\{A =< B\#1, C =< A\#2, B =< C\#3, B =< C\#4\}, C = 7, \emptyset, 4\rangle$$
$$\langle \{A =< B\#1, C =< A\#2, B =< C\#3, B =< C\#4\}, C = 7, \emptyset, 4, \emptyset$$
$$\{A =< C\#5, A =< B\#1, C =< A\#2, B =< C\#3, B =< C\#4\}, C = 7, \{trs@1, 3\}, 5\rangle$$
$$\langle \{A =< C\#5, A =< B\#1, C =< A\#2, B =< C\#3, B =< C\#4\}, C = 7, \{trs@1, 3\}, 5, \emptyset$$
$$\{A = C, A =< B\#1, B =< C\#3, B =< C\#4\}, C = 7, \{trs@1, 3\}, 5\rangle$$
$$\langle \{A = C, A =< B\#1, B =< C\#3, B =< C\#4\}, C = 7, \{trs@1, 3\}, 5, \emptyset$$
$$\{A =< B\#1, B =< C\#3, B =< C\#4\}, (A = C, C = 7), \{trs@1, 3\}, 5\rangle$$
$$\langle \{A =< B\#1, B =< C\#3, B =< C\#4\}, (A = C, C = 7), \{trs@1, 3\}, 5, \emptyset$$
$$\{B = C, B =< C\#4\}, (A = C, C = 7), \{trs@1, 3\}, 5\rangle$$
$$\langle \{B = C, B =< C\#4\}, (A = C, C = 7), \{trs@1, 3\}, 5, \emptyset$$
$$\{B =< C\#4\}, (B = C, A = C, C = 7), \{trs@1, 3\}, 5\rangle$$
$$\langle \{B =< C\#4\}, (B = C, A = C, C = 7), \{trs@1, 3\}, 5, \emptyset$$
$$\{B =< C\#4\}, (B = C, A = C, C = 7), \{trs@1, 3\}, 5\rangle$$

We can then define formally the concrete sequences as follows.

Definition 4 (Concrete sequences). *The set Seq containing all the possible (concrete) sequences is defined as the set*

$$Seq = \{\langle \tilde{G}_1, c_1, T_1, m_1, \tilde{K}_1, \tilde{G}_2, d_1, T_1', m_1'\rangle\langle \tilde{G}_2, c_2, T_2, m_2, \tilde{K}_2, \tilde{G}_3, d_2, T_2', m_2'\rangle \cdots$$
$$\langle \tilde{G}_n, c_n, T_n, m_n, \emptyset, \tilde{G}_n, c_n, T_n, m_n\rangle \mid$$
$$n \geq 1, \text{ for each } j, 1 \leq j \leq n \text{ and for each } i, 1 \leq i \leq n - 1,$$
$$\tilde{G}_j \text{ are identified CHR goals, } \tilde{K}_i \text{ are sets of identified CHR constraints,}$$
$$T_j, T_j' \text{ are sets of tokens, } m_j, m_i' \text{ are natural numbers and}$$
$$c_j, d_i \text{ are built-in constraints such that}$$
$$T_i' \supseteq T_i, \ T_{i+1} \supseteq T_i', \ m_i' \geq m_i, \ m_{i+1} \geq m_i',$$
$$CT \models d_i \rightarrow c_i, \ CT \models c_{i+1} \rightarrow d_i \text{ and}$$
$$\text{either } c_n = \texttt{false} \text{ or } \tilde{G}_n \text{ is a set of identified CHR constraints}\}.$$

From these concrete sequences we extract some more abstract sequences which are the objects of our semantic domain. If $\langle \tilde{G}, c, T, m, \tilde{K}, \tilde{G}', d, T', m'\rangle$ is a tuple, different from the last one, appearing in a sequence $\delta \in \mathcal{S}eq$, we extract from it a tuple of the form $\langle c, \tilde{K}, \tilde{H}, d \rangle$ where c and d are the input and output store respectively, $\tilde{K}$ are the assumptions and $\tilde{H}$ the stable atoms (these are the identified constraints in $\tilde{G}$ that will not be used any more in δ to fire a rule, see the definition below). The output goal $\tilde{G}'$ is no longer considered. Intuitively, $\tilde{H}$ contains those atoms which are available for satisfying assumptions of other goals, when composing two different sequences (representing two derivations of different goals). If $\langle c_i, \tilde{K}_i, \tilde{H}_i, d_i \rangle \langle c_{i+1}, \tilde{K}_{i+1}, \tilde{H}_{i+1}, d_{i+1} \rangle$ is in a sequence we also assume that $\tilde{H}_i \subseteq \tilde{H}_{i+1}$ holds, since the set of those atoms which will not be rewritten in the derivation can only increase.

Moreover, if $\langle \tilde{G}, c, T, m, \emptyset, \tilde{G}, c, T, m \rangle$ is the last tuple in δ, we extract a tuple of the form $\langle c, \tilde{G}, T \rangle$, where we consider the input store c (the output store is equal), the input goal $\tilde{G}$ and the token store T. We can then define our semantic domain as follows:

Definition 5 (Sequences). *The semantic domain $\mathcal{D}$ containing all the possible sequences is defined as the set*

$$\mathcal{D} = \{ \langle c_1, \tilde{K}_1, \tilde{H}_1, d_1 \rangle \langle c_2, \tilde{K}_2, \tilde{H}_2, d_2 \rangle \dots \langle c_m, \tilde{H}_m, T \rangle \mid$$
$$m \geq 1, \text{ for each } j, \ 1 \leq j \leq m \text{ and for each } i, 1 \leq i \leq m-1,$$
$$\tilde{H}_j \text{ and } \tilde{K}_i \text{ are sets of identified CHR constraints,}$$
$$T \text{ is a set of tokens and } c_j, d_i \text{ are built-in constraints such that}$$
$$\tilde{H}_i \subseteq \tilde{H}_{i+1}, \ CT \models d_i \rightarrow c_i \text{ and } CT \models c_{i+1} \rightarrow d_i \}.$$

In order to define our semantics we need two more notions: the first one is an abstraction operator α, which extracts from the concrete sequences in $\mathcal{S}eq$ (representing exactly derivation steps) the sequences used in our semantic domain. To this aim we need the notion of stable atom.

Definition 6 (Stable atoms and Abstraction). *Let*

$$\delta = \langle \tilde{G}_1, c_1, T_1, n_1, \tilde{K}_1, \tilde{G}_2, d_1, T_2, n'_1 \rangle \dots \langle \tilde{G}_m, c_m, T_m, n_m, \emptyset, \tilde{G}_m, c_m, T_m, n_m \rangle$$
$$\in \mathcal{S}eq.$$

We say that an identified atom $g \# l$ is stable in δ if $g \# l$ appears in $\tilde{G}_j$ and the identifier l does not appear in $T_j \setminus T_1$, for each $1 \leq j \leq m$. The abstraction operator $\alpha : \mathcal{S}eq \rightarrow \mathcal{D}$ is then defined inductively as

$$\alpha(\langle \tilde{G}, c, T, n, \emptyset, \tilde{G}, c, T, n \rangle) = \langle c, \tilde{G}, T \rangle$$
$$\alpha(\langle \tilde{G}_1, c_1, T_1, n_1, \tilde{K}_1, \tilde{G}_2, d_1, T_2, n'_1 \rangle \cdot \delta') = \langle c_1, \tilde{K}_1, \tilde{H}, d_1 \rangle \cdot \alpha(\delta')$$

where $\tilde{H}$ is the set consisting of all the identified atoms which are stable in
$\langle \tilde{G}_1, c_1, T_1, n_1, \tilde{K}_1, \tilde{G}_2, d_1, T_2, n'_1 \rangle \cdot \delta'$.

The following example illustrates the use of the abstraction function α.

Example 4. The application of the function α to the (concrete) sequence in Example 3 gives the following abstract sequence:

$\langle \texttt{true}, \emptyset, \{ B =< C \# 4 \}, C = 7 \rangle \ \langle C = 7, \emptyset, \{ B =< C \# 4 \}, C = 7 \rangle \ \langle C = 7, \emptyset, \{ B =< C \# 4 \}, C = 7 \rangle$
$\langle C = 7, \emptyset, \{ B =< C \# 4 \}, (A = C \wedge C = 7) \rangle \ \langle (A = C \wedge C = 7), \emptyset, \{ B =< C \# 4 \}, (A = C \wedge C = 7) \rangle$
$\langle (A = C \wedge C = 7), \emptyset, \{ B =< C \# 4 \}, (B = C \wedge A = C \wedge C = 7) \rangle$
$\langle (B = C \wedge A = C \wedge C = 7), \{ B =< C \# 4 \}, \{ trs@1, 3 \} \rangle.$

Before defining the compositional semantics we need a further notion of compatibility. Given a sequence

$$\delta = \langle \tilde{G}_1, c_1, T_1, n_1, \tilde{K}_1, \tilde{G}_2, d_1, T_2, n'_1 \rangle \dots \langle \tilde{G}_m, c_m, T_m, n_m, \emptyset, \tilde{G}_m, c_m, T_m, n_m \rangle$$
$$\in Seq$$

and a derivation step $t = \langle \tilde{G}, c, T, n, \tilde{K}, \tilde{G}', d, T', n' \rangle$, we define

$V_{loc}(t) = Fv(G', d) \setminus Fv(G, c, K)$ (the local variables of t),

$V_{ass}(\delta) = \bigcup_{i=1}^{m-1} Fv(K_i)$ (the variables in the assumptions of δ) and

$V_{loc}(\delta) = \bigcup_{i=1}^{m-1} Fv(G_{i+1}, d_i) \setminus Fv(G_i, c_i, K_i)$ (the local variables of δ, namely the variables in the clauses used in the derivation δ).

The following example gives some instances of the previously introduced sets of variables.

Example 5. Let us consider the concrete derivation introduced in Example 2 which here we denote by γ. Then $V_{loc}([\gamma]_i) = V_{ass}(\gamma) = V_{loc}(\gamma) = \emptyset$, for $1 \le i \le 7$, where $[\gamma]_i$ represents the ith tuple of γ. Let us consider a program P composed only by the following rule

$$P = \{r@X =< Y, Y =< Z, Z =< T \Leftrightarrow X! = Y, Z! = T | X < F, F < T\}$$

where the constraint "$! =$" (*is different from*) is considered as a built-in and let us apply P to the goal $\{X =< Y, Z =< T, X! = Y, Z! = T\}$. We obtain the derivation:

$$\langle \{X =< Y\#1, Z =< T\#2, X! = Y, Z! = T\}, \text{true}, \emptyset \rangle_2 \longrightarrow^{\emptyset} \quad Solve'$$
$$\langle \{X =< Y\#1, Z =< T\#2, Z! = T\}, X! = Y, \emptyset \rangle_2 \longrightarrow^{\emptyset} \quad Solve'$$
$$\langle \{X =< Y\#1, Z =< T\#2, \}, \{X! = Y, Z! = T\}, \emptyset \rangle_2 \longrightarrow^{Y =< Z} r@1, 2, 3$$
$$\langle \{X < F\#4, F =< Z\#5, \}, \{X! = Y, Z! = T\}, \emptyset \rangle_5$$

and therefore the concrete sequence

$$\gamma' = \langle \{X =< Y\#1, Z =< T\#2, X! = Y, Z! = T\}, \text{true}, \emptyset, 2, \emptyset,$$
$$\{X =< Y\#1, Z =< T\#2, Z! = T\}, X! = Y, \emptyset, 2 \rangle$$
$$\langle \{X =< Y\#1, Z =< T\#2, Z! = T\}, X! = Y, \emptyset, 2, \emptyset,$$
$$\{X =< Y\#1, Z =< T\#2, \}, \{X! = Y, Z! = T\}, \emptyset, 2 \rangle$$
$$\langle \{X =< Y\#1, Z =< T\#2, \}, \{X! = Y, Z! = T\}, \emptyset, 2, \{Y =< Z\},$$
$$\{X < F\#4, F =< Z\#5, \}, \{X! = Y, Z! = T\}, \emptyset, 5 \rangle$$
$$\langle \{X < F\#4, F =< Z\#5, \}, \{X! = Y, Z! = T\}, \emptyset, 5, \emptyset,$$
$$\{X < F\#4, F < Z\#5, \}, \{X! = Y, Z! = T\}, \emptyset, 5 \rangle$$

Then $V_{loc}([\gamma']_i) = \emptyset$ with $i \in \{1, 2, 4\}$ while $V_{loc}([\gamma']_3) = \{F\}$. Naturally, $V_{loc}(\gamma') = \{F\}$ because it is the union of all the local variable introduced in the single tuples of γ'. $V_{ass}(\gamma') = \{Y, Z\}$ where both the variables can be seen in the third tuple.

We can now defined the compatibility as follows.

Definition 7 (Compatibility). *[7,11] Let* $t = \langle \tilde{G}_1, c_1, T_1, n_1, \tilde{K}_1, \tilde{G}_2, d_1, T_2, n'_1 \rangle$ *a tuple representing a derivation step for the goal* G_1 *and let*

$$\delta = \tilde{G}_2, c_2, T_2, n_2, \tilde{K}_2, \tilde{G}_3, d_2, T_3, n'_2 \rangle \dots \langle \tilde{G}_m, c_m, T_m, n_m, \emptyset, \tilde{G}_m, c_m, T_m, n_m \rangle$$
$$\in Seq$$

be a sequence of derivation steps for G_2. *We say that* t *is compatible with* δ *if the following holds:*

1. $V_{loc}(\delta) \cap Fv(t) = \emptyset$,
2. $V_{loc}(t) \cap V_{ass}(\delta) = \emptyset$ *and*
3. for $i \in [2, m]$, $V_{loc}(t) \cap Fv(c_i) \subseteq \bigcup_{j=1}^{i-1} Fv(d_j)$.

The three conditions of Definition 7 reflect the following facts: 1) The clauses in a derivation are separately renamed; 2) The variables in the assumptions are disjointed from the variables in the clauses used in a derivation; 3) Each of the local variables appearing in an input constraint has already appeared in an output constraint. These conditions ensure that, by using the notation of the definition above, if t is compatible with δ then $t \cdot \delta \in Seq$ is a sequence of derivation steps for G_1. Moreover, the local variables in a derivation δ and in the abstraction of δ are the same (Lemma 1). We have now all the tools for defining the compositional semantics.

Definition 8 (Compositional semantics). *Let* P *be a program and let* G *be a goal. The compositional semantics of* G *in the program* P, $\mathcal{S}_P : Goals \to \wp(\mathcal{D})$, *is defined as*

$$\mathcal{S}_P(G) = \alpha(\mathcal{S}'_P(G))$$

where α *is the pointwise extension to sets of the abstraction operator given in Definition 6 and* $\mathcal{S}'_P : Goals \to \wp(Seq)$ *is inductively defined as follows:*

$$\mathcal{S}'_P(G) = \{\langle \tilde{G}_1, c_1, T_1, n_1, \tilde{K}_1, \tilde{G}_2, d_1, T_2, n'_1 \rangle \cdot \delta \in Seq \mid$$
$$\tilde{G}_1 \text{ is an identified version of } G,$$
$$CT \not\models c_1 \leftrightarrow \texttt{false}, \langle \tilde{G}_1, c_1, T_1 \rangle_{n_1} \longrightarrow_P^{K_1} \langle \tilde{G}_2, d_1, T_2 \rangle_{n'_1}$$
$$\text{and } \delta \in \mathcal{S}'_P(G_2) \text{ for some } \delta \text{ such that}$$
$$\langle \tilde{G}_1, c_1, T_1, n_1, \tilde{K}_1, \tilde{G}_2, d_1, T_2, n'_1 \rangle \text{ is compatible with } \delta\} \cup$$
$$\{\langle \tilde{G}, c, T, n, \emptyset, \tilde{G}, c, T, n \rangle \in Seq\}.$$

It can be observed that $\mathcal{S}'_P(G)$ is also the least fix-point of the corresponding operator $\Phi \in (Goals \to \wp(Seq)) \to Goals \to \wp(Seq)$ defined by

$$\Phi(I)(G) = \{\langle \tilde{G}_1, c_1, T_1, n_1, \tilde{K}_1, \tilde{G}_2, d_1, T_2, n'_1 \rangle \cdot \delta \in Seq \mid$$
$$\tilde{G}_1 \text{ is an identified version of } G,$$
$$CT \not\models c_1 \leftrightarrow \texttt{false}, \langle \tilde{G}_1, c_1, T_1 \rangle_{n_1} \longrightarrow_P^{K_1} \langle \tilde{G}_2, d_1, T_2 \rangle_{n'_1}$$
$$\text{and } \delta \in I(G_2) \text{ for some } \delta \text{ such that}$$
$$\langle \tilde{G}_1, c_1, T_1, n_1, \tilde{K}_1, \tilde{G}_2, d_1, T_2, n'_1 \rangle \text{ is compatible with } \delta\} \cup$$
$$\{\langle \tilde{G}, c, T, n, \emptyset, \tilde{G}, c, T, n \rangle \in Seq\}.$$

where $I : Goals \to \wp(Seq)$ stands for a generic interpretation, assigning a set of sequences to a goal. The ordering of the set of interpretations $Goals \to \wp(Seq)$ is that of point-wise extended set-inclusion. It is straightforward to check that Φ is continuous on a CPO, thus, standard results ensure that the fix-point can be calculated by $\bigsqcup_{n \geq 0} \phi^n(\bot)$, where ϕ^0 is the identity map and for $n > 0$, $\phi^n = \phi \circ \phi^{n-1}$ (see for example [6]).

Before proving the compositionality of the above semantics we give an example which illustrates derivations and abstract sequences.

Example 6. The goal in Example 2 can be divided in the sub-goals $(A =< B, C =< A)$ and $(C = 7, B =< C, B =< C)$ (this division will be used in the next section to illustrate the composition of sequences). by using the program in Example 1 the goal $(A =< B, C =< A)$ has the derivation

$$\langle\{A =< B\#1, C =< A\#2\}, C = 7, \emptyset\rangle_4 \rightarrow^{\{B=<C\}} \qquad\qquad trs@1, 5$$
$$\langle\{A =< C\#6, B =< C\#5, A =< B\#1, C =< A\#2\}, C = 7, \{trs@1, 5\}\rangle_6 \rightarrow^\emptyset \; asx@6, 2$$
$$\langle\{A = C, B =< C\#5, A =< B\#1\}, C = 7, \{trs@1, 5\}\rangle_6 \rightarrow^\emptyset \qquad Solve'$$
$$\langle\{B =< C\#5, A =< B\#1\}, (A = C \wedge C = 7), \{trs@1, 5\}\rangle_6 \rightarrow^\emptyset \qquad asx@5, 1$$
$$\langle\{B = C\}, (A = C \wedge C = 7), \{trs@1, 5\}\rangle_6 \rightarrow^\emptyset \qquad\qquad Solve'$$
$$\langle\emptyset, (B = C \wedge A = C \wedge C = 7), \{trs@1, 5\}\rangle_6$$

and denoting by δ the (concrete) sequence arising from such a computation we obtain the abstract sequence $\alpha(\delta) =$

$$\langle C = 7, \{B =< C\#5\}, \emptyset, C = 7\rangle \qquad\qquad (a)$$
$$\langle C = 7, \emptyset, \emptyset, C = 7\rangle \qquad\qquad (b)$$
$$\langle C = 7, \emptyset, \emptyset, (A = C \wedge C = 7)\rangle \qquad\qquad (c)$$
$$\langle (A = C \wedge C = 7), \emptyset, \emptyset, (A = C \wedge C = 7)\rangle \qquad (d)$$
$$\langle (A = C \wedge C = 7), \emptyset, \emptyset, (B = C \wedge A = C \wedge C = 7)\rangle \; (e)$$
$$\langle (B = C \wedge A = C \wedge C = 7), \emptyset, \{trs@1, 5\}\rangle \qquad (f)$$

Moreover, we have the following derivation step for $(C = 7, B =< C, B =< C)$

$$\langle\{C = 7, B =< C\#3, B =< C\#4\}, \texttt{true}, \emptyset\rangle_4 \rightarrow^\emptyset \quad Solve'$$
$$\langle\{B =< C\#3, B =< C\#4\}, C = 7, \emptyset\rangle_4$$

and therefore we can say that

$$\gamma = \langle \; \{C = 7, B =< C\#3, B =< C\#4\}, \texttt{true}, \emptyset, 4, \emptyset, \{B =< C\#3, B =< C\#4\}, C = 7, \emptyset, 4\rangle$$
$$\langle \; \{B =< C\#3, B =< C\#4\}, (B = C \wedge A = C \wedge C = 7), \emptyset, 4, \emptyset,$$
$$\{B =< C\#3, B =< C\#4\}, (B = C \wedge A = C \wedge C = 7), \emptyset, 4\rangle$$

is a (concrete) sequence for the goal $(C = 7, B =< C, B =< C)$. Then $\alpha(\gamma)$ is the following sequence

$$\langle\texttt{true}, \emptyset, \{B =< C\#3, B =< C\#4\}, C = 7\rangle \qquad (g)$$
$$\langle (B = C \wedge A = C \wedge C = 7), \{B =< C\#3, B =< C\#4\}, \emptyset\rangle \; (h)$$

4   Compositionality and Correctness

In this section we prove that the semantics defined above is and-compositional and correct w.r.t. the observables $\mathcal{SA}_P$.

4.1   Compositionality

In order to prove the compositionality result we need to define how to compose two sets of sequences corresponding to a conjunction (i.e. parallel composition) of two goals. This is the content of Definition 12, which has the following intuitive explanation: If S_1 and S_2 are the sets we want to compose, first of all every sequence $\sigma_1 \in S_1$ is interleaved with every sequence $\sigma_2 \in S_2$. Then an η operator (defined in Definition 11) is applied to the resulting sequences in order to satisfy the assumptions by means of stable atoms (and suitable substitutions for the identifiers, see Definition 10).

In the following we will then introduce the various definitions needed to obtain the composition operator for sets of sequences. We first need some more notation. Assuming that

$$\sigma = \langle c_1, \tilde{K}_1, \tilde{H}_1, d_1\rangle\langle c_2, \tilde{K}_2, \tilde{H}_2, d_2\rangle \cdots \langle c_m, \tilde{H}_m, T\rangle \in \mathcal{D}$$

is the abstraction of a sequence for the goal G, we define the overloaded operator $id(\sigma) = id(\bigcup_{i=1}^{m-1} \tilde{K}_i) \cup id(\bigcup_{i=1}^{m} \tilde{H}_i)$ as the set of identification values of all CHR constraints in σ. We define the following operators, some of which are analogous to those already introduced for concrete sequences:

$V_{ass}(\sigma) = \bigcup_{i=1}^{m-1} Fv(K_i)$ (the variables in the assumptions of σ),
$V_{stable}(\sigma) = Fv(H_m) = \bigcup_{i=1}^{m} Fv(H_i)$ (the variables in the stable sets of σ),
$V_{constr}(\sigma) = \bigcup_{i=1}^{m-1} Fv(d_i) \setminus Fv(c_i)$ (the variables in the output constraints of σ
  which are not in the corresponding input constraints),
$V_{loc}(\sigma) = (V_{constr}(\sigma) \cup V_{stable}(\sigma)) \setminus (V_{ass}(\sigma) \cup Fv(G))$ (the local variables of a
  sequence σ, which are the local variables of the derivations δ such that $\alpha(\delta) = \sigma$
  (by using Definition 7 and by Lemma 1)).

Then we define the $\|$ operator which performs the interleaving of two sequences.

Definition 9 (Composition of sequences). *The operator* $\|: \mathcal{D} \times \mathcal{D} \to \wp(\mathcal{D})$ *is defined as follows. Let* $\sigma_1, \sigma_2 \in \mathcal{D}$ *be sequences for the goals H and G, respectively, such that* $id(\sigma_1) \cap id(\sigma_2) = \emptyset$ *and*

$$(V_{loc}(\sigma_1) \cup Fv(H)) \cap (V_{loc}(\sigma_2) \cup Fv(G)) = Fv(H) \cap Fv(G). \tag{1}$$

Then $\sigma_1 \| \sigma_2$ *is defined by cases as follows:*

i. *If both σ_1 and σ_2 have length 1 and have the same built-in store, say* $\sigma_1 = \langle c, \tilde{H}, T \rangle$ *and* $\sigma_2 = \langle c, \tilde{G}, T' \rangle$, *then*

$$\sigma_1 \| \sigma_2 = \{\langle c, \tilde{H} \cup \tilde{G}, T \cup T' \rangle \in \mathcal{D}\}.$$

ii. *If* $\sigma_2 = \langle e, \tilde{G}, T' \rangle$ *has length 1 and* $\sigma_1 = \langle c_1, \tilde{K}_1, \tilde{H}_1, d_1 \rangle \cdot \sigma_1'$ *has length* > 1 *then*

$$\sigma_1 \| \sigma_2 = \{\langle c_1, \tilde{K}_1, \tilde{H}_1 \cup \tilde{G}, d_1 \rangle \cdot \sigma \in \mathcal{D} \mid \sigma \in \sigma_1' \| \sigma_2\}.$$

iii. *If* $\sigma_1 = \langle c, \tilde{H}, T \rangle$ *has length 1 and* $\sigma_2 = \langle e_1, \tilde{J}_1, \tilde{Y}_1, f_1 \rangle \cdot \sigma_2'$ *has length* > 1 *then*

$$\sigma_1 \| \sigma_2 = \{\langle e_1, \tilde{J}_1, \tilde{H} \cup \tilde{Y}_1, f_1 \rangle \cdot \sigma \in \mathcal{D} \mid \sigma \in \sigma_1 \| \sigma_2'\}.$$

iv. *If both* $\sigma_1 = \langle c_1, \tilde{K}_1, \tilde{H}_1, d_1 \rangle \cdot \sigma_1'$ *and* $\sigma_2 = \langle e_1, \tilde{J}_1, \tilde{Y}_1, f_1 \rangle \cdot \sigma_2'$ *have length* > 1
then
$$\sigma_1 \| \sigma_2 = \{\langle c_1, \tilde{K}_1, \tilde{H}_1 \cup \tilde{Y}_1, d_1 \rangle \cdot \sigma \in \mathcal{D} \mid \sigma \in \sigma_1' \| \sigma_2\}$$
$$\cup$$
$$\{\langle e_1, \tilde{J}_1, \tilde{H}_1 \cup \tilde{Y}_1, f_1 \rangle \cdot \sigma \in \mathcal{D} \mid \sigma \in \sigma_1 \| \sigma_2'\}.$$

It is worth noting that the condition $id(\sigma_1) \cap id(\sigma_2) = \emptyset$ in the above definition avoids the capture of identifiers, while the condition (1) ensures that the two sequences σ_1 and σ_2 do not share local variables names, thus avoiding variable capture in the composition of the two sequences. Note also that the condition **i** requires that both the two sequences have the same built-in constraint store in the last tuples (otherwise the sequences could not be the in interleaved components of the same unique derivation, as the last tuple is different from the others).

Next we define the η operator which allows to "satisfy" (i.e. eliminate from sequences) assumptions by using stable atoms. In general one can satisfy the assumption $g\#j$ by using the stable atom $h\#i$, provided that the identifier j is replaced everywhere in the sequence by the identifier i and provided that the token set cardinality does not decrease. This is made precise by the following two definitions, where the first one defines this substitution operation on identifiers.

Definition 10 (Substitution operators). *Let T be a token set, S be a set of identified atoms, $id_1, \ldots, id_o, id'_1, \ldots, id'_o$ be identification values and let $g_1\#id_1, \ldots, g_o\#id_o, h_1\#id'_1, \ldots, h_o\#id'_o$ be identified atoms.*
Moreover, let $\sigma = \langle c_1, \tilde{K}_1, \tilde{H}_1, d_1 \rangle \langle c_2, \tilde{K}_2, \tilde{H}_2, d_2 \rangle \cdots \langle c_m, \tilde{H}_m, T \rangle \in \mathcal{D}$.

- $T' = T[id_1/id'_1, \ldots, id_o/id'_o]$ *is the token set obtained from T, by substituting each occurrence of the identifier id_l with id'_l, for $1 \leq l \leq o$. The operation is defined if T and T' have the same cardinality (namely, there are no elements in T, which collapse when we apply the substitution).*
- $S[g_1\#id_1/h_1\#id'_1, \ldots, g_o\#id_o/h_o\#id'_o]$ *is the set of identified atoms obtained from S by substituting each occurrence of the identified atom $g_l\#id_l$ with $h_l\#id'_l$, for $1 \leq l \leq o$.*
- $\sigma' = \sigma[g_1\#id_1/h_1\#id'_1, \ldots, g_o\#id_o/h_o\#id'_o]$ *is defined only if $T' = T[id_1/id'_1, \ldots, id_o/id'_o]$ is defined and in this case*

$$\sigma' = \langle c_1, \tilde{K}'_1, \tilde{H}'_1, d_1 \rangle \langle c_2, \tilde{K}'_2, \tilde{H}'_2, d_2 \rangle \cdots \langle c_m, \tilde{H}'_m, T' \rangle \in \mathcal{D},$$

with $1 \leq l \leq m-1$, $1 \leq p \leq m$, $\tilde{K}'_l = \tilde{K}_l[g_1\#id_1/h_1\#id'_1, \ldots, g_o\#id_o/h_o\#id'_o]$ and $\tilde{H}'_p = \tilde{H}_p[g_1\#id_1/h_1\#id'_1, \ldots, g_o\#id_o/h_o\#id'_o]$.

Definition 11 (η operator). *Let $\tilde{W}$ be a set of identified CHR atoms, let σ be a sequence in $\mathcal{D}$ of the form*

$$\langle c_1, \tilde{K}_1, \tilde{H}_1, d_1 \rangle \langle c_2, \tilde{K}_2, \tilde{H}_2, d_2 \rangle \ldots \langle c_m, \tilde{H}_m, T \rangle.$$

We denote the sequence

$$\langle c_1, \tilde{K}_1, \tilde{H}_1 \setminus \tilde{W}, d_1 \rangle \langle c_2, \tilde{K}_2, \tilde{H}_2 \setminus \tilde{W}, d_2 \rangle \ldots \langle c_m, \tilde{H}_m \setminus \tilde{W}, T \rangle,$$

by $\sigma \setminus \tilde{W} \in \mathcal{D}$ (where the sets' difference $\tilde{H}_j \setminus \tilde{W}$ considers identifications, with $1 \leq j \leq m$).
The operator $\eta : \wp(\mathcal{D}) \to \wp(\mathcal{D})$ is defined as follows. Given $S \in \wp(\mathcal{D})$, $\eta(S)$ is the minimal set satisfying the following conditions:

- $S \subseteq \eta(S)$;
- *if $\sigma' \cdot \langle c, \tilde{K}, \tilde{H}, d \rangle \cdot \sigma'' \in \eta(S)$ and there exist two sets of identified atoms $\tilde{K}' = \{g_1\#id_1, \ldots, g_o\#id_o\} \subseteq \tilde{K}$ and $\tilde{W} = \{h_1\#id'_1, \ldots, h_o\#id'_o\} \subseteq \tilde{H}$ such that*
  1. *for $1 \leq l \leq o$, $CT \models (c \wedge g_l) \leftrightarrow (c \wedge h_l)$ and*
  2. $\bar{\sigma} = ((\sigma' \cdot \langle c, \tilde{K} \setminus \tilde{K}', \tilde{H}, d \rangle \cdot \sigma'') \setminus \tilde{W})[g_1\#id_1/h_1\#id'_1, \ldots, g_o\#id_o/h_o\#id'_o]$
     is defined,
  then $\bar{\sigma} \in \eta(S)$.

Note that previous definition introduces an upper closure operator[2] which saturates a set of sequences S by adding new sequences where redundant assumptions can be removed. In fact, according to previous definition, an assumption $g\#i$ in $\tilde{K}$ can be removed if $h\#j$ appears as a stable atom in $\tilde{H}$ and the built-in store c implies that g is equivalent to h. This has the intuitive explanations that stable atoms are, by definition, those atoms which will never be "consumed" in the sequence, hence it is safe to assume that they are used to fulfil an assumption (on some atoms appearing in a head). Once a stable atom is consumed for satisfying an assumption it is removed from (the sets of stable atoms of) all the tuples appearing in the sequence, to avoid multiple uses of the same atom.

We can now define the composition operator $\|$ for sets of sequences. To simplify the notation we denote by $\|$ both the operator acting on sequences and the one acting on sets of sequences.

Definition 12 (Composition of sets of sequences). *The composition of sets of sequences is the partial fucntion* $\|: \wp(\mathcal{D}) \times \wp(\mathcal{D}) \to \wp(\mathcal{D})$ *defined by:*

$$S_1 \| S_2 = \{\sigma \in \mathcal{D} \mid \text{there exist } \sigma_1 \in S_1 \text{ and } \sigma_2 \in S_2 \text{ such that}$$
$$\sigma = \langle c_1, \tilde{K}_1, \tilde{H}_1, d_1\rangle \cdots \langle c_m, \tilde{H}_m, T\rangle \in \eta(\sigma_1 \| \sigma_2),$$
$$(V_{loc}(\sigma_1) \cup V_{loc}(\sigma_2)) \cap V_{ass}(\sigma) = \emptyset \text{ and for } i \in [1, m]$$
$$(V_{loc}(\sigma_1) \cup V_{loc}(\sigma_2)) \cap Fv(c_i) \subseteq \bigcup_{j=1}^{i-1} Fv(d_j)\}.$$

The first condition on variables ensures that local variables of σ, that are the ones used in the derivation of which σ is an abstraction, are different from the ones used by assumptions of σ. The second condition ensures that σ is the abstraction of a derivation that satisfies condition 3 of Definition 7. The next example illustrate Definition 12.

Example 7. We consider the two abstract sequences of Example 6 and show that their composition produces the sequence in Example 4. First of all, by using the interleaving (see Definition 9) we can compose the abstract sequences $\alpha(\delta)$ and $\alpha(\gamma)$ to obtain (among others) the sequence

$$
\begin{array}{ll}
\langle \text{true}, \emptyset, \{B =< C\#3, B =< C\#4\}, C = 7\rangle & g(a) \\
\langle C = 7, \{B =< C\#5\}, \{B =< C\#3, B =< C\#4\}, C = 7\rangle & a(h) \\
\langle C = 7, \emptyset, \{B =< C\#3, B =< C\#4\}, C = 7\rangle & b(h) \\
\langle C = 7, \emptyset, \{B =< C\#3, B =< C\#4\}, (A = C, C = 7)\rangle & c(h) \\
\langle (A = C, C = 7), \emptyset, \{B =< C\#3, B =< C\#4\}, (A = C, C = 7)\rangle & d(h) \\
\langle (A = C, C = 7), \emptyset, \{B =< C\#3, B =< C\#4\}, (B = C, A = C, C = 7)\rangle & e(h) \\
\langle (B = C, A = C, C = 7), \{B =< C\#3, B =< C\#4\}, \{trs@1, 5\}\rangle & f \text{ and } h
\end{array}
$$

where $g(a)$ means that the tuple g and the stable atoms of tuple (a) are used (analogously for the other steps). Then the application of Definition 11 produces the sequence

$$
\begin{array}{ll}
\langle \text{true}, \emptyset, \{\cancel{B =< C\#3}, B =< C\#4\}, C = 7\rangle & g(a) \\
\langle C = 7, \{\cancel{B =< C\#5}\}, \{\cancel{B =< C\#3}, B =< C\#4\}, C = 7\rangle & a(h) \\
\langle C = 7, \emptyset, \{\cancel{B =< C\#3}, B =< C\#4\}, C = 7\rangle & b(h) \\
\langle C = 7, \emptyset, \{\cancel{B =< C\#3}, B =< C\#4\}, (A = C, C = 7)\rangle & c(h) \\
\langle (A = C, C = 7), \emptyset, \{\cancel{B =< C\#3}, B =< C\#4\}, (A = C, C = 7)\rangle & d(h) \\
\langle (A = C, C = 7), \emptyset, \{\cancel{B =< C\#3}, B =< C\#4\}, (B = C, A = C, C = 7)\rangle & e(h) \\
\langle (B = C, A = C, C = 7), \{\cancel{B =< C\#3}, B =< C\#4\}, \{trs@1, 5 \to 3\}\rangle & f \text{ and } h
\end{array}
$$

---

[2] $S \subseteq \eta(S)$ holds by definition, and it is easy to see that $\eta(\eta(S)) = \eta(S)$ holds and that $S \subseteq S'$ implies $\eta(S) \subseteq \eta(S')$.

where some assumptions are removed since they are satisfied by some stable atoms (this is represented by crossing both constraints). Note that identifier #5 is substitued by #3 (by using Definition 10) when satisfying the assumption $B =< C\#5$.

Using this notion of composition we can show that the semantics S_P is compositional. Before proving the main result we need some technical lemmas whose proofs are deferred to the Appendix.

The following Lemma states that abstraction operator α on sequences (see Definition 6) does not affect the variables in the assumptions and the local variables of the sequence.

Lemma 1. *Let G be a goal, $\delta \in S'_P(G)$ and let $\sigma = \alpha(\delta)$. Then $V_r(\delta) = V_r(\sigma)$ holds, where $r \in \{ ass, loc \}$.*

Since identifiers are used only to distinguish two different occurrences of the same atom we can freely rename them. We recall that a renaming is a substitution of the form $[j_1/i_1, \ldots, j_o/i_o]$, where $j_1, \ldots, j_o$ are distinct identification values and $i_1, \ldots, i_o$ is a permutation of $j_1, \ldots, j_o$. We will use ρ, $\rho', \ldots$ to denote renamings. The following definition introduces some specific notation for renamings of indexes.

Definition 13. *Let $\sigma \in \mathcal{D}$ and let $\rho = [j_1/i_1, \ldots, j_o/i_o]$ be a renaming. $\sigma\rho$ is defined as the sequence obtained from σ by substituting each occurrence of the identification value j_l with the corresponding i_l, for $l \in [1, o]$. Moreover, given $\sigma, \sigma_1, \sigma_2 \in \mathcal{D}$ and $S_1, S_2 \in \wp(\mathcal{D})$, we define:*

- *$\sigma_1 \simeq \sigma_2$ if there exists a renaming ρ such that $\sigma_1 = \sigma_2\rho$.*
- *$S_1 \ll S_2$ if for each $\sigma_1 \in S_1$ there exists $\sigma_2 \in S_2$ such that $\sigma_1 \simeq \sigma_2$.*
- *$S_1 \simeq S_2$ if $S_1 \ll S_2$ and $S_2 \ll S_1$.*

From the definition of renaming follows also immediately that if there exists a renaming $\rho = [i_1/j_1, \ldots i_o/j_o]$ such that $\sigma_1 = \sigma_2\rho$ then there also exists a renaming $\rho^{-1} = [j_1/i_1, \ldots j_o/i_o]$ such that $\sigma_1\rho^{-1} = \sigma_2$.

The next lemma states that once a concrete sequence for the goal (H, G) has been fixed, there exist two concrete sequences for the two goals H and G whose abstraction can be composed to obtain a sequence that is equal to the abstraction of the fixed sequence.

Lemma 2. *Let P be a program, H and G be two goals and assume that $\delta \in S'_P(H, G)$. There then exist $\delta_1 \in S'_P(H)$ and $\delta_2 \in S'_P(G)$, and $\sigma \in \eta(\alpha(\delta_1) \| \alpha(\delta_2))$ such that, for $i = 1, 2$, $V_{loc}(\delta_i) \subseteq V_{loc}(\delta)$ and $\sigma \simeq \alpha(\delta)$.*

Under some more assumptions a vice versa of the previous lemma is obtained by the following:

Lemma 3. *Let P be a program, let H and G be two goals and assume that $\delta_1 \in S'_P(H)$ and $\delta_2 \in S'_P(G)$ are two sequences such that the following holds:*

1. *$\alpha(\delta_1) \| \alpha(\delta_2)$ is defined,*
2. *$\sigma = \langle c_1, \tilde{K}_1, \tilde{W}_1, d_1 \rangle \cdots \langle c_m, \tilde{W}_m, T_m \rangle \in \eta(\alpha(\delta_1) \| \alpha(\delta_2))$,*

3. $(V_{loc}(\alpha(\delta_1)) \cup V_{loc}(\alpha(\delta_2))) \cap V_{ass}(\sigma) = \emptyset$,
4. *for* $i \in [1, m]$, $(V_{loc}(\alpha(\delta_1)) \cup V_{loc}(\alpha(\delta_2))) \cap Fv(c_i) \subseteq \bigcup_{j=1}^{i-1} Fv(d_j)$.

There then exists $\delta \in S'_P(H, G)$ *such that* $\alpha(\delta) \simeq \sigma$.

We can eventually prove the main result of this section which states the compositionality of the semantics.

Theorem 1 (Compositionality). *Let* P *be a program and let* H *and* G *be two goals. Then*

$$S_P(H, G) \simeq S_P(H) \parallel S_P(G).$$

Proof. We prove the two inclusions separately.

$(S_P(H, G) \ll S_P(H) \parallel S_P(G))$. Let $\sigma \in S_P(H, G)$. By definition of S_P, there exists $\delta \in S'_P(H, G)$ such that $\sigma = \alpha(\delta)$. According to Lemma 2 there exist $\delta_1 \in S'_P(H)$ and $\delta_2 \in S'_P(G)$ such that for $i = 1, 2$, $V_{loc}(\delta_i) \subseteq V_{loc}(\delta)$, $\sigma' \in \eta(\alpha(\delta_1) \parallel \alpha(\delta_2))$ and $\sigma' \simeq \sigma$. Let

$$\delta = \langle (\tilde{H}, \tilde{G}), c_1, T_1, n_1, \tilde{K}_1, \tilde{B}_2, d_1, T_2, n'_1 \rangle \cdots$$
$$\cdots \langle \tilde{B}_m, c_m, T_m, n_m, \emptyset, \tilde{B}_m, c_m, T_m, n_m \rangle$$

and let $\sigma' = \langle c_1, \tilde{K}_1, \tilde{W}_1, d_1 \rangle \cdots \langle c_m, \tilde{W}_m, T_m \rangle$. First note that if $\sigma \simeq \sigma'$ then $V_{ass}(\sigma) = V_{ass}(\sigma')$ holds. Hence, since $\sigma \simeq \sigma'$ holds, in order to prove the thesis we have only to show that

$$(V_{loc}(\alpha(\delta_1)) \cup V_{loc}(\alpha(\delta_2))) \cap V_{ass}(\sigma) = \emptyset \text{ and}$$
$$\text{for } i \in [1, m], (V_{loc}(\alpha(\delta_1)) \cup V_{loc}(\alpha(\delta_2))) \cap Fv(c_i) \subseteq \bigcup_{j=1}^{i-1} Fv(d_j),$$

the two conditions which are missing and thus fail to satisfy all the ones of Definition 12. Firstly, observe that according to Lemma 1 and by hypothesis, we can conclude respectively that

$$V_{ass}(\sigma) = V_{ass}(\delta) \text{ and for } i \in \{1, 2\}, V_{loc}(\alpha(\delta_i)) = V_{loc}(\delta_i) \subseteq V_{loc}(\delta). \quad (2)$$

Then according to the previous results and the properties of the derivations (point 2 of Definition 7 (Compatibility))

$$(V_{loc}(\alpha(\delta_1)) \cup V_{loc}(\alpha(\delta_2))) \cap V_{ass}(\sigma) \subseteq V_{loc}(\delta) \cap V_{ass}(\delta) = \emptyset.$$

Furthermore, by hypothesis and point 3 of Definition 7 (Compatibility), for $i \in [1, m]$,

$$(V_{loc}(\alpha(\delta_1)) \cup V_{loc}(\alpha(\delta_2))) \cap Fv(c_i) \subseteq V_{loc}(\delta) \cap Fv(c_i) \subseteq \bigcup_{j=1}^{i-1} Fv(d_j)$$

holds and this completes the proof of the first inclusion.

$(S_P(H) \parallel S_P(G) \ll S_P(H, G))$. Let $\sigma \in S_P(H) \parallel S_P(G)$. According to definition of S_P and of $\parallel$ there exist $\delta_1 \in S'_P(H)$ and $\delta_2 \in S'_P(G)$, such that $\sigma_1 = \alpha(\delta_1)$, $\sigma_2 = \alpha(\delta_2)$, $\sigma_1 \parallel \sigma_2$ is defined, $\sigma = \langle c_1, \tilde{K}_1, \tilde{H}_1, d_1 \rangle \cdots \langle c_m, \tilde{H}_m, T_m \rangle \in \eta(\sigma_1 \parallel \sigma_2)$, $(V_{loc}(\sigma_1) \cup V_{loc}(\sigma_2)) \cap V_{ass}(\sigma) = \emptyset$ and for $i \in [1, m]$, $(V_{loc}(\sigma_1) \cup V_{loc}(\sigma_2)) \cap Fv(c_i) \subseteq \bigcup_{j=1}^{i-1} Fv(d_j)$. The proof is then straightforward by using Lemma 3. $\square$

4.2   Correctness

In order to show the correctness of the semantics $\mathcal{S}_P$ w.r.t. the (input/output) observables $\mathcal{S}A_P$ we first introduce a different characterization of $\mathcal{S}A_P$, obtained by using the new transition system defined in Table 2.

Definition 14. *Let P be a program and let G be a goal and let $\longrightarrow_P$ be (the minimal relation), defined by the rules in Table 2. We define*

$$\mathcal{S}A'_P(G) = \{\exists_{-Fv(G)}c \mid \langle \tilde{G}, \texttt{true}, \emptyset \rangle_{n_1} \longrightarrow_P^{\emptyset} \cdots \longrightarrow_P^{\emptyset} \langle \emptyset, c, T_m \rangle_{n_m}\}$$
$$\cup$$
$$\{\texttt{false} \mid \langle \tilde{G}, \texttt{true}, \emptyset \rangle_{n_1} \longrightarrow_P^{\emptyset} \cdots \longrightarrow_P^{\emptyset} \langle \tilde{G}', c, T \rangle_{n_m} \text{ and }$$
$$CT \models c \leftrightarrow \texttt{false}\}.$$

The correspondence of $\mathcal{S}A'$ with the original notion $\mathcal{S}A$ is stated by the following proposition, whose proof is immediate.

Proposition 1. *Let P be a program and let G be a goal. Then*

$$\mathcal{S}A_P(G) = \mathcal{S}A'_P(G).$$

Then to prove the correctness of the compositional semantics w.r.t. $\mathcal{S}A_P$ it is sufficient to show that the observables $\mathcal{S}A'_P$ can be obtained from $\mathcal{S}_P$. To this aim we have first to identify those sequences in $\mathcal{S}_P$ which correspond to real computations. These are those sequences, called connected, which do not perform assumptions neither on CHR constraints nor on built-in constraints: The first condition means that the second component of tuples of the sequence of our compositional semantics ($\langle c, \tilde{K}, \tilde{H}, d \rangle$) must be empty, while the second one means that the assumed constraint at step i must be equal to the produced constraint of steps $i - 1$. The following is the precise definition.

Definition 15 (Connected sequences). *Let*

$$\sigma = \langle c_1, \tilde{K}_1, \tilde{H}_1, d_1 \rangle \langle c_2, \tilde{K}_2, \tilde{H}_2, d_2 \rangle \ldots \langle c_m, \tilde{H}_m, T_m \rangle \in \mathcal{D}.$$

We say that σ is connected if for each j, $1 \leq j \leq m - 1$, $\tilde{K}_j = \emptyset$ and $d_j = c_{j+1}$.

The proof of the next result derives from the definition of connected sequence and an easy inductive argument. If $\sigma = \langle c_1, \tilde{K}_1, \tilde{H}_1, d_1 \rangle \ldots \langle c_m, \tilde{H}_m, T_m \rangle$ is a sequence, we denote by $instore(\sigma)$ and $store(\sigma)$ the built-in constraint c_1 and c_m respectively and by $lastg(\sigma)$ the goal $\tilde{H}_m$.

Proposition 2. *Let P be a program and let G be a goal. Then*

$$\mathcal{S}A'_P(G) = \{\exists_{-Fv(G)}c \mid \text{ there exists } \sigma \in \mathcal{S}_P(G) \text{ such that } instore(\sigma) = \emptyset,$$
$$\sigma \text{ is connected}, lastg(\sigma) = \emptyset \text{ and } c = store(\sigma)\}$$
$$\cup$$
$$\{\texttt{false} \mid \text{ there exists } \sigma \in \mathcal{S}_P(G) \text{ such that } instore(\sigma) = \emptyset,$$
$$\sigma \text{ is connected and } CT \models store(\sigma) \leftrightarrow \texttt{false}\}.$$

The following corollary follows immediately from previous two propositions.

Corollary 1 (Correctness). *Let P be a program and let G be a goal. Then*

$$\mathcal{SA}_P(G) = \{\exists_{-Fv(G)}c \mid \text{ there exists } \sigma \in \mathcal{S}_P(G) \text{ such that } instore(\sigma) = \emptyset,$$
$$\sigma \text{ is connected, } lastg(\sigma) = \emptyset \text{ and } c = store(\sigma)\}$$
$$\cup$$
$$\{\texttt{false} \mid \text{ there exists } \sigma \in \mathcal{S}_P(G) \text{ such that } instore(\sigma) = \emptyset,$$
$$\sigma \text{ is connected and } CT \models store(\sigma) \leftrightarrow \texttt{false}\}.$$

5   Conclusions

In this paper we have defined a semantics for CHR which is compositional w.r.t. the conjunction of goals, which is correct w.r.t data sufficient answers and which takes into account the token store used in the theoretical operational semantics ω_t [1]. in order to avoid trivial non-termination due to propagation rules.

This paper can be seen as a completion of [7,11], where the approach we follow here was first defined. These papers however did not treat in a satisfactory way the propagation rules, since they considered the original "naive" operational semantics of CHR, thus allowing trivial non-termination. The need to model the token store is then the main technical difference of this work with [7,11]. This need, together with the presence of multiple heads, leads to a semantic model which is rather involved, even though the basic idea is simple. However, it is difficult to avoid this complication if one wants to model precisely and in a compositional way the observables we are interested in. In fact, any compositional semantics for modeling the I/O behaviour of CHR programs has to use semantic structures essentially as complicated as the present ones, since in any case one needs traces (as in the case of any other concurrent asynchronous language) and assumptions (which can be expressed in many different ways). Of course, it would be desirable to introduce in the semantics the minimum amount of information needed to obtain compositionality, while preserving correctness. In other words, it would be desirable to obtain a fully abstract semantics for data sufficient answers. A similar full abstraction result is left for future work and appears to be not easy (again, mainly due to the presence of multiple heads). However it is worth noting that obtaining a fully abstract model does not mean to obtain a substantially simpler model: in fact, full abstraction results are typically obtained by introducing suitable abstraction (or saturation) operators on a compositional model. A simpler (compositional) model could be obtained by considering a more abstract, imprecise, semantics which characterizes a superset of observables. Such an abstract semantics could perhaps be useful for program analysis, along the lines of the abstract interpretation theory.

Another issue which is left for future work is the compositional characterization of qualified answers, as formalized in Definition 3. The compositional semantics, as presented in this paper, is not refined enough to model these answers for the following reason. The acceptance of a non-empty final store in the concrete semantics means that a non-empty stable atom set remains in the abstract semantics. This can permit the interleaving with other abstract sequences which possibly present assumptions which can be satisfied by such a stable atom set, thus introducing a clear difficulty in the determination of when an abstract sequence is terminated. An example could clarify this point. Let $P = \{r@p, q \Leftrightarrow m\}$ be a CHR program. The two sequences of one element $\langle \emptyset, p, \emptyset \rangle$ and $\langle \emptyset, p, \emptyset \rangle$ would be in the semantics modeling the qualified answers of p and of q, respectively (because $p \in \mathcal{QA}_P(p)$ and $q \in \mathcal{QA}_P(q)$). However $\langle \emptyset, (p, q), \emptyset \rangle$, obtained by composing the two one element sequences, should not be in the semantics of p, q, since p, q is not a qualified answer for the goal p, q (that is, $(p, q) \notin \mathcal{QA}_P(p, q)$). This problem could probably be solved by introducing a set which contains the names of rules that can not be applied from a certain point onwards, however this would further complicate the semantics.

Acknowledgments. We thank Michael Maher for having initially suggested the problem of compositionality for CHR semantics. We also thank the anonymous reviewers for their many precise and useful comments.

References

1. Abdennadher, S.: Operational semantics and confluence of constraint propagation rules. In: Smolka, G. (ed.) CP 1997. LNCS, vol. 1330, pp. 252–266. Springer, Heidelberg (1997)
2. Abdennadher, S., Krämer, E., Saft, M., Schmauss, M.: JACK: a Java constraint kit. Electronic Notes in Theoretical Computer Science, vol. 64. Elsevier, Amsterdam (2000)
3. de Boer, F.S., Gabbrielli, M., Meo, M.C.: Semantics and expressive power of a timed concurrent constraint language. In: Smolka, G. (ed.) CP 1997. LNCS, vol. 1330, pp. 47–61. Springer, Heidelberg (1997)
4. de Boer, F.S., Palamidessi, C.: A Fully Abstract Model for Concurrent Constraint Programming. In: Abramsky, S. (ed.) CAAP 1991 and TAPSOFT 1991. LNCS, vol. 493, pp. 296–319. Springer, Heidelberg (1991)
5. Brookes, S.: A fully abstract semantics of a shared variable parallel language. In: Proc. of the Eighth IEEE Symposium on Logic In Computer Science, pp. 98–109. IEEE Computer Society Press, Los Alamitos (1993)
6. Davey, B.A., Priestley, H.A.: Introduction to Lattices and Order. Cambridge University Press, Cambridge (1990)
7. Delzanno, G., Gabbrielli, M., Meo, M.C.: A Compositional Semantics for CHR. In: PPDP 2005: Proc. of the 7th International ACM SIGPLAN Conference on Principles and Practice of Declarative Programming, pp. 209–217. ACM, New York (2005)
8. Duck, G.J., Stuckey, P.J., de la Banda, M.G., Holzbaur, C.: The Refined Operational Semantics of Constraint Handling Rules. In: Demoen, B., Lifschitz, V. (eds.) ICLP 2004. LNCS, vol. 3132, pp. 90–104. Springer, Heidelberg (2004)
9. Frühwirth, T.: Theory and practice of Constraint Handling Rules. Journal of Logic Programming 37(1-3), 95–138 (1998)
10. Frühwirth, T.: Constraint Handling Rules: The Story So Far. In: PPDP 2006: Proc. of the 8th ACM SIGPLAN symposium on Principles and practice of declarative programming, pp. 13–14. ACM, New York (2006)
11. Gabbrielli, M., Meo, M.C.: A Compositional Semantics for CHR. In: ACM Transactions on Computational Logic (to appear, 2008)
12. Garcia de la Banda, M., Demoen, B., Mariott, K., Stuckey, P.J.: To the gates of HAL: a HAL tutorial. In: Hu, Z., Rodríguez-Artalejo, M. (eds.) FLOPS 2002. LNCS, vol. 2441, pp. 47–66. Springer, Heidelberg (2002)

13. Hanus, M.: Adding Constraint Handling Rules to Curry. In: Proc. of the 20th Workshop on Logic Programming (WLP 2006), pp. 81–90. INFSYS Research Report 1843-06-02, TU Wien (2006)
14. Holzbaur, C., Frühwirth, T.: A Prolog constraint handling rules compiler and runtime system. Journal of Applied Artificial Intelligence 14(4) (2000)
15. Jaffar, J., Maher, M.: Constraint logic programming: a survey. Journal of Logic Programming 19/20, 503–582 (1994)
16. Jonsson, B.: A model and a proof system for asynchronous processes. In: Proc. of the 4th ACM Symp. on Principles of Distributed Computing, pp. 49–58. ACM Press, New York (1985)
17. Schrijvers, T.: Analyses, Optimizations and Extensions of Constraint Handling Rules. Ph.D thesis, Katholieke Universiteit Leuven (June 2005)
18. Sulzmann, M., Lam, E.S.L.: Compiling Constraint Handling Rules with Lazy and Concurrent Search Techniques. In: Proc. of Fourth Workshop on Constraint Handling Rules, pp. 139–149 (2007)
19. Sneyers, J., Schrijvers, T., Demoen, B.: The Computational Power and Complexity of Constraint Handling Rules. ACM Transactions on Programming Languages and Systems (to appear, 2008)
20. Wuille, P., Schrijvers, T., Demoen, B.: CCHR: the fastest CHR Implementation, in C. In: Proc. of Fourth Workshop on Constraint Handling Rules, pp. 123–137 (2007)

Appendix

In this appendix we provide the proofs of Lemmata 1, 2 and 3 that are used in the proof of Theorem 1. These proofs use some auxiliary lemmata that are introduced below. We also need some more notation.

In the following, given a sequence γ, where $\gamma \in \mathcal{S}eq \cup \mathcal{D}$, we will denote by $lenght(\gamma)$, $instore(\gamma)$, $Ass(\gamma)$ and $Stable(\gamma)$ the length of sequence γ, the first input built-in constraint of γ, the set of non-identified assumptions of γ and the set of non-identified atoms in the last goal of γ respectively. Moreover, let δ be a sequence of derivation steps

$$\delta = \langle \tilde{B}_1, c_1, T_1, n_1, K_1, \tilde{B}_2, d_1, T_2, n_1' \rangle \ldots \langle \tilde{B}_m, c_m, T_m, n_m, \emptyset, \tilde{B}_m, c_m, T_m, n_m \rangle.$$

We denote by $InG(\delta)$, $Intok(\delta)$ and $Inid(\delta)$ the identified goal $\tilde{B}_1$, the token set T_1 and the counter n_1, respectively. Moreover $Inc(\delta)$ denotes the set of all the input built-in constraints $\{c_1, \ldots, c_n\}$ of δ.

Finally, we denote by $Aloc(\delta)$ the set of the CHR-atoms in the (renamed) clauses used in the derivation represented by δ.

Now, let $\tilde{W}$ and $\tilde{B}_1$ be sets of identified CHR-constraints and let n_1 be an integer, such that for each $i \in id(\tilde{W})$ and $j \in id(\tilde{B}_1)$, we have that $i < n_1$ and $i \neq j$. We denote by $\delta \oplus \tilde{W}$ the sequence

$$\langle (\tilde{B}_1, \tilde{W}), c_1, T_1, n_1, \tilde{K}_1, (\tilde{B}_2, \tilde{W}), d_1, T_2, n_1' \rangle \cdots$$
$$\langle (\tilde{B}_m, \tilde{W}), c_m, T_m, n_m, \emptyset, (\tilde{B}_m, \tilde{W}), c_m, T_m, n_m \rangle.$$

The following Lemma states that, when considering a sequence δ in the concrete semantics, the variables in the assumptions and the local variables in δ are the same as those in the abstraction of δ.

Lemma 1. *Let G be a goal, $\delta \in S'_P(G)$ and let $\sigma = \alpha(\delta)$. Then $V_r(\delta) = V_r(\sigma)$ holds, where $r \in \{ ass, loc \}$.*

Proof. Let us consider the following two sequences (where $\tilde{G}_1$ is an identified version of G):

$$\delta = \langle \tilde{G}_1, c_1, T_1, n_1, \tilde{K}_1, \tilde{G}_2, d_1, T_2, n'_1 \rangle \ldots \langle \tilde{G}_m, c_m, T_m, n_m, \emptyset, \tilde{G}_m, c_m, T_m, n_m \rangle$$

and

$$\sigma = \langle c_1, \tilde{K}_1, \tilde{H}_1, d_1 \rangle \ldots \langle c_m, \tilde{H}_m, T_m \rangle,$$

where $\tilde{H}_m = \tilde{G}_m$. Moreover, let $t = \langle \tilde{G}_1, c_1, T_1, n_1, \tilde{K}_1, \tilde{G}_2, d_1, T_2, n'_1 \rangle$.

By definition we have $V_{ass}(\delta) = \bigcup_{i=1}^{m-1} Fv(K_i) = V_{ass}(\sigma)$ holds. Let us also recall the definitions of V_{loc}:

$$V_{loc}(t) = Fv(G_2, d_1) \setminus Fv(G_1, c_1, K_1)$$

$$V_{loc}(\delta) = \bigcup_{i=1}^{m-1} Fv(G_{i+1}, d_i) \setminus Fv(G_i, c_i, K_i)$$

$$V_{loc}(\sigma) = (V_{constr}(\sigma) \cup V_{stable}(\sigma)) \setminus (V_{ass}(\sigma) \cup Fv(G))$$

We prove now that $V_{loc}(\delta) = V_{loc}(\sigma)$. The proof is by induction on $m = length(\delta)$.

$m = 1$) In this case $\delta = \langle \tilde{G}, c, T, n, \emptyset, \tilde{G}, c, T, n \rangle$, $\sigma = \langle c, \tilde{G}, T \rangle$, and therefore, by definition $V_{loc}(\delta) = V_{loc}(\sigma) = \emptyset$.

$m \geq 1$) Let

$$\delta = \langle \tilde{G}_1, c_1, T_1, n_1, \tilde{K}_1, \tilde{G}_2, d_1, T_2, n'_1 \rangle \langle \tilde{G}_2, c_2, T_2, n_2, \tilde{K}_2, \tilde{G}_3, d_2, T_3, n'_2 \rangle \cdots$$
$$\langle \tilde{G}_m, c_m, T_m, n_m, \emptyset, \tilde{G}_m, c_m, T_m, n_m \rangle.$$

By definition of $S'_P(G)$, there exists $\delta' \in S'_P(G_2)$ such that

$$t = \langle \tilde{G}_1, c_1, T_1, n_1, \tilde{K}_1, \tilde{G}_2, d_1, T_2, n'_1 \rangle$$

is compatible with δ' and $\delta = t \cdot \delta' \in Seq$.

By inductive hypothesis, we have that $V_{loc}(\delta') = V_{loc}(\sigma')$, where $\sigma' = \alpha(\delta')$. Moreover, by definition of α, $\sigma = \langle c_1, \tilde{K}_1, \tilde{H}_1, d_1 \rangle \cdot \sigma'$, where $\tilde{H}_1$ is the set consisting of all the identified atoms that are stable in δ.

By definition of V_{loc} and by inductive hypothesis

$$V_{loc}(\delta) = \bigcup_{i=1}^{m-1} Fv(G_{i+1}, d_i) \setminus Fv(G_i, c_i, K_i)$$
$$= V_{loc}(\delta') \cup (Fv(G_2, d_1) \setminus Fv(G_1, c_1, K_1))$$
$$= V_{loc}(\sigma') \cup (Fv(G_2, d_1) \setminus Fv(G_1, c_1, K_1)). \tag{3}$$

Moreover, by definition of $V_{loc}(\sigma)$ and since $V_{stable}(\sigma) = V_{stable}(\sigma')$, we have that

$$V_{loc}(\sigma') = (V_{constr}(\sigma') \cup V_{stable}(\sigma)) \setminus (V_{ass}(\sigma') \cup Fv(G_2)). \tag{4}$$

Therefore, considering the equations (3) and (4), using the properties of $\cup$ and observing that $Fv(G_2) \cap Fv(G_1, c_1, K_1) = Fv(G_2) \cap Fv(G_1, K_1)$ because of the behavior of $Solve'$ and $Apply'^3$, we are in position to write:

$$V_{loc}(\delta) = ((V_{constr}(\sigma') \cup V_{stable}(\sigma)) \setminus (V_{ass}(\sigma') \cup Fv(G_2)))$$
$$\cup (Fv(G_2) \setminus Fv(G_1, K_1)) \cup (Fv(d_1) \setminus Fv(G_1, c_1, K_1)). \quad (5)$$

Now, let $x \in Fv(K_1)$. By definition $x \in Fv(t)$, since t is compatible with δ' and by point 1 of Definition 7 (Compatibility), that is $V_{loc}(\delta') \cap Fv(t) = \emptyset$, we have that $x \notin V_{loc}(\delta') = V_{loc}(\sigma')$ and therefore considering (4) we can add x to $V_{ass}(\sigma') \cup Fv(G_2)$. Then by (5) it follows that

$$V_{loc}(\delta) = ((V_{constr}(\sigma') \cup V_{stable}(\sigma)) \setminus (V_{ass}(\sigma) \cup Fv(G_2)))$$
$$\cup (Fv(G_2) \setminus Fv(G_1, K_1)) \cup (Fv(d_1) \setminus Fv(G_1, c_1, K_1). \quad (6)$$

We will now only consider the first part of the equation (6): by properties of $\cup$, and considering that the variables that we can add using $Fv(G_2) \cap Fv(G_1, K_1)$ instead of $Fv(G_2)$ are yet added by $Fv(G_2) \setminus Fv(G_1, K_1)$, we have that

$$((V_{constr}(\sigma') \cup V_{stable}(\sigma)) \setminus (V_{ass}(\sigma) \cup Fv(G_2))) \cup$$
$$(Fv(G_2) \setminus Fv(G_1, K_1)) =$$
$$((V_{constr}(\sigma') \cup V_{stable}(\sigma)) \setminus (V_{ass}(\sigma) \cup (Fv(G_2) \cap Fv(G_1, K_1)))) \cup$$
$$(Fv(G_2) \setminus Fv(G_1, K_1)) =$$
$$((V_{constr}(\sigma') \cup V_{stable}(\sigma)) \setminus (V_{ass}(\sigma) \cup (Fv(G_2) \cap Fv(G_1)))) \cup$$
$$(Fv(G_2) \setminus Fv(G_1, K_1)), \quad (7)$$

where the last equality follows by observing that $Fv(K_1) \subseteq V_{ass}(\sigma)$.

Now let $x \in Fv(G_1) \setminus Fv(G_2)$ and let us assume that $x \in V_{constr}(\sigma') \cup V_{stable}(\sigma)$. Then $x \notin V_{loc}(\delta') = V_{loc}(\sigma')$ because $x \in Fv(t)$ and by Definition 7 point 1 (Compatibility) $V_{loc}(\delta') \cap Fv(t) = \emptyset$. Therefore since $x \notin Fv(G_2)$, by considering the equation (4) we can say that $x \in V_{ass}(\sigma') \subseteq V_{ass}(\sigma)$. According to the previous results, by (6) and (7), we have that

$$V_{loc}(\delta) = ((V_{constr}(\sigma') \cup V_{stable}(\sigma)) \setminus (V_{ass}(\sigma) \cup Fv(G_1)))$$
$$\cup (Fv(G_2) \setminus Fv(G_1, K_1)) \cup (Fv(d_1) \setminus Fv(G_1, c_1, K_1)). \quad (8)$$

Now let $x \in (Fv(d_1) \setminus Fv(c_1)) \cap V_{ass}(\sigma')$. Since by point 2 of Definition 7 (Compatibility) $V_{loc}(t) \cap V_{ass}(\sigma') = \emptyset$, we have that $x \in Fv(G_1, K_1)$. Then

$$Fv(d_1) \setminus Fv(G_1, c_1, K_1) = (Fv(d_1) \setminus Fv(c_1)) \setminus Fv(G_1, K_1)$$
$$= (Fv(d_1) \setminus Fv(c_1)) \setminus (Fv(G_1, K_1) \cup V_{ass}(\sigma'))$$
$$= (Fv(d_1) \setminus Fv(c_1)) \setminus (Fv(G_1) \cup V_{ass}(\sigma)).$$

---

[3] **Solve'** : $Fv(G_2) \cap Fv(G_1, c_1, K_1) = Fv(G_2) \cap Fv(G_1)$;
Apply' : fresh variable of the rule can not be in c_1.

Considering the previous result we can further say that

$$V_{loc}(\delta) = ((V_{constr}(\sigma) \cup V_{stable}(\sigma)) \setminus (V_{ass}(\sigma) \cup Fv(G_1))) \cup (Fv(G_2) \setminus Fv(G_1, K_1)). \tag{9}$$

Finally observe that if $x \in Fv(G_2) \setminus Fv(G_1, K_1)$ then an *Apply'* step occurred, $x \in V_{loc}(t)$ and therefore, by point 2 of Definition 7 (Compatibility), $x \notin V_{ass}(\sigma)$. Now, let $\{a_1, \ldots, a_l\} \subseteq G_2$ the set of atoms in G_2 such that $x \in Fv(a_j)$, for each $j \in [1, l]$. We have two cases:

1. there exists $v \in [1, l]$ such that a_v is a CHR constraint and $a_v \notin Stable(\sigma) = Stable(\delta)$. Then, by definition of derivation, there exists $j \in [1, n-1]$ such that $x \in Fv(d_j)$. Let h be the least index $j \in [1, n-1]$ such that $x \in Fv(d_h)$. Since by hypothesis $x \in V_{loc}(t)$, we have that $x \notin Fv(c_h)$, otherwise by point 3 of Definition 7 (Compatibility) there exists $j \in [1, h-1]$ such that $x \in Fv(d_j)$ and this contradicts the hypothesis that h is the least index $j \in [1, n-1]$ such that $x \in Fv(d_h)$. Then $x \in Fv(d_h) \setminus Fv(c_h) \subseteq V_{constr}(\sigma)$ and therefore by (9), by the previous result and by definition of V_{loc},

$$V_{loc}(\delta) = (V_{constr}(\sigma) \cup V_{stable}(\sigma)) \setminus (V_{ass}(\sigma) \cup Fv(G_1)) = V_{loc}(\sigma)$$

and then the thesis holds

2. for each $v \in [1, l]$, a_v is a built-in constraint. Now, we have two further cases:
   (a) c_n is satisfiable. In this case, by Definition 4 (Concrete sequences) we have that a_v is evaluated in δ, for each $v \in [1, l]$. Analogously to the previous case, by point 3 of Definition 7 (Compatibility), we have that $x \in V_{constr}(\sigma)$.
   (b) $c_n = \mathtt{false}$. In this case, by definition of the operational semantics, we can assume without loss of generality that δ evaluates at least a constraint in $\{a_1, \ldots, a_l\}$. Therefore, as before, $x \in V_{constr}(\sigma)$.
   Now the proof is the same of the previous case.   □

We have now three auxiliary lemmas whose proofs are immediate (from the definition of derivation and of $\simeq$) and therefore omitted.

The first one states that we can always obtain two concrete sequences that differ only in the same fixed subset of token in each tuple.

Lemma 4. *Let G be a goal, $\delta \in \mathcal{S}'_P(G)$ such that*

$$\delta = \langle \tilde{G}, c_1, T_1, n_1, \tilde{K}_1, \tilde{G}_2, d_1, T_2, n'_1 \rangle \langle \tilde{G}_2, c_2, T_2, n_2, \tilde{K}_2, \tilde{G}_3, d_2, T_3, n'_2 \rangle \cdots \langle \tilde{G}_m, c_m, T_m, n_m, \emptyset, \tilde{G}_m, c_m, T_m, n_m \rangle,$$

where $\tilde{G}$ is an identified version of G. Let $T'_1 \subseteq T_1$. There then exists a derivation $\delta' \in \mathcal{S}'_P(G)$

$$\delta' = \langle \tilde{G}, c_1, T'_1, n_1, \tilde{K}_1, \tilde{G}_2, d_1, T'_2, n'_1 \rangle \langle \tilde{G}_2, c_2, T'_2, n_2, \tilde{K}_2, \tilde{G}_3, d_2, T'_3, n'_2 \rangle \cdots \langle \tilde{G}_m, c_m, T'_m, n_m, \emptyset, \tilde{G}_m, c_m, T'_m, n_m \rangle,$$

such that $T_m \setminus T'_m = T_1 \setminus T'_1$.

The following lemma shows that if a concrete sequence δ is obtained from the goal (H, G) and the first step is made by an *Apply'* rule, then δ, up to the first tuple and an index renaming, can be obtained from the goal H by assuming in the first step all the constraints in G that are used in the *Apply'* rule.

Lemma 5. *Let H, G be goals and let $\delta \in \mathcal{S}'_P(H, G)$ such that*

$$\delta = \langle (\tilde{H}, \tilde{G}), c_1, T_1, n_1, \tilde{K}_1, \tilde{R}_2, d_1, T_2, n'_1 \rangle \langle \tilde{R}_2, c_2, T_2, n_2, \tilde{K}_2, \tilde{R}_3, d_2, T_3, n'_2 \rangle$$
$$\cdots \langle \tilde{R}_m, c_m, T_m, n_m, \emptyset, \tilde{R}_m, c_m, T_m, n_m \rangle$$
$$= \langle (\tilde{H}, \tilde{G}), c_1, T_1, n_1, \tilde{K}_1, \tilde{R}_2, d_1, T_2, n'_1 \rangle \cdot \delta_1$$

*where $\tilde{H} = (\tilde{H}', \tilde{H}'')$ and $\tilde{G}$ are identified versions of $H = (H', H'')$ and G, respectively, $H'' \neq \emptyset$ and the first tuple of the sequence δ represents a derivation step s, which uses the **Apply'** rule and rewrites only and all the atoms in $(\tilde{H}'', \tilde{G})$. There then exists a derivation $\delta' \in \mathcal{S}'_P(H)$,*

$$\delta' = \langle \tilde{H}, c_1, T_1, n_1, \tilde{K}'_1 \cup \tilde{G}', \tilde{R}'_2, d_1, T'_2, l'_1 \rangle \langle \tilde{R}'_2, c_2, T'_2, l_2, \tilde{K}'_2, \tilde{R}'_3, d_2, T'_3, l'_2 \rangle$$
$$\cdots \langle \tilde{R}'_m, c_m, T'_m, l_m, \emptyset, \tilde{R}'_m, c_m, T'_m, l_m \rangle,$$
$$= \langle \tilde{H}, c_1, T_1, n_1, \tilde{K}'_1 \cup \tilde{G}', \tilde{R}'_2, d_1, T'_2, l'_1 \rangle \cdot \delta'_1$$

and there further exists a renaming ρ such that $\delta'_1 = \delta_1 \rho$, $\tilde{K}'_1 = \tilde{K}_1 \rho$ and $\tilde{G}' = \tilde{G} \rho$.

Finally the third immediate lemma shows that by adding a set of identified constraints to the goal store we obtain a concrete sequence, provided that the addition is possible (that is, provided there are enough free indexes).

Lemma 6. *Let G be a goal, $\tilde{W}$ be a set of identified atoms and let $\delta \in \mathcal{S}'_P(G)$ such that $\delta \oplus \tilde{W}$ is defined and $Fv(\tilde{W}) \cap V_{loc}(\delta) = \emptyset$. Then $\delta \oplus \tilde{W} \in \mathcal{S}'_P(G, chr(\tilde{W}))$.*

We have now two more lemmas (used in the proof of Lemma 2) whose proofs are not immediate. The following one states that we can obtain the same concrete semantics both from a goal and from one part of it, with a resort of identifier.

Lemma 7. *Let P be a program and let H and G be two goals such that there exists a derivation step*

$$s = \langle (\tilde{H}, \tilde{G}), c_1, T_1 \rangle_{n_1} \longrightarrow^{K_1}_P \langle (\tilde{B}, \tilde{G}), d_1, T_2 \rangle_{n'_1},$$

where $\tilde{H}$ and $\tilde{G}$ are identified versions of H and G respectively and only the atoms in $\tilde{H}$ are rewritten in s.
Assume that there exists $\delta \in \mathcal{S}'_P(H, G)$ such that $\delta = t \cdot \delta' \in Seq$, where

$$t = \langle (\tilde{H}, \tilde{G}), c_1, T_1, n_1, \tilde{K}_1, (\tilde{B}, \tilde{G}), d_1, T_2, n'_1 \rangle,$$

$\delta' \in \mathcal{S}'_P(B, G)$ and t is compatible with δ'. Moreover, assume that there exists $\delta'_1 \in \mathcal{S}'_P(B)$ and $\delta'_2 \in \mathcal{S}'_P(G)$, such that

1. *$InG(\delta'_1) = \tilde{B}$, $InG(\delta'_2) = \tilde{G}$, $Intok(\delta'_1) = Intok(\delta'_2) = T_2$, for $i \in [1, 2]$, $Inid(\delta'_i) \geq n'_1$, $V_{loc}(\delta'_i) \subseteq V_{loc}(\delta')$ and $Inc(\delta'_i) \subseteq Inc(\delta')$.*

2. $Ass(\delta_1') \subseteq Ass(\delta') \cup Aloc(\delta_2') \cup InG(\delta_2')$ and $Ass(\delta_2') \subseteq Ass(\delta')$,
3. $\alpha(\delta_1') \parallel \alpha(\delta_2')$ is defined and that there exists $\sigma' \in \eta(\alpha(\delta_1') \parallel \alpha(\delta_2'))$ such that $\sigma' \simeq \alpha(\delta')$.

Then $\delta_1 = t' \cdot \delta_1' \in S_P'(H)$, where $t' = \langle \tilde{H}, c_1, T_1, n_1, \tilde{K}_1, \tilde{B}, d_1, T_2, n_1' \rangle$, $\alpha(\delta_1) \parallel \alpha(\delta_2')$ is defined and there exists $\sigma \in \eta(\alpha(\delta_1) \parallel \alpha(\delta_2'))$ such that $\sigma \simeq \alpha(\delta)$.

Proof. In the following proof we assume that

$$\delta_1' = \langle \tilde{B}_1, e_1, T_2, h_1, \tilde{M}_1, \tilde{B}_2, f_1, T_2', h_1' \rangle \cdots \langle \tilde{B}_l, e_l, T_l', h_l, \emptyset, \tilde{B}_l, e_l, T_l', h_l \rangle$$
$$\delta_2' = \langle \tilde{G}_1, r_1, S_2, j_1, \tilde{N}_1, \tilde{G}_2, s_1, S_2', j_1' \rangle \cdots \langle \tilde{G}_p, r_p, S_p', j_p, \emptyset, \tilde{G}_p, r_p, S_p', j_p \rangle$$
$$\delta' = \langle \tilde{R}_2, c_2, T_2, n_2, \tilde{K}_2, \tilde{R}_3, d_2, T_3, n_2' \rangle \cdots \langle \tilde{R}_m, c_m, T_m, n_m, \emptyset, \tilde{R}_m, c_m, T_m, n_m \rangle,$$

where $B_1 = \tilde{B}$, $G_1 = \tilde{G}$, $R_2 = (\tilde{B}, \tilde{G})$ and $e_l = r_p = c_m$ (our sequence needs the last condition to close the composition, see Definition 9). The proof is divided in four parts.

(a) t' **represents the derivation step** $s' = \langle \tilde{H}, c_1, T_1 \rangle_{n_1} \longrightarrow_P^{K_1} \langle \tilde{B}, d_1, T_2 \rangle_{n_1'}$. The proof of this part is straightforward by observing that t represents the derivation step

$$s = \langle (\tilde{H}, \tilde{G}), c_1, T_1 \rangle_{n_1} \longrightarrow_P^{K_1} \langle (\tilde{B}, \tilde{G}), d_1, T_2 \rangle_{n_1'},$$

which uses only atoms in $\tilde{H}$.

(b) $\delta_1 \in S_P'(H)$. By considering the previous point, by hypothesis and by definition of $S_P'(H)$, we have to prove that $\delta_1 \in Seq$ and that Definition 7 is satisfied. According to the hypothesis $InG(\delta_1') = \tilde{B}$, $Intok(\delta_1') = T_2$, $Inid(\delta_1') = h_1 \geq n_1'$ and $Inc(\delta_1') \subseteq Inc(\delta')$ (and then $CT \models instore(\delta_1') \rightarrow instore(\delta')$). Moreover, since $\delta = t \cdot \delta' \in Seq$, we have that $CT \models instore(\delta') \rightarrow d_1$ and therefore $CT \models instore(\delta_1') \rightarrow d_1$ by transitivity. Then we have only to prove that t' is compatible with δ_1' and so that the three conditions of Definition 7 hold. The following points then hold:

1. According to the hypothesis $V_{loc}(\delta_1') \subseteq V_{loc}(\delta')$ and the construction $Fv(t') \subseteq Fv(t)$. Then $V_{loc}(\delta_1') \cap Fv(t') \subseteq V_{loc}(\delta') \cap Fv(t) = \emptyset$, where the last equality follows since t is compatible with δ'.
2. We have that:

$$V_{loc}(t') \cap V_{ass}(\delta_1') \subseteq$$
   (since by construction $V_{loc}(t') = V_{loc}(t)$ and
   by hypothesis $Ass(\delta_1') \subseteq Ass(\delta') \cup Aloc(\delta_2') \cup InG(\delta_2'))$
$$V_{loc}(t) \cap (V_{ass}(\delta') \cup V_{loc}(\delta_2') \cup Fv(G)) \subseteq$$
   (since by hypothesis $V_{loc}(\delta_2') \subseteq V_{loc}(\delta')$ and
   by construction $V_{loc}(t) \cap Fv(G) = \emptyset$)
$$V_{loc}(t) \cap (V_{ass}(\delta') \cup V_{loc}(\delta')) =$$
   (since t is compatible with δ' and $V_{loc}(t) \subseteq Fv(t)$)
$$\emptyset$$

3. We have to prove that with $1 \leq i \leq l$,

$$V_{loc}(t') \cap Fv(e_i) \subseteq \bigcup_{j=1}^{i-1} Fv(f_j) \cup Fv(d_1).$$

First of all, observe that since t is compatible with δ', by construction $x \in V_{loc}(t') = V_{loc}(t)$ and $V_{loc}(\delta_2') \subseteq V_{loc}(\delta')$ we have that

$$x \notin Fv(G) \cup V_{loc}(\delta_2') \cup V_{ass}(\delta'). \tag{10}$$

Moreover, since by hypothesis $Inc(\delta_1') \subseteq Inc(\delta')$, there exists the least index $h \in [2, m]$ such that $e_i = c_h$. Therefore, since, by construction, $V_{loc}(t') = V_{loc}(t)$ and, by hypothesis, t is compatible with δ', considering a generic variable $x \in V_{loc}(t') \cap Fv(e_i)$, we have that

$$x \in \bigcup_{j=1}^{h-1} Fv(d_j).$$

Then, to prove the thesis, we have to prove that if $x \in \bigcup_{j=1}^{h-1} Fv(d_j)$ then $x \in \bigcup_{j=1}^{i-1} Fv(f_j) \cup Fv(d_1)$. If $x \in Fv(d_1)$ then the thesis holds.

Let us assume that $x \notin Fv(d_1)$, $x \in \bigcup_{j=2}^{h-1} Fv(d_j)$ and let k be the least index $j \in [2, h-1]$ such that $x \in Fv(d_j)$. Now, we have two possibilities:

(a) d_k is an output constraint of δ_1', i.e. there exists $j \in [1, i-1]$ such that $d_k = f_j$, then we have the proof.

(b) d_k is an output constraint of δ_2', namely there exists $w \in [1, p]$ such that $d_k = s_w$. Then, since k is the least index j such that $x \in Fv(d_j)$, $x \in V_{loc}(t)$ and, by hypothesis, t is compatible with δ', we have that $x \notin Fv(c_k)$ and therefore $x \notin Fv(r_w)$.

Moreover, since by (10) and by point 2 of the hypothesis, $x \notin Fv(G) \cup V_{loc}(\delta_2') \cup V_{ass}(\delta_2')$, we have that $x \notin Fv(G_w)$.

Then by definition of derivation step, we have a contradiction, since $x \in Fv(s_w) \setminus (Fv(r_w) \cup Fv(G_w) \cup V_{loc}(\delta_2') \cup V_{ass}(\delta_2'))$.

(c) $\alpha(\delta_1) \parallel \alpha(\delta_2')$ **is defined.** Now we consider Definition 9. First of all, observe that $id(\delta_1) \cap id(\delta_2') = \emptyset$ since $\alpha(\delta_1') \parallel \alpha(\delta_2')$ is defined (and therefore $id(\delta_1') \cap id(\delta_2') = \emptyset$) and since by hypothesis $Inid(\delta_2') = j_1 \geq n_1'$. Then we only have to prove that

$$(V_{loc}(\alpha(\delta_1)) \cup Fv(H)) \cap (V_{loc}(\alpha(\delta_2')) \cup Fv(G)) = Fv(H) \cap Fv(G).$$

By Lemma 1

$$V_{loc}(\alpha(\delta_1)) = V_{loc}(\alpha(\delta_1')) \cup V_{loc}(t'). \tag{11}$$

and since $\alpha(\delta_1') \parallel \alpha(\delta_2')$ is defined, we can say that

$$(V_{loc}(\alpha(\delta_1')) \cup Fv(B)) \cap (V_{loc}(\alpha(\delta_2')) \cup Fv(G)) = Fv(B) \cap Fv(G).$$

From the above equality, we have that

$$V_{loc}(\alpha(\delta_1')) \cap (V_{loc}(\alpha(\delta_2')) \cup Fv(G)) = \emptyset. \tag{12}$$

Now observe that, since t is compatible with δ', by point 1 of Definition 7, $V_{loc}(\delta') \cap Fv(t) = \emptyset$ holds, by construction $V_{loc}(t') = V_{loc}(t)$ and by Lemma 1, we can conclude that $V_{loc}(t') \cap V_{loc}(\alpha(\delta')) = \emptyset$. Furthermore, by hypothesis $V_{loc}(\alpha(\delta_2')) \subseteq$

$V_{loc}(\alpha(\delta'))$ and according to the definition of t, we have that $Fv(G) \cap V_{loc}(t') = Fv(G) \cap V_{loc}(t) = \emptyset$. Then

$$V_{loc}(\alpha(\delta_1)) \cap (V_{loc}(\alpha(\delta_2')) \cup Fv(G)) =$$
$$(V_{loc}(\alpha(\delta_1')) \cup V_{loc}(t')) \cap (V_{loc}(\alpha(\delta_2')) \cup Fv(G)) = \emptyset. \qquad (13)$$

Finally, since t is compatible with δ', by point 1 of Definition 7 $V_{loc}(\delta') \cap Fv(t) = \emptyset$), by construction $Fv(H) \subseteq Fv(t)$ and by hypothesis $V_{loc}(\alpha(\delta_2')) \subseteq V_{loc}(\alpha(\delta'))$. Then we have that

$$Fv(H) \cap V_{loc}(\alpha(\delta_2')) \subseteq Fv(H) \cap V_{loc}(\alpha(\delta')) = \emptyset \qquad (14)$$

and then the thesis holds by(11), (13), (14) and by properties of set operators.

(d) There exists $\sigma \in \eta(\alpha(\delta_1) \parallel \alpha(\delta_2'))$ **such that** $\sigma \simeq \alpha(\delta)$. By inductive hypothesis $\alpha(\delta') \simeq \sigma' \in \eta(\alpha(\delta_1') \parallel \alpha(\delta_2'))$. By the definition of $\simeq$, there exists a renaming ρ such that

$$\alpha(\delta') = \sigma'\rho. \qquad (15)$$

Since by hypothesis $InG(\delta') = (InG(\delta_1'), InG(\delta_2'))$ and $Intok(\delta_1') = Intok(\delta_2') = Intok(\delta')$, without loss of generality, we can assume that

$$t'\rho = t'. \qquad (16)$$

Moreover, by definition of $\parallel$ there exists $\sigma_1 \in \alpha(\delta_1') \parallel \alpha(\delta_2')$ such that $\sigma' \in \eta(\{\sigma_1\})$ and

$$\langle c_1, \tilde{K}_1, (\tilde{J}_1 \cup \tilde{Y}_1), d_1 \rangle \cdot \sigma_1 \in \alpha(\delta_1) \parallel \alpha(\delta_2'),$$

where $\tilde{J}_1$ is the set of atoms in $\tilde{H}$ which are not rewritten in δ_1 and $\tilde{Y}_1$ the set of atoms in $\tilde{G}$ which are not rewritten in δ_2'.

Let us denote
- $\tilde{J}_2$ as the set of atoms in $\tilde{B}$ which are not rewritten in δ_1';
- $\tilde{W}_1$ as the set of atoms in $(\tilde{H}, \tilde{G})$ which are not rewritten in δ;
- $\tilde{W}_2$ as the set of atoms in $(\tilde{B}, \tilde{G})$ which are not rewritten in δ'.

According to the definition of α,

$$\alpha(\delta) = \langle c_1, \tilde{K}_1, \tilde{W}_1, d_1 \rangle \cdot \alpha(\delta'). \qquad (17)$$

According to the definition of η and since $\sigma' \in \eta(\{\sigma_1\})$,

$$\langle c_1, \tilde{K}_1, (\tilde{J}_1 \cup \tilde{Y}_1) \setminus S, d_1 \rangle \cdot \sigma' \in \eta(\alpha(\delta_1) \parallel \alpha(\delta_2')), \qquad (18)$$

where the sets difference $(\tilde{J}_1 \cup \tilde{Y}_1) \setminus S$ considers identification values and S is such that $(\tilde{J}_2 \cup \tilde{Y}_1) \setminus S = \tilde{W}_2$. Since $(\tilde{J}_1 \cup \tilde{Y}_1) \subseteq (\tilde{J}_2 \cup \tilde{Y}_1)$, we can assume that $\tilde{W} = (\tilde{J}_1 \cup \tilde{Y}_1) \setminus S = (\tilde{J}_1 \cup \tilde{Y}_1) \cap \tilde{W}_2$. Then by definition, $\tilde{W}$ contains all and only the atoms in $(\tilde{H}, \tilde{G})$ which are not rewritten in t and in δ' and therefore $\tilde{W} = \tilde{W}_1$. Therefore by (18)

$$\langle c_1, \tilde{K}_1, \tilde{W}_1, d_1 \rangle \cdot \sigma' \in \eta(\alpha(\delta_1) \parallel \alpha(\delta_2')).$$

Then

$$\begin{aligned}
(\langle c_1, \tilde{K}_1, \tilde{W}_1, d_1 \rangle \cdot \sigma')\, \rho &= \text{(by (16))} \\
\langle c_1, \tilde{K}_1, \tilde{W}_1, d_1 \rangle \cdot (\sigma'\rho) &= \text{(by (15))} \\
\langle c_1, \tilde{K}_1, \tilde{W}_1, d_1 \rangle \cdot \alpha(\delta') &= \text{(by (17))} \\
\alpha(\delta) &
\end{aligned}$$

and this completes the proof.   □

Lemma 8. *Let P be a program and let H and G be two goals such that there exists a derivation step*

$$s = \langle (\tilde{H}, \tilde{G}), c_1, T_1 \rangle_{n_1} \longrightarrow_P^{K_1} \langle (\tilde{B}, \tilde{G}), d_1, T_2 \rangle_{n_1'},$$

where $\tilde{H}$ and $\tilde{G}$ are identified versions of H and G respectively and only the atoms in $\tilde{G}$ are rewritten in s.

Assume that there exists $\delta \in \mathcal{S}_P'(H, G)$ such that $\delta = t \cdot \delta' \in \mathcal{S}eq$, where

$$t = \langle (\tilde{H}, \tilde{G}), c_1, T_1, n_1, \tilde{K}_1, (\tilde{H}, \tilde{B}), d_1, T_2, n_1' \rangle,$$

$\delta' \in \mathcal{S}_P'(B, G)$ and t is compatible with δ'. Moreover assume that there exists $\delta_1' \in \mathcal{S}_P'(H)$ and $\delta_2' \in \mathcal{S}_P'(B)$, such that

1. *$InG(\delta_1') = \tilde{H}$, $InG(\delta_2') = \tilde{B}$, $Intok(\delta_1') = Intok(\delta_2') = T_2$, for $i \in [1, 2]$, $Inid(\delta_i') \geq n_1'$, $V_{loc}(\delta_i') \subseteq V_{loc}(\delta')$ and $Inc(\delta_i') \subseteq Inc(\delta')$.*
2. *$Ass(\delta_1') \subseteq Ass(\delta') \cup Aloc(\delta_2') \cup InG(\delta_2')$ and $Ass(\delta_2') \subseteq Ass(\delta')$,*
3. *$\alpha(\delta_1') \parallel \alpha(\delta_2')$ is defined and there exists $\sigma' \in \eta(\alpha(\delta_1') \parallel \alpha(\delta_2'))$ such that $\sigma' \simeq \alpha(\delta')$.*

Then $\delta_2 = t' \cdot \delta_2' \in \mathcal{S}_P'(G)$, where $t' = \langle \tilde{G}, c_1, T_1, n_1, \tilde{K}_1, \tilde{B}, d_1, T_2, n_1' \rangle$, $\alpha(\delta_1') \parallel \alpha(\delta_2)$ is defined and there exists $\sigma \in \eta(\alpha(\delta_1') \parallel \alpha(\delta_2))$ such that $\sigma \simeq \alpha(\delta)$.

Proof. The proof is analogous to that one of Lemma 7 and therefore omitted.

We can now prove the second lemma used in the proof of the compositionality theorem. This lemma states that the abstraction of a concrete sequence for the goal (H, G) can be reconstructed (up to the indexes) by the abstract composition of two sequences for the goals H and G, respectively.

Lemma 2. *Let P be a program, H and G be two goals and let $\delta \in \mathcal{S}_P'(H, G)$. Then there exist $\delta_1 \in \mathcal{S}_P'(H)$, $\delta_2 \in \mathcal{S}_P'(G)$ and $\sigma \in \eta(\alpha(\delta_1) \parallel \alpha(\delta_2))$ such that for $i = 1, 2$, $V_{loc}(\delta_i) \subseteq V_{loc}(\delta)$ and $\sigma \simeq \alpha(\delta)$.*

Proof. In order to prove this result we construct, by induction on $l = length(\delta)$, two sequences $\delta \uparrow_{(H,G)} = (\delta_1, \delta_2)$, where $\delta_1 \in \mathcal{S}_P'(H)$, $\delta_2 \in \mathcal{S}_P'(G)$ and $i \in \{1, 2\}$ with the following features:

1. *$InG(\delta) = (InG(\delta_1), InG(\delta_2))$, $V_{loc}(\delta_i) \subseteq V_{loc}(\delta)$, $Inid(\delta_i) \geq Inid(\delta)$, $Intok(\delta_i) = Intok(\delta)$ and $Inc(\delta_i) \subseteq Inc(\delta)$ (and then $CT \models instore(\delta_i) \to instore(\delta)$);*
2. *$Ass(\delta_1) \subseteq Ass(\delta) \cup Aloc(\delta_2) \cup InG(\delta_2)$ and $Ass(\delta_2) \subseteq Ass(\delta)$;*

3. $\alpha(\delta_1) \parallel \alpha(\delta_2)$ is defined and $\alpha(\delta) \simeq \sigma \in \eta(\alpha(\delta_1) \parallel \alpha(\delta_2))$ (where identifiers of atoms in σ are resorted with respect to the δ ones).

(l=1). In this case $\delta = \langle (\tilde{H}, \tilde{G}), c, T, n, \emptyset, (\tilde{H}, \tilde{G}), c, T, n \rangle$, so

$$\delta \uparrow_{(H,G)} = (\langle \tilde{H}, c, T, n, \emptyset, \tilde{H}, c, T, n \rangle, \langle \tilde{G}, c, T, n, \emptyset, \tilde{G}, c, T, n \rangle)$$
$$= (\delta_1, \delta_2)$$

where $\delta_1 \in \mathcal{S}'_P(H)$, $\delta_2 \in \mathcal{S}'_P(G)$. Note that, by definition of sequence, $id(\tilde{H}) \cap id(\tilde{G}) = \emptyset$ and by construction $V_{loc}(\delta_1) = V_{loc}(\delta_2) = \emptyset$, so $\alpha(\delta_1) \parallel \alpha(\delta_2)$ is defined. Then

$$\alpha(\delta_1) = \langle c, \tilde{H}, T \rangle, \ \alpha(\delta_2) = \langle c, \tilde{G}, T \rangle \text{ and}$$
$$\alpha(\delta) = \sigma = \langle c, (\tilde{H}, \tilde{G}), T \rangle \in \alpha(\delta_1) \parallel \alpha(\delta_2).$$

Moreover the following holds

1. $InG(\delta) = (\tilde{H}, \tilde{G}) = (InG(\delta_1), InG(\delta_2))$, $V_{loc}(\delta) = V_{loc}(\delta_i) = \emptyset$ so $V_{loc}(\delta_i) \subseteq V_{loc}(\delta) = \emptyset$, $Inid(\delta_i) = Inid(\delta)$, $Intok(\delta_i) = T = Intok(\delta)$ and $Inc(\delta_i) = Inc(\delta)$;
2. $Ass(\delta_1) = \emptyset$ so $Ass(\delta_1) \subseteq Ass(\delta) \cup Aloc(\delta_2) \cup InG(\delta_2)$ and $Ass(\delta_2) = \emptyset$ so $Ass(\delta_2) \subseteq Ass(\delta)$;
3. $\alpha(\delta_1) \parallel \alpha(\delta_2)$ is defined and $\alpha(\delta) \in \eta(\alpha(\delta_1) \parallel \alpha(\delta_2))$: the proof is straightforward by definition of $\parallel$.

(l>1). If $\delta \in \mathcal{S}'_P(H, G)$, by definition

$$\delta = \langle (\tilde{H}, \tilde{G}), c_1, T_1, n_1, \tilde{K}_1, \tilde{B}_2, d_1, T_2, n'_1 \rangle \cdot \delta',$$

where $\tilde{H}$, $\tilde{G}$ and $\tilde{B}_2$ are identified versions of the goals H, G and B_2, respectively, $id(\tilde{H}) \cap id(\tilde{G}) = \emptyset$, $\delta' \in \mathcal{S}'_P(B_2)$ and $t = \langle (\tilde{H}, \tilde{G}), c_1, T_1, n_1, \tilde{K}_1, \tilde{B}_2, d_1, T_2, n'_1 \rangle$ is compatible with δ'. We recall that, by definition, the tuple t represents a derivation step

$$s = \langle (\tilde{H}, \tilde{G}), c_1, T_1 \rangle_{n_1} \longrightarrow_P^{K_1} \langle \tilde{B}_2, d_1, T_2 \rangle_{n'_1}.$$

Now we distinguish various cases according to the structure of the derivation step s.

Solve'. If the derivation step s uses a *Solve'* rule we can assume, without loss of generality, that $H = (c, H')$ and $\tilde{H} = (c, \tilde{H}')$ so:

$$s = \langle (\tilde{H}, \tilde{G}), c_1, T_1 \rangle_{n_1} \rightarrow_P^\emptyset \langle (\tilde{H}', \tilde{G}), d_1, T_1 \rangle_{n_1},$$

$CT \models c_1 \wedge c \leftrightarrow d_1$, $t = \langle (\tilde{H}, \tilde{G}), c_1, T_1, n_1, \emptyset, (\tilde{H}', \tilde{G}), d_1, T_1, n_1 \rangle$ and $\delta' \in \mathcal{S}'_P(H', G)$. Furthermore, $\alpha(\delta) = \langle c_1, \emptyset, \tilde{W}, d_1 \rangle \cdot \alpha(\delta')$ where $\tilde{W}$ is the first stable identified atoms set of $\alpha(\delta')$, because the application of *Solve'* does not modify the next stable identified atoms set.

By inductive hypothesis there exists $\delta'_1 \in \mathcal{S}'_P(H')$ and $\delta_2 \in \mathcal{S}'_P(G)$ such that $\delta' \uparrow_{(H',G)} = (\delta'_1, \delta_2)$ and $\alpha(\delta') \simeq \sigma' \in \eta(\alpha(\delta'_1) \parallel \alpha(\delta_2))$. We may now define:

$$\delta \uparrow_{(H,G)} = (\delta_1, \delta_2) \text{ where } \delta_1 = \langle \tilde{H}, c_1, T_1, n_1, \emptyset, \tilde{H}', d_1, T_1, n_1 \rangle \cdot \delta'_1.$$

By definition, $\langle \tilde{H}, c_1, T_1 \rangle_{n_1} \rightarrow_P^\emptyset \langle \tilde{H}', d_1, T_1 \rangle_{n_1}$ represents a derivation step for H and so we can write the tuple $t' = \langle \tilde{H}, c_1, T_1, n_1, \emptyset, \tilde{H}', d_1, T_1, n_1 \rangle$, $Fv(d_1) \subseteq Fv(H) \cup Fv(c_1)$ and therefore $V_{loc}(t') = \emptyset$. Then the following holds:

1. By inductive hypothesis $InG(\delta_2) = \tilde{G}$ and therefore $InG(\delta) = (\tilde{H}, \tilde{G}) = (InG(\delta_1), InG(\delta_2))$. Now, let $i \in \{1, 2\}$. $V_{loc}(\delta_i) \subseteq V_{loc}(\delta')$ by inductive hypothesis and by construction; $V_{loc}(\delta') = V_{loc}(\delta)$ by previous observation (that is $V_{loc}(t') = \emptyset$), then $V_{loc}(\delta_i) \subseteq V_{loc}(\delta)$.

   $Intok(\delta_i) = T_1 = Intok(\delta)$, $Inid(\delta_1) = n_1 = Inid(\delta)$ and by inductive hypothesis $Inid(\delta_2) \geq Inid(\delta') \geq Inid(\delta)$, where the last inequality follows from the definition of sequence.

   By inductive hypothesis and by construction $Inc(\delta_i) \subseteq Inc(\delta') \cup \{c_1\} = Inc(\delta)$.

2. By construction $Ass(\delta_1) = Ass(\delta'_1)$ and $Ass(\delta) = Ass(\delta')$ and by inductive hypothesis $Ass(\delta'_1) \subseteq Ass(\delta') \cup Aloc(\delta_2) \cup InG(\delta_2)$. Then $Ass(\delta_1) \subseteq Ass(\delta) \cup Aloc(\delta_2) \cup InG(\delta_2)$ and $Ass(\delta_2) \subseteq Ass(\delta') = Ass(\delta)$.

3. The proof follows according to Lemma 7 and by inductive hypothesis.

Apply' - only atoms of H. In the derivation step s we use the $Apply'$ rule and we assume that only atoms deriving from $H = (H', H'')$ are used: $H'' \neq \emptyset$ is used by $Apply'$ rule and $\tilde{H} = (\tilde{H}', \tilde{H}'')$.

In this case we can assume that

$$s = \langle (\tilde{H}, \tilde{G}), c_1, T_1 \rangle_{n_1} \rightarrow_P^{K_1} \langle (\tilde{H}', \tilde{B}, \tilde{G}), d_1, T_2 \rangle_{n'_1}$$

so $\delta' \in \mathcal{S}'_P(H', B, G)$ and $t = \langle (\tilde{H}, \tilde{G}), c_1, T_1, n_1, \tilde{K}_1, (\tilde{H}', \tilde{B}, \tilde{G}), d_1, T_2, n'_1 \rangle$. By inductive hypothesis there exist $\delta'_1 \in \mathcal{S}'_P(H', B)$ and $\delta'_2 \in \mathcal{S}'_P(G)$ such that $\delta' \uparrow_{((H', B), G)} = (\delta'_1, \delta'_2)$ and $\alpha(\delta') \simeq \sigma' \in \eta(\alpha(\delta'_1) \parallel \alpha(\delta'_2))$. By the definition of $\uparrow$, $Intok(\delta'_2) = T_2 \supseteq T_1$.

Thus, according to Lemma 4, there exists a derivation $\delta_2 \in \mathcal{S}'_P(G)$ such that

$$V(\delta_2) = V(\delta'_2), \text{ for } V \in \{length, Aloc, Ass, V_{loc}, Stable\},$$
$$Intok(\delta_2) = T_1 \text{ and } \alpha(\delta') \in \eta(\alpha(\delta'_1) \parallel \alpha(\delta_2)). \tag{19}$$

We may then define:

$$\delta \uparrow_{(H,G)} = (\delta_1, \delta_2) \text{ where } \delta_1 = \langle \tilde{H}, c_1, T_1, n_1, \tilde{K}_1, (\tilde{H}', \tilde{B}), d_1, T_2, n'_1 \rangle \cdot \delta'_1$$

By definition $s' = \langle \tilde{H}, c_1, T_1 \rangle_{n_1} \longrightarrow_P^{K_1} \langle (\tilde{H}', \tilde{B}), d_1, T_2 \rangle_{n'_1}$ is a derivation step for H, $t' = \langle \tilde{H}, c_1, K_1, T_1, n_1, (\tilde{H}', \tilde{B}), d_1, T_2, n'_1 \rangle$ represents the derivation step s' and $V_{loc}(t') = V_{loc}(t)$. Now the following holds, with $i \in \{1, 2\}$:

1. By construction $InG(\delta) = (InG(\delta_1), InG(\delta_2)) = (\tilde{H}, \tilde{G})$. By inductive hypothesis, construction, property of union and by (19), $V_{loc}(\delta_i) \subseteq V_{loc}(\delta') \cup V_{loc}(t)$.

   Moreover, by inductive hypothesis, the definition of δ, (19) and by construction $V_{loc}(\delta') \cup V_{loc}(t) = V_{loc}(\delta)$ and $Inc(\delta_i) \subseteq Inc(\delta') \cup \{c_1\} = Inc(\delta)$ so $V_{loc}(\delta_i) \subseteq V_{loc}(\delta)$ and $Inc(\delta_i) \subseteq Inc(\delta)$. $Inid(\delta_1) = n_1 = Inid(\delta)$ and $Inid(\delta_2) \geq Inid(\delta') \geq Inid(\delta)$. Finally, by construction and inductive hypothesis $Intok(\delta_i) = T_1 = Intok(\delta)$.

2. By inductive hypothesis, (19) and construction,

$$Ass(\delta_1) = Ass(\delta_1') \cup \{K_1\}$$
$$\subseteq Ass(\delta') \cup Aloc(\delta_2) \cup InG(\delta_2) \cup \{K_1\}$$
$$= Ass(\delta) \cup Aloc(\delta_2) \cup InG(\delta_2)$$

and

$$Ass(\delta_2) = Ass(\delta_2') \subseteq Ass(\delta') \subseteq Ass(\delta).$$

3. The proof follows according to Lemma 7 and inductive hypothesis.

Apply' - only atoms of G. The proof is the same as that one of the previous case (by using by Lemma 8 instead of by Lemma 7) hence it is omitted.

Apply' - atoms of H and G. In the derivation step s we use the *Apply'* rule and let us assume that in s some atoms deriving both from H and G are used. In this case, we can assume that $H = (H', H'')$, $G = (G', G'')$, $H'' \neq \emptyset$, $G'' \neq \emptyset$, $\tilde{H} = (\tilde{H}', \tilde{H}'')$, $\tilde{G} = (\tilde{G}', \tilde{G}'')$ and $(\tilde{H}'', \tilde{G}'')$ are the atoms in the goal $(\tilde{H}, \tilde{G})$, which are used in s.

$$s = \langle(\tilde{H}, \tilde{G}), c_1, T_1\rangle_{n_1} \longrightarrow_P^{K_1} \langle(\tilde{H}', \tilde{G}', \tilde{B}), d_1, T_2\rangle_{n_1'},$$

so $\delta' \in S_P'(H', G', B)$ and $t = \langle(\tilde{H}, \tilde{G}), c_1, T_1, n_1, \tilde{K}_1, (\tilde{H}', \tilde{G}', \tilde{B}), d_1, T_2, n_1'\rangle$. Moreover $\alpha(\delta) = \langle c_1, \tilde{K}_1, \tilde{W}, d_1\rangle \cdot \alpha(\delta')$, where $\tilde{W}$ is the set of stable atoms of δ' restricted to the atoms in $(\tilde{H}', \tilde{G}')$.

Using the same arguments of the previous point we can show that there exist $\delta_1' \in S_P'(H, G'')$ and $\delta_2' \in S_P'(G')$ such that $\delta \uparrow_{((H,G''),G')} = (\delta_1', \delta_2')$.

Now, observe that, according to Lemma 5 and the definition of $\uparrow$, there exists $\delta_1 \in S_P'(H)$ such that

$$InG(\delta_1) = \tilde{H}, \ Ass(\delta_1) = Ass(\delta_1') \cup \{G''\},$$
$$\alpha(\delta_1') = \langle c_1, \tilde{K}_1, \tilde{W}_1, d_1\rangle \cdot \sigma_1, \ \ \alpha(\delta_1) = \langle c_1, \tilde{K}_1' \cup \tilde{G}_2, \tilde{W}_1', d_1\rangle \cdot \sigma_1',$$
$$V(\delta_1) = V(\delta_1') \text{ for } V \in \{Intok, Inid, V_{loc}, Inc, Stable, Aloc\} \qquad (20)$$

where $\sigma_1 \simeq \sigma_1'$, and $\tilde{K}_1'$, $\tilde{W}_1'$ and $\tilde{G}_2$ are an identified version of K_1, of W_1 and of G'', respectively.

Moreover, since $\delta \in S_P'(H, G)$ and $V_{loc}(\delta_2') \subseteq V_{loc}(\delta)$, we have that $Fv(G'') \cap V_{loc}(\delta_2') = \emptyset$ and for each $i \in id(\tilde{G}'')$ and $j \in id(\tilde{G}')$, we can further say that $i \leq n_1$ and $i \neq j$. Then according to Lemma 6, we can assume that $\delta_2 = \delta_2' \oplus \tilde{G}'' \in S_P'(G)$. By construction

$$InG(\delta_2) = \tilde{G}, \ Stable(\delta_2) = Stable(\delta_2') \cup \{G''\} \text{ and}$$
$$V(\delta_2) = V(\delta_2') \text{ for } V \in \{Intok, Inid, V_{loc}, Inc, Ass, Aloc\}. \quad (21)$$

Without loss of generality, we can choose δ_1 and δ_2 in such a way that $id(\delta_1) \cap id(\delta_2) = \emptyset$.

Then, we define

$$\delta \uparrow_{(H,G)} = (\delta_1, \delta_2).$$

Now the following holds, with $i \in \{1, 2\}$:

1. By construction $InG(\delta) = (InG(\delta_1), InG(\delta_2))$. By definition of $\uparrow$ and by previous observation $V_{loc}(\delta_i) = V_{loc}(\delta_i') \subseteq V_{loc}(\delta)$, $Intok(\delta_i) = Intok(\delta_i') = Intok(\delta)$, $Inid(\delta_i) = Inid(\delta_i') \geq Inid(\delta)$ and $Inc(\delta_i) = Inc(\delta_i') \subseteq Inc(\delta)$.

2. By (20), by definition of $\uparrow$ and by (21)

$$Ass(\delta_1) = Ass(\delta_1') \cup \{G''\}$$
$$\subseteq Ass(\delta) \cup Aloc(\delta_2') \cup InG(\delta_2') \cup \{G''\}$$
$$= Ass(\delta) \cup Aloc(\delta_2) \cup InG(\delta_2).$$

Moreover by (21) and by definition of $\uparrow$, we have that

$$Ass(\delta_2) = Ass(\delta_2') \subseteq Ass(\delta).$$

3. $\alpha(\delta_1) \parallel \alpha(\delta_2)$ is defined and there exists $\sigma \in \eta(\alpha(\delta_1) \parallel \alpha(\delta_2))$ such that $\alpha(\delta) \simeq \sigma$. The proof that $\alpha(\delta_1) \parallel \alpha(\delta_2)$ is defined follows by observing that, by definition of derivation, $V_{loc}(\delta_1') \cap Fv(G'') = \emptyset$, by construction for $i \in \{1, 2\}$, $V_{loc}(\delta_i) = V_{loc}(\delta_i')$ and by definition of $\uparrow$, $\alpha(\delta_1') \parallel \alpha(\delta_2')$ is defined.

Now, we prove that $\alpha(\delta) \simeq \sigma \in \eta(\alpha(\delta_1) \parallel \alpha(\delta_2))$. First of all, observe that by construction, by (20) and by (21) for each $\bar{\sigma}_1 \in \eta(\alpha(\delta_1') \parallel \alpha(\delta_2'))$ there exists $\bar{\sigma}_2 \in \eta(\alpha(\delta_1) \parallel \alpha(\delta_2))$ such that $\bar{\sigma}_1 \simeq \bar{\sigma}_2$ (namely, $\eta(\alpha(\delta_1') \parallel \alpha(\delta_2')) \ll \eta(\alpha(\delta_1) \parallel \alpha(\delta_2)))$.

Moreover, by definition of $\uparrow$, $\alpha(\delta) \simeq \bar{\sigma} \in \eta(\alpha(\delta_1') \parallel \alpha(\delta_2'))$. Then the proof follows by the transitivity of $\simeq$ and this completes the proof. □

Now we have three more auxiliary lemmas which are needed in the proof of Lemma 3. In the following, given a derivation

$$\delta = \langle \tilde{R}_1, c_1, T_1, n_1, \tilde{K}_1, \tilde{R}_2, d_1, T_2, n_1' \rangle \cdots \langle \tilde{R}_m, c_m, T_m, n_m, \emptyset, \tilde{R}_m, c_m, T_m, n_m \rangle,$$

we define $id(\delta) = id(\bigcup_{i=1}^{m} \tilde{R}_i) \cup id(\bigcup_{i=1}^{m-1} \tilde{K}_i)$.

The following lemma considers a derivation step s and allows to replace the assumptions of s by unused constraints in the input goal of s.

Lemma 9. *Let P be a program and let R be a goal, such that there exists a derivation step $s = \langle \tilde{R}, c, T, n, \tilde{L}_1, \tilde{R}', d, T', n' \rangle$ for R. We suppose that $\tilde{L}_1$ has k CHR constraints. Assume that there exist*

$$\tilde{L}' = \{h_1 \# id_1', \ldots, h_o \# id_o'\} \subseteq \tilde{R} \text{ and } \tilde{L} = \{g_1 \# id_1, \ldots, g_o \# id_o\} \subseteq \tilde{L}_1$$

such that

- *the identified atoms in $\tilde{L}'$ are not used by s,*
- *for each $j \in [1, o]$, $CT \models c \wedge h_j \leftrightarrow c \wedge g_j$ and*
- *$T'[id_1/id_1', \ldots, id_o/id_o']$ is defined.*

There then exists a derivation step

$$s' = \langle \tilde{R}, c, T, n, \tilde{L}'_1, \tilde{R}'', d, T'', n'' \rangle,$$

whereby

- $\{n+1, \ldots, n+k\} = id(\tilde{L}_1)$, $\rho = [n+1/j_1, \ldots, n+k/j_k]$ *is a renaming,*
- $\tilde{L}'_1 = (\tilde{L}_1 \setminus \tilde{L})\rho$,
- $\tilde{R}'' = (\tilde{R}' \setminus \tilde{L}')[g_1\#id_1/h_1\#id'_1, \ldots, g_o\#id_o/h_o\#id'_o]\rho$,
- $T'' = T'[id_1/id'_1, \ldots, id_o/id'_o]\rho$, $n'' \leq n'$ *and*
- $V_{loc}(s) = V_{loc}(s')$.

Proof. Straightforward by definition of derivation step.   □

The following lemma allows to substitute constraints in the input goal (and possibly also in the output goal) by other constraints having a different label. This lemma is used in order to propagate the substitution of an assumption with a stable atom in all of the computational steps of a sequence.

Lemma 10. *Let P be a program. R be a goal,*

$$s = \langle \tilde{R}_1, c, T_1, n, \tilde{L}_1, \tilde{R}_2, d, T_2, n' \rangle$$

be a derivation step for R, where $\tilde{R}_1$ is an identified version of R and let $\tilde{L}'=\{h_1\#id'_1, \ldots, h_o\#id'_o\}$ and $\tilde{L}=\{g_1\#id_1, \ldots, g_o\#id_o\}$ be two sets of identified atoms such that for each $j \in [1, o]$ the following then holds

- $CT \models c \wedge h_j \leftrightarrow c \wedge g_j$,
- $id'_j \notin id(\tilde{R}_1) \cup id(\tilde{R}_2) \cup id(\tilde{L}_1)$
- *Either $g_j\#id_j \in \tilde{R}_1$ or $id_j \notin id(\tilde{R}_1) \cup id(\tilde{R}_2) \cup id(\tilde{L}_1)$ and*
- $T_2[id_1/id'_1, \ldots, id_o/id'_o]$ *is defined.*

There then exists a derivation step

$$s' = \langle \tilde{R}'_1, c, T'_1, n, \tilde{L}_1, \tilde{R}'_2, d, T'_2, n' \rangle$$

where for $i \in \{1, 2\}$, $\tilde{R}'_i = \tilde{R}_i[g_1\#id_1/h_1\#id'_1, \ldots, g_o\#id_o/h_o\#id'_o]$, $T'_i = T_i[id_1/id'_1, \ldots, id_o/id'_o]$ and $V_{loc}(s) = V_{loc}(s')$.

Proof. Straightforward by the definition of derivation step.   □

We need the following definition which extend the substitution operator defined in Definition 10 to concrete sequences.

Definition 16. *Assume the notation of definition 10. Let the sequence*

$$\delta = \langle \tilde{R}_1, c_1, T_1, n_1, \tilde{L}_1, \tilde{R}_2, d_1, T_2, n'_1 \rangle \cdots \langle \tilde{R}_m, c_m, T_m, n_m, \emptyset, \tilde{R}_m, c_m, T_m, n_m \rangle.$$

then $\delta' = \delta[g_1\#id_1/h_1\#id'_1, \ldots, g_o\#id_o/h_o\#id'_o]$ with for each $j \in [1, o]$, $id_j \leq n_1$ and $id'_j \leq n_1$ is:

$$\delta' = \langle \tilde{R}^*_1, c_1, T^*_1, n_1, \tilde{L}^*_1, \tilde{R}^*_2, d_1, T^*_2, n'_1 \rangle \cdots \langle \tilde{R}^*_m, c_m, T^*_m, n_m, \emptyset, \tilde{R}^*_m, c_m, T^*_m, n_m \rangle.$$

where $\tilde{R}^*_i=\tilde{R}_i[g_1\#id_1/h_1\#id'_1, \ldots, g_o\#id_o/h_o\#id'_o]$, $T^*_i=T_i[id_1/id'_1, \ldots, id_o/id'_o]$ and $\tilde{L}^*_j=\tilde{L}_j[g_1\#id_1/h_1\#id'_1, \ldots, g_o\#id_o/h_o\#id'_o]$ with $1 \leq i \leq m$, $1 \leq j \leq m-1$.

The following lemma allows to substitute constraints of a goal by other constraints that differ only for the identifier used. This will be used to substitute the assumptions by stable atoms in a sequence.

Lemma 11. *Let P be a program and R be a goal,*

$$\delta = \langle \tilde{R}_1, c_1, T_1, n_1, \tilde{L}_1, \tilde{R}_2, d_1, T_2, n'_1 \rangle \cdots \langle \tilde{R}_m, c_m, T_m, n_m, \emptyset, \tilde{R}_m, c_m, T_m, n_m \rangle$$
$$\in \mathcal{S}'_P(R),$$

where $\tilde{R}_1$ is an identified version of R, and let $\tilde{L}' = \{h_1 \# id'_1, \ldots, h_o \# id'_o\}$ and let $\tilde{L} = \{g_1 \# id_1, \ldots, g_o \# id_o\}$ be two sets of identified atoms such that for each $j \in [1, o]$ the following holds

- $id_j \leq n_1$ and $id'_j \leq n_1$
- $CT \models c \wedge h_j \leftrightarrow c \wedge g_j$,
- $id'_j \notin id(\delta)$
- *either $g_j \# id_j \in \tilde{R}_1$ or $id_j \notin id(\delta)$ and*
- $T_m[id_1/id'_1, \ldots, id_o/id'_o]$ *is defined.*

Then $\delta[g_1 \# id_1/h_1 \# id'_1, \ldots, g_o \# id_o/h_o \# id'_o] \in \mathcal{S}'_P(R')$, where $R' = chr(\tilde{R}_1[g_1 \# id_1/h_1 \# id'_1, \ldots, g_o \# id_o/h_o \# id'_o])$.

Proof. Straightforward by Lemma 10 and by induction on the length of δ. $\qquad \square$

Finally we can prove Lemma 3 which shows that fixed two concrete sequences for the goals H and G, there exists a concrete sequence for (H, G), whose abstraction is equal to the abstraction of the composition of the two given sequences.

Lemma 3. *Let P be a program, let H and G be two goals and assume that $\delta_1 \in \mathcal{S}'_P(H)$ and $\delta_2 \in \mathcal{S}'_P(G)$ are two sequences such that the following holds:*

1. $\alpha(\delta_1) \parallel \alpha(\delta_2)$ *is defined,*
2. $\sigma = \langle c_1, \tilde{K}_1, \tilde{W}_1, d_1 \rangle \cdots \langle c_m, \tilde{W}_m, T_m \rangle \in \eta(\alpha(\delta_1) \parallel \alpha(\delta_2))$,
3. $(V_{loc}(\alpha(\delta_1)) \cup V_{loc}(\alpha(\delta_2))) \cap V_{ass}(\sigma) = \emptyset$,
4. *For $i \in [1, m]$, $(V_{loc}(\alpha(\delta_1)) \cup V_{loc}(\alpha(\delta_2))) \cap Fv(c_i) \subseteq \bigcup_{j=1}^{i-1} Fv(d_j)$.*

Then there exists $\delta \in \mathcal{S}'_P(H, G)$ such that $\alpha(\delta) \simeq \sigma$.

Proof. The proof is by induction on length of δ. First we consider two concrete sequences (elements of $\mathcal{S}eq$): $\delta_1 \in \mathcal{S}'_p(H)$ and $\delta_2 \in \mathcal{S}'_p(G)$ and their composition. Then we will prove that the first concrete tuple whose abstraction provide the first abstract tuple of the composed abstract sequence, represents a derivation step for (H, G). Afterward we will prove that the inductive abstract sequence satisfies the four properties described in the hypothesis of the lemma. Then the existence of $\delta \in \mathcal{S}'_p(H, G)$ will follow by compatibility. Finally the existence of a rename ρ such that $\sigma = \alpha(\delta)\rho$ will be proven.

First of all, observe that since $\alpha(\delta_1) \parallel \alpha(\delta_2)$ is defined, we can assume without loss of generality, that the following holds:

i. $InG(\delta_1) = \tilde{H}$, $InG(\delta_2) = \tilde{G}$. $Intok(\delta_1) = T_1'$, $Intok(\delta_2) = T_1''$ and $Inid(\delta_1) = p_1$ and $Inid(\delta_2) = q_1$ such that

ii. for each $h \in id(\tilde{H})$ and $k \in id(\tilde{G})$, $h \neq k$, $h \leq q_1$, $k \leq p_1$ and

iii. for each $j \in [1, l]$ and $r@i_1, \ldots, i_l \in T_1'$, $\{i_1, \ldots, i_l\} \not\subseteq id(\delta_2)$ and $i_j \leq q_1$ and for each $r@i_1, \ldots, i_l \in T_1''$, $\{i_1, \ldots, i_l\} \not\subseteq id(\delta_1)$ and $i_j \leq p_1$.

In the remaining part of the proof, given two derivations $\delta_1 \in S_P'(H)$ and $\delta_2 \in S_P'(G)$, which verify the previous conditions, we can construct by induction on the $l = length(\sigma)$ a derivation $\delta \in S_P'(H, G)$ such that the following conditions hold

1. $InG(\delta)=(\tilde{H}, \tilde{G})=(InG(\delta_1), InG(\delta_2))$, $V_{loc}(\delta) \subseteq V_{loc}(\delta_1) \cup V_{loc}(\delta_2)$, $Intok(\delta) = T_1' \cup T_1''$, $Inid(\delta) = n_1$, where n_1 is the minimum between p_1 and q_1, $Inc(\delta) \subseteq Inc(\delta_1) \cup Inc(\delta_2)$,

2. $Ass(\delta) \subseteq Ass(\delta_1) \cup Ass(\delta_2)$ and

3. there exists a renaming ρ such that $\sigma = \alpha(\delta)\rho$ (and therefore $\sigma \simeq \alpha(\delta)$) and $\rho(id) = id$ for each $id \leq Inid(\delta)$.

$(l = 1)$. In this case $\delta_1 = \langle \tilde{H}, c, T', p, \emptyset, \tilde{H}, c, T', p \rangle$, $\delta_2 = \langle \tilde{G}, c, T'', q, \emptyset, \tilde{G}, c, T'', q \rangle$, $\alpha(\delta_1) = \langle c, \tilde{H}, T' \rangle$, $\alpha(\delta_2) = \langle c, \tilde{G}, T'' \rangle$, $\sigma = \langle c, (\tilde{H}, \tilde{G}), T' \cup T'' \rangle$ and $\delta = \langle (\tilde{H}, \tilde{G}), c, T, n, \emptyset, (\tilde{H}, \tilde{G}), c, T, n \rangle$, where $T = T' \cup T''$ and (by using assumptions **ii** and **iii**) n is the minimum between p and q.

$(l > 1)$. Without loss of generality, we can assume that

$$\delta_1 = t' \cdot \delta_1', \quad \delta_2 = \langle \tilde{G}, e_1, T_1'', q_1, \tilde{J}_1, \tilde{G}_2, f_1, T_2'', q_1' \rangle \cdot \delta_2'$$

where the following holds

- $t' = \langle \tilde{H}, c_1, T_1', p_1, \tilde{L}_1, \tilde{H}_2, d_1, T_2', p_1' \rangle$, $\delta_1' \in S_P'(H_2)$, t' is compatible with δ_1' and $\sigma_1 = \alpha(\delta_1) = \langle c_1, \tilde{L}_1, \tilde{N}_1, d_1 \rangle \cdot \alpha(\delta_1')$ where $\tilde{N}_1$ is the set of stable atoms for σ_1.

- $\delta_2' \in S_P'(G_2) \cup \varepsilon$ and if $\delta_2' \in S_P'(G_2)$ then $\sigma_2 = \alpha(\delta_2) = \langle e_1, \tilde{J}_1, \tilde{M}_1, f_1 \rangle \cdot \alpha(\delta_2')$ and $\tilde{M}_1$ is the set of stable atoms for σ_2, else $\sigma_2 = \alpha(\delta_2) = \langle e_1, \tilde{M}_1, T_1'' \rangle$ and $\tilde{M}_1 = \tilde{G}$.

- $\sigma \in \eta(\langle c_1, \tilde{L}_1, \tilde{N}_1 \cup \tilde{M}_1, d_1 \rangle \cdot \sigma')$ and $\sigma' \in \eta(\alpha(\delta_1') \parallel \sigma_2)$.

where we denote by ε the empty sequence.

In this case, without loss of generality, we can assume that $p_1' \leq q_1$.

By definition of η, there exist the sets of identified atoms $\tilde{L}', \tilde{L}'', \tilde{L}$ such that

$$\tilde{L} = \{g_1 \# id_1, \ldots, g_o \# id_o\} \subseteq \tilde{L}_1 \text{ and}$$
$$\tilde{L}' = \{h_1 \# id_1', \ldots, h_o \# id_o'\} \subseteq ((\tilde{N}_1 \cup \tilde{M}_1) \setminus \tilde{L}''),$$

where

1. $\tilde{L}''$ is the set of stable atoms of $(\tilde{N}_1 \cup \tilde{M}_1)$ used in $\eta(\alpha(\delta_1') \parallel \sigma_2)$, in order to obtain σ'.

2. for $1 \leq j \leq o$, $CT \models (c_1 \wedge g_j) \leftrightarrow (c_1 \wedge h_j)$ and

3. $\sigma = (\langle c_1, \tilde{K}_1, \tilde{W}_1, d_1 \rangle \cdot (\sigma' \setminus \tilde{L}'))[g_1 \# id_1 / h_1 \# id_1', \ldots, g_o \# id_o / h_o \# id_o']$ is defined, where $\tilde{K}_1 = \tilde{L}_1 \setminus \tilde{L}$ and $\tilde{W}_1 = (\tilde{N}_1 \cup \tilde{M}_1) \setminus (\tilde{L}' \cup \tilde{L}'')$.

Now observe that the following holds:

- Since $t' = \langle \tilde{H}, c_1, T'_1, p_1, \tilde{L}_1, \tilde{H}_2, d_1, T'_2, p'_1 \rangle$ represents a derivation step for H and since by hypothesis for each $k \in id(G)$, $k \leq p_1$ and for each $r@i_1, \ldots, i_l \in T''_1$, $\{i_1, \ldots, i_l\} \not\subseteq id(\delta_1)$, we can conclude that

$$t'' = \langle (\tilde{H}, \tilde{G}), c_1, T'_1 \cup T''_1, p_1, \tilde{L}_1, (\tilde{H}_2, \tilde{G}), d_1, T'_2 \cup T''_1, p'_1 \rangle$$

represents a derivation step for (H, G).

- Since

$$\sigma = (\langle c_1, \tilde{K}_1, \tilde{W}_1, d_1 \rangle \cdot (\sigma' \setminus \tilde{L}')) [g_1 \# id_1 / h_1 \# id'_1, \ldots, g_o \# id_o / h_o \# id'_o]$$

is defined and by definition of $\|$, we have that $(T'_2 \cup T''_1)[id_1/id'_1, \ldots, id_o/id'_o]$ is defined

- By previous observations and Lemma 9,

$$t = \langle (\tilde{H}, \tilde{G}), c_1, T'_1 \cup T''_1, p_1, \tilde{K}'_1, \tilde{B}, d_1, T'', p''_1 \rangle$$

represents a derivation step for (H, G), where
  - $\{p_1 + 1, \ldots, p_1 + k\} = id(\tilde{L}_1)$ and $\rho_1 = [p_1 + 1/j_1, \ldots, p_1 + k/j_k]$ is a renaming,
  - $\tilde{K}'_1 = (\tilde{L}_1 \setminus \tilde{L})\rho_1 = \tilde{K}_1 \rho_1$,
  - $\tilde{B} = ((\tilde{H}_2, \tilde{G}) \setminus \tilde{L}')[g_1 \# id_1 / h_1 \# id'_1, \ldots, g_o \# id_o / h_o \# id'_o]\rho_1$,
  - $T'' = (T'_2 \cup T''_1)[id_1/id'_1, \ldots, id_o/id'_o]\rho_1$, $p''_1 \leq p'_1$ and $V_{loc}(t) = V_{loc}(t')$.

Moreover, the following holds:

$\alpha(\delta'_1) \| \alpha(\delta_2)$ **is defined.** Since $\alpha(\delta_1) \| \alpha(\delta_2)$ is defined, we can assume that $id(\delta_1) \cap id(\delta_2) = \emptyset$ and so $id(\delta'_1) \cap id(\delta_2) = \emptyset$. Then by definition, we have only to prove that

$$(V_{loc}(\alpha(\delta'_1)) \cup Fv(H_2)) \cap (V_{loc}(\alpha(\delta_2)) \cup Fv(G)) = Fv(H_2) \cap Fv(G).$$

First of all, observe that since $V_{loc}(\alpha(\delta'_1)) \subseteq V_{loc}(\alpha(\delta_1))$ and $\alpha(\delta_1) \| \alpha(\delta_2)$ is defined, we have that $V_{loc}(\alpha(\delta'_1)) \cap (V_{loc}(\alpha(\delta_2)) \cup Fv(G)) = \emptyset$ and $(Fv(H) \cup V_{loc}(\alpha(\delta_1))) \cap (V_{loc}(\alpha(\delta_2))) = \emptyset$.

Now, observe that according to definition of derivation

$$Fv(H_2) \subseteq Fv(H) \cup V_{loc}(\alpha(\delta_1)) \cup Fv(L_1)$$

and therefore, $Fv(H_2) \cap V_{loc}(\alpha(\delta_2)) = Fv(L_1) \cap V_{loc}(\alpha(\delta_2))$. Then by previous observations

$$(V_{loc}(\alpha(\delta'_1)) \cup Fv(H_2)) \cap (V_{loc}(\alpha(\delta_2)) \cup Fv(G))$$
$$= (Fv(H_2) \cap Fv(G)) \cup (Fv(L_1) \cap V_{loc}(\alpha(\delta_2))).$$

We now, assume that there exists $x \in Fv(L_1) \cap V_{loc}(\alpha(\delta_2))$ and that $g \in L_1$ such that $x \in Fv(g)$. Since as seen in Point 3. of the hypothesis $V_{loc}(\alpha(\delta_2)) \cap V_{ass}(\sigma) = \emptyset$, we can maintain that $g \notin K_1$ and therefore there exists $g' \in G$ such that $CT \models c_1 \wedge g \leftrightarrow c_1 \wedge g'$. Now, observe that, since $g' \in G$ and $x \in V_{loc}(\alpha(\delta_2))$, we have that $x \notin Fv(g')$ and therefore we can further say that $x \in Fv(c_1)$ and $CT \not\models \exists_x c_1 \leftrightarrow c_1$. Then, since by definition of $\|$, $CT \models e_1 \rightarrow c_1$, either $x \in Fv(e_1)$ or $CT \models e_1 \leftrightarrow \texttt{false}$. In both cases $x \notin V_{loc}(\alpha(\delta_2))$ and it then follows that $Fv(L_1) \cap V_{loc}(\alpha(\delta_2)) = \emptyset$.

$\sigma' = \langle c_2, \tilde{K}_2, \tilde{W}_2 \cup \tilde{L}', d_2 \rangle \cdots \langle c_m, \tilde{W}_m \cup \tilde{L}', T_m \rangle \in \eta(\alpha(\delta_1') \parallel \alpha(\delta_2))$. The proof is straightforward, by definition of $\parallel$.

$(V_{loc}(\alpha(\delta_1')) \cup V_{loc}(\alpha(\delta_2))) \cap V_{ass}(\sigma') = \emptyset$. According to the definition, the hypothesis and Lemma 1, we have that

$$(V_{loc}(\alpha(\delta_1')) \cup V_{loc}(\alpha(\delta_2))) \cap V_{ass}(\sigma') \subseteq$$
$$(V_{loc}(\alpha(\delta_1)) \cup V_{loc}(\alpha(\delta_2))) \cap V_{ass}(\sigma) = \emptyset.$$

for $i \in [2, m]$, $(V_{loc}(\alpha(\delta_1')) \cup V_{loc}(\alpha(\delta_2))) \cap Fv(c_i) \subseteq \bigcup_{j=2}^{i-1} Fv(d_j)$.

To prove this statement, observe that by hypothesis and Lemma 1, for $i \in [2, m]$,

$$(V_{loc}(\alpha(\delta_1')) \cup V_{loc}(\alpha(\delta_2))) \cap Fv(c_i) \subseteq$$
$$(V_{loc}(\alpha(\delta_1)) \cup V_{loc}(\alpha(\delta_2))) \cap Fv(c_i) \subseteq$$
$$\bigcup_{j=1}^{i-1} Fv(d_j).$$

Let $i \in [2, m]$, such that there exists $x \in (V_{loc}(\alpha(\delta_1')) \cup V_{loc}(\alpha(\delta_2))) \cap Fv(c_i) \cap Fv(d_1)$. By the hypothesis $x \notin Fv(c_1)$. Then, since $x \in Fv(d_1) \subseteq Fv(t')$ and t' is compatible with δ_1', we may conclude that $x \notin V_{loc}(\alpha(\delta_1'))$ and therefore $x \in V_{loc}(\alpha(\delta_2))$. By Lemma 1 and since $\alpha(\delta_1) \parallel \alpha(\delta_2)$ is defined, we have that $x \notin Fv(H)$ and therefore, by definition of derivation, we can say that $CT \not\models \exists_x d_1 \leftrightarrow d_1$. According to the definition of $\parallel$, $CT \models e_1 \rightarrow d_1$ and therefore, since $x \in Fv(d_1)$ and $CT \not\models \exists_x d_1 \leftrightarrow d_1$, either $x \in Fv(e_1)$ or $CT \models e_1 \leftrightarrow \texttt{false}$. In both the cases $x \notin V_{loc}(\alpha(\delta_2))$. As in previous observations

$$(V_{loc}(\alpha(\delta_1')) \cup V_{loc}(\alpha(\delta_2))) \cap Fv(c_i) \subseteq \bigcup_{j=2}^{i-1} Fv(d_j)$$

and then the thesis holds.

Moreover, by construction the following holds

- $Intok(\delta_1') = T_2'$ and $Inid(\delta_1') = p_2$. Since by definition of derivation $p_2 \geq p_1$ and by hypothesis for each $k \in id(\tilde{G})$, $k \leq p_1$, we have that for each $h \in id(\tilde{H}_2)$, $h \neq k$ and $k \leq p_2$. Moreover, without loss of generality, we can assume that for each $h \in id(\tilde{H}_2)$, $h \leq q_1$.
- by definition of derivation, if $T_2' \neq T_1'$, $T_2' = T_1' \cup \{r@id_1, \ldots, id_l\}$ such that $\{id_1, \ldots, id_l\} \subseteq id(\delta_1)$. Then since by hypothesis $id(\delta_1) \cap id(\delta_2) = \emptyset$ and for each $r@i_1, \ldots, i_l \in T_1'$, $\{i_1, \ldots, i_l\} \not\subseteq id(\delta_2)$, we have that for each $r@i_1, \ldots, i_l \in T_2'$, $\{i_1, \ldots, i_l\} \not\subseteq id(\delta_2)$.

By previous results and by inductive hypothesis, we have that there exists $\delta' \in S_P'(H_2, G)$ such that

1. $InG(\delta') = (InG(\delta_1'), InG(\delta_2)) = (\tilde{H}_2, \tilde{G})$, $V_{loc}(\delta') \subseteq V_{loc}(\delta_1') \cup V_{loc}(\delta_2)$, $Intok(\delta') = T_2' \cup T_1''$, $Inid(\delta') = m_2$, where m_2 is the minimum between p_2 and q_1, $Inc(\delta') \subseteq Inc(\delta_1') \cup Inc(\delta_2)$,
2. $Ass(\delta') \subseteq Ass(\delta_1') \cup Ass(\delta_2)$ and
3. there exists a renaming ρ' such that $\sigma' = \alpha(\delta')\rho'$ (and therefore $\sigma' \simeq \alpha(\delta')$) and $\rho'(id) = id$ for each $id \leq Inid(\delta')$.

Moreover by definition of η, $\tilde{L}' \subseteq (\tilde{H}, \tilde{G})$ is a set of atoms which are stable in δ'. Let $\delta'' \in \mathcal{S}'_P(R')$ the derivation obtained form δ' by deleting from each goal in δ' the atoms in $\tilde{L}'$, where $\tilde{R}' = (\tilde{H}_2, \tilde{G}) \setminus \tilde{L}'$ and $R' = chr(\tilde{R}')$.

By construction and by Lemma 11

$$\bar{\delta} = \delta''[g_1\#id_1/h_1\#id'_1, \ldots, g_o\#id_o/h_o\#id'_o]\rho_1 \in \mathcal{S}'_P(R),$$

where

- $InG(\bar{\delta}) = \tilde{R} = \tilde{R}'[g_1\#id_1/h_1\#id'_1, \ldots, g_o\#id_o/h_o\#id'_o]\rho_1$, $R = chr(\tilde{R})$,
- $Intok(\bar{\delta}) = (T'_2 \cup T''_1)[id_1/id'_1, \ldots, id_o/id'_o]\rho_1$ and
- $V_{loc}(\bar{\delta}) = V_{loc}(\delta'') = V_{loc}(\delta')$.

Let us denote by δ the sequence $t \cdot \bar{\delta}$.

Then, to prove the thesis, we have to prove that $t \cdot \bar{\delta} \in \mathcal{S}eq$, t is compatible with $\bar{\delta}$ (and therefore $\delta \in \mathcal{S}'_P(H, G)$), $V_{loc}(\delta) \subseteq V_{loc}(\delta_1) \cup V_{loc}(\delta_2)$, $Inc(\delta) \subseteq Inc(\delta_1) \cup Inc(\delta_2)$, $Ass(\delta) \subseteq Ass(\delta_1) \cup Ass(\delta_2)$ and $\sigma \simeq \alpha(\delta)$.

$(t \cdot \bar{\delta} \in \mathcal{S}eq)$. By construction, we have only to prove that $CT \models instore(\bar{\delta}) \rightarrow d_1$. The proof is straightforward, since by construction either $instore(\bar{\delta}) = instore(\delta'_1)$ or $instore(\bar{\delta}) = instore(\delta_2)$.

$(t$ **is compatible with** $\bar{\delta})$. The following holds.

1. $V_{loc}(\bar{\delta}) \cap Fv(t) = \emptyset$. By construction and by inductive hypothesis

$$V_{loc}(t) = V_{loc}(t'), \quad Fv(t) \subseteq Fv(t') \cup Fv(G) \text{ and}$$
$$V_{loc}(\bar{\delta}) = V_{loc}(\delta') \subseteq V_{loc}(\delta'_1) \cup V_{loc}(\delta_2). \tag{22}$$

Since t' is compatible with δ'_1 (Definition 7 point 1) and $\alpha(\delta'_1) \parallel \alpha(\delta_2)$ is defined, we have that

$$V_{loc}(\delta'_1) \cap (Fv(t') \cup Fv(G)) = \emptyset. \tag{23}$$

By points 3. and 4. of the hypothesis $Fv(K_1, c_1) \cap V_{loc}(\delta_2) = \emptyset$ and by definition of derivation $Fv(G) \cap V_{loc}(\delta_2) = \emptyset$. Moreover, by point 1. of the hypothesis we have that $\alpha(\delta_1) \parallel \alpha(\delta_2)$ is defined and therefore $(Fv(H) \cup V_{loc}(t')) \cap V_{loc}(\delta_2) = \emptyset$. Then by definition and by the first statement in (22)

$$Fv(t) \cap V_{loc}(\delta_2) = (Fv(c_1, H, G, K_1) \cup V_{loc}(t')) \cap V_{loc}(\delta_2) = \emptyset. \tag{24}$$

Then

$V_{loc}(\bar{\delta}) \cap Fv(t)$	$\subseteq$ (by the last statement in (22))
$(V_{loc}(\delta'_1) \cup V_{loc}(\delta_2)) \cap Fv(t)$	$\subseteq$ (by the second statement in (22) and by (23))
$V_{loc}(\delta_2) \cap Fv(t)$	$=$ (by (24))
$\emptyset.$	

2. $V_{loc}(t) \cap V_{ass}(\bar{\delta}) = \emptyset$. The proof is immediate by point 3. of the hypothesis.
3. for $i \in [2, n]$, $V_{loc}(t) \cap Fv(c_i) \subseteq \bigcup_{j=1}^{i-1} Fv(d_j)$. The proof is immediate by construction and by point 4. of hypothesis.

$(V_{loc}(\delta) \subseteq V_{loc}(\delta_1) \cup V_{loc}(\delta_2))$. By construction

$$
\begin{aligned}
V_{loc}(\delta) & = \text{(by construction)} \\
V_{loc}(t) \cup V_{loc}(\bar{\delta}) & = \text{(by construction)} \\
V_{loc}(t') \cup V_{loc}(\delta') & \subseteq \text{(by previous results)} \\
V_{loc}(t') \cup V_{loc}(\delta_1') \cup V_{loc}(\delta_2) & = \text{(by construction)} \\
V_{loc}(\delta_1) \cup V_{loc}(\delta_2). &
\end{aligned}
$$

$(Inc(\delta) \subseteq Inc(\delta_1) \cup Inc(\delta_2))$

$$
\begin{aligned}
Inc(\delta) & = \text{(by construction)} \\
\{c_1\} \cup Inc(\bar{\delta}) & = \text{(by construction)} \\
\{c_1\} \cup Inc(\delta') & \subseteq \text{(by previous results)} \\
\{c_1\} \cup Inc(\delta_1') \cup Inc(\delta_2) & = \text{(by construction)} \\
Inc(\delta_1) \cup Inc(\delta_2). &
\end{aligned}
$$

$(Ass(\delta) \subseteq Ass(\delta_1) \cup Ass(\delta_2))$

$$
\begin{aligned}
Ass(\delta) & = \text{(by construction)} \\
Ass(t) \cup Ass(\bar{\delta}) & = \text{(by definition of } Ass(t)) \\
(\tilde{L}_1 \setminus \tilde{L}) \cup Ass(\bar{\delta}) & \subseteq \text{(by definition of } \setminus) \\
\tilde{L}_1 \cup Ass(\bar{\delta}) & \subseteq \text{(by definition of } \bar{\delta}) \\
\tilde{L}_1 \cup Ass(\delta') & \subseteq \text{(by previous results)} \\
\tilde{L}_1 \cup Ass(\delta_1') \cup Ass(\delta_2) & = \text{(by construction)} \\
Ass(\delta_1) \cup Ass(\delta_2). &
\end{aligned}
$$

(there exists a renaming ρ such that $\sigma = \alpha(\delta)\rho$ (and therefore $\sigma \simeq \alpha(\delta)$) and $\rho(id) = id$ for each $id \leq n_1$). By inductive hypothesis there exists a renaming ρ' such that $\sigma' = \alpha(\delta')\rho'$ and $\rho'(id) = id$ for each $id \leq n_2$. Since by definition of derivation, for each $j \in id(\tilde{L}')$, $j \leq n_2$ we have that $\rho'(j) = j$ for each $j \in id(\tilde{L}')$. Then

$$
\begin{aligned}
\sigma' \setminus \tilde{L}' & = \text{(since } \sigma' = \alpha(\delta')\rho') \\
\alpha(\delta')\rho' \setminus \tilde{L}' & = \text{(by previous observation)} \\
(\alpha(\delta') \setminus \tilde{L}')\rho' & = \text{(by definition of } \setminus \text{ and } \alpha) \\
(\alpha(\delta' \setminus \tilde{L}'))\rho' & = \text{(by definition of } \delta'') \\
(\alpha(\delta''))\rho'. &
\end{aligned}
$$

Moreover, since for $i \in [1, o]$ and for $r \in [1, k]$, $id_i \leq n_2$ $id_i' \leq n_2$, $p_1 + r \leq n_2$ and $j_r \leq n_2$, we have that

$$
\begin{aligned}
(\alpha(\delta''))\rho'[g_1 \# id_1/h_1 \# id_1', \ldots, g_o \# id_o/h_o \# id_o']\rho_1 = \\
(\alpha(\delta''))[g_1 \# id_1/h_1 \# id_1', \ldots, g_o \# id_o/h_o \# id_o']\rho_1\rho'
\end{aligned}
$$

and therefore

$$
\begin{aligned}
(\sigma' \setminus \tilde{L}')[g_1 \# id_1/h_1 \# id_1', \ldots, g_o \# id_o/h_o \# id_o']\rho_1 = \\
\text{(by previous result)} \\
(\alpha(\delta''))\rho'[g_1 \# id_1/h_1 \# id_1', \ldots, g_o \# id_o/h_o \# id_o']\rho_1 = \\
\text{(by previous observation)}
\end{aligned}
$$

$$(\alpha(\delta''))[g_1\#id_1/h_1\#id'_1, \ldots, g_o\#id_o/h_o\#id'_o]\rho_1\rho' =$$
$$\text{(by definition of } \bar{\delta})$$
$$(\alpha(\bar{\delta}))\rho'.$$

Then, by definition of renaming

$$(\sigma' \setminus \tilde{L}')[g_1\#id_1/h_1\#id'_1, \ldots, g_o\#id_o/h_o\#id'_o] = (\alpha(\bar{\delta}))\rho \qquad (25)$$

where $\rho = \rho'\rho_2$ and $\rho_2 = [j_1/p_1 + 1, \ldots, j_k/p_1 + k] = \rho_1^{-1}$.

By definition, we have that ρ is a renaming and by construction $\rho(j) = j$ for each $j \leq n_1$.

By definition of δ, we have that

$$\alpha(\delta)\rho \qquad\qquad\quad = \text{(by definition of } \alpha \text{ and } \delta)$$
$$\langle c_1, \tilde{K}'_1\rho, \tilde{W}'_1\rho, d_1 \rangle \cdot \alpha(\bar{\delta})\rho = \text{(by definition of renaming and by (25))}$$
$$\langle c_1, \tilde{K}'_1\rho, \tilde{W}'_1\rho, d_1 \rangle \cdot (\sigma' \setminus \tilde{L}')[g_1\#id_1/h_1\#id'_1, \ldots, g_o\#id_o/h_o\#id'_o]. \quad (26)$$

where $\tilde{W}'_1 = \tilde{B}_1 \cap \tilde{B}_2$, where $\tilde{B}_1$ and $\tilde{B}_2$ are the sets of atoms in $(\tilde{H}, \tilde{G})$ which are not rewritten by t and by $\bar{\delta}$, respectively. Now observe that since $\tilde{K}'_1 = \tilde{K}_1\rho_1$ and since $\rho'(j) = j$ for each $j \leq n_2$, we have that

$$\tilde{K}'_1\rho = \tilde{K}_1\rho_1\rho = \tilde{K}_1\rho_1\rho'\rho_2 = \tilde{K}_1\rho_1\rho_2 = \tilde{K}_1. \qquad (27)$$

Moreover, by construction $\tilde{B}_1 = ((\tilde{N}_1 \cup \tilde{M}_1) \setminus \tilde{L}')$ and by (25) $\tilde{B}_2 = (\tilde{W}'_2 \setminus \tilde{L}')[g_1\#id_1/h_1\#id'_1, \ldots, g_o\#id_o/h_o\#id'_o]\rho^{-1}$, where $\tilde{W}'_2$ is the first stable set of σ'. Then

$$\tilde{W}'_1 = ((\tilde{N}_1 \cup \tilde{M}_1) \setminus \tilde{L}') \cap$$
$$(\tilde{W}'_2 \setminus \tilde{L}')[g_1\#id_1/h_1\#id'_1, \ldots, g_o\#id_o/h_o\#id'_o]\rho^{-1}. \quad (28)$$

Now, observe that $\rho(j) = j$ for each $j \leq n_1$ and for each $i \in id((\tilde{N}_1 \cup \tilde{M}_1) \setminus \tilde{L}')$, we have that $i \leq n_1$. Then by (28)

$$\tilde{W}'_1 = ((\tilde{N}_1 \cup \tilde{M}_1) \setminus \tilde{L}') \cap$$
$$(\tilde{W}'_2 \setminus \tilde{L}')[g_1\#id_1/h_1\#id'_1, \ldots, g_o\#id_o/h_o\#id'_o]. \quad (29)$$

By construction for each $i \in [1, o]$, we have that $id_i > n_1$ and $id'_i \in id(\tilde{L}')$. Then by (29)
$$\tilde{W}'_1 = ((\tilde{N}_1 \cup \tilde{M}_1) \setminus \tilde{L}') \cap (\tilde{W}'_2 \setminus L').$$

By construction and by definition of $\|$, $W'_2 = ((\tilde{N}_2 \cup \tilde{M}_1) \setminus \tilde{L}'')$, where $\tilde{N}_2$ is the set of stable atoms of $\alpha(\delta'_1)$, and therefore, by the previous result

$$\tilde{W}'_1 = ((\tilde{N}_1 \cup \tilde{M}_1) \setminus \tilde{L}') \cap ((\tilde{N}_2 \cup \tilde{M}_1) \setminus \tilde{L}''). \qquad (30)$$

Moreover, since for each $i \in [1, o]$, $id_i \in id(\tilde{L})$ we have that

$$\tilde{W}_1 = \tilde{W}_1[g_1\#id_1/h_1\#id'_1, \ldots, g_o\#id_o/h_o\#id'_o] \text{ and}$$
$$\tilde{K}_1 = \tilde{K}_1[g_1\#id_1/h_1\#id'_1, \ldots, g_o\#id_o/h_o\#id'_o] \qquad (31)$$

Then

$$
\begin{array}{ll}
\tilde{W}_1'\rho & = \text{(since } \rho(i) = i \text{ for each } i \le n_1) \\
\tilde{W}_1' & = \text{(by (30))} \\
((\tilde{N}_1 \cup \tilde{M}_1) \setminus \tilde{L}') \cap (((\tilde{N}_2 \cup \tilde{M}_1) \setminus \tilde{L}'') & = \text{(by properties of set operators)} \\
((\tilde{N}_1 \cup \tilde{M}_1) \cap (\tilde{N}_2 \cup \tilde{M}_1)) \setminus (\tilde{L}' \cup \tilde{L}'') & = \text{(since by definition } \tilde{N}_1 \subseteq \tilde{N}_2) \\
(\tilde{N}_1 \cup \tilde{M}_1) \setminus (\tilde{L}' \cup \tilde{L}'') & = \text{(by construction)} \\
\tilde{W}_1 &
\end{array}
$$

and therefore

$$
\begin{array}{ll}
\alpha(\delta)\rho & = \\
\quad \text{(by (26))} & \\
\langle c_1, \tilde{K}_1'\rho, \tilde{W}_1'\rho, d_1 \rangle \cdot (\sigma' \setminus L')[g_1 \# id_1 / h_1 \# id_1', \dots, g_o \# id_o / h_o \# id_o'] & = \\
\quad \text{(by (27) and previous result)} & \\
\langle c_1, \tilde{K}_1, \tilde{W}_1, d_1 \rangle \cdot (\sigma' \setminus L')[g_1 \# id_1 / h_1 \# id_1', \dots, g_o \# id_o / h_o \# id_o'] & = \\
\quad \text{(by (31))} & \\
(\langle c_1, \tilde{K}_1, \tilde{W}_1, d_1 \rangle \cdot (\sigma' \setminus L'))[g_1 \# id_1 / h_1 \# id_1', \dots, g_o \# id_o / h_o \# id_o'] & = \\
\quad \text{(by definition)} & \\
\sigma &
\end{array}
$$

and then the thesis holds.   □

CHR for Imperative Host Languages

Peter Van Weert*, Pieter Wuille, Tom Schrijvers**, and Bart Demoen

Department of Computer Science, K.U.Leuven, Belgium
FirstName.LastName@cs.kuleuven.be

Abstract. In this paper, we address the different conceptual and technical difficulties encountered when embedding CHR into an imperative host language. We argue that a tight, natural integration leads to a powerful programming language extension, intuitive to both CHR and imperative programmers. We show how to compile CHR to highly optimized imperative code. To this end, we first review the well-established CHR compilation scheme, and survey the large body of possible optimizations. We then show that this scheme, when used for compilation to imperative target languages, leads to stack overflows. We therefore introduce new optimizations that considerably improve the performance of recursive CHR programs. Rules written using tail calls are even guaranteed to run in constant space. We implemented systems for both Java and C, following the language design principles and compilation scheme presented in this paper, and show that our implementations outperform other state-of-the-art CHR compilers by several orders of magnitude.

1 Introduction

Constraint Handling Rules (CHR) [1, 2, 3] is a high-level programming language extension based on guarded, multi-headed, committed-choice multiset rewrite rules. Originally designed for writing user-defined constraint solvers, CHR has matured as a powerful and elegant general purpose language used in a wide range of application domains.

CHR is usually embedded in a CLP host language, such as Prolog [4, 5, 6] or HAL [7, 8]. Real world, industrial software however is mainly written in imperative or object-oriented programming languages. For many problems, however, declarative approaches are more effective. Applications such as planning and scheduling often lead to special-purpose constraint solvers. These are mostly written in the mainstream language itself because a seamless cooperation with existing components is indispensable. Such ad-hoc constraint solvers are notoriously difficult to maintain, modify and extend.

A multiparadigmatic integration of CHR and mainstream programming languages therefore offers powerful synergetic advantages to the software developer. A user-friendly and efficient CHR system lightens the design and development effort required for application-tailored constraint systems considerably. Adhering

---

* Research Assistant of the Research Foundation– Flanders (FWO-Vlaanderen).
** Post-Doctoral Researcher of the Research Foundation– Flanders (FWO-Vlaanderen).

T. Schrijvers and T. Frühwirth (Eds.): Constraint Handling Rules, LNAI 5388, pp. 161–212, 2008.
© Springer-Verlag Berlin Heidelberg 2008

to common CHR semantics further facilitates the reuse of numerous constraint handlers already written in CHR. A proper embedding of CHR in a mainstream language conversely enables the use of innumerous existing software libraries and components in CHR programs.

In the past decade there has been a renewed interest in the integration and use of the rule-based paradigm, in particular *business rules*. Business rules are a technology derived from *production rules*, and are used extensively in real world applications. CHR, with its well-studied clean operational semantics and efficient implementation techniques presents a valid alternative for these tools. Arguably, for CHR to play a role here, embeddings in mainstream languages are required.

Existing CHR embeddings in imperative languages either lack performance [9, 10], or are designed to experiment with specific extensions of CHR [11]. Also, in our opinion, these systems do not provide a sufficiently natural integration of CHR with the imperative host language. Instead of incorporating the specifics of the new host into a combined language, these systems port part of the (C)LP host environment as well. This needlessly enlarges the paradigm shift for the programmers of the imperative host language. We will show that a tighter integration of both worlds leads to a useful and powerful language extension, intuitive to both CHR adepts and imperative programmers.

1.1   Overview and Contributions

Our contributions can be summarized as follows:

- We show how CHR can be integrated effectively with an imperative host language. In Section 3, we first outline the different language design issues faced when integrating these two different paradigms. Next, Section 4 outlines our solution, aimed at a tight and natural integration of both worlds. The approaches taken by related systems are discussed in Section 7.
- In Section 5 we present a compilation scheme from CHR to efficient, optimized imperative host language code. We survey generic optimizations, and show how they can be ported to the imperative setting. We also focus on implementation aspects and optimizations specific to imperative target languages.
- We developed mature and efficient implementations of the proposed language design for both Java and C, available at respectively [12] and [13]. The design of both language extensions is presented in Section 4, and their implementations are evaluated in Section 6.

The focus of this article is thus on the design and implementation of CHR systems for imperative host languages. First, we briefly introduce a generic, host language independent syntax and semantics of CHR. For a gentler introduction to CHR, we refer the reader to [2, 5, 7, 14].

2   Preliminaries: CHR Syntax and Semantics

CHR is embedded in a host language that provides a number of predefined constraints, called *built-in constraints*, and a number of data types. The traditional host language of CHR is Prolog. Its only built-in constraint is equality over its data types, logical variables and Herbrand terms. Asides from built-in constraints, practical implementations mostly allow arbitrary host language procedures to be called as well. Whilst most CHR systems are embedded in Prolog, efficient implementations also exist for Java, Haskell, and C (see Section 7). In this section we only consider the generic, host language independent syntax and semantics of CHR.

2.1 Syntax and Informal Semantics

A CHR program is called a *CHR handler*. It declares a number of user-defined *CHR constraints* and a sequence of *CHR rules*. The rules determine how the handler's CHR constraints are simplified and propagated. A *constraint*, either built-in or CHR, is written $c(X_1, \ldots, X_n)$. Here c is the constraint's *type*, and the X_i's are the constraint's *arguments*. The arguments are elements of a host language data type. The number of arguments, n, is called the constraint's *arity*, and c is called an n-ary constraint, commonly denoted c/n. For nullary constraints the empty argument list is omitted. Trivial nullary built-in constraints are **true** and **false**. Depending on the system, other symbolic notations can be used to express constraints. Equality for instance is mostly written using an infix notation, that is, '$X = Y$' is used instead of e.g. '$eq(X, Y)$'.

There are three kinds of CHR rules ($n, n_g, n_b \geq 1$ and $n \geq r > 1$):

- Simplification rules: $h_1, \ldots, h_n \Leftrightarrow g_1, \ldots, g_{n_g} \mid b_1, \ldots, b_{n_b}.$
- Propagation rules: $h_1, \ldots, h_n \Rightarrow g_1, \ldots, g_{n_g} \mid b_1, \ldots, b_{n_b}.$
- Simpagation rules: $h_1, \ldots, h_{r-1} \setminus h_r, \ldots, h_n \Leftrightarrow g_1, \ldots, g_{n_g} \mid b_1, \ldots, b_{n_b}.$

The *head* of a CHR rule is a sequence, or conjunction, of CHR constraints '$h_1, \ldots, h_n$'. A rule with n head constraints is called an n-*headed* rule; when $n > 1$ it is a *multi-headed* rule. The conjuncts h_i of the head are called *occurrences*. Both the occurrences in a simplification rule and the occurrences '$h_r, \ldots, h_n$' in a simpagation rule are called *removed occurrences*. All other occurrences are *kept occurrences*. The *body* of a CHR rule is a conjunction of CHR constraints and built-in constraints '$b_1, \ldots, b_{n_b}$'. The part of the rule between the arrow and the body is called the *guard*. It is a conjunction of built-in constraints. The guard '$g_1, \ldots, g_{n_g} \mid$' is optional; if omitted, it is considered to be '**true** $\mid$'. A rule is optionally preceded by a unique *rule identifier*, followed by the '@' symbol.

Example 1. The program LEQ, see Fig. 1, is a classic example CHR handler. It defines one CHR constraint, a less-than-or-equal constraint, using four CHR rules. All three kinds of rules are present. The constraint arguments are logical variables. The handler uses one built-in constraint, namely equality. If the *antisymmetry* is applied, its body adds a new built-in constraint to the built-in constraint solver provided by the host environment. The body of the *transitivity* rule adds a CHR constraint, which will be handled by the CHR handler itself. The informal operational semantics of the rules is explained below, in Example 2.

```
reflexivity   @ leq(X, X) ⇔ true.
antisymmetry  @ leq(X, Y), leq(Y, X) ⇔ X = Y.
idempotence   @ leq(X, Y) \ leq(X, Y) ⇔ true.
transitivity  @ leq(X, Y), leq(Y, Z) ⇒ leq(X, Z).
```

Fig. 1. The CHR program LEQ, a handler for the less-than-or-equal constraint

Informal Semantics. An execution starts from an initial query: a sequence of constraints, given by the user. The *multiset* of all CHR constraints of a CHR handler is called its *constraint store*. The execution proceeds by applying, or *firing*, the handler's rules. A rule is applicable if there are constraints matching the rule's occurrences present in the constraint store for which the guard condition holds. When no more rules can be applied, the execution stops; the final constraint store is called the *solution*.

Rules modify the constraint store as follows. A simplification rule removes the constraints that matched its head, and replaces them with those in its body. The double arrow indicates that the head is logically equivalent to the body, which justifies the replacement. Often, the body is a simpler, or more canonical form of the head. In propagation rules, the body is a consequence of the head: given the head, the body may be added (if the guard holds). As the body is implied by the head, it is redundant. However, adding redundant constraints may allow more rewriting later on. Simpagation rules are a hybrid between simplification and propagation rules: only the constraints matching its removed occurrences, i.e. those after the backslash, are removed if the rule is applied.

Example 2. The first rule of the LEQ handler of Fig. 1, *reflexivity*, replaces a leq(X,X) constraint by the trivial built-in constraint true. Operationally, this entails removing this constraint from the constraint store. The *antisymmetry* rule states that leq(X,Y) and leq(Y,X) are logically equivalent to X = Y. When firing this rule, the two constraints matching the left-hand side are removed from the store, after which the built-in equality constraint solver is told that X and Y are equal. The third rule, *idempotence*, removes redundant copies of the same leq constraint. It is necessary to do this explicitly since CHR has a *multiset semantics*: multiple instances of the same constraint can reside in the constraint store at the same time. The last rule, *transitivity*, is a propagation rule that computes the transitive closure of the leq relation.

2.2   The Refined Operational Semantics

The operational semantics introduced informally in the previous section corresponds to the so-called *high-level* or *theoretical operational semantics* of CHR [2, 15]. In this highly non-deterministic semantics, rules are applied in arbitrary order. Most CHR systems though implement a particular, significantly more deterministic instance of this semantics, called the *refined operational semantics*

[15]. This semantics is commonly denoted by ω_r. In ω_r, queries and bodies are executed *left-to-right*, treating the execution of each constraint as a procedure call. When a CHR constraint is executed, this constraint becomes *active*, and looks for matching rules in a *top-to-bottom* order. If a rule fires, the constraints in its body become active first. Only when these are fully handled, the control returns to the formerly active constraint.

The compilation scheme presented in Section 5 implements ω_r, and its optimizations are often justified by properties of this semantics. A sufficiently detailed introduction to this formalism is therefore warranted. For a more complete discussion, we refer the reader to [7, 15].

The ω_r semantics is formulated as a state transition system. Transition rules define the relation between subsequent execution states in a CHR execution. Sets, multisets and sequences (ordered multisets) are defined as usual.

Execution State. Formally, an execution state of ω_r is a tuple $\langle \mathbb{A}, \mathbb{S}, \mathbb{B}, \mathbb{T} \rangle_n$. The first element, the *execution stack* $\mathbb{A}$, is explained below, in the subsection on ω_r's transition rules. The CHR *constraint store* $\mathbb{S}$ is a set of *identified CHR constraints* that can be matched with the rules. An identified CHR constraint $c\#i$ is a CHR constraint c associated with a unique *constraint identifier* i. We introduce the mapping operators $chr(c\#i) = c$ and $id(c\#i) = i$, and extend them to sequences and sets in the obvious manner. The constraint identifier is used to distinguish otherwise identical constraints. This is why, even though $chr(\mathbb{S})$ is a multiset of constraints, $\mathbb{S}$ is indeed a set. The *built-in constraint store* $\mathbb{B}$ is the logical conjunction of all built-in constraints passed to the underlying constraint solvers. The *propagation history* $\mathbb{T}$ is a set of tuples, each recording a sequence of constraint identifiers of the CHR constraints that fired a rule, together with that rule's identifier. Its primary function is to prevent trivial non-termination for propagation rules. The integer counter n, finally, represents the next free constraint identifier.

Notation. In the following, we use $\mathbin{+\!\!+}$ for *sequence concatenation* and $\sqcup$ for *disjoint set union*[1]. For logical expressions X and Y, $vars(X)$ denotes the set of *free variables*, and $\bar{\exists}_Y(X) \leftrightarrow \exists v_1, \ldots, v_n : X$ with $\{v_1, \ldots, v_n\} = vars(X) \backslash vars(Y)$. A *variable substitution* θ is defined as usual. The expression '$\mathcal{D}_b \models \mathbb{B} \rightarrow \bar{\exists}_{\mathbb{B}} \theta(G)$' formally states that modelling the *built-in constraint domain* $\mathcal{D}_b$ (see e.g. [5] for a rigorous definition of constraint domains), the built-in store $\mathbb{B}$ entails the guard G after application of substitution θ. For CHR rules a generic simpagation notation is used: '$H_1 \setminus H_2 \Leftrightarrow G \mid B$'. For propagation rules, H_1 is the empty sequence; for simplification rules H_2 is empty.

Transition Rules. The transition rules of ω_r are listed in Fig. 3. Given an initial query Q, the *initial execution state* σ_0 is $\langle Q, \emptyset, true, \emptyset \rangle_1$. Execution proceeds by exhaustively applying transitions to σ_0, until the built-in store is unsatisfiable or no more transitions are applicable.

---

[1] Let X, Y, and Z be sets, then $X = Y \sqcup Z \leftrightarrow X = Y \cup Z \wedge Y \cap Z = \emptyset$.

---

reflexivity   @ leq[1](X, X) ⇔ true.
antisymmetry @ leq[3](X, Y), leq[2](Y, X) ⇔ X = Y.
idempotence @ leq[5](X, Y) \ leq[4](X, Y) ⇔ true.
transitivity @ leq[7](X, Y), leq[6](Y, Z) ⇒ leq(X, Z).

Fig. 2. The LEQ handler annotated with occurrence numbers

A central concept in this semantics is the *active constraint*, the top-most element on the execution stack $\mathbb{A}$. Each newly added CHR constraint causes an **Activate** transition, which initiates a sequence of searches for partner constraints to match rule heads. Adding a built-in constraint initiates similar searches for applicable rules: a built-in constraint is passed to the underlying solver in a **Solve** transition, which causes **Reactivate** transitions for all constraints whose arguments might be affected. We say these constaints are *reactivated*. CHR constraints whose arguments are *fixed* are not reactivated, the additional built-in constraint cannot alter the entailment of guards on these arguments; formally:

Definition 1. *A variable v is fixed by a conjunction of built-in constraints B, denoted $v \in fixed(B)$, iff $\mathcal{D}_b \models \forall \rho(\bar{\exists}_v(B) \wedge \bar{\exists}_{\rho(v)}\rho(B) \rightarrow v = \rho(v))$ for arbitrary renaming ρ.*

The order in which occurrences are traversed is fixed by ω_r. Each active constraint tries its occurrences in a CHR program in a top-down, right-to-left order. The constraints on the execution stack can therefore become *occurrenced* (in **Activate** and **Reactivate** transitions). An *occurrenced* identified CHR constraint $c\#i:j$ indicates that only matches with the j'th occurrence of constraint c are considered when the constraint is active.

Example 3. Fig. 2 shows the LEQ program, with all occurrences annotated with their *occurrence number*. Rules are tried from *top-to-bottom*. In this example, this means simplification is tried prior to propagation. Furthermore, occurrences in the same rule are matched with the active constraint from *right-to-left*, ensuring that the active constraint is removed as soon as possible. Both properties can be essential for an efficient execution.

Each active CHR constraint traverses its different occurrences through a sequence of **Default** transitions, followed by a **Drop** transition. During this traversal all applicable rules are fired in **Propagate** and **Simplify** transitions. As with a procedure, when a rule fires, other constraints (its body) are executed, and execution does not return to the original active constraint until after these calls have finished. The different conjuncts of the body are solved (for built-in constraints) or activated (for CHR constraints) in a left-to-right order.

The approach taken by ω_r thus closely corresponds to the execution of the stack-based programming languages to which CHR is commonly compiled. This is why the semantics feels familiar, and why it allows a natural interleaving with host language code (see Section 4). It is also an important reason why the semantics can be implemented very efficiently (see Section 5).

3   Impedance Mismatch

CHR was originally designed to use a (C)LP language as a host. Integrating it with imperative languages gives rise to particular challenges. Imperative host languages do not provide certain language features used by many CHR programs, such as logical variables, search, and pattern matching (Section 3.1). Conversely, the CHR system must be made compatible with the properties of the imperative host. Unlike Prolog, many imperative languages are statically typed, and allow destructive update (Section 3.2).

3.1   (C)LP Language Features

Logical Variables. Imperative languages do not provide *logical variables*. No reasoning is possible over imperative variables, unless they have been assigned a value. Many algorithms written in CHR however use constraints over unbound

---

1. Solve $\langle [b|\mathbb{A}], S_0 \sqcup S_1, \mathbb{B}, \mathbb{T} \rangle_n \rightarrowtail \langle S_1 + \!\!\!+ \, \mathbb{A}, S_0 \sqcup S_1, b \wedge \mathbb{B}, \mathbb{T} \rangle_n$ where b is a built-in constraint and $vars(S_0) \subseteq fixed(\mathbb{B})$, the variables fixed by $\mathbb{B}$. This causes all CHR constraints affected by the newly added built-in constraint b to be reconsidered.

---

2. Activate $\langle [c|\mathbb{A}], S, \mathbb{B}, \mathbb{T} \rangle_n \rightarrowtail \langle [c\#n:1|\mathbb{A}], \{c\#n\} \sqcup S, \mathbb{B}, \mathbb{T} \rangle_{n+1}$ where c is a CHR constraint (which has not yet been active).

---

3. Reactivate $\langle [c\#i|\mathbb{A}], S, \mathbb{B}, \mathbb{T} \rangle_n \rightarrowtail \langle [c\#i:1|\mathbb{A}], S, \mathbb{B}, \mathbb{T} \rangle_n$ where c is a CHR constraint (re-added to $\mathbb{A}$ by a **Solve** transition but not yet active).

---

4. Simplify $\langle [c\#i:j|\mathbb{A}], \{c\#i\} \sqcup H_1 \sqcup H_2 \sqcup H_3 \sqcup S, \mathbb{B}, \mathbb{T} \rangle_n \rightarrowtail$
$\langle B + \!\!\!+ \, \mathbb{A}, H_1 \sqcup S, \theta \wedge \mathbb{B}, \mathbb{T}' \rangle_n$ where the j-th occurrence of c is d, an occurrence in a (renamed apart) rule ρ of the form:

$$\rho \, @ \, H_1' \setminus H_2', d, H_3' \Leftrightarrow G \mid B$$

and there exists a matching substitution θ such that $c = \theta(d)$, $chr(H_k) = \theta(H_k')$ for $1 \le k \le 3$, and $\mathcal{D}_b \models \mathbb{B} \to \bar{\exists}_\mathbb{B} \theta(G)$. Let $t = (\rho, id(H_1) + \!\!\!+ \, id(H_2) + \!\!\!+ \, [i] + \!\!\!+ \, id(H_3))$, then $t \notin \mathbb{T}$ and $\mathbb{T}' = \mathbb{T} \cup \{t\}$.

---

5. Propagate $\langle [c\#i:j|\mathbb{A}], \{c\#i\} \sqcup H_1 \sqcup H_2 \sqcup H_3 \sqcup S, \mathbb{B}, \mathbb{T} \rangle_n \rightarrowtail$
$\langle B + \!\!\!+ \, [c\#i:j|\mathbb{A}], \{c\#i\} \sqcup H_1 \sqcup H_2 \sqcup S, \theta \wedge \mathbb{B}, \mathbb{T}' \rangle_n$ where the j-th occurrence of c is d, an occurrence in a (renamed apart) rule ρ of the form:

$$\rho \, @ \, H_1', d, H_2' \setminus H_3' \Leftrightarrow G \mid B$$

and there exists a matching substitution θ such that $c = \theta(d)$, $chr(H_k) = \theta(H_k')$ for $1 \le k \le 3$, and $\mathcal{D}_b \models \mathbb{B} \to \bar{\exists}_\mathbb{B} \theta(G)$. Let $t = (\rho, id(H_1) + \!\!\!+ \, [i] + \!\!\!+ \, id(H_2) + \!\!\!+ \, id(H_3))$, then $t \notin \mathbb{T}$ and $\mathbb{T}' = \mathbb{T} \cup \{t\}$.

---

6. Drop $\langle [c\#i:j|\mathbb{A}], S, \mathbb{B}, \mathbb{T} \rangle_n \rightarrowtail \langle \mathbb{A}, S, \mathbb{B}, \mathbb{T} \rangle_n$ if there is no j-th occurrence of c.

---

7. Default $\langle [c\#i:j|\mathbb{A}], S, \mathbb{B}, \mathbb{T} \rangle_n \rightarrowtail \langle [c\#i:j+1|\mathbb{A}], S, \mathbb{B}, \mathbb{T} \rangle_n$ if the current state cannot fire any other transition.

Fig. 3. The transition rules of the refined operational semantics ω_r

variables, or require two, possibly unbound variables to be asserted equal. The latter feature of (C)LP languages is called *variable aliasing*.

Example 4. The constraints of the LEQ handler in Fig. 1 range over logical variables. The body of the *antisymmetry* rule contains an example of aliasing.

The unavailability of a corresponding feature would limit the usefulness of a CHR system in imperative languages. A logical data type, together with library routines to maintain it, therefore has to be implemented in the host language.

Built-in Constraint Solvers. More general than variable aliasing, (C)LP languages provide *built-in constraint solvers* for CHR. Prolog provides only one true built-in constraint, namely equality over Herbrand terms. More powerful CLP systems such as HAL offer multiple types of constraint solvers (see [16]). Imperative languages on the other hand offer no built-in constraint support. To allow high level programming with constraints in CHR guards and bodies, underlying constraint solvers need to be implemented from scratch. We refer to Section 4.2 for more information.

Pattern Matching. CHR uses pattern matching to find applicable rules. In logical languages, pattern matching is readily available through unification[2], even on elements of compound data structures (Herbrand terms). These matches are referred to as *structural matches*. Imperative hosts typically do not provide a suited language construct to perform pattern matching on its (compound) data types. Of course, it is possible to implement a library for Herbrand terms and their unification in the host language. A natural CHR embedding, however, also allows constraints and pattern matching over native data types of the imperative host. Section 3.2 discusses some complications that arise in this context.

Search. To solve non-trivial constraint problems constraint simplification and propagation alone is not always enough. Many constraint solvers also require search. As pure CHR does not provide search, many CHR systems therefore implement CHR$^\vee$ (pronounced "CHR-or"), an extension of CHR with disjunctions in rule bodies [17, 18]. The built-in support for chronological backtracking typically offered by Prolog and other (C)LP languages makes the implementation of these disjunctions trivial. Providing search for a CHR system embedded in an imperative host, however, requires an explicit implementation of the choice and backtracking facilities.

We do not address this issue in this article. Earlier work extensively studies the combination of CHR with search [19, 20] (see Section 7). There remain however some interesting challenges for future work, as undoing changes made after a choice-point becomes particularly challenging if arbitrary imperative data types and operations are allowed. The only practical solution seems to be a limitation of the host language code used in CHR handlers that need to support search.

---

[2] Although CHR's pattern matching (sometimes also referred to as *one-way unification*) is different from unification, it is relatively easy to implement matching using the built-in unification facilities of a typical logical language.

3.2   Imperative Language Features

Static Typing. Unlike Prolog, many imperative languages are statically typed. A natural implementation of CHR in a typed host language would also support typed constraint arguments, and perform the necessary type checking. Calling arbitrary external host language code is only possible if the CHR argument types have a close correspondence with those of the host language.

Complex Data Types. The data types provided by imperative languages are typically much more diverse and complex than those used in logical languages. An effective embedding of CHR should support host language data types as constraint arguments as much as possible.

In Section 3.1 we saw that in (C)LP embeddings, CHR handlers use structural matches to specify the applicability of rules on compound data. Providing structural pattern matching on arbitrary compound data structures provided by imperative languages would require specific syntax, and has certain semantical issues, as discussed in the next three subsections.

Modification Problem. Contrary to logical languages, imperative languages allow side effects and destructive update. When executing imperative code, arbitrary values may therefore change. If these values are referred to by CHR guards, these modifications may require the reactivation of one or more constraints. Modifications to a constraint's arguments could also render inconsistent the index data structures used by an efficient CHR implementation (see Section 5). In general it can be very hard or impossible for the CHR handler to know when the content of values has changed. In the production rule literature this is referred to as the *Modified Problem* [21, 22, 23] (we prefer the term modification problem, as modified problem wrongfully suggests the problem is modified).

Non-monotonicity. The traditional specification of CHR and its first order logical reading (see e.g. [2]) assumes monotonicity of the built-in constraints, that is: once a constraint is entailed, it remains entailed. If non-monotonic host-language statements are used in a guard, the corresponding rule no longer has a logical reading. This issue is not exclusive to an imperative host language, but certainly more prominent due to the possibility of destructive updates. A consequence of using imperative data structures as constraint arguments is indeed that, often, these values change non-monotonically. CHR rules that were applicable before, or even rules that have been applied earlier, can thus become inapplicable again by executing host language code. This problem is related to the modification problem, but is more a semantical issue than a practical one.

Behavioral Matches. As structural matches over imperative data types are often impractical (see above), guards will test for properties of constraint arguments using procedure calls. This is particularly the case for object-oriented host languages: if constraints range over objects, structural matches are impossible if encapsulation hides the objects' internal structure. Guards are then forced to use public inspector methods instead. Matching of objects using such guards has been coined *behavioral matches* [24]. So, not only can it be difficult to determine when the structure of values changes (the modification problem), it can be difficult to determine which changes affect which guards.

4 Language Design

A CHR system for an imperative host language should aim for an intuitive and familiar look and feel for users of both CHR and the imperative language. This entails a combination of the declarative aspects of CHR — high-level programming in terms of rules and constraints, both built-in and user-defined — with aspects of the host language. As outlined in Section 3, such a combination leads to a number of language design challenges. In this section we outline our view on these issues, and illustrate with two CHR system case studies: one for Java [25] and one for C [26].

4.1 Embedding CHR in an Imperative Host Language

A natural integration of CHR with a host language should allow CHR rules to contain arbitrary host language expressions. For the operational semantics, the refined operational semantics is therefore a good choice (see Section 2.2). The left-to-right execution of guards and bodies is familiar to imperative programmers, and eases the interleaving with imperative host language statements. Moreover, to allow an easy porting of existing CHR solvers, support for the same familiar semantics is at least as important as a similar syntax.

Because calling imperative code typically requires typed arguments, it follows that CHR constraints best range over regular host language data types. In our opinion, this is also the most natural for imperative programmers. Logical variables and other (C)LP data types, such as finite domain variables or Herbrand terms, can always be encoded as host language data types. The CHR compiler could however provide syntactic sugar for (C)LP data types and built-in constraints to retain CHR's high-level, declarative nature of programming.

Our philosophy is contrary to the one adopted by related systems, such as HCHR, JaCK and DJCHR. As seen in Section 7, these systems limit the data types used in CHR rules to typed logical variables (JaCK) or Herbrand terms (HCHR and DJCHR). Host language data then has to be encoded as logical variables or terms, whereas we propose the opposite: not only is using the host's types is more intuitive to an imperative programmer, it also avoids the performance penalty incurred by constantly encoding and decoding of data when switching between CHR and host language. Partly due to the data type mismatch, some of the aforementioned systems simply do not allow CHR rules to call host language code, or only in a very limited manner (see also Section 7).

The limitations imposed by systems such as JaCK and DJCHR, however, could be motivated by the fact that they need to be able to undo changes made in CHR bodies. This language design choice is reasonable for constraint solvers that require either search or adaptation. Practice shows, however, that even Prolog

CHR systems are for general purpose programming (see e.g. [3] for a recent survey of CHR applications). These CHR programs do not always use search or adaptation, and can often be expressed naturally without term encodings.

We therefore focus on providing a tight, natural integration of imperative host language features with CHR. The goal is to facilitate a seemless cooperation with software components written in the host language (see also Section 1). We argue that constraints should therefore range over host language data types, and that arbitrary host language expressions must be allowed in rule guards and bodies.

As seen in Section 3, allowing arbitrary imperative data types and expressions in rule guards leads to the *modification problem*. An important aspect of the interaction between a CHR handler and its host is thus that the CHR handler has to be notified of any relevant modifications to the constrained data values. A first, simple solution is for a CHR handler to provide an operation to reactivate all constraints in its store (see Section 5.2). In Section 5.3, we discuss the performance issues with this solution, and propose several optimizations. Where possible, these notifications should furthermore occur transparently, relieving the programmer of the responsibility of notifying after each change.

4.2   Built-in Constraints and Solvers

In the previous section, we argued that arbitrary host language expressions should be allowed. In this section, we show that it remains worthwhile to consider constraints separately. An important motivation will be that the modification problem can be solved effectively for built-in constraints.

The semantics of CHR assumes an arbitrary underlying constraint system (see Section 2). Imperative languages however offer hardly any built-in constraint support (Section 3). Typically, only asking whether two data values are equal is supported natively, or asking disequality over certain ordered data types. Solvers for more advanced constraints have to be implemented explicitly.

In any case — whether they either built in the host language itself, or realized as a host language library, or even by another CHR constraint handler (see below) — we call these solvers *built-in constraint solvers*, and their constraints *built-in constraints*. The interaction between a CHR handler and the underlying constraint solvers is well defined (after [16]):

- A built-in constraint solver may provide procedures for *telling* new constraints. Using these procedures, new constraints can be added to the solver's constraint store in bodies of CHR rules and the initial query.
- For constraints that occur in guards, the constraint solver must provide a procedure for *asking* whether the constraint is entailed by its current constraint store or not.
- Thirdly, a built-in constraint solver must alert CHR handlers when changes in their constraint store might cause entailment tests to succeed. The CHR handler then checks whether more rules can be fired. Constraint solvers should relieve the user from the responsibility of notifying the CHR handlers, and notify the CHR solver to only reconsider affected constraints. For

efficiency reasons, this is typically solved by adding observers [27] to the constrained variables. This is discussed in more detail in Section 5.3.

Example 5. Reconsider the LEQ handler of Example 1. The handler uses one built-in constraint, namely equality over logical variables. For an imperative host language, this constraint will not be natively supported, but implemented as a library. The *antisymmetry* rule is the only rule that uses the *tell* version of this constraint. All rules though use the *ask* version of this built-in constraint to check whether the equality of certain logical variables is entailed (this is more clearly seen when the rules are rewritten to their Head Normal Form, as introduced in Section 5.2: see Fig. 8 of Example 9). Also, when new built-in constraints are told, e.g. by the *antisymmetry* rule, the entailment of these guards may change, and the necessary `leq/2` constraints must be reactivated.

We do not require all built-in constraints to have both an ask and a tell version. Constraints natively supported by an imperative host language for instance, such as built-in equality and disequality checks, typically only have an ask version. Also, traditionally, built-in constraints implemented by a CHR handler only have a tell version. For a CHR constraint to be used in a guard, it requires both an entailment check, and a mechanism to reactivate constraints when the constraint becomes entailed (as explained above). In [28], an approach to automatic entailment checking is introduced, whilst [29] proposes a programming discipline where the programmer is responsible for specifying the entailment checks. Currently though, no system provides *ask* versions of CHR constraints.

A first reason to distinguish constraints from arbitrary host language code is thus that the modification problem is solved efficiently, and transparently to the user. Built-in constraints can therefore safely be used in guards. A second reason is that a CHR compiler may support specific syntactic sugar to ask and tell these constraints (as assumed in the LEQ handler of the previous example).

Cooperating Constraint Systems. Multiple CHR handlers and built-in solvers may need to cooperate to solve problems. CHR handlers can for instance share variables constrained by the same built-in constraint solvers, or one CHR handler can be used as a built-in solver for another CHR handler. When implementing multiple solvers and handlers that have to work together, often the need for global data structures arises. Examples include the data structures required for the implementation of search, or an explicit call stack representation (see Section 5). We therefore group such cooperative constraint components under a single *constraint system*. Only solvers and handlers in the same constraint system are allowed to work together.

4.3 CCHR

CCHR [26] is an integration of CHR with the programming language C [30]. CHR code is embedded into C code by means of a `cchr` block. This block can not only contain CCHR constraint declarations and rule definitions, but also additional data-type definitions and imports of host language symbols. Host

```
cchr {
    logical log_int_t int;
    constraint leq(log_int_t,log_int_t);

    reflexivity   @ leq(X,X) <=> true;
    antisymmetry  @ leq(X,Y), leq(Y,X) <=> {telleq(X,Y);};
    idempotence   @ leq(X,Y) \ leq(X,Y) <=> true;
    transitivity  @ leq(X,Y), leq(Y,Z) ==> leq(X,Z);
}

void test(void) {
    cchr_runtime_init();
    log_int_t a=log_int_t_create(), b=log_int_t_create(),
        c=log_int_t_create();
    leq(a,b); leq(b,c); leq(c,a);
    int nLeqs=0; cchr_consloop(j,leq_2,{ nLeqs++; });
    assert(nLeqs==0);
    assert(log_int_t_testeq(a,b));
    assert(log_int_t_testeq(b,c));
    assert(log_int_t_testeq(c,a));
    log_int_t_destruct(a);
    log_int_t_destruct(b);
    log_int_t_destruct(c);
    cchr_runtime_free();
}
```

Fig. 4. The CHR program LEQ implemented in CCHR

language integration is achieved by allowing arbitrary C expressions as guards, and by allowing arbitrary C statements in bodies. Functions to add or reactivate CHR constraints are made available to the host language environment, so they can be called from within C.

Constraint arguments are typed, and can be of any C data type except arrays. Support for logical data types is provided, both in the host language and within CHR blocks. CCHR does not have a concept of built-in constraints as introduced in Section 4.2. All 'ask' requests are simply host-language expressions, and 'tell' constraints are host-language statements, which have to be surrounded by curly brackets. It is however possible to declare macro's providing shorter notations for certain operations, a workaround for C's lack of polymorphism. When a data type is declared as logical, such macro's are generated automatically.

Rules follow the normal Prolog-CHR syntax, yet are delimited by a semicolon instead of a dot. This latter would cause ambiguities since the dot is a C operator.

Example 6. In Figure 4 an example is given how to implement the LEQ handler in CCHR. The first line starts the cchr block. The next line declares log_int_t as a logical version of the built-in C data type int. The third line declares a leq

```
package examples.leq;

import runtime.Logical;
import runtime.EqualitySolver;

public handler leq<T> {
    public solver EqualitySolver<T> builtin;

    public constraint leq(Logical<T>, Logical<T>) infix =<;

    rules {
        reflexivity  @ X =< X <=> true;
        antisymmetry @ X =< Y, Y =< X <=> X = Y;
        idempotence  @ X =< Y \ X =< Y <=> true;
        transitivity @ X =< Y, Y =< Z ==> X =< Z;
    }
}
```

Fig. 5. The LEQ handler using K.U.Leuven JCHR syntax

constraint that takes two logical integers as argument. The four rules of the LEQ handler look very similar to those of Fig. 1. Equality of logical variables is told using the generated `telleq()` macro.

The `test()` function shows how to interact with the CHR handler from within C. The first line of the function initializes the CHR runtime. The next line creates three `log_int_t` variables (a, b and c), and is followed by a line that adds the three `leq` constraints `leq(a,b)`, `leq(b,c)` and `leq(c,a)`. The next line counts the number of `leq` constraints left in the store. The next four lines assert that no CHR constraints are left, and that all logical variables are equal (in C, if the argument of `assert` evaluates to 0, the program is aborted and a diagnostic error message is printed). The function ends with the destruction of the logical variables used, and the release of all memory structures created by the CCHR runtime.

4.4 The K.U.Leuven JCHR System

This section outlines and illustrates the most important language design choices made for the K.U.Leuven JCHR System [12, 25]. For a more detailed description of the language extension we refer to the system's user's manual [31].

A handler declaration in K.U.Leuven JCHR is designed to be very similar to a class declaration in Java. Language features such as `package` and `import` declarations, and the access modifiers `public`, `private` and `protected`, are defined exactly as their Java counterparts [32]. To ease the transition from untyped Prolog to strongly typed Java, we further fully support Java's generic types [32, 33]. To the best of our knowledge the K.U.Leuven JCHR system is the first typed CHR-system that adequately deals with polymorphic handlers this way.

A JCHR handler declares one or more constraints. As in CCHR, constraint arguments are typed. In principle, any valid Java-type, including primitive types and generic types, can be used. For each handler, and for each of its declared constraints, a corresponding Java class is generated. A handler class contains methods to add non-`private` constraints, and to inspect the constraint store. The latter methods return standard Java `Collection` or `Iterator` objects [34]. The handler class itself also implements the `Collection<Constraint>` interface.

Example 7. Fig. 5 shows a polymorphic K.U.Leuven JCHR implementation of the canonical LEQ example. Note that JCHR allows constraints, both built-in and CHR constraints, to be written using infix notation. Fig. 6 shows how the generated classes are used to solve `leq` constraints over `Integer` objects.

```
...
EqualitySolver<Integer> builtin = new EqualitySolverImpl<Integer>();
LeqHandler<Integer> handler = new LeqHandler<Integer>(builtin);

Logical<Integer> A = new Logical<Integer>(),
  B = new Logical<Integer>(), C = new Logical<Integer>();

handler.tellLeq(A, B);  // A ≤ B
handler.tellLeq(B, C);  // B ≤ C
handler.tellLeq(C, A);  // C ≤ A

// all CHR constraints are simplified to built-in equalities:
assert handler.getLeqConstraints().size() == 0;
assert builtin.askEqual(A, B);
assert builtin.askEqual(B, C);
assert builtin.askEqual(A, C);
...
```

Fig. 6. A code snippet illustrating how the JCHR LEQ handler and equality built-in solvers are called from Java code

JCHR supports user-defined incremental, built-in constraint solvers. The design follows the principles outlined in Section 4.2. Using annotations, a regular Java type is annotated with meta-data that allows the JCHR compiler to derive which built-in constraints are solved by a solver, and which methods to use for asking and telling these constraints. A JCHR handler has to declare all built-in constraint solvers it uses.

Example 8. The K.U.Leuven JCHR System contains an efficient reference implementation for equality over logical variables. Its interface declaration is shown in Fig. 7. It declares a single `eq` constraint, that can also be written using infix notation. This built-in solver is used in the LEQ example of Fig. 5. The `solver` declaration tells the JCHR compiler to use the `EqualitySolver<T>` interface

```
@JCHR_Constraint (identifier = "eq", arity = 2, infix = "=")
public interface EqualitySolver<T> {
    @JCHR_Tells ("eq")
    public void tellEqual(Logical<T> X, T val);
    @JCHR_Tells ("eq")
    public void tellEqual(T val, Logical<T> X);
    @JCHR_Tells ("eq")
    public void tellEqual(Logical<T> X, Logical<T> Y);

    @JCHR_Asks ("eq")
    public void askEqual(Logical<T> X, T val);
    @JCHR_Asks ("eq")
    public void askEqual(T val, Logical<T> X);
    @JCHR_Asks ("eq")
    public void askEqual(Logical<T> X, Logical<T> Y);
}
```

Fig. 7. The declaration of a built-in equality constraint solver interface using annotations

as a built-in solver. Using the annotations, the JCHR compiler knows to use the `askEqual` method to check the implicit equality guards, and to use the `tellEqual` method in the body of the *antisymmetry* rule. Fig. 6 shows how a built-in constraint solver is used to verify that all JCHR constraints are simplified to built-in equalities after adding three `leq` constraints to the handler.

Next to high-level constraint programming, the K.U.Leuven JCHR also allows arbitrary Java objects and methods to be used. An adequate, efficient solution for the modification problem though, which would allow behavioral matches over arbitrary Java Bean objects [35], is an important part of future work. Interaction with Java already possible though: the user simply needs to reactivate all constraints in case of relevant changes explicitly.

5   Optimized Compilation

Considerable research has been devoted to the efficient compilation and execution of CHR programs, mostly with Prolog as the host language. An early, very influential implementation was the SICStus implementation described in [4]. Its operational semantics was the basis for the refined operational semantics ω_r (see Section 2.2), and its compilation scheme has been adopted by state-of-the-art systems such as HALCHR [7, 8] and K.U.Leuven CHR [5, 6].

   We show how this compilation scheme can be ported to the imperative setting. The structure of this section is similar to that of [5, Chapter 5: *The Implementation of CHR: A Reconstruction*]. Section 5.2 presents a simple compilation scheme for CHR. This naive scheme, whilst obviously correct with respect to ω_r, is fairly inefficient. In Sections 5.3 and 5.4, we gradually transform it into a very efficient CHR compilation scheme. Equivalents of most optimizations discussed in Section 5.3 are also implemented in the Prolog and HAL systems. Section 5.4 however addresses an important technical issue that only arises when adapting the scheme to imperative host languages.

For the compilation scheme presented below, we use imperative pseudo-code. It can easily be instantiated for any concrete imperative language. The instance used by the K.U.Leuven JCHR system to compile CHR to Java is described in detail in [36].

Before the compilation scheme is introduced, Section 5.1 abstractly describes the data structures and the operations it uses. The efficient implementation of these data structures is beyond the scope of this article.

5.1   Basic Data Structures and Operations

The Constraint Store. The main data structure of a CHR handler is the *constraint store*. Each stored CHR constraint is represented as a *constraint suspension* in the constraint store. For each constraint, a constraint suspension data type is generated containing the following fields:

`type`. The type of the constraint.

`args`. A list of fields containing the constraint's arguments. The type of these arguments is derived from the constraint's declaration.

`id`. Each constraint suspension is uniquely identified by a *constraint identifier*, as in the refined operational semantics.

`alive`. A boolean field indicating whether the constraint is *alive* or not.

`activated`. A boolean indicating whether the constraint has been (re)activated. This field is used for optimizations (see Sections 5.3 and 5.4).

`stored`. A boolean field set to `true` if the constraint is stored in the constraint store. Due to the *Late Storage* optimization (Section 5.3), suspensions may represent constraints that are not stored in the constraint store.

`hist`. A constraint suspension may contain fields related to the propagation history. More details can be found in Section 5.3.

The constraint suspension may contain further fields, used for instance for constant time removal from the constraint store data structures. These implementation details are beyond the scope of this article though.

In the pseudo-code used throughout this article, a constraint suspension of an n-ary constraint is denoted as $c(X_1, \ldots, X_a)\#\text{ID}$. We assume the transition from a constraint identifier ID to its corresponding constraint suspension can be made, and we often make this transition implicitly. In other words, a constraint identifier is very similar to a pointer to a constraint suspension.

The basic constraint store operations are as follows:

`create(c, [args])`. Creates a constraint suspension for a constraint with given type `c` and argument list *args*, and returns its constraint identifier.

Because arity and argument types are constraint specific, concrete implementations most likely offer specific `create_c` operations for each constraint type *c*.

`store(ID)`. Adds the referenced constraint suspension (created earlier with the `create` operation) to the constraint store.

`reactivateAll`. Reactivates all constraints in the store, using the `reactivate`(ID) operation. Optionally, only constraints whose arguments are modifiable are reactivated (as in ω_r's **Solve** transition, see Fig. 3).

`reactivate(ID)`. Reactivates the constraint with the given identifier.

`kill(ID)`. Removes the identified constraint suspension from the constraint store data structures, and sets its `alive` field to `false`.

`alive(ID)`. Tests whether the corresponding constraint is alive or not.

`lookup(c)`. Returns an iterator (see below) over all stored constraint suspensions of constraint type *c*.

To iterate over candidate partner constraints, we use *iterators* [27]. This common abstraction can easily be implemented in any imperative language. Even though probably all CHR implementations rely on some form of iterators, their necessary requirements have never been fixed explicitly. We require the iterators returned by `lookup` operations to have at least the following properties:

robustness. The iterators are robust under constraint store modifications. If constraints are added or removed whilst a constraint iteration is suspended, iteration can be resumed from the point where it was suspended.

correctness. The iterators only return constraint suspensions that are alive.

completeness. All constraints that are stored at the moment of the iterator's creation are returned at least once in the iteration.

weak termination. A contiguous iteration does not contain duplicate suspensions. Only if constraint store modifications occur whilst an iteration is suspended, constraints returned prior to this suspension are allowed to be returned once more.

Iterators are preferred to satisfy a stronger termination property, namely **strong termination**, which requires that an iterator returns a constraint suspension at most once.

Iterators offered by predefined data structures typically do not have all required properties. Iterators returned by most standard Java data structures [34], for instance, are not robust under modifications.

The Propagation History. A second important data structure for any CHR implementation is the *propagation history*. Abstractly, the propagation history contains *tuples*, each containing a rule identifier and a non-empty sequence of constraint identifiers (denoted '[ID+]'). We assume the following two operations:

`addToHistory(rule, [ID+])` Adds a tuple to the propagation history.

`notInHistory(rule, [ID+])` Tests whether a given tuple is in the propagation history or not.

```
1   procedure occurrence_c_i_j_i(ID_i,X_{i,1},...,X_{i,a_i})
2     foreach c_1(X_{1,1},...,X_{1,a_1})#ID_1 in lookup(c_1)
3         ⋱
4           foreach c_{i-1}(X_{i-1,1},...,X_{i-1,a_{i-1}})#ID_{i-1} in lookup(c_{i-1})
5             foreach c_{i+1}(X_{i+1,1},...,X_{i+1,a_{i+1}})#ID_{i+1} in lookup(c_{i+1})
6                 ⋱
7                   foreach c_h(X_{h,1},...,X_{h,a_h})#ID_h in lookup(c_h)
8                     if alive(ID_1) and ... and alive(ID_h)
9                       if ID_1 ≠ ID_2 and ... and ID_1 ≠ ID_h
10                          ⋱
11                            if ID_{h-1} ≠ ID_h
12                              if g_1 and ... and g_{n_g}
13                                if notInHistory(ρ,ID_1,...,ID_h)
14                                  addToHistory(ρ,ID_1,...,ID_h)
15                                  kill(ID_r)
16                                      ⋮
17                                  kill(ID_h)
18                                  b_1
19                                      ⋮
20                                  b_{n_b}
21                            end
22                          end
23                        end
24                      ⋱
25                    end
26                  end
27                end
28              ⋱
29            end
30          end
31        ⋱
32      end
33  end
```

Listing 1. The compilation scheme for a single occurrence. The active constraint is $c_i(X_{i,1},...,X_{i,a_i})$, with constraint identifier ID_i.

5.2   Basic Compilation Scheme

A CHR rule ρ with h occurrences in its head has the following generic form:

$$\rho @ c_1^{[j_1]}(X_{1,1}, ..., X_{1,a_1}), ..., c_{r-1}^{[j_{r-1}]}(X_{r-1,1}, ..., X_{r-1,a_{r-1}}) \setminus$$
$$c_r^{[j_r]}(X_{r,1}, ..., X_{r,a_r}), ..., c_h^{[j_h]}(X_{h,1}, ..., X_{h,a_h}) \Leftrightarrow g_1, ..., g_{n_g} \mid b_1, ..., b_{n_b}.$$

The occurrences in a rule are numbered from left to right, with r the index of the first removed occurrence. For a simplification rule there are no kept occurrences (i.e., $r = 1$), for a propagation rule there are no removed occurrences

($h = r-1$). The *occurrence number* j_i in $c_i^{[j_i]}$ denotes that this occurrence is the j_i'th occurrence of constraint c_i in the program, when numbered according to the top-to-bottom, right-to-left order determined by ω_r, as defined in Section 2.2.

In this generic form, also called the *Head Normal Form (HNF)*, all arguments $X_{\alpha,\beta}$ in a rule's head are variables. Moreover, variables never occur more than once in a rule's head, that is: all equality guards implicitly present in the head are written explicitly in the guard.

Example 9. Fig. 8 shows the normalized version of the LEQ handler, with occurrence numbers added for illustration purposes.

```
reflexivity    @ leq⁽¹⁾(X, X₁) ⟺ X = X₁ | true.
antisymmetry   @ leq⁽³⁾(X, Y), leq⁽²⁾(Y₁, X₁) ⟺ X = X₁, Y = Y₁ | X = Y.
idempotence    @ leq⁽⁵⁾(X, Y) \ leq⁽⁴⁾(X₁, Y₁) ⟺ X = X₁, Y = Y₁ | true.
transitivity   @ leq⁽⁷⁾(X, Y), leq⁽⁶⁾(Y₁, Z) ⟹ Y = Y₁ | leq(X, Z).
```

Fig. 8. The LEQ handler in *Head Normal Form*. Occurrence numbers are added for illustration purposes (as in Fig. 2).

Listing 1 shows the compilation scheme for an occurrence $c_i^{[j_i]}$ in such a rule. Lines 2–7 constitute a nested iteration over all $h-1$ candidate partner constraints. A rule is applicable on some combination of constraints if all constraints are alive (line 8) and mutually distinct (lines 9–11), and if the guard is satisfied (line 12). After verifying that the rule has not fired before with the same combination of constraints (line 13), the rule is fired: the propagation history is updated (line 14), the constraints that matched removed occurrences are removed from the constraint store (lines 15–17), and the body is executed (lines 18–20).

For each n-ary constraint c a procedure $c(X_1, \ldots, X_n)$ is then generated by the compiler as depicted in Listing 2. These procedures are used for executing CHR constraints in the body of rules, or for calling CHR from the host language. Also for each constraint c an instance of the (polymorphic) procedure $\texttt{activate}(c(X_1, \ldots, X_n)\#\texttt{ID})$ is generated. Called by both $c(X_1, \ldots, X_n)$ and $\texttt{reactivate(ID)}$, it deals with trying all occurrence procedures in order.

With the basic compilation scheme, it is the responsibility of the built-in constraint solvers to call $\texttt{reactivateAll}$ each time a built-in constraint is added. This operation calls the $\texttt{reactivate(ID)}$, also shown in Listing 2, for all constraints in the store (see also Section 5.1). As a simple optimization, constraints without modifyable arguments should not be reactivated, as indicated in the corresponding **Solve** transition of ω_r.

Correctness. The basic compilation scheme of Listings 1–2 closely follows the refined operational semantics (see Section 2.2). It is therefore not hard to see it is correct. Lines 1–2 of Listing 2 correspond with an **Activate** transition: the constraint is assigned a constraint identifier and stored in the constraint

```
1   procedure c(X₁,...,Xₙ)
2       ID = create(c, [X₁,...,Xₙ])
3       store(ID)
4       activate(ID)
5   end
6
7   procedure reactivate(ID)
8       activate(ID)
9   end
10
11  procedure activate(c(X₁,...,Xₙ)#ID)
12      occurrence_c_1(ID,X₁,...,Xₙ)
13      ...
14      occurrence_c_m(ID,X₁,...,Xₙ)
15  end
```

Listing 2. Compilation scheme for an n-ary constraint c with m occurrences throughout the program. For each occurrence, lines 4–6 call the corresponding occurrence procedure (see Listing 1).

store. The remaining lines constitute a sequence of **Default** transitions, chaining together the different occurrence procedures.

Each occurrence procedure, as shown in Listing 1, has to perform all applicable **Propagate** or **Simplify** transitions. The body is executed left-to-right as a sequence of host language statements, thus mapping the activation stack onto the host's implicit call stack.

The only subtlety is showing that in a sequence of **Propagate** transitions, all required partner constraint combinations are effectively found by the nested iterations of lines 2–7. The order in which the partners have to be found is not determined by ω_r. The **completeness** and **correctness** properties of the iterators guarantee that an iteration contains at least all constraints that existed at the creation of the iterator, and that are still alive on the moment the iterator is advanced. However, constraints that are added to the store *after* the creation of an iterator, i.e. by an execution of the body, are not required to appear in the iteration. These constraints, however, have been active themselves, so any combination involving them has already been tried or applied. As the propagation history prevents any re-application, not including these constraints in iterations is correct.

Running Example. The following example will be used as a running example for illustrating the different optimizations throughout the next section:

Example 10. Consider the following rule from the RAM simulator example [37]:

```
add @ mem(B,Y), prog(L,ADD,B,A) \
    mem(A,X), pc(L) <=> mem(A,X+Y), pc(L+1).
```

```
1    procedure occurrence_pc_1(ID₄,L)
2      foreach mem(B,Y)#ID₁ in lookup(mem)
3        foreach prog(L₁,$₁,B₁,A)#ID₂ in lookup(prog)
4          foreach mem(A₁,X)#ID₃ in lookup(mem)
5            if alive(ID₁) and alive(ID₂) and alive(ID₃) and alive(ID₄)
6              if ID₁ ≠ ID₂ and ID₁ ≠ ID₃ and ID₁ ≠ ID₄
7                if ID₂ ≠ ID₃ and ID₂ ≠ ID₄
8                  if ID₃ ≠ ID₄
9                    if A = A₁ and B = B₁ and L = L₁ and $₁ = ADD
10                     if notInHistory(add,ID₁,ID₂,ID₃,ID₄)
11                       addToHistory(add,ID₁,ID₂,ID₃,ID₄)
12                       kill(ID₃)
13                       kill(ID₄)
14                       mem(A,X+Y)
15                       pc(L+1)
16                   end
17               end
18              ...
```

Listing 3. Naive compilation of the pc(L) occurrence of the RAM simulator rule

This rule simulates the ADD instruction of a *Random Access Machine*. The full program can be found in Appendix A. The program of the simulated RAM machine is represented as prog constraints. The current program counter L is maintained in a pc constraint. If L refers to an ADD instruction, the above rule is applicable. It looks up two cells of the RAM machine's memory, and replaces one of them with a cell containing the sum of their values, before advancing to the next instruction by adding an incremented program counter.

After HNF transformation, the *add* rule becomes:

add @ mem(B,Y), prog(L₁,$₁,B₁,A) \ mem(A₁,X), pc(L)
    <=> A = A₁, B = B₁, L = L₁, $₁ = ADD | mem(A,X+Y), pc(L+1).

The code for the pc occurrence in this rule, using the basic compilation scheme, is shown in Listing 3.

5.3   Optimizations

This section describes a number of optimizations for the basic compilation scheme presented in the previous section. Most of these optimizations are not new, and have been applied for compiling CHR to (C)LP as well. Our contribution is a first clear survey that places the many optimizations mentioned in recent literature [5, 7, 8, 38, 39, 40, 41, 42, 43] in one coherent framework. Even though introduced and illustrated for an imperative host language, the overview provided in this section is useful for any reader interested in optimized compilation of CHR, or any other forward chaining rule-based language. Implementation aspects more specific to imperative target languages are discussed in Section 5.4.

```
1    procedure occurrence_pc_1(ID4,L)
2       foreach mem(B,Y)#ID1 in lookup(mem)
3          foreach prog(L1,$1,B1,A)#ID2 in lookup(prog)
4             if B = B1 and L = L1 and $1 = ADD
5                foreach mem(A1,X)#ID3 in lookup(mem)
6                   if ID1 ≠ ID3
7                      if A = A1
8                         if alive(ID1) and alive(ID2) ... and alive(ID4)
9                            if notInHistory(add,ID1,ID2,ID3,ID4)
10                              ⋮
```

Listing 4. The compilation of the RAM simulator example of Listing 3 after *Loop-Invariant Code Motion*

Loop-Invariant Code Motion. The tests on lines 9–12 of Listing 1 should be performed as early as possible. Otherwise a phenomenon denoted *trashing* could occur, where tests depending only on outer loops fail for all iterations of the inner loops. So guards are scheduled as soon as all required variables are present[3], and the identifiers of new candidate partner constraints are immediately compared to those of the candidates already found. Only identifiers of constraints of the same type have to be compared.

The alive tests on line 8 are not yet moved, since the liveness of partner constraints may change when the rule is committed. Failure to test the liveness of all partners before the next body execution might result in a rule being applied with dead constraints. The optimization of the alive tests is addressed later.

Example 11. The optimized compilation of the RAM simulator example introduced in the previous section is listed in Listing 4. Scheduling the 'L = L_1' on line 4 avoids enumerating all mem(A,X) memory cells before the right program instruction is found. The search for partner constraints is not yet optimal though. Further optimizations will address several remaining issues.

Indexing. The efficient, selective lookup of candidate partner constraints is indispensable. To achieve this, *indexes* on constraints are used.

Example 12. In Listing 4 of the RAM simulator example, line 3 iterates over all prog constraints, each time immediately testing the 'L = L_1' guard. There will however be only one prog constraint with the given instruction label L (see also the *Set Semantics* optimization). Using an index to retrieve this single constraint, reduces the linear time complexity of this part of the partner constraint search to constant time. A similar reasoning applies to line 5 of Listing 4.

---

[3] Note that we assume all guards to be monotonic (see Section 3.2). If a satisfied guard might become unsatisfied by executing a body, scheduling this guard early is not allowed for **Propagate** transitions.

```
1    procedure occurrence_pc_1(ID₄,L)
2       foreach mem(B,Y)#ID₁ in lookup(mem)
3          foreach prog(L₁,$₁,B₁,A)#ID₂ in lookup(prog,{B=B₁,L=L₁,$₁=ADD})
4             foreach mem(A₁,X)#ID₃ in lookup(mem,{A=A₁})
5                if ID₁ ≠ ID₃
6                   ⋱
```

Listing 5. Compilation of the RAM simulator's pc(L) occurrence. This version improves Listing 4 by incorporating the *Indexing* optimization.

For lookups of partner constraints via known arguments, tree-, hash-, or array-based indexes are used (see e.g. [5, 7, 8, 44]). Tree-based indexes can be used not only for equality-based lookups, but also for pruning the partner constraint search space in case of disequality guards (see [16]). The other two indexing types are particularly interesting as they offer (amortized) constant time constraint store operations. Care must be taken that indexes remain consistent after modifications to the indexed arguments. These techniques are therefore often only used for unmodifiable constraint arguments.

One indexing technique for unbound logical variables commonly used by CHR implementations is *attributed variables* [4, 45]. With this technique, variables contain references to all constraints in which they occur. This allows constant time lookups of partner constraints via shared variables.

Imperative host languages naturally allow for direct and efficient implementations of index data structures [25, 26]. In fact, performance-critical parts of the hash indexes of the K.U.Leuven CHR system for SWI-Prolog [5, 6] have recently been reimplemented in C for efficiency.

Indexes are incorporated into the general compilation scheme by extending the **lookup** operation. The extended operation accepts an additional set of conditions, allowing the combination of a **lookup** with one or more subsequent guards. This operation may make use of existing indexes to obtain all constraints satisfying the requested conditions, or any superset thereof. In the latter case, the conditions not guaranteed by the index are checked within the iterator. This way, constraints returned by the iterator are always guaranteed to satisfy the provided guard conditions. By using index lookups that only return the requested constraints, suitable candidate partner constraints are looked up far more efficiently.

Example 13. Listing 5 shows the optimized compilation of our running example. If the specialized **lookup** operations on lines 3–4 use array- or hash-based indexing, both partner constraints are found in $\mathcal{O}(1)$ time. Without indexing, the time complexity is $\mathcal{O}(p \times m)$, with p the number of lines of the RAM program, and m the number memory cells used by the RAM machine.

Join Ordering. The time complexity of executing a CHR program is often determined by the *join ordering* — the order in which partner constraints are looked up in order to find matching rules. So far this order was determined by the order they occur in the rule.

```
1   procedure occurrence_pc_1(ID₄,L)
2      foreach prog(L₁,$₁,B₁,A)#ID₂ in lookup(prog,{L=L₁,$₁=ADD})
3         foreach mem(A₁,X)#ID₃ in lookup(mem,{A=A₁})
4            foreach mem(B,Y)#ID₁ in lookup(mem,{B=B₁})
5               if ID₁ ≠ ID₃
6                  ⋱
```

Listing 6. Compilation of the pc(L) occurrence of Listing 5 with optimal *Join Ordering*

The join order determines the earliest position where guards, and thus indexes, may be used. The general principle behind *Join Ordering* is to maximize the usage of indexes, in order to minimize the number of partner constraints tried. The optimal join order may depend on dynamic properties, such as the number of constraints in the store for which certain guards are entailed. Sometimes *functional dependency analysis* [7, 8, 39] can determine statically that certain indexed lookups return at most one constraint (see also the *Set Semantics* optimization). Without functional dependencies though (or without proper indexing), a compiler must rely on heuristics to determine the join order. The most comprehensive treatment of the join ordering problem is [38].

Example 14. Line 2 of Listing 5 iterates over all mem constraints. Lacking any information on B and L, there is no possibility to use an index using the standard join order. The join order depicted in Listing 6, on the other hand, first looks up the prog constraint using the known L. Next both mem partners are looked up using the known A and B. In all three cases, if proper indexing is used, only one partner constraint is retrieved (see also Example 15), as the first argument of both the prog/4 and the mem/2 constraint are unique identifiers. The latter property may be derived statically from the full RAM program as listed in Appendix A using functional dependency analysis.

Set Semantics. The functional dependency analysis may show at compile time that a certain lookup will result in at most one constraint [8, 39]. In this case, more efficient data structures can be used for the constraint store and its indexes, and specialized lookup routines can be used that return a single suspension instead of an iterator. Such specialized routines are denoted lookup_single.

Example 15. In our running example, all lookups have set semantics after applying *Join Ordering* (see Example 14). All loops can thus be turned into simple conditionals, as shown in Listing 7. As an index on prog's first argument alone already yields at most one result, the test on $₁$ is placed outside the lookup.

Early Drop and Backjumping. As seen in Section 5.1, iterators are guaranteed not to return dead constraints. Constraints may be removed though when

```
1   procedure occurrence_pc_1(ID₄,L)
2       prog(L₁,$₁,B₁,A)#ID₂ = lookup_single(prog,{L=L₁})
3       if ID₂ ≠ nil
4           if $₁ = ADD
5               mem(A₁,X)#ID₃ = lookup_single(mem,{A=A₁})
6               if ID₃ ≠ nil
7                   mem(B,Y)#ID₁ = lookup_single(mem,{B=B₁})
8                   if ID₁ ≠ nil and ID₁ ≠ ID₃
9                       ⋱
```

Listing 7. The compilation scheme for the RAM simulator rule occurrence after applying *Set Semantics* to Listing 6

```
1   procedure activate(c(X₁,…,Xₙ)#ID)
2       if occurrence_c_1(ID,X₁,…,Xₙ) return
3           …
4       if occurrence_c_m(ID,X₁,…,Xₙ) return
5   end
```

Listing 8. Compilation scheme for an n-ary constraint c with m occurrences throughout the program. This is an updated version of the activate procedure of Listing 2, performing an *Early Drop* for the active constraint if required.

matching removed occurrences, or indirectly during the execution of the body. In the naive compilation scheme of Listing 1, this leads to many useless iterations where the active constraint, or certain partner constraints, are no longer alive.

Once the active constraint is killed, we should stop handling it. We call this an *Early Drop*. For this optimization, the activate operation of Listing 2 is replaced with the version of Listing 8. Occurrence routines are modified to return a boolean: true if trying further occurrences is no longer necessary; false otherwise. The alive test for the active constraint is thus removed from line 8 of Listing 1, and replaced with a 'if not alive(ID$_i$) return true' statement *right after* the body. At the end of the occurrence code finally (i.e., after line 32 of Listing 1), a 'return false' is added. This is the default case, signifying that any remaining occurrences must still be tested for the current active constraint.

A similar optimization is possible for the partner constraints. When using the scheme of Listing 1, a form of trashing similar to the one seen in *Loop-Invariant Code Motion* may occur. If, for instance, the first partner constraint dies by executing the body, all nested loops are still fully iterated. Since the first partner is already dead, all these lookups and iterations are useless. So, if a constraint dies, we should instead immediately continue with the next constraint for the corresponding loop. The alive tests for the partner constraints are therefore moved after the alive test for the active constraint (i.e., after the body as well). The constraint of the outermost iterator is tested first. If one of the partner constraints tests dead after the execution of the body, a jump is used to resume the corresponding iteration. This optimization, known as *Backjumping*, avoids the form of trashing described above.

All alive tests are now placed after the body instead of before it. This is allowed because at the start of a body execution, each partner was either just returned by an iterator (which guarantees liveness), or tested for liveness after the previous body execution.

In case of a **Simplify** transition, the active constraint is always killed. The *Early Drop* therefore becomes unconditional ('**return true**'), and all further alive become unreachable, and should be omitted. Similarly, removed partner constraints will always be dead after the body. The alive test of the outermost removed partner constraint can therefore be omitted, and replaced with an unconditional backjump. All following alive tests thus becomes redundant. If static analysis shows the active constraint or certain partner constraints cannot be killed during the execution of the body, the corresponding alive tests can be dropped. One trivial case is when the body is empty.

Example 16. In the RAM simulator example, the active pc constraint is removed by the rule, so all alive tests can be replaced by a single unconditional '**return true**' after the rule body. See Listing 9.

Non-Robust Iterators. Due to the highly dynamic nature of the CHR constraint store, the robustness property of iterators, as specified in Section 5.2, is hard to implement and often has a considerable performance penalty. There are however cases where this property is not required:

1. If after the execution of a rule body an iterator is never resumed due to an unconditional early drop, or an unconditional backjump over the corresponding loop, introduced by the previous optimization.
2. If static analysis shows the body of a rule is guaranteed not to modify the CHR constraint store.

Robust and non-robust iterators are sometimes called *universal* and *existential* iterators [5, 8]. We prefer the term *non-robust iterator*, because they can also be used to iterate over more than one partner constraint (see case 2 above). Non-robust iterators are used where possible because they can typically be implemented more efficiently.

Example 17. In case of the RAM simulator example, all iterators are already superseded by the single-constraint lookups since *Set Semantics* was applied; otherwise, they could have been replaced by non-robust iterators because of the unconditional *Early Drop* in the body.

Late Storage. In the default compilation scheme, see Listing 2, constraints are stored immediately after they are told, as in ω_r. A constraint's lifetime, however, is often very short. This is most apparent when the active constraint is removed shortly after activation. The goal of the *late storage* optimization is to postpone adding the constraint to the constraint store as long as possible. In many cases the constraint will then be killed before it is stored. This avoids the considerable overhead of adding and removing the constraint to the constraint store. The performance gain is particularly significant if indexes are used.

During the execution of a body in a **Propagate** transition the formerly active constraint might be required as a partner constraint, or it might have to be reactivated. A straightforward implementation of the optimization therefore stores the active constraint prior to every non-empty body in **Propagate** transitions. To further delay constraint storage the *observation analysis* [5, 40] can be used. This static program analysis determines whether a specific body requires a constraint to be stored or not. Finally, if not stored earlier, the active constraint is stored after all occurrence procedures are called (i.e. line 3 is moved after line 4 in Listing 2).

Late Allocation. As constraints are not always stored, constraint suspensions do not always have to be created either. Late allocation and late storage are considered separately, because a distributed propagation history maintenance (cf. next optimization) might require allocation earlier than storage. In the optimized compilation schemes of Section 5.4, a constraint suspension may also be allocated earlier if needed as a continuation.

Propagation History Maintenance. In the basic compilation scheme, tuples are added to the propagation history, but never removed (line 14 of Listing 1). However, it is obvious that tuples referring to removed constraints are redundant. Tuples added for simplification and simpagation rules, immediately become redundant in lines 15–17, so a propagation history is only kept for propagation rules. The propagation history remains a memory problem nevertheless.

There exist several techniques to overcome this problem. Immediately removing all propagation history tuples a constraint occurs in once it is removed is a first possibility. Practice shows however that this is difficult to implement efficiently. CHR implementations therefore commonly use ad-hoc garbage collection techniques, which in theory could result in excessive memory use, but perform adequately in practice. A first such technique is to remove tuples referring to dead constraints during `notInHistory` checks (see [7]). A second is denoted *distributed propagation history* maintenance, for which suspensions contain propagation history tuples they occur in (see [5]). When a constraint suspension is removed, part of the propagation history is removed as well. These techniques can easily be combined. Other, more advanced garbage collection techniques could be applied as well.

Example 18. The add rule of the RAM example is a simpagation rule, so maintaining a propagation history for it is unnecessary. This is reflected in Listing 9.

Propagation History Elimination. Despite the above techniques, the maintenance of a propagation history remains expensive, and has a considerable impact on both the space and time performance of a CHR program [43]. For rules

```
1    procedure occurrence_pc_1(ID₄,L)
2       prog(L₁,$₁,B₁,A)#ID₂ = lookup_single(prog,{L=L₁})
3       if ID₂ ≠ nil
4          if $₁ = ADD
5             mem(A₁,X)#ID₃ = lookup_single(mem,{A=A₁})
6             if ID₃ ≠ nil
7                mem(B,Y)#ID₁ = lookup_single(mem,{B=B₁})
8                if ID₁ ≠ nil and ID₁ ≠ ID₃
9                   kill(ID₃)
10                  kill(ID₄)
11                  mem(A,X+Y)
12                  pc(L+1)
13                  return true
14               end
15            end
16         end
17      end
18      return false
19   end
```

Listing 9. The compilation scheme for the `pc(L)` occurrence after applying *Early Drop* to Listing 7. Also, no propagation history is kept since the occurrence is part of a simpagation rule.

that are never matched by reactivated constraints, however, [43] proves that the history can either be eliminated, or replaced by very cheap constraint identifier comparisons. The same paper moreover shows that reapplication is generally more efficient than maintaining a propagation history, and presents a static analysis that determines when rule reapplication has no observable effect. Together, these optimizations cover most propagation rules occurring in practice.

Guard Simplification. For each occurrence, guard simplification looks at earlier removed occurrences to infer superfluous conjuncts in the guard. This optimization is best described in [41]. The expected performance gain for guard simplification in itself is limited. Simplifying guards, however, does improve results of other analyses, such as the detection of passive occurrences described in the next optimization.

Passive Occurrences. An important goal of several CHR analyses is to detect *passive occurrences*. An occurrence is passive if it can be derived that the corresponding rule can never fire with the active constraint matching it. Detecting passive occurrences is important, not only because superfluous searches for partner constraints are avoided, but also because any index structures only required for these searches do not have to be maintained.

Subsumption Analysis. Where guard simplification tries to replace guards with `true`, subsumption analysis uses similar techniques to replace guards with `false`.

An occurrence is *subsumed* by another occurrence if each constraint that matches the former constraint also matches the latter (taking into account guards and partner constraints). An occurrence that is subsumed by an earlier removed occurrence can be made passive. More information can be found in [41].

Example 19. In the LEQ handler of Fig. 1, the kept occurrence of the *idempotence* rules is clearly subsumed by the removed one (recall from Section 2.2 that ω_r specifies that removed occurrences are tried first). By symmetry, one of the occurrences of the *antisymmetry* rule can be made passive as well (as ω_r considers occurrences from right-to-left, the first occurrence will be made passive).

Never Stored Analysis. If one of the partners of an occurrence is known never to be stored in the constraint store, that occurrence can also be made passive. The basic analysis [7, 8] determines that a constraint is never stored if:

- The constraint occurs in a single-headed, guardless simplification rule. The *Guard Simplification* optimization helps considerably by removing redundant guards in these rules.
- The *Late Storage* analysis shows that the constraint is never stored prior to the execution of a body.

Never stored constraints also do not require any constraint store data structures.

Example 20. Given the complete RAM handler program (Appendix A), a CHR compiler can derive that the pc constraint is never stored. All other occurrences in the add rule of Example 10 are therefore passive. Because most occurrences of mem constraints are thus found passive, a compiler can also derive that less indexes have to be built for looking up prog constraints.

Selective Constraint Reactivation. The naive approach reactivates all suspended constraints (with modifiable arguments) for each modification to a constrained value. This corresponds to the unoptimized **Solve** transition in the refined operational semantics. Reconsidering always *all* constraints though is clearly very inefficient. An obvious optimization is to reactivate only those constraints whose arguments are affected. For an efficient interaction with CHR, constrained data values should therefore maintain references to the CHR constraints they occur in. In terms of the well-known observer pattern [27]: CHR constraints have to observe their arguments.

As explained in Section 4.2, built-in constraint solvers should perform selective reactivation transparently to the user. Changes in a built-in constraint store can typically be reduced to a limited set of variables. This allows the reactivation of only those CHR constraints that are affected by a change in the constraint store. This is analogous to a typical implementation of a constraint solver: constrained variables contain references to all constraints they occur in (see e.g. [46]). When extending logic programming languages with constraint solvers, *attributed variables* are typically used for this [47].

Several further optimizations are possible to avoid more redundant work on reactivation:

- If two unbound (logical) variables are told equal, only the constraints observing one of these variables have to be reactivated. This is correct because all rules that become applicable by telling this equality constraint necessarily contain constraints over both variables.
- So-called *wake conditions* can be used to reconsider only those occurrences whose guard might be affected. This becomes particularly interesting for more complex built-in constraints, such as finite domain constraints. For more information we refer to [16]. Closely related are the *events* used in efficient implementations of constraint propagators [48].

As argued in Sections 3–4, the modification problem should also be addressed for arbitrary host language values. Asides from the `reactivateAll` operation, more selective constraint reactivation needs to be possible. Possible solutions include a well-defined use of the observer pattern, or reactivate operations with user-definable filter functions.

Delay Avoidance. By the previous optimization, a constraint is reactivated each time one of its arguments is modified. If the compiler can prove though that these modifications cannot affect the outcome of a rule's guard, there is no need to reactivate. This is the case if a particular argument does not occur in any guard, or only in anti-monotonous guards (see [49]). A constraint does not have to observe one of its arguments if none of its occurrences has to be reconsidered when it is modified. More details can be found in [49] and [50, Appendix A].

Memory Reuse. The memory reuse optimizations of [42] can also be ported to the imperative setting. Two classes of optimizations are distinguished:

- *Suspension reuse*: Memory used by suspensions of removed constraints can be reused for newly added constraints.
- *In-place updates*: In-place updates go one step further. If a constraint is removed and immediately replaced in the rule's body, it is possible to reuse the suspension of the former. This is particularly interesting if the new constraint is of the same constraint type, and only slightly different from the removed constraint. It could then be that the suspension does not have to be removed and re-added to certain indices.

There are subtle issues when implementing this optimization. For more details, we refer to [42].

Example 21. In the RAM simulator example, both constraints added in the body are replacing removed constraints. Using a `replace(ID, indexes, values)` that assigns new values to the arguments on the specified indices, lines 9–13 of Listing 9 can safely be replaced by:

```
⋮
replace(ID₃, [2], [X+Y])
replace(ID₄, [1], [L+1])
⋮
```

We assume the `replace` operation also activates the updated constraint. In this case, updating these arguments should not require any constraint store operations. The only index on the `mem` constraint for instance is on its first argument. Updating the X argument of the `mem(A,X)#`ID$_3$ suspension does not require this index to be adjusted.

Drop After Reactivation. If a rule fires, the refined operational semantics determines that the active constraint is suspended — i.e., pushed on the activation stack — until the body is completely executed. During the execution of the body this constraint may be reactivated. In this case, when the execution continues with the suspended constraint, all applicable rules matching it have already been tried or fired by this reactivation. Searching for more partner constraints, and continuing with further occurrences, is then superfluous.

Traditionally, this optimization is implemented using an integer field incremented each time the constraint is reactivated (see e.g. [5], which also contains a correctness proof). Here, we propose a slightly more efficient implementation, which also generalizes better when considering the optimized compilation scheme presented in Section 5.4. We use a boolean field, `activated`, in the constraint suspension, which is set to `true` *after* each reactivation. Prior to a **Propagate** transition, the active constraint's `activated` field is set to `false`. If after the execution of the body, it has become `true`, the constraint must have been reactivated, and the handling of this active constraint can safely be terminated using an early drop (i.e., by returning `true`, as in the *Early Drop* optimization).

This optimization is not applied if static analysis determines that the body never reactivates the active constraint. Obvious instances include when the body is empty, or, if all arguments of the active constraint are unmodifiable. In all other cases, this optimization may save a lot of redundant work.

5.4   Recursion Optimizations

Any non-trivial CHR program contains recursion, i.e., directly or indirectly, there are rules with an occurrence of c/n in the head that activate a body that add a constraint of the same type c/n to the store. In such a case, the compilation schema presented in the previous two sections generates a set of mutually recursive host language procedures. We rely on the host language compiler for generating the final executable, or on the host language interpreter for the eventual execution of our generated code. If the host language does not adequately deal with recursion, the naive compilation scheme leads to stack overflow issues.

Prolog implementations perform tail call optimization since the early days of Prolog. This optimization consists in reusing the execution frame of the caller for the last call in of a clause's body. Prolog thus executes tail calls in constant stack space. For a host language like Prolog, recursion is therefore less of a problem: to solve call stack overflows during the execution of a CHR program it mostly suffices to rewrite the CHR program to use tail calls for the recursive constraints. The notion of tail calls in the context of CHR is explained later.

Even though similar tail call optimizations are possible in imperative host languages [51], in practice, most compilers for imperative languages do not perform them, or only in certain situations. The GCC C compiler [52], for instance, only optimizes tail calls in specific cases [53]. Most implementations of the Java Virtual Machine [54], including Sun's reference implementation HotSpot [55], do not perform (recursive) tail call optimizations at all[4]. Indeed, in practice we have observed that our naive compilation schema to Java overflows the execution stack very quickly. For C the situation is only slightly better.

Since improving the optimizations in the host language compilers is seldom an option, we designed novel compilation schemes that avoids execution stack overflows. Stack overflow can only occur when calling arbitrary host language code. Our new schema keeps data structures for the control flow of a CHR program on the heap. It might seem that the overflow is just shifted from the stack to the heap. However, in the new schema we guarantee that these data structures remain constant size for CHR programs that are tail recursive. Moreover, in a language like Java, the heap is substantially larger than the call stack. So in any case, even for non-tail recursive CHR programs, the memory limits will be reached considerably later. This is also experimentally validated in Section 6.

Tail Calls in CHR. In CHR, a *tail call* occurs when the active constraint matches a removed occurrence, and the body ends with the addition of a CHR constraint. If the active constraint is not removed, the last body conjunct is not considered a tail call, as the search for partner constraints has to be resumed after the execution for the body, or more occurrences have to be tried for the previously active constraint.

Example 22. Recall the *add* rule of Example 10. For an active pc(L) constraint, the execution of this rule's body results in a tail call. The leq(Y,Z) constraint added by the body of the *transitivity* rule of Fig. 1, however, is not a tail call.

Using the optimized compilation schemes presented below, tail calls no longer consume space.

Trampoline. Tail calls in CHR can be optimized such that they no longer consume stack space. A CHR constraint added by a tail call is no longer activated immediately by calling the corresponding occurrence procedures. Instead, a constraint suspension is returned that represents this constraint. Control then always returns to a loop that activates these suspensions as long tail calls occur. This technique is called *trampoline* [57, 58].

So tail calls are replaced by a **return** of the newly created constraint. The 'return true' statements introduced for the *Early Drop* and *Drop after Reactivation* optimizations (cf. Section 5.3) are replaced by 'return DROP', the default 'return false' statements by 'return nil'. These are the only changes required to the occurrence procedures. All optimizations of Section 5.3 remain applicable.

---

[4] Supporting tail call optimization would interfere with Java's stack walking security mechanism (though this security folklore has recently been challenged in [56]).

```
1              ⋮
2              kill(ID₃)
3              kill(ID₄)
4              mem(A,X+Y)
5              return create(pc,[L+1])
6          end
7        ⋰
8      end
9      return nil
10   end
```

Listing 10. The compilation scheme for the RAM simulator rule occurrence, modifying Listing 9 for use in the trampoline scheme of Listing 11

Example 23. The RAM handler contains many tail calls. The compilation of the pc(L) occurrence of its *add* rule (see Example 10) using the trampoline compilation scheme is shown in Listing 10.

Next we modify the $c(X_1, \ldots, X_n)$ and reactivate(ID) procedures of Listing 2 to loop as long as the occurrence procedure returns a constraint suspension to activate. The looping is done by a separate procedure trampoline, called from both c and reactivate. The resulting compilation scheme is shown in Listing 11. The listing also shows the modified activate procedure. In the default case, nil, the next occurrence procedure is tried. Otherwise, the control returns to the trampoline (lines 11–15). The returned value is either a constraint suspension in case of a tail call, or the special DROP value. The latter case corresponds with a **Drop** transition of the current active constraint, so the trampoline exits. In the former case though, the constraint from the tail call is activated. By always returning to the trampoline this way, tail calls no longer consume stack space.

Explicit Stack. This subsection presents a more general solution. Whilst trampoline-style compilation deals with tail calls only, the new compilation scheme deals with all instances of recursion. Instead of mapping the refined semantics' activation stack onto the host's implicit call stack, it maintains an explicit *continuation stack* on the heap. The elements on this stack are called *continuations*, and represent "the rest of the computation for an active constraint".

If a conjunction of multiple CHR constraints has to be executed, a *continuation* is pushed onto this stack, containing all information required to execute all but the first body conjunct. Next, the first conjunct is executed by returning to an outer control loop, similar to the trampoline scheme. After this conjunct has been handled completely, the continuation is popped from the stack, and the remainder of the body is executed in a similar, conjunct-by-conjunct fashion. If the remaining body is empty, and the active occurrence is alive, more partner constraints are searched, or the next occurrence is tried. Similar techniques are used to solve recursion involving built-in constraints or host language code.

```
1    procedure c(X₁,...,Xₙ)
2       ID = create(c, [X₁,...,Xₙ])
3       trampoline(ID)
4    end
5
6    procedure reactivate(ID)
7       trampoline(ID)
8    end
9
10   procedure trampoline(cont)
11      do
12          cont = activate(cont)
13      while cont ≠ DROP
14   end
15
16   procedure activate(c(X₁,...,Xₙ)#ID)
17      ret = occurrence_c_1(ID,X₁,...,Xₙ)
18      if ret ≠ nil
19         return ret
20      end
21      ⋮
22      ret = occurrence_c_m(ID,X₁,...,Xₙ)
23      if ret ≠ nil
24         return ret
25      end
26      store(ID)
27      return DROP
28   end
```

Listing 11. Compilation scheme for an n-ary constraint c with m occurrences throughout the program, replacing Listing 2. A *trampoline* loop is added around the call to `activate`. The latter procedure is further modified to return either a constraint suspension, in case of a tail call, or the special DROP value otherwise.

We treat constraint suspensions as a special case of continuations. If *called* (see below), the corresponding constraint is simply activated. The following operations are introduced:

push($\langle$ID, *occurrence number, body index, vars*$\rangle$). Pushes a new *continuation* onto the continuation stack. This continuation contains the identifier of the active constraint, the number of the occurrence that caused the rule application, the index of the next body conjunct to be executed, and the variables required to execute the remainder of the body.

push(ID). Pushes a constraint suspension on the continuation stack.

pop(). Removes the most recently pushed continuation from the continuation stack and returns it.

```
1    procedure c(X_1,...,X_n)
2        push(SENTINEL)
3        cont = create(c, [X_1,...,X_n])
4        do
5            cont = call(cont)
6            if cont = DROP
7                cont = pop()
8            end
9        while cont ≠ SENTINEL
10   end
11
12   procedure reactivate(ID)
13       push(ID)
14   end
```

Listing 12. Compilation scheme for telling a CHR constraint using a continuation stack

call(*continuation*). An extension of the `activate` operation of Listing 11. For constraint suspensions, `call` is equivalent to `activate`. Calling another constraint suspension resumes the handling of a suspended active constraint. This entails executing any remaining body conjuncts, resuming a search for partner constraints, or advancing to the next occurrence. The implementation of this operation is discussed below.

The compilation scheme is listed in Listing 12. Similar to the trampoline compilation scheme, recursion is solved by always returning to an outer control loop. The main differences with Listing 11 are the generalization of constraint suspensions to continuations, and the use of the continuation stack. As before, a constraint suspension for the newly told constraint is created (line 3), followed by a loop that repeatedly calls continuations (lines 4–9). Calling a continuation still returns the next continuation to be executed, which is DROP if the handling of the previously active constraint is finished. In the latter case, a next continuation is popped from the stack (lines 6–8).

To overcome recursion involving multiple constraint CHR handlers, or interleaving with host language code (see later), all cooperating CHR handlers of the same constraint system share the same continuation stack (cf. Section 4.2). In order to know when to return from the procedure of Listing 12, a special SENTINEL continuation is pushed on line 2. Popping a SENTINEL continuation means the **Drop** transition for the constraint initially told by the procedure was reached (line 6), and the procedure must return.

In the remainder of this section, we focus on the compilation scheme for the piecewise execution of the body. For a more complete discussion of the compilation scheme and the call operation, we refer to [36].

Recall the generic form of a CHR rule ρ introduced in Section 5.2:

$$\rho @ c_1^{[j_1]}(X_{1,1}, \ldots, X_{1,a_1}), \ldots, c_{r-1}^{[j_{r-1}]}(X_{r-1,1}, \ldots, X_{r-1,a_{r-1}}) \setminus$$
$$c_r^{[j_r]}(X_{r,1}, \ldots, X_{r,a_r}), \ldots, c_h^{[j_h]}(X_{h,1}, \ldots, X_{h,a_h}) \Leftrightarrow g_1, \ldots, g_{n_g} \mid b_1, \ldots, b_{n_b}.$$

Suppose an applicable rule was found with the active constraint matching the $c_i^{[j_i]}$ occurrence. Suppose the body conjuncts that still have to be executed are $b_k, \ldots, b_{n_b}$, with $k \leq n_b$. At the **Propagate** or **Simplify** transition itself, k will be equal to one, but when calling a continuation k can be larger than one. We distinguish three different cases:

(1) b_k *is a CHR constraint*
Let $b_k = c(Y_1, \ldots, Y_a)$, then this case is simply implemented as:

> $\vdots$
> **push**(ID_i, j_i, $k+1$, $vars\langle b_{k+1}, \ldots, b_{n_b}\rangle$)
> **return** create(c, $[Y_1, \ldots, Y_a]$)
> $\cdot\cdot\cdot$

The constraint suspension of the first conjunct is returned, after pushing a continuation on the stack. The expression $vars\langle b_{k+1}, \ldots, b_{n_b}\rangle$ returns all variables required in the remainder of the body. This way, after the returned constraint is activated and fully handled, the execution continues handling the currently active constraint. First, the remaining body will be piecewise executed, using the compilation scheme presented in this section. If the body is completely executed, and the active constraint is still alive, more applicable rules are searched, starting at the occurrence that caused the previous rule application.

Example 24. In Listing 13 the full generated pseudocode for our running example is given. Only the code for the occurrence of the pc constraint in the *add* rule is given. The body of the occurrence first creates a continuation on the stack, and then returns the mem constraint that needs to be activated next. Eventually, after this constraint is completely handled, the continuation will be popped from the stack and executed. The code for this continuation, given in lines 45–47, simply returns the new pc constraint.

(2) b_k *is a Built-In Constraint*
Calling a built-in constraint from a body may reactivate CHR constraints, which could cause recursive applications of the same rule. To avoid this, the reactivate(ID) procedure of Listing 12 is simply implemented as push(ID). Reactivations are thus not performed immediately, but instead pushed onto the continuation stack. A built-in constraint b_k in a body is then compiled as:

> $\vdots$
> **push**(ID_i, j_i, $k+1$, $vars\langle b_{k+1}, \ldots, b_{n_b}\rangle$)
> b_k
> **return** pop()
> $\cdot\cdot\cdot$

```
1    procedure pc(L)
2       push(SENTINEL)
3       cont = create(pc, [L])
4       do
5          cont = call(cont)
6          if cont = DROP
7             cont = pop()
8          end
9       while cont ≠ SENTINEL
10   end
11
12   procedure call(pc(L)#ID)
13      ret = occurrence_pc_1(ID,L)
14      if ret ≠ nil
15         return ret
16      end
17         ⋮
18      ret = occurrence_pc_m(ID,L)
19      if ret ≠ nil
20         return ret
21      end
22      store(ID)
23      return DROP
24   end
25
26   procedure occurrence_pc_1(ID₄,L)
27      prog(L₁,$₁,B₁,A)#ID₂ = lookup_single(prog,{L=L₁})
28      if ID₂ ≠ nil
29         if $₁ = ADD
30            mem(A₁,X)#ID₃ = lookup_single(mem,{A=A₁})
31            if ID₃ ≠ nil
32               mem(B,Y)#ID₁ = lookup_single(mem,{B=B₁})
33               if ID₁ ≠ nil and ID₁ ≠ ID₃
34                  kill(ID₃)
35                  kill(ID₄)
36                  push(⟨pc,1,2,[L]⟩)
37                  return create(mem,[A,X+Y])
38               end
39            end
40         end
41      end
42      return false
43   end
44
45   procedure call(⟨pc,1,2,[L]⟩)
46      return create(pc,[L+1])
47   end
```

Listing 13. Full example of generated code for the pc(L) constraint in the RAM simulator. Included are the pc(L) procedure for adding a constraint to the store from host language, occurrence code for first occurrence, and a polymorphic call dispatcher for both pc suspensions and continuations of the first occurrence body.

The continuation is pushed, the built-in constraint is executed, and the top of the stack is returned. If the built-in constraint triggered reactivations these are executed first. If not, the continuation itself is popped and executed. Notice that compared to the scheme that used the native call stack, this scheme reverses the order in which constraints are reactivated. This is allowed because the refined operational semantics does not determine this order.

If built-in constraints only rarely reactivate constraints, the above scheme is overly expensive. The creation, pushing and popping of the continuation can be avoided. One possible optimization uses the following two stack operations:

stackSize() Returns the number of continuations currently on the stack.
replace(index, ID, *occurrence number, body index, vars*)
>   Similar to push, but adds the continuation on a given index rather than on top of the stack. The operation returns the continuation that was previously on the given index.

The stack indexes start from zero, so the index of the next continuation to be pushed is equal to stackSize. In other words, 'replace(stackSize(), ...)' is equivalent to 'push(...)'. The compilation scheme becomes:

```
    ⋮
SS = stackSize()
    ⋮
b_k
if (stackSize() > SS)
    return replace(SS, ID_i, j_i, k + 1, vars⟨b_{k+1}, ..., b_{n_b}⟩)
    ⋮ /* remainder of the body, starting with b_{k+1} */
```

This way, a continuation is only created and pushed, if a built-in constraint causes reactivations. By remembering the old stack size, this continuation is inserted exactly on the same location as before. The result of the call to replace will be a reactivation continuation. If no reactivations are pushed though, the control simply continues with the remainder of the body, or with the search for partner constraints.

(3) b_k *is a Host Language Statement*
Recursion where CHR code is interleaved with host language code is more difficult to eliminate. Firstly, host language code may not only reactivate CHR constraints, it can also add new CHR constraints. The scheme used for built-in constraints therefore cannot be used, as reversing the activation order of CHR constraints told from host language code is not allowed by the refined operational semantics. Secondly, CHR handlers and built-in constraint solvers are *incremental*: executing a built-in or CHR constraint has to immediately perform all required changes, before returning control. By default, CHR constraint solvers should remain incremental, as host language code may rely on this property. This is also why the SENTINEL continuation is pushed on line 2 of Listing 12:

this way multiple activations that have to return control after their activation can be handled using the same stack.

The implicit call stack can still overflow if a CHR handler and host language code recursively call each other. Arguably, this behavior is acceptable. One possibility to safeguard against these stack overflows though is to abandon incrementality. A queue can then be used to collect all constraints told whilst executing a host language statement in a body. Once the control returns to the CHR handler, the enqueued continuations are pushed, *in reverse order*, on the continuation stack. We refer to [36] for more details.

Optimizations. If the active constraint is still alive after the execution of a body, remaining partner constraints have to be searched. The naive explicit stack scheme outlined in the previous subsection simply restarts all iterations, relying on the propagation history to avoid duplicate rule applications. This results in many redundant lookups, iterations, and history checks. The optimized scheme includes the constraint iterators into the continuations of the explicit stack, and uses them to efficiently resume the search for partner constraints.

Explicitly maintaining a stack unavoidably entails constant time overheads when compared to the traditional, call-based compilation scheme. The host environment's call stack is able to use more specialized low level mechanisms. This is particularly the case for high-level host languages such as Java. Possible optimizations to reduce these overheads include:

- Pushing a continuation can sometimes be avoided,for instance in the case of a tail call. Also, if there are no more partner constraints to be searched due to set semantics, the pushing of a continuation at the end of the body can be improved. These specializations can be done either statically, or by simple runtime checks.
- If static analysis shows activating a constraint does not result in recursion, the constraint can simply be activated using the compilation scheme of Sections 5.2–5.3.
- Continuations can sometimes be reused.
- The *Drop after Reactivation* optimization can be generalized to not only drop if a constraint is reactivated during an activation, but also if it is reactivated during an earlier reactivation. As constraint reactivations are not executed immediately, but instead scheduled on the continuation stack. This can again lead to the same constraint occurring multiple times on the continuation stack. In the scheme outlined above, these redundant reactivations can easily be avoided[5].

For a more detailed description of these and other optimizations, we refer to [36].

Example 25. In Listing 13, creating the continuation on line 36 is not necessary. As the remaining body is a tail call, simply pushing the constraint suspension representing the pc(L+1) constraint suffices.

---

[5] This optimization is not specific to the compilation scheme with an explicit stack. The implementation for the scheme presented in Sections 5.2–5.3 however is less straightforward.

Furthermore, after application of the *Passive Occurrences* optimization (see Section 5.3), most occurrences of the *mem* constraint are passive in the RAM handler (Appendix A). Static analysis therefore easily derives that adding a *mem* never causes recursion. A *mem* constraint can therefore safely be activated using the host's call stack.

When combining these optimizations, Listing 13 essentially reduces to Listing 10. For the RAM handler the explicit call stack is thus never used.

Conclusion. The implicit call stack of the host environment is replaced by an explicitly maintained stack on the host's heap. If the explicit stack is not used though, the compilation scheme of Listing 12 becomes equivalent to the trampoline scheme of Listing 11. CHR tail calls therefore do not consume space. Also, even if tail optimizations are not possible, the heap of imperative hosts such as Java or C is considerably larger than their stack. We refer to Section 6 for an experimental evaluation.

6   Evaluation

Using the compilation scheme given in Section 5, we implemented a CHR embedding for two imperative host languages, Java and C. These implementations are briefly discussed in Section 6.1, and their performance is evaluated in Section 6.2.

Table 1. Summary of all listed optimizations and their implementations in K.U.Leuven CHR for SWI- and YAP Prolog, K.U.Leuven JCHR and CCHR (development versions of March 1, 2008). Optimizations that are implemented only partially or in an ad-hoc fashion are indicated with '±'.

Optimization	Prolog	JCHR	CCHR
Loop-Invariant Code Motion	✓	✓	✓
Indexing	✓	✓	✓
Join Ordering	✓	✓	✓
Set Semantics		✓	
Early Drop	✓	✓	✓
Backjumping		✓	✓
Non-Robust Iterators	✓	✓	✓
Late Storage	✓	✓	±
Late Allocation	✓		±
Distributed Propagation History	✓	✓	✓
History Elimination	✓	✓	
Guard Simplification	✓		
Passive Occurrences	✓	✓	±
Selective Constraint Reactivation	✓	✓	✓
Delay Avoidance	✓	✓	
Memory Reuse			±
Generations	✓	✓	✓
Recursion optimization		✓	✓

6.1   Implementations

In this section we briefly discuss the implementation of two imperative embeddings of CHR, namely the K.U.Leuven JCHR system [25] for Java and CCHR [26] for C. These implementations are available at respectively [12] and [13].

The most important language design issues taken for both systems are discussed in Section 4. Our implementations do not provide search. We are convinced though that search can be added effectively to our CHR systems as a mostly orthogonal component, as shown by related systems [19, 20].

Both systems implement the compilation scheme presented in Section 5. The implemented optimizations are listed in Table 1. As a reference, the table also lists the optimizations implemented by the K.U.Leuven CHR system [5, 6] for SWI-Prolog [59] (in the version of SWI used, the memory reuse optimizations of [42] were not implemented).

As discussed in Section 5.3, the recursion optimizations are less relevant for a Prolog implementation, as the Prolog runtime performs tail call optimizations. Both JCHR and CCHR explicitly maintain an explicit continuation stack when necessary (see Section 5.3). In CCHR continuations are efficiently implemented using `goto` statements. In Java this is not possible. For a detailed discussion of the compilation scheme used by JCHR, we refer to [36].

6.2   Performance

To verify our implementation's competitiveness, we benchmarked the performance of some typical CHR programs. The following benchmarks were used[6]:

- Calculating $tak(500, 450, 405)$ with a tabling Takeuchi function evaluator.
- Using Dijkstra's algorithm to find the shortest path in a sparse graph with 16,384 nodes and 65,536 edges. A Fibonacci heap, also implemented in CHR, is used to obtain the optimal complexity (see [44] for a description of the Dijkstra and Fibonacci heap handlers).
- Solving a circular set of 100 less-or-equal-than constraints (see Fig. 1).
- Calculating 25,000 resp. 200,000 Fibonacci numbers using the RAM simulator (see Appendix A), with the addition replaced by a multiplication to avoid arithmetic operations on large numbers (when using multiplication all Fibonacci numbers are equal to one).

The results[7] can be found in Table 2. We compared our two systems with the K.U.Leuven CHR system implementation for SWI-Prolog, and its port to YAP Prolog [60], a more efficient Prolog system. The YAP implementation used an older version of K.U.Leuven CHR. Execution times for native implementations in C and Java were added for reference.

---

[6] Benchmarks available at http://www.cs.kuleuven.be/~petervw/bench/lnai2008/

[7] The benchmarks were performed on a Intel® Core™2 Duo 6400 system with 2 GiB of RAM. SWI-Prolog 5.6.50 and YAP 5.1.2 were used. All C programs were compiled with GCC 4.1.3 [52]. K.U.Leuven JCHR 1.6.0 was used; the generated Java code was compiled with Sun's JDK 1.6.0 and executed with HotSpot JRE 1.6.0.

Table 2. Benchmark comparing performance in some typical CHR programs in several systems. The average CPU runtime in milliseconds is given and, between parentheses, the relative performance with YAP Prolog as the reference system.

	Takeuchi	Dijkstra	leq	RAM	
				25k	**200k**
YAP	2,310 (100%)	44,000 (100%)	4,110 (100%)	1,760 (100%)	15,700 (100%)
SWI	3,930 (170%)	6,620 (15%)	17,800 (433%)	1,000 (57%)	*stack overflow*
CCHR	48 (2.1%)	1,170 (2.7%)	189 (4.5%)	416 (24%)	3,540 (23%)
JCHR	183 (7.9%)	704 (1.6%)	68 (1.7%)	157 (8.9%)	1,714 (11%)
C	10 (0.4%)	-	2 (.05%)	1.3 (.07%)	12.7 (.08%)
Java	11 (0.5%)	-	2 (.05%)	2 (.11%)	16 (.10%)

The imperative systems are significantly faster than both Prolog systems, up to one or two orders of magnitude, depending on the benchmark. This is partly due to the fact that the generated Java and C code is (just-in-time) compiled, whereas the Prolog code is interpreted. In SWI the RAM benchmark consumes linear stack space as the SWI runtime does not perform the necessary tail call optimizations. The RAM benchmark for 200k Fibonacci numbers therefore results in a stack overflow.

The native C and Java implementations remain two orders of magnitude faster than their CHR counterparts. The main reason is that these programs use specialized, low-level data structures, or exploit domain knowledge difficult to derive from the CHR program. The Dijkstra algorithm was not implemented natively.

To show the necessity for the recursion optimizations of Section 5.4 in Java and C, we also benchmarked the limits on recursion. A simple program was tested that recursively adds a single constraint. If this happened using a tail call, JCHR runs out of stack space after 3,200 steps when using the unoptimized compilation scheme (i.e., without recursions optimizations). For CCHR, the GCC compiler was able to perform tail call optimization. Both YAP and SWI performed tail call optimization as well. For these systems, the test therefore ran in constant stack space, without limits. Using the optimized compilation scheme of Section 5.4, the same applies of course for JCHR (and CCHR).

If the recursive call was not a tail call, the different systems showed the following limits. Both SWI's and Java's native call stack have static size. In SWI, the test resulted in a stack overflow after 3.3 million recursive calls, in JCHR, without recurions optimization, already after 3,200 calls (the same as when a tail call was used). These numbers clearly show the necessity for the recursion optimizations when compiling to Java. If using an explicit call stack, JCHR is only limited by available heap memory, which is substantially larger than the stack. Using standard heap size, more than 1.8 million calls were possible. As the Java system used can be configured to use larger heap sizes, JCHR became essentially only limited by available (virtual) memory. The size of Java's call stack could not be configured.

The results for C were similar to those for Java: when using the unoptimized scheme the C call stack overflowed after around half a million recursive calls, whereas with the explicit stack optimization, CCHR permits over 40 million recursive calls. YAP Prolog's call stack grows dynamically, so YAP is also only limited by available (virtual) memory.

7   Related Work

Even though (C)LP remains the most common CHR host language paradigm (see e.g. [4, 5, 6, 7, 8]), an increasing number of other CHR implementations have appeared. In this section we discuss several CHR embeddings in functional and imperative host languages (Sections 7.1 and 7.2 respectively), focussing on how they deal with the issues raised in Section 3.

Of course, countless other declarative paradigms have been integrated and compiled to imperative host languages. We only consider *production rules* (Section 7.3), as this formalism is most closely related to CHR.

7.1   CHR in Functional Languages

When embedding CHR in functional languages, many of the same challenges are met. Typically, functional languages are statically typed, and do not provide search or built-in constraints. Structural matching on compound data on the other hand is mostly readily available.

HCHR provides a type-safe embedding of CHR in Haskell, leveraging the the built-in Haskell type checker to type check HCHR programs [61]. HCHR constraints only range over typed logical variables and terms, encoded as a polymorphic Haskell data type. Unification and matching functions are generated automatically for each type (this is similar to the approach taken by CCHR, cf. Section 4.3). Haskell data structures therefore have to be encoded as terms when used in a HCHR constraint, and reconstructed again when retrieving answers. No Haskell functions can be called from HCHR rule bodies, probably due to this data type mismatch.

The Chameleon system [62] is a Haskell-style language that incorporates CHR. It has been applied successfully to experiment with advanced type system extensions [63]. Chameleon's back-end CHR solver is HaskellCHR [64]. To allow Prolog-style terms with variables, this system includes a WAM implementation for Haskell, written in C. It is the only Haskell CHR system to provide chronological backtracking. HaskellCHR is not intended to be used stand-alone, but simply as a back-end to Chameleon.

With the advent of software transactional memories (STM) in Haskell, two systems with parallel execution strategies have recently been developed: Concurrent CHR [65] and STMCHR[66]. These systems are currently the only known CHR implementations that exploit the inherent parallelism in CHR programs.

Even though both HCHR and Chameleon provide syntactic preprocessing, both Haskell implementations are fairly naive interpreters. Their performance cannot compete with the optimizing CHR compilers for logic and imperative programming host languages. Similarly, the STM implementations are still early prototypes, whose performance is not yet competitive with sequential state-of-the-art implementations (unless of course when multiple processors are used for highly parallelizable CHR programs).

7.2   CHR in Imperative Languages

Aside from the systems discussed in this article, there exist at least three other CHR systems in Java. The oldest is the Java Constraint (JaCK) [9, 17]. The main issue with JaCK is probably its lacking performance (see e.g. [25]). The JaCK framework consists of three major components:

JCHR. A CHR dialect intended to be very similar to Java, in order to provide an intuitive programming language [67]. The semantics of the language are unspecified, and are known to deviate from other CHR implementations. CHR constraints only range over typed logical variables. All Java objects thus have to be wrapped in logical variables. Only static Java methods can be called from a rule's body.

VisualCHR. An interactive tool visualizing the execution of JCHR [68]. It can be used to debug and to improve the performance of constraint solvers.

JASE. The Java Abstract Search Engine, allows for a flexible specification of tree-based search strategies [19]. JCHR bodies do not contain disjunctions, as in (C)LP implementations of CHR$^\vee$. Instead, JASE is added to JaCK as an orthogonal component. The JASE library provides a number of utility classes that help the user to implement a search algorithm in Java. A typical algorithm consists of the following two operations, executed in a loop: first, a JCHR handler is run until it reaches a fix-point, after which a new choice is made. If an inconsistency is found, chronological backtracking is used to return to the previous choice point. JASE aids in maintaining the search tree, and can be configured to use either trailing or copying.

The CHORD system (Constraint Handling Object-oriented Rules with Disjunctive bodies) [10], developed as part of the ORCAS project [69], is a Java implementation of CHR$^\vee$ [70]. Its implementation seems to build on that of JaCK, but adds the possibility to include disjunction in rule bodies.

A last CHR system for Java is DJCHR (Dynamic JCHR) [11], which implements an extension of CHR known as adaptive CHR [71]. Constraint solving in a dynamic environment often requires immediate adaptation of solutions when constraints are added or removed. By nature, CHR solvers already support efficient adaptation on constraint addition. Adaptive CHR is an extension of CHR capable of adapting CHR derivations after constraint deletions as well [71].

Constraints in DJCHR range only over Herbrand terms. Integration of the host language in the CHR rules is not supported. The system seems mainly created to experiment with the incremental adaptation algorithm of [71]. Like JaCK, DJCHR was later extended to support a wide range of search strategies [20]. Search is again implemented orthogonally to the actual CHR handlers. Interestingly, [20] clearly shows that the use of advanced search strategies can be more efficient than a low-level, host language implementation of chronological backtracking (as in Prolog).

7.3   Production Rules

Production rules, or *business rules* as they are often called, are a forward chaining rule-based programming language extension, very similar to CHR. Most of the many commercial and open-source implementations of this paradigm are based on the classical RETE algorithm [72]. This algorithm eagerly computes and maintains all possible joins and applicable rules. As the first rule fired with a fact (the equivalent of a CHR constraint) often already removes this fact (see also Section 5.3), RETE can be very costly. A lazy algorithm that fires applicable rules as it finds them, is usually more efficient in both time and memory. Even though this fact has been recognized in the production rule literature [73], the RETE algorithm remains the most widely used implementation technique. We believe that the compilation scheme developed for CHR, as presented in this article, is the first rigorously studied lazy execution mechanism for forward chaining rules. It would be interesting to compare the performance of CHR with that of state-of-the-art, RETE based production rule engines.

Modern production rule systems such as Jess [74] and Drools [75] allow arbitrary host language code to be called. To solve the modification problem, a technique called *shadow facts* is commonly used. Consistency of the RETE network is maintained by keeping a clone of any modifiable object referred to by facts in an internal data structure. The user is responsible for notifying the rule engine of any changes to these objects. This solution however does not work for arbitrary objects (e.g. only for Java Bean objects [35]), and is fairly inefficient.

8   Conclusions and Future Work

In this work we presented our approach to solve the impedance mismatch between CHR and imperative languages. We outlined the different language design issues faced when embedding CHR into an imperative host language. In our approach, we advocated a tight and natural integration of both paradigms. We illustrated with two case studies, the K.U.Leuven JCHR system and CCHR, and showed that our approach leads to a programming language extension intuitive and useful to adepts of both CHR and the intuitive host language.

We ported the standard CHR compilation scheme to an imperative setting, and showed how the many existing optimizations can be incorporated. The result is a first comprehensive survey of the vast, recent literature on optimized CHR compilation. Many of the presented compilation and optimization techniques are applicable for any implementation of CHR, or any similar rule-based language.

More specific to imperative target languages, we showed that the standard call-based compilation scheme of CHR results in call stack overflows when used to compile to imperative host languages. We proposed a novel, optimized compilation scheme using which CHR programs written using tail calls are guaranteed to execute in constant space. Where tail call optimization is not possible, an explicitly maintained stack is used instead of the host's call stack. By maintaining the stack on the heap, memory limits are reached considerably later for all recursive CHR programs.

We created efficient, state-of-the-art implementations for Java and C, and showed that they outperform other CHR systems up to several orders of magnitude. We also showed the effectiveness of our recursion optimizations.

8.1 Future Work

Certain issues raised in Section 3 are not yet adequately solved by current, imperative CHR systems. The modification problem is only solved effectively for built-in constraints. Similarly, the combination of arbitrary host language code with search requires more investigation. The integration of search in an efficient compilation scheme is also an interesting topic for future research.

The current compilation scheme considers each occurrence separately. However, we believe that more efficient code can be generated with a more global compilation scheme. For instance, the entire RAM handler of Appendix A could be compiled to a single switch statement in a loop. Rather than linearly going through all possible operations for each program counter, the applicable rule would be found in constant time using a switch. Sharing partial joins for overlapping rules among different occurrences is another example.

Over the past decade there has been an increase in the number of CHR systems. The support for advanced software development tools, such as debuggers, refactoring tools, and automated analysis tools, lags behind, and remains an important challenge, not only for the systems embedding CHR in imperative hosts, but for the entire CHR community.

References

1. The Constraint Handling Rules (CHR) programming language homepage, http://www.cs.kuleuven.be/~dtai/projects/CHR/
2. Frühwirth, T.: Theory and practice of Constraint Handling Rules. J. Logic Programming, Special Issue on Constraint Logic Programming 37(1–3), 95–138 (1998)
3. Sneyers, J., Van Weert, P., Schrijvers, T., De Koninck, L.: As time goes by: Constraint Handling Rules — a survey of CHR research between 1998 and 2007. Journal of Theory and Practice of Logic Programming (submitted, 2008)
4. Holzbaur, C., Frühwirth, T.: A Prolog Constraint Handling Rules compiler and runtime system. In: [76], pp. 369–388
5. Schrijvers, T.: Analyses, optimizations and extensions of Constraint Handling Rules. Ph.D thesis, K.U.Leuven, Belgium (June 2005)
6. Schrijvers, T., Demoen, B.: The K.U.Leuven CHR system: Implementation and application. In: [77], pp. 8–12
7. Duck, G.J.: Compilation of Constraint Handling Rules. Ph.D thesis, University of Melbourne, Australia (December 2005)
8. Holzbaur, C., García de la Banda, M., Stuckey, P.J., Duck, G.J.: Optimizing compilation of Constraint Handling Rules in HAL. In: [78], pp. 503–531
9. Abdennadher, S., Krämer, E., Saft, M., Schmauß, M.: JACK: A Java Constraint Kit. In: Hanus, M. (ed.) WFLP 2001: Proc. 10th Intl. Workshop on Functional and (Constraint) Logic Programming, Kiel, Germany. ENTCS, vol. 64, pp. 1–17. Elsevier, Amsterdam (2002), http://pms.ifi.lmu.de/software/jack/

10. Vitorino, J., Aurelio, M.: Chord (2005), http://chord.sourceforge.net/
11. Wolf, A.: Adaptive constraint handling with CHR in Java. In: Walsh, T. (ed.) CP 2001. LNCS, vol. 2239, pp. 256–270. Springer, Heidelberg (2001)
12. Van Weert, P.: The K.U.Leuven JCHR system (2008), http://www.cs.kuleuven.be/~petervw/JCHR/
13. Wuille, P.: CCHR: The fastest CHR implementation, in C (2008), http://www.cs.kuleuven.be/~pieterw/CCHR/
14. Frühwirth, T.: Constraint Handling Rules. Cambridge University Press, Cambridge (to appear, 2008)
15. Duck, G.J., Stuckey, P.J., García de la Banda, M., Holzbaur, C.: The refined operational semantics of Constraint Handling Rules. In: Demoen, B., Lifschitz, V. (eds.) ICLP 2004. LNCS, vol. 3132, pp. 90–104. Springer, Heidelberg (2004)
16. Duck, G.J., Stuckey, P.J., García de la Banda, M., Holzbaur, C.: Extending arbitrary solvers with Constraint Handling Rules. In: PPDP 2003, Uppsala, Sweden, pp. 79–90. ACM Press, New York (2003)
17. Abdennadher, S.: Rule-based Constraint Programming: Theory and Practice. Habilitationsschrift, Institute of Computer Science, LMU, Munich, Germany (July 2001)
18. Abdennadher, S., Schütz, H.: CHR$^\vee$, a flexible query language. In: Andreasen, T., Christiansen, H., Larsen, H. (eds.) FQAS 1998. LNCS, vol. 1495, pp. 1–14. Springer, Heidelberg (1998)
19. Krämer, E.: A generic search engine for a Java Constraint Kit. Diplomarbeit, Institute of Computer Science, LMU, Munich, Germany (January 2001)
20. Wolf, A.: Intelligent search strategies based on adaptive Constraint Handling Rules. In: [78], pp. 567–594 (2005)
21. da Figueira Filho, C.S., Ramalho, G.L.: JEOPS - the java embedded object production system. In: Monard, M.C., Sichman, J.S. (eds.) SBIA 2000 and IBERAMIA 2000. LNCS, vol. 1952, p. 53. Springer, Heidelberg (2000)
22. Pachet, F.: On the embeddability of production rules in object-oriented languages. Journal of Object-Oriented Programming 8(4), 19–24 (1995)
23. Pachet, F. (ed.): EOOPS 1994: Proc. OOPSLA 1994 Workshop on Embedded Object-Oriented Production Systems, Portland, Oregon, USA (October 2004)
24. Bouaud, J., Voyer, R.: Behavioral match: Embedding production systems and objects. In: [23]
25. Van Weert, P., Schrijvers, T., Demoen, B.: K.U.Leuven JCHR: a user-friendly, flexible and efficient CHR system for Java. In: [79], pp. 47–62
26. Wuille, P., Schrijvers, T., Demoen, B.: CCHR: the fastest CHR implementation, in C. In: [80], pp. 123–137
27. Gamma, E., Helm, R., Johnson, R., Vlissides, J.: Design Patterns: Elements of Reusable Object-Oriented Software. Addison-Wesley, Reading (1995)
28. Schrijvers, T., Demoen, B., Duck, G.J., Stuckey, P.J., Frühwirth, T.: Automatic implication checking for CHR constraints. In: RULE 2005: 6th Intl. Workshop on Rule-Based Programming, Nara, Japan, January 2006. ENTCS, vol. 147(1), pp. 93–111. Elsevier, Amsterdam (2006)
29. Fages, F., de Oliveira Rodrigues, C.M., Martinez, T.: Modular chr with ask and tell. In: [81], pp. 95–110
30. Kernighan, B.W., Ritchie, D., Ritchie, D.M.: C Programming Language, 2nd edn. Prentice Hall PTR, Englewood Cliffs (1988)

31. Van Weert, P.: K.U.Leuven JCHR User's Manual (2008). In: [12]
32. Gosling, J., Joy, B., Steele, G., Bracha, G.: The Java Language Specification, 3rd edn. The Java Series. Prentice Hall, Englewood Cliffs (2005)
33. Bracha, G.: Generics in the Java Programming Language (July 2004) (Tutorial)
34. Sun Microsystems, Inc.: The Collections framework: API's and developer guides (2008), http://java.sun.com/javase/6/docs/technotes/guides/collections/
35. Sun Microsystems, Inc.: JavaBeans (2008), http://java.sun.com/products/javabeans/
36. Van Weert, P.: Compiling Constraint Handling Rules to Java: A reconstruction. Technical Report CW 521, K.U.Leuven, Dept. Comp. Sc. (August 2008)
37. Sneyers, J., Schrijvers, T., Demoen, B.: The computational power and complexity of Constraint Handling Rules. In: [79], pp. 3–17
38. De Koninck, L., Sneyers, J.: Join ordering for Constraint Handling Rules. In: [80], pp. 107–121
39. Duck, G.J., Schrijvers, T.: Accurate functional dependency analysis for Constraint Handling Rules. In: [79], pp. 109–124
40. Schrijvers, T., Stuckey, P.J., Duck, G.J.: Abstract interpretation for Constraint Handling Rules. In: Barahona, P., Felty, A. (eds.) PPDP 2005, Lisbon, Portugal, July 2005, pp. 218–229. ACM Press, New York (2005)
41. Sneyers, J., Schrijvers, T., Demoen, B.: Guard reasoning in the refined operational semantics of CHR. In: Schrijvers, T., Frühwirth, T. (eds.) Constraint Handling Rules. LNCS(LNAI), vol. 5388, pp. 213–244. Springer, Heidelberg (2008)
42. Sneyers, J., Schrijvers, T., Demoen, B.: Memory reuse for CHR. In: Etalle, S., Truszczyński, M. (eds.) ICLP 2006. LNCS, vol. 4079, pp. 72–86. Springer, Heidelberg (2006)
43. Van Weert, P.: Optimization of CHR propagation rules. In: ICLP 2008: Proc. 24rd Intl. Conf. Logic Programming, Udine, Italy, December 2008. LNCS. Springer, Heidelberg (accepted, 2008)
44. Sneyers, J., Schrijvers, T., Demoen, B.: Dijkstra's algorithm with Fibonacci heaps: An executable description in CHR. In: [82], pp. 182–191
45. Holzbaur, C., Frühwirth, T.: Compiling Constraint Handling Rules into Prolog with attributed variables. In: Nadathur, G. (ed.) PPDP 1999. LNCS, vol. 1702, pp. 117–133. Springer, Heidelberg (1999)
46. Rossi, F., van Beek, P., Walsh, T. (eds.): Handbook of Constraint Programming. Foundations of Artificial Intelligence. Elsevier, Amsterdam (2006)
47. Holzbaur, C.: Metastructures versus attributed variables in the context of extensible unification. In: Proc. 4th Intl. Symposium on Programming Language Implementation and Logic Programming, pp. 260–268. Springer, Heidelberg (1992)
48. Schulte, C., Stuckey, P.J.: Efficient constraint propagation engines. Under consideration for ACM Transactions on Programming Languages and Systems (2008)
49. Schrijvers, T., Demoen, B.: Antimonotony-based delay avoidance for CHR. Technical Report CW 385, K.U.Leuven, Dept. Comp. Sc (July 2004)
50. Van Weert, P.: A tale of histories. In: [81], pp. 79–94
51. Probst, M.: Proper tail recursion in C. Diplomarbeit, Institute of Computer Languages, Vienna University of Technology (2001)
52. Free Software Foundation: GCC, the GNU Compiler Collection (2008), http://gcc.gnu.org/
53. Bauer, A.: Compilation of functional programming languages using GCC—Tail calls. Master's thesis, Institut für Informatik, Technische Univ. München (2003)
54. Lindholm, T., Yellin, F.: The Java™ Virtual Machine Specification, 2nd edn. Prentice Hall, Englewood Cliffs (1999)

55. Sun Microsystems, Inc.: Java SE HotSpot at a glance (2008),
    http://java.sun.com/javase/technologies/hotspot/
56. Clements, J., Felleisen, M.: A tail-recursive machine with stack inspection. ACM
    Trans. on Prog. Languages and Systems (TOPLAS) 26(6), 1029–1052 (2004)
57. Baker, H.G.: CONS should not CONS its arguments, part II: Cheney on the M.T.A.
    SIGPLAN Notices 30(9), 17–20 (1995)
58. Ganz, S.E., Friedman, D.P., Wand, M.: Trampolined style. In: Intl. Conf. on Func-
    tional Programming, pp. 18–27 (1999)
59. Wielemaker, J.: An overview of the swi-prolog programming environment. In: Proc.
    13th Intl. Workshop on Logic Programming Environments, Mumbai, India (2003),
    http://www.swi-prolog.org/
60. Santos Costa, V., et al.: YAP Prolog, http://www.ncc.up.pt/yap/
61. Chin, W.N., Sulzmann, M., Wang, M.: A type-safe embedding of Constraint Han-
    dling Rules into Haskell. Honors thesis, School of Computing, National University
    of Singapore (2003)
62. Stuckey, P.J., Sulzmann, M., Wazny, J.: The Chameleon system. In: [77], pp. 13–32
63. Stuckey, P.J., Sulzmann, M.: A theory of overloading. ACM TOPLAS 27(6), 1216–
    1269 (2005)
64. Duck, G.J.: HaskellCHR (2004), http://www.cs.mu.oz.au/~gjd/haskellchr/
65. Lam, E.S., Sulzmann, M.: A concurrent Constraint Handling Rules semantics and
    its implementation with software transactional memory. In: DAMP 2007: Proc.
    ACM SIGPLAN Workshop on Declarative Aspects of Multicore Programming,
    Nice, France. ACM Press, New York (2007)
66. Stahl, M.: STMCHR. In: CHR Homepage [1] (2007)
67. Schmauß, M.: An implementation of CHR in Java. Diplomarbeit, Institute of Com-
    puter Science, LMU, Munich, Germany (November 1999)
68. Abdennadher, S., Saft, M.: A visualization tool for Constraint Handling Rules. In:
    Kusalik, A. (ed.) WLPE 2001, Paphos, Cyprus (December 2001)
69. Robin, J., Vitorino, J.: ORCAS: Towards a CHR-based model-driven framework
    of reusable reasoning components. In: [82], pp. 192–199
70. Menezes, L., Vitorino, J., Aurelio, M.: A high performance CHR$^\vee$ execution engine.
    In: [79], pp. 35–45
71. Wolf, A., Gruenhagen, T., Geske, U.: On incremental adaptation of CHR deriva-
    tions. In: [76], pp. 389–416
72. Forgy, C.: Rete: A fast algorithm for the many pattern/many object pattern match
    problem. Artificial Intelligence 19, 17–37 (1982)
73. Miranker, D.P., Brant, D.A., Lofaso, B., Gadbois, D.: On the performance of lazy
    matching in production systems. In: Proc. 8th Intl. Conf. on Artificial Intelligence,
    pp. 685–692 (1990)
74. Friedman-Hill, E., et al.: Jess, the rule engine for the Java platform (2008),
    http://www.jessrules.com/
75. JBoss: Drools (2008), http://labs.jboss.com/drools/
76. Holzbaur, C., Frühwirth, T. (eds.): Special Issue on Constraint Handling Rules.
    Journal of Applied Artificial Intelligence 14(4) (2000)
77. Frühwirth, T., Meister, M. (eds.): CHR 2004: 1st Workshop on Constraint Handling
    Rules: Selected Contributions, Ulm, Germany (May 2004)
78. Abdennadher, S., Frühwirth, T., Holzbaur, C.: Special Issue on Constraint Han-
    dling Rules. Theory and Practice of Logic Programming, vol. 5(4–5). Cambridge
    University Press, Cambridge (2005)

79. Schrijvers, T., Frühwirth, T. (eds.): CHR 2005: Proc. 2nd Workshop on Constraint Handling Rules. CHR 2005. K.U.Leuven, Dept. Comp. Sc., Technical report CW 421, Sitges, Spain (2005)
80. Djelloul, K., Duck, G.J., Sulzmann, M. (eds.): CHR 2007: Proc. 4th Workshop on Constraint Handling Rules. CHR 2007, Porto, Portugal (September 2007)
81. Schrijvers, T., Raiser, F., Frühwirth, T. (eds.): CHR 2008: Proc. 5th Workshop on Constraint Handling Rules. CHR 2008. RISC Report Series 08-10, University of Linz, Austria, Hagenberg, Austria (July 2008)
82. Fink, M., Tompits, H., Woltran, S. (eds.): WLP 2006: Proc. 20th Workshop on Logic Programming. T.U.Wien, Austria, INFSYS Research report 1843-06-02, Vienna, Austria (February 2006)

A   A RAM Simulator Written in CHR

Fig. 9 contains a CHR handler that implements a simulator for a standard RAM machine. The memory of the simulated RAM machine is represented as `mem` constraints, the instructions of the program it is executing as `prog` constraints. The current program counter is maintained as a `pc` constraint. Different CHR

```
// enforce functional dependencies:
mem(A,_), mem(A,_) <=> fail.
prog(L,_,_,_), prog(L,_,_,_) <=> fail.
pc(_), pc(_) <=> fail.

prog(L,ADD,B,A), mem(B,Y) \ mem(A,X), pc(L) <=> mem(A,X+Y), pc(L+1).
prog(L,SUB,B,A), mem(B,Y) \ mem(A,X), pc(L) <=> mem(A,X-Y), pc(L+1).
prog(L,MULT,B,A), mem(B,Y) \ mem(A,X), pc(L) <=> mem(A,X*Y), pc(L+1).
prog(L,DIV,B,A), mem(B,Y) \ mem(A,X), pc(L) <=> mem(A,X/Y), pc(L+1).

prog(L,MOVE,B,A), mem(B,X) \ mem(A,_), pc(L) <=> mem(A,X), pc(L+1).
prog(L,I_MOV,B,A), mem(B,C), mem(C,X) \ mem(A,_), pc(L) <=> mem(A,X), pc(L+1).
prog(L,MOV_I,B,A), mem(B,X), mem(A,C) \ mem(C,_), pc(L) <=> mem(C,X), pc(L+1).

prog(L,CONST,B,A) \ mem(A,_), pc(L) <=> mem(A,B), pc(L+1).
prog(L,INIT,A,_), mem(A,B) \ pc(L) <=> mem(B,0), pc(L+1).

prog(L,JUMP,_,A) \ pc(L) <=> pc(A).
prog(L,CJMP,R,A), mem(R,X) \ pc(L) <=> X == 0 | pc(A).
prog(L,CJMP,R,_), mem(R,X) \ pc(L) <=> X != 0 | pc(L+1).

prog(L,HALT,_,_) \ pc(L) <=> true.

// Safeguard against invalid program counter:
pc(_) <=> fail.
```

Fig. 9. A RAM machine simulator written in CHR

rule declares what has to be done for each instruction type. Example 10 in Section 5.2 discusses the rule for an ADD instruction in more detail.

Four extra rules are added to the original program, as it first appeared in [37]. The first three rules ensure that illegal combinations of constraints cannot occur; the last rule safeguards against invalid program counters. These four extra rules allow static program analysis to defer certain program properties essential for an efficient compilation of the program, as shown in Section 5.3.

Guard Reasoning in the Refined Operational Semantics of CHR

Jon Sneyers[*], Tom Schrijvers[**], and Bart Demoen

Dept. of Computer Science, K.U.Leuven, Belgium
{jon,toms,bmd}@cs.kuleuven.be

Abstract. Constraint Handling Rules (CHR) is a high-level programming language based on multi-headed guarded rules. The original high-level operational semantics of CHR is very nondeterministic. Recently, instantiations of the high-level operational semantics have been proposed and implemented, removing sources of nondeterminism and hence allowing better execution control. Rule guards may be redundant under a more instantiated semantics while being necessary in the general high-level semantics. Expert CHR programmers tend to remove such redundant guards. Although this tends to improve the performance, it also destroys the local logical reading of CHR rules: in order to understand the meaning of a rule, the entire program and the details of the instantiated operational semantics have to be taken into account. As a solution, we propose compiler optimizations that automatically detect and remove redundant guards.

1 Introduction

Constraint Handling Rules (CHR) is a high-level multi-headed rule-based programming language extension commonly used to write constraint solvers. We assume that the reader is familiar with the syntax and semantics of CHR, referring to [6,17] for an overview. Although examples are given for CHR(Prolog), the optimizations can be applied in any host language.

The (original) theoretical operational semantics (ω_t) of CHRs, as defined in [6], is nondeterministic. For instance, the order in which rules are applied is not specified. All implementations of CHR are an instantiation of the ω_t semantics of CHRs. Any of these instantiations are completely deterministic, since they compile CHR programs to (eventually) instructions of a deterministic RAM machine. Although for any given (version of a) CHR system the execution strategy is completely fixed, only a partial instantiation of ω_t is guaranteed by the developers of CHR compilers. In other words, most CHR systems exclude many

---

[*] This work was partly supported by project G.0144.03 funded by the Research Foundation - Flanders (F.W.O.-Vlaanderen). Jon Sneyers is currently funded by Ph.D. grants of the Institute for the Promotion of Innovation through Science and Technology in Flanders (IWT-Vlaanderen).

[**] Post-Doctoral Researcher of the Research Foundation Flanders (FWO-Vlaanderen).

T. Schrijvers and T. Frühwirth (Eds.): Constraint Handling Rules, LNAI 5388, pp. 213–244, 2008.
© Springer-Verlag Berlin Heidelberg 2008

choices allowed by ω_t but at the same time they do not completely specify their exact deterministic operational semantics since it may change in later versions or with certain compiler optimizations switched on or off.

Most CHR systems instantiate the *refined* operational semantics (ω_r) [5] of CHR. In ω_r, the concept of an *active* constraint is introduced: its occurrences are tried top-to-bottom, removed-before-kept, left-to-right, while rule bodies are executed depth-first and left-to-right. In a sense, this generalizes the standard Prolog execution strategy. Recently, other (partial) instantiations of the ω_t semantics have been proposed; most notably, the priority semantics ω_p [3].

Experienced CHR programmers know the operational semantics specified by the CHR system they use. They take that knowledge into account to improve the performance of their program. However, the resulting CHR programs may well be no longer correct in all ω_t execution strategies. The dilemma experienced CHR programmers face is the following: either they make sure their programs are valid under ω_t semantics, or they write programs that only work correctly under a more instantiated operational semantics. The former may result in a performance penalty, while the latter results in a program for which the logical reading of the rules is no longer clear. CHR rules have a (linear or classical) logic reading which is local: a rule always has the same reading, whatever its context. When the specifics of the operational semantics are implicitly assumed, the locality of the logic reading is lost. For instance, under ω_r semantics, CHR programmers often omit the rule guards that are implicitly entailed by the rule order. In this work we show how to overcome this problem by using optimizing compilation.

Automatic code generation and source-to-source transformations are typically implemented by applying a general scheme. Such approaches often introduce many redundant guards or redundant rules. Once more, the optimizations introduced in this paper can be used to improve the output code. By allowing the user to declare background knowledge about the CHR constraints and host-language predicates that are used, even more redundant code can be avoided.

Our contributions are as follows:

1. We formalize the implicit pre-conditions of a constraint occurrence in the refined operational semantics (see Section 4). Our formalization not only considers the rules in the program, but also user-provided declarations for types, modes and general background knowledge (see also Section 3).

2. We establish the usefulness of these pre-conditions for optimized compilation with two program transformations: *guard simplification* and *occurrence subsumption* (see Sections 3 and 4).

3. We describe our implementation of these optimizations (see Section 6), and the common component for entailment checking (see Section 5). The implementation is available in the K.U.Leuven CHR System.

4. Experimental evaluation shows that our optimizations yield compact and efficient code (see Section 7).

5. We sketch a similar approach for the priority semantics (see Section 8).

This paper is a revised and extended version of [16] and [15]. In the next section we briefly introduce CHR and its formal semantics. The body of this paper is structured as outlined above.

2 Constraint Handling Rules

We use $[H|T]$ to denote the first (H) and remaining elements (T) of a sequence, $+\!\!+$ for sequence concatenation, ϵ for empty sequences, $\uplus$ for multiset union, and $\subseteq$ for multiset subset. We shall sometimes omit existential quantors to get a lighter notation. Constraints are either CHR constraints or *built-in* constraints in some constraint domain $\mathcal{D}$. The former are manipulated by the CHR execution mechanism while the latter are handled by an underlying constraint solver. We will assume this underlying solver supports at least equality, `true` and `fail`. We consider all three types of CHR rules to be special cases of simpagation rules:

Definition 1 (CHR program). *A CHR program P is a sequence of CHR rules R_i of the form*

$$\text{(rulename @)} \quad H_i^k \setminus H_i^r \iff g_i \mid B_i$$

where H_i^k (kept head constraints) and H_i^r (removed head constraints) are sequences of CHR constraints with $H_i^k +\!\!+ H_i^r \neq \epsilon$, g_i (guard) is a conjunction of built-in constraints, and B_i (body) is a conjunction of constraints. We will write H_i as a shorthand for $H_i^k +\!\!+ H_i^r$.

If H_i^k is empty, then the rule R_i is a *simplification* rule. If H_i^r is empty, then R_i is a *propagation* rule. Otherwise the rule is a *simpagation* rule. We assume all arguments of the CHR constraints in H_i to be unique variables, making any head matchings explicit in the guard. This head normalization procedure is explained in [4] and an illustrating example can be found in section 2.1 of [12].

We number the occurrences of each CHR constraint predicate p appearing in the heads of the rules of some CHR program P following the top-down rule order and right-to-left constraint order. The latter is aimed at ordering first the constraints after the backslash ($\setminus$) and then those before it, since this gives the refined operational semantics a clearer behavior. We number the rules in the same top-down way.

2.1 The Theoretical Operational Semantics ω_t

The operational semantics ω_t of CHR, sometimes also called *theoretical* or *high-level* operational semantics, is highly nondeterministic. It is formulated as a state transition system.

Definition 2 (Identified constraint). *An* identified *CHR constraint $c\#i$ is a CHR constraint c associated with some unique integer i, the constraint identifier. This number serves to differentiate between copies of the same constraint. We introduce the functions $\mathsf{chr}(c\#i) = c$ and $\mathsf{id}(c\#i) = i$, and extend them to sequences and sets of identified CHR constraints in the obvious manner, e.g. $\mathsf{id}(S) = \{i|c\#i \in S\}$.*

---

1. **Solve** $\langle \{c\} \uplus \mathbb{G}, \mathbb{S}, \mathbb{B}, \mathbb{T} \rangle_n \overset{\omega_t}{\rightarrowtail}_{\mathcal{P}} \langle \mathbb{G}, \mathbb{S}, c \wedge \mathbb{B}, \mathbb{T} \rangle_n$
where c is a built-in constraint and $\mathcal{D}_{\mathcal{H}} \models \bar{\exists}_{\emptyset} \mathbb{B}$.

---

2. **Introduce** $\langle \{c\} \uplus \mathbb{G}, \mathbb{S}, \mathbb{B}, \mathbb{T} \rangle_n \overset{\omega_t}{\rightarrowtail}_{\mathcal{P}} \langle \mathbb{G}, \{c\#n\} \cup \mathbb{S}, \mathbb{B}, \mathbb{T} \rangle_{n+1}$
where c is a CHR constraint and $\mathcal{D}_{\mathcal{H}} \models \bar{\exists}_{\emptyset} \mathbb{B}$.

---

3. **Apply** $\langle \mathbb{G}, H_1 \uplus H_2 \uplus \mathbb{S}, \mathbb{B}, \mathbb{T} \rangle_n \overset{\omega_t}{\rightarrowtail}_{\mathcal{P}} \langle C \uplus \mathbb{G}, H_1 \uplus \mathbb{S}, \theta \wedge \mathbb{B}, \mathbb{T} \cup \{h\} \rangle_n$
where $\mathcal{P}$ contains a (renamed apart) rule of the form $r @ H_1' \setminus H_2' \iff g \mid C$,
θ is a matching substitution such that $chr(H_1) = \theta(H_1')$ and $chr(H_2) = \theta(H_2')$,
$h = (r, \mathsf{id}(H_1), \mathsf{id}(H_2)) \notin \mathbb{T}$, and $\mathcal{D}_{\mathcal{H}} \models (\bar{\exists}_{\emptyset} \mathbb{B}) \wedge (\mathbb{B} \rightarrow \bar{\exists}_{\mathbb{B}} (\theta \wedge g))$.

Fig. 1. The transitions of the theoretical operational semantics ω_t

Definition 3 (ω_t execution state). *An ω_t execution state σ is a tuple $\langle \mathbb{G}, \mathbb{S}, \mathbb{B}, \mathbb{T} \rangle_n$. The goal $\mathbb{G}$ is a multiset of constraints to be rewritten to solved form. The CHR constraint store $\mathbb{S}$ is a set of identified CHR constraints that can be matched with rules in the program $\mathcal{P}$. Note that $\mathsf{chr}(\mathbb{S})$ is a multiset although $\mathbb{S}$ is a set. The built-in constraint store $\mathbb{B}$ is the conjunction of all built-in constraints that have been posted to the underlying solver. These constraints are assumed to be solved (implicitly) by the host language $\mathcal{H}$. The propagation history $\mathbb{T}$ is a set of tuples, each recording the identities of the CHR constraints that fired a rule, and the name of the rule itself. The propagation history is used to prevent trivial non-termination for propagation rules: a propagation rule is allowed to fire on a set of constraints only if the constraints have not been used to fire the same rule before. Finally, the counter $n \in \mathbb{N}$ represents the next integer that can be used to number a CHR constraint. We use $\sigma, \sigma_0, \sigma_1, \dots$ to denote execution states.*

For a given CHR program $\mathcal{P}$, the transitions are defined by the binary relation $\overset{\omega_t}{\rightarrowtail}_{\mathcal{P}}$ shown in Figure 1. Execution proceeds by exhaustively applying the transition rules, starting from an initial state. Given an initial goal G, the *initial state* is: $\langle G, \emptyset, true, \emptyset \rangle_1$.

2.2   The Refined Operational Semantics ω_r

Duck et al. [5] introduced the refined operational semantics ω_r of CHR. It formally captures the behavior of many CHR implementations.

The refined operational semantics uses a stack of constraints: when a new constraint arrives in the constraint store it is pushed on the stack. The constraint on top of the stack is called the *active* constraint. The active constraint is used to find matching rules, in the order in which this constraint occurs in the program. When all occurrences have been tried, the constraint is popped from the stack. When a rule fires, its body is executed immediately from left to right, thereby potentially suspending the active constraint because of newly arriving constraints. When a constraint becomes topmost again, it resumes its search for matching clauses.

1. **Solve** $\langle[c|\mathbb{A}], \mathbb{S}' \uplus \mathbb{S}, \mathbb{B}, \mathbb{T}\rangle_n \stackrel{\omega_r}{\rightarrowtail}_{\mathcal{P}} \langle\mathbb{S} +\!\!+ \mathbb{A}, \mathbb{S}' \uplus \mathbb{S}, c \wedge \mathbb{B}, \mathbb{T}\rangle_n$
   if c is a built-in constraint and $\mathbb{B}$ fixes the variables of $\mathbb{S}'$.

2. **Activate** $\langle[c|\mathbb{A}], \mathbb{S}, \mathbb{B}, \mathbb{T}\rangle_n \stackrel{\omega_r}{\rightarrowtail}_{\mathcal{P}} \langle[c\#n\!:\!1|\mathbb{A}], \mathbb{S}', \mathbb{B}, \mathbb{T}\rangle_{(n+1)}$
   if c is a CHR constraint, where $\mathbb{S}' = \{c\#n\} \uplus \mathbb{S}$.

3. **Reactivate** $\langle[c\#i|\mathbb{A}], \mathbb{S}, \mathbb{B}, \mathbb{T}\rangle_n \stackrel{\omega_r}{\rightarrowtail}_{\mathcal{P}} \langle[c\#i\!:\!1|\mathbb{A}], \mathbb{S}, \mathbb{B}, \mathbb{T}\rangle_n$

4. **Drop** $\langle[c\#i\!:\!j|\mathbb{A}], \mathbb{S}, \mathbb{B}, \mathbb{T}\rangle_n \stackrel{\omega_r}{\rightarrowtail}_{\mathcal{P}} \langle\mathbb{A}, \mathbb{S}, \mathbb{B}, \mathbb{T}\rangle_n$
   if there is no j^{th} occurrence of c in $\mathcal{P}$.

5. **Simplify** $\langle[c\#i\!:\!j|\mathbb{A}], \{c\#i\} \uplus H_1 \uplus H_2 \uplus H_3 \uplus \mathbb{S}, \mathbb{B}, \mathbb{T}\rangle_n$
   $\stackrel{\omega_r}{\rightarrowtail}_{\mathcal{P}} \langle C +\!\!+ \mathbb{A}, H_1 \uplus \mathbb{S}, \theta \wedge \mathbb{B}, \mathbb{T} \cup \{h\}\rangle_n$
   if the jth occurrence of the constraint c is d_j in a rule r in $\mathcal{P}$ of the form
   $r @ H_1' \setminus H_2', d_j, H_3' \iff g \mid C$ and $\exists \theta : c = \theta(d_j)$, $chr(H_k) = \theta(H_k')$ $(k = 1, 2, 3)$,
   $\mathcal{D} \models \mathbb{B} \to \bar{\exists}_\mathbb{B}(\theta \wedge g)$, and $T \not\ni h = (\mathsf{id}(H_1), \mathsf{id}(H_2 +\!\!+ c\#i +\!\!+ H_3), r)$.

6. **Propagate** $\langle[c\#i\!:\!j|\mathbb{A}], \{c\#i\} \uplus H_1 \uplus H_2 \uplus H_3 \uplus \mathbb{S}, \mathbb{B}, \mathbb{T}\rangle_n$
   $\stackrel{\omega_r}{\rightarrowtail}_{\mathcal{P}} \langle C +\!\!+ [c\#i\!:\!j|\mathbb{A}], \{c\#i\} \uplus H_1 \uplus H_2 \uplus \mathbb{S}, \theta \wedge \mathbb{B}, \mathbb{T} \cup \{h\}\rangle_n$
   if the jth occurrence of the constraint c is d_j in a rule r in $\mathcal{P}$ of the form
   $r @ H_1', d_j, H_2' \setminus H_3' \iff g \mid C$ and $\exists \theta : c = \theta(d_j)$, $chr(H_k) = \theta(H_k')$ $(k = 1, 2, 3)$,
   $\mathcal{D} \models \mathbb{B} \to \bar{\exists}_\mathbb{B}(\theta \wedge g)$, and $T \not\ni h = (\mathsf{id}(H_1 +\!\!+ c\#i +\!\!+ H_2), \mathsf{id}(H_3), r)$.

7. **Default** $\langle[c\#i\!:\!j|\mathbb{A}], \mathbb{S}, \mathbb{B}, \mathbb{T}\rangle_n \stackrel{\omega_r}{\rightarrowtail}_{\mathcal{P}} \langle[c'|\mathbb{A}], \mathbb{S}, \mathbb{B}, \mathbb{T}\rangle_n$
   if no other transition applies, where $c' = c\#i\!:\!(j+1)$.

Fig. 2. The transitions of the refined operational semantics ω_r

Definition 4 (Occurrenced identified constraint). *An occurrenced identified CHR constraint $c\#i : j$ is an identified constraint $c\#i$ annotated with an occurrence number j. This annotation indicates that only matches with occurrence j of constraint c are considered at this point in the execution.*

Definition 5 (ω_r execution state). *An ω_r execution state σ is a tuple $\langle\mathbb{A}, \mathbb{S}, \mathbb{B}, \mathbb{T}\rangle_n$, where $\mathbb{S}$, $\mathbb{B}$, $\mathbb{T}$, and n represent the CHR store, the built-in store, the propagation history and the next free identity number just like before. The execution stack $\mathbb{A}$ is a sequence of constraints, identified CHR constraints and occurrenced identified CHR constraints, with a strict.*

Execution in ω_r proceeds by exhaustively applying transitions from figure 2 to the initial execution state until the built-in store is unsatisfiable or no transitions are applicable. Initial states are defined in the same way as in ω_t.

3   Guard Reasoning

Consider the following example CHR program, which computes the greatest common divisor using Euclid's algorithm.

Example 1 (gcd).

```
gcd(N) <=> N =:= 0 | true.
gcd(N) \ gcd(M) <=> N =\= 0, M >= N | gcd(M-N).
```

A query containing two (or more) gcd/1 constraints with positive integer arguments, will eventually result in a constraint store containing one gcd(k) constraint where k is their greatest common divisor. For example, the query gcd(9),gcd(15) causes the second rule to fire, resulting in gcd(9),gcd(6). This rule keeps firing until the store contains gcd(3),gcd(0). Now the first rule fires, removing gcd(0) from the store. The remaining constraint does indeed contain the greatest common divisor of 9 and 15, namely 3.   □

Taking the refined operational semantics into account, the above CHR program can also be written as

```
gcd(N) <=> N =:= 0 | true.
gcd(N) \ gcd(M) <=> M >= N | gcd(M-N).
```

because if the second rule is tried, the guard of the first rule must have failed – otherwise the active constraint would have been removed. Hence the condition N =\= 0 is redundant. Under ω_t semantics, this second version of the CHR program is no longer guaranteed to terminate, since applying the second rule indefinitely (which is a valid execution strategy under ω_t semantics) when the constraint store contains e.g. gcd(0),gcd(3) results in an infinite loop.

3.1 Guard Simplification

When a simpagation rule or a simplification rule fires, some or all of its head constraints are removed. As a result, for every rule R_i, we know that when this rule is tried, any non-propagation rule R_j with $j < i$, where the set of head constraints of rule R_j is a (multiset) subset of that of rule R_i, did not fire for some reason. Either the heads did not match, or the guard failed. Let us illustrate this general principle with some simple examples.

Example 2 (entailed guard).

```
pos  @ sign(P,S) <=> P > 0 | S = positive.
zero @ sign(Z,S) <=> Z =:= 0 | S = zero.
neg  @ sign(N,S) <=> N < 0 | S = negative.
```

If the third rule, neg, is tried, we know pos and zero did not fire, because otherwise, the sign/2 constraint would have been removed. Because the first rule, pos, did not fire, its guard must have failed, so we know that $N \leq 0$. From the failing of the second rule, zero, we can derive $N \neq 0$. Now we can combine these results to get $N < 0$, which trivially entails the guard of the third rule. Because this guard always succeeds, we can safely remove it. This results in slightly more efficient generated code, and — maybe more importantly — it might also be useful for other analyses. In this example, guard optimization reveals that all sign/2 constraints are removed after the third rule, allowing the *never-stored* analysis [14] to detect that sign/2 is never-stored.   □

Example 3 (rule that can never fire).

```
neq   @ p(A) \ q(B) <=> A \== B | ...
eq    @ q(C) \ p(D) <=> C == D | ...
prop @ p(X), q(Y) ==> ...
```

In this case, we can detect that the third rule, prop, will never fire. Indeed, because the first rule, neq, did not fire, we know that X and Y are equal and because the second rule, eq, did not fire, we know X and Y are not equal. This is a contradiction, so we know the third rule can never fire.   □

Generalizing from the previous examples, we can summarize guard simplification as follows: If (part of) a guard is entailed by knowledge given by the negation of earlier guards, we can replace it by true, thus removing it. However, if the *negation* of (part of a) guard is entailed by that knowledge, we know the rule will never fire and we can remove the entire rule.

In handwritten programs, such never firing rules most often indicate bugs in the CHR program – there is no reason to write rules that cannot fire – so it seems appropriate for the CHR compiler to give a warning message when it encounters such rules. Automatic program generation and source-to-source transformations often introduce never firing rules and redundant guards, so it certainly makes sense to apply guard simplification in that context.

3.2   Head Matching Simplification

Matchings in the arguments of head constraints can be seen as an implicit guard condition that can also be simplified. Consider the following example:

Example 4 (head matching simplification).

```
p(X,Y) <=> X \== Y | ...
p(X,X) <=> ...
```

We can rewrite the second rule to p(X,Y) <=> ..., because the (implicit) condition X == Y is entailed by the negation of the guard of the first rule. In the refined operational semantics, this does not change the behavior of the program. However, in a sense the second rule has become simpler: it imposes less conditions on the head constraint arguments. As a result, p/2 can now easily be seen to be never-stored, so more efficient code can be generated by the compiler.   □

3.3   Type and Mode Declarations

Head matching simplification can be much more effective if the types of constraints arguments are known.

Example 5 (sum).

```
:- chr_type list(T) ---> [] ; [T | list(T)].
:- constraints sum(+list(int), ?int).

sum([],S) <=> S = 0.
sum([X|Xs],S) <=> sum(Xs,S2), S is X + S2.
```

Since we know the first argument of constraint sum/2 is a (ground) list, these two rules cover all possible cases and thus the constraint is never-stored.   □

Note that the first declaration is a recursive and generic type definition for lists of some type T, a variable that can be instantiated with built-in types like int, float, the general type any, or any user-defined type. The constraint declaration on the second line includes mode and type information. It is read as follows: sum/2 is a CHR constraint which has two arguments: a ground list of integers and an integer, which can be ground or a variable.

Using this knowledge, we can rewrite the second rule of the example program to "sum(A,S) <=> A = [X|Xs], sum(Xs,S2), S is X + S2.". Again, under ω_r semantics this does not affect any computation, but since sum/2 is now clearly never-stored, the program can be compiled to more efficient Prolog code.

3.4   Domain Knowledge Declarations

In addition to type and mode information, we have added the possibility to add domain knowledge declarations. Suppose for instance that a Prolog fact v/1 is used to indicate the verbosity of the program, which can be "verbose", "normal", or "quiet". Consider the following program:

```
foo(X) <=> v(verbose) | writeln(verbose_foo(X)).
foo(X) <=> v(normal) | write(f).
foo(X), bar(X) ==> \+ v(quiet) | writeln(same_foo_bar(X)).
```

Under the refined operational semantics, the last rule can never fire. The following declaration allows the guard reasoning system to detect this:

```
:- chr_declaration  v(verbose) ; v(normal) ; v(quiet).
```

In general such a declaration should be ground and always true. We also allow slightly more general declarations of the form

```
:- chr_declaration predicate(X) ---> expression(X).
```

where all variables occurring on the right hand side should also occur on the left hand side. The left hand side should be either a CHR constraint predicate or a Prolog predicate. For example, if the Prolog predicates male/1 and female/1 are used in the guards of rules involving person/1 constraints, the expected behavior of those predicates could be declared as follows:

```
:- chr_declaration person(X) ---> male(X) ; female(X).
```

This declaration ensures that in a program like

```
person(X) <=> male(X) | person(X,m).
person(X) <=> female(X) | person(X,f).
person(X), person(Y) ==> maybe_marry(X,Y).
```

the last rule is automatically removed.

3.5   Occurrence Subsumption

If the head of a rule contains multiple occurrences of the same constraint, we can test for *occurrence subsumption*. We know that when a certain occurrence is tried, all earlier occurrences in constraint removing rules must have failed. If the rule containing this occurrence is not a propagation rule, this also holds for earlier occurrences inside that rule.

The K.U.Leuven CHR compiler already had two optimizations that can be considered to be special cases of occurrence subsumption. *Symmetry analysis* checks rules R with a head containing two constraints c_1 and c_2 that are symmetric, in the sense that there is a variable renaming θ such that $\theta(c_1) = c_2$ and $\theta(c_2) = c_1$ and $\theta(R) = R$. In such rules, one of the c_i's is made passive. This means the occurrence can be skipped. In terms of the ω_r semantics: the Default transition can be immediately applied for that occurrence, since the Simplify or Propagate transitions are never applicable for that occurrence. The second optimization looks at rules which make a constraint have *set semantics*, of the form $c_1 \backslash c_2 \Leftrightarrow true|B$, without head matchings, where c_1 and c_2 are identical. In this case, c_1 can be made passive (or c_2, but it is better to keep the occurrence which immediately removes the active constraint). A more efficient constraint store can be used for c if it has set semantics.

In section 4.1 of [8,9], a concept called *continuation optimization* is introduced. *Fail* continuation optimization is essentially the same as occurrence subsumption, while *success* continuation optimization uses similar reasoning to improve the generated code for occurrences in propagation rules. The HAL CHR compiler, discussed in [9], performs a simple fail continuation optimization, which only considers rules without guards and does not use information derived from the failing of earlier guards.

Example 6 (simple case).

```
c(A,B),  c(B,A) <=> p(A),p(B) | true.
```

Suppose the active constraint is `c(X,Y)`. For brevity, we use the phrase "occurrence x fires" as a shortcut for "occurrence x of the active constraint causes rule application". If the first occurrence does not fire, this means that either `c(Y,X)` is not in the constraint store, or `p(X),p(Y)` fails. If the second occurrence fires, then `c(Y,X)` must be in the constraint store, and the guard `p(Y),p(X)` must succeed. So it is impossible for the second occurrence to fire if the first one did not[1]. If the first occurrence did fire, it removes the active constraint so the second occurrence is not even tried. From the above reasoning it follows that the second occurrence is redundant, so we could as well change the rule to `c(A,B),` `c(B,A)#passive <=> p(A),p(B) | true.`   □

In the following examples, the general occurrence subsumption analysis is able to find much more redundant occurrences than the earlier symmetry and set semantics analyses. Underlined occurrences can be made passive so they can be

---

[1] We assume conjunctions in guards to be commutative: if `p(X),p(Y)` fails, then `p(Y),p(X)` must also fail.

skipped (i.e. the compiler does not need to generate a clause for such an occurrence). All these redundant occurrences are detected by the current K.U.Leuven CHR compiler.

Example 7 (more complicated cases).

1. `a(X,Y,Z),a(Y,Z,X),a(Z,X,Y) <=> ...`
2. `b(X,Y,Z),b(Y,Z,X),b(Z,X,Y) <=> (p(X); p(Y)) | ...`
3. `c(A,B,C),c(A,C,B),c(B,A,C),c(B,C,A),c(C,A,B),c(C,B,A) <=> ...`
4. `d(A,B,C),d(A,C,B),d(B,A,C),d(B,C,A),d(C,A,B),d(C,B,A)`
           `<=> p(A),p(B) | ...`
5. `e(A,B,C),e(A,C,B),e(B,A,C),e(B,C,A),e(C,A,B),e(C,B,A)`
           `<=> p(A) | ...`
6. `f(A,B), f(B,C) <=> A \== C | ...`
   `f(A,B), f(B,C) <=> ...`   □

A strong occurrence subsumption analysis takes away the need for CHR programmers to write `passive` pragmas to improve efficiency, since the compiler is able to add them automatically if it can prove that making the occurrence passive is justified, i.e. does not change the program's behavior. Because of this, the CHR source code contains much less of these non-declarative operational pragmas, improving the compactness and logical readability.

Of course, not every redundant occurrence can be detected by our analysis. Consider the last rule in this classic CHR version of the Sieve of Eratosthenes:

Example 8 (too complicated case).

```
candidate(1) <=> true.
candidate(N) <=> prime(N), candidate(N-1).
prime(Y) \ prime(X) <=> 0 =:= X mod Y | true.
```

In this program, the last occurrence of `prime/1` can be declared to be passive, provided that user queries are of the form `candidate`(n), with $n \geq 1$. Because `prime/1` constraints are added in reverse order, the guard `0 =:= X mod Y` will always fail if `prime(X)` is the active constraint. Indeed, for all possible partner constraints `prime(Y)` we have `Y > X > 1` because of the order in which `prime/1` constraints are added, so `X mod Y = X ≠ 0`. Our implementation of occurrence subsumption lacks the reasoning capability to detect this kind of situations. Not only does the current implementation lack a mechanism for the CHR programmer to indicate which kind of user queries are allowed, it also does not try to investigate rule bodies to derive the kind of information needed in this example. Furthermore, it is far from trivial to automatically detect complicated entailments like $Y > X > 1 \rightarrow X \bmod Y \neq 0$.   □

4   Formalization

In this section we formalize the guard simplification transformation that was intuitively described above. First we introduce some additional notation for the functor/arity of constraints:

Definition 6 (Functor). *For every CHR constraint* $c = p(t_1, \ldots, t_n)$, *we define* functor$(c) = p/n$. *For every multiset* C *of CHR constraints we define* functor(C) *to be the multiset* $\{$functor$(c) | c \in C\}$.

4.1 Implicit Preconditions

We consider rules that must have been tried (according to the refined operational semantics) before some rule R_i is tried, calling them *earlier subrules* of R_i.

Definition 7 (Earlier subrule). *The rule* R_j *is an* earlier subrule *of rule* R_i *(notation:* $R_j \prec R_i$*) iff* $j < i$ *and* functor$(H_j) \not\subseteq$ functor(H_i).

Now we can define a logical expression $\mathsf{nesr}(R_i)$ ("**n**o **e**arlier **s**ubrule (fired)") stating the implications of the fact that all constraint-removing earlier subrules of rule R_i have been tried unsuccessfully.

Definition 8 (Nesr). *For every rule* R_i, *we define:*

$$\mathsf{nesr}(R_i) = \bigwedge \left\{ \left(\neg(\theta_j \wedge g_j) \right) \mid R_j \prec R_i \wedge H_j^r \neq \epsilon \right\}$$

where θ_j *is a matching substitution mapping the head constraints of* R_j *to corresponding head constraints of* R_i.

If mode, type or domain knowledge information is available for head constraints of R_i, it can be added to the $\mathsf{nesr}(R_i)$ conjunction without affecting the following definitions and proofs, as long as this information is correct at any given point in any derivation starting from a legal query. This information is encoded as follows:

modes. Each mode is translated to its corresponding Prolog built-in: the + mode yields a `ground/1` condition, the - mode a `var/1` condition, and the ? mode a `true/0` precondition. For instance, for the constraint `c(X,Y,Z)` the mode declaration `c(+,-,?)` results in the precondition `ground(X)` $\wedge$ `var(Y)` $\wedge$ `true`.

types. Each type declaration results in a compound precondition, based on the type definition. Take for instance the type definition for the boolean type:
   `:- chr_type boolean ---> true ; false.`
The precondition for constraint `p(X)`, whose argument is of type `boolean`, is:
`var(X)` $\vee$ `(nonvar(X)` $\wedge$ `(X = true` $\vee$ `X = false))`. Note that this precondition explicitly distinguishes between different instantiations of the argument.

   Type definitions are recursively unfolded into the formula. Unrestrained unfolding is problematic for recursive types like `list(T)`: its leads to an infinite formula. Hence, we stop the unfolding at a fixed depth.

domain knowledge. The unconditional and fully ground domain knowledge is added as is. For the conditional form *Pattern* `--->` *Formula* we consider all predicate occurrences in $\mathsf{nesr}(R_i)$ and all the heads of R_i. For each occurrence that matches *Pattern*, we add the corresponding instance of *Formula*.

4.2   Definition of Guard Simplification

Consider a CHR program P with rules R_i which have guards $g_i = \bigwedge_k g_{i,k}$. Applying guard simplification to this program means rewriting some parts of the guards to `true`, if they are entailed by the "no earlier subrule fired" condition (and already evaluated parts of the guard). The entire guard is rewritten to `fail`, if the *negation* of some part of it is entailed by that condition. This effectively removes the rule. Because head matchings are made explicit, head matching simplification (section 3.2) is an implicit part of guard simplification.

Definition 9 (Guard Simplification). *Applying the guard simplification transformation to a CHR program P (with rules $R_i = H_i \Leftrightarrow \bigwedge_k g_{i,k}|B_i$) results in a new CHR program $P' = GS(P)$ which is identical to P except for the guards, i.e. its rules R'_i are of the form $H_i \Leftrightarrow g'_i|B_i$, where*

$$g'_i = \begin{cases} \texttt{fail} & \text{if } \exists k\ \mathcal{D} \models \mathsf{nesr}(R_i) \wedge \bigwedge_{m<k} g_{i,m} \rightarrow \neg g_{i,k}; \\ \bigwedge_k g'_{i,k} & \text{otherwise.} \end{cases}$$

In the second case, the $g'_{i,k}$ are defined by

$$g'_{i,k} = \begin{cases} \texttt{true} & \text{if } \mathcal{D} \models \mathsf{nesr}(R_i) \wedge \bigwedge_{m<k} g_{i,m} \rightarrow g_{i,k}; \\ g_{i,k} & \text{otherwise.} \end{cases}$$

Note that this definition is slightly stronger compared to the definition given in [16], because it takes into account the left-to-right evaluation of the guard. As a result, internally inconsistent guards like `X > Y, Y > X` can be simplified to `fail`, and internally redundant guards can be simplified, e.g. the condition `X >= Y` can be removed from `X > Y, X >= Y`.

Theorem 1 (Guard simplification & transitions). *Given a CHR program P and its guard-simplified version $P' = GS(P)$. Given an execution state $s = \langle A, S, B, T \rangle_n$ occurring in some derivation for the P program under ω_r semantics, exactly the same transitions are possible from s for P and for P'. In other words, $\rightarrowtail_P \equiv \rightarrowtail_{P'}$.*

See Appendix A for the proof.

4.3   Definition of Occurrence Subsumption

Although occurrence subsumption can be seen as a source to source transformation (inserting `passive` pragmas), we use a slightly different approach to define occurrence subsumption formally because the common formal definitions of CHR programs and ω_r derivations do not include pragmas. Instead of introducing the concept of `passive` occurrences in the formal refined operational semantics, we define *occurrence subsumable* occurrences and then we show that trying rule application on a subsumed occurrence is redundant. First we define this auxiliary condition:

Definition 10 (Neocc). *Given a non-propagation rule R_i containing in its head multiple occurrences $c_m, \ldots, c_n$ of the same constraint c and other partner constraints d. We define for every c_k ($m \leq k \leq n$):*

$$\text{neocc}(R_i, c_k) = \bigwedge \left\{ \neg\theta_l\big(\text{fc}(R_i, c_l)\big) \mid m \leq l < k, \theta_l(c_l) = c_k \right\}$$

where $\text{fc}(R_i, c_l) = (g_i \wedge d \wedge c_m \wedge \ldots \wedge c_{l-1} \wedge c_{l+1} \wedge \ldots \wedge c_n)$.

As the reader can verify, $\text{fc}(R_i, c_l)$ is the firing condition for rule R_i to fire if c_l is the active constraint. The condition $\text{neocc}(R_i, c_k)$ ("**no e**arlier **occ**urrence (fired)") describes that if the kth occurrence of c is tried, i.e. application of rule R_i is tried, the earlier occurrences inside rule R_i must have failed (since R_i is not a propagation rule). Now we can define formally which occurrences can be made passive.

Definition 11 (Occurrence subsumption). *Given a rule R_i as in the previous definition. We say c_k ($m < k \leq n$) is occurrence subsumable iff*

$$\mathcal{D} \models \text{nesr}(R_i) \wedge \text{neocc}(R_i, c_k) \rightarrow \neg\text{fc}(R_i, c_k)$$

In the next section we present a formal correctness proof of both the guard simplification transformation from the previous section and occurrence subsumption.

Theorem 2 (Correctness of Occ. Subsumption). *Given a CHR program P and an ω_r derivation for P in which an execution state $s = \langle [c\#i : j|A], S, B, T \rangle_n$ occurs. If c_j is occurrence subsumable, **Simplify** and **Propagate** transition cannot (directly) be applied on state s.*

See Appendix A for the proof.

5 Entailment Checking

The core component for guard reasoning is a logical entailment checker. In this section we discuss our implementation, in CHR, of such an entailment checker. This implementation is used in the guard simplification analysis to test whether one condition B (e.g. $X < Z$) is entailed by another condition A (e.g. $X < Y \wedge Y < Z$), i.e. whether $A \rightarrow B$ holds. The entailment checker only considers (a fragment of the) host-language built-ins. In particular, it does not try to discover implications of user-defined predicates, which would require a complex analysis of the host-language program.

5.1 Overview

As the entailment checking problem is generally undecidable, our entailment checker is incomplete. It tries to prove that B is entailed by A; if it succeeds, $A \rightarrow B$ must hold, but if it fails, either $A \not\rightarrow B$ holds or $A \rightarrow B$ holds but could not be shown. The core of the entailment checker is written in CHR. When the entailment $A \rightarrow B$ needs to be checked, we call the entailment checker with the query known(A), test(B). Schematically, it works as follows:

1. normalize;
   e.g. apply De Morgan's laws, convert $\geq, >, <$ to $\leq$ and $\neq$
2. evaluate ground expressions;
   e.g. replace `known`$(5 \leq 3)$ by `known(fail)`
3. propagate entailed information;
   e.g. if you find both `known`$(X \leq Y)$ and `known`$(Y \leq Z)$, then add `known`$(X \leq Z)$
4. succeed whenever `known`(B) is added;
5. succeed if B is entailed;
   e.g. `test`$(X \neq 3)$ is entailed by `known`$(X \leq 0)$
6. if there is a disjunction `known`$(A_1 \vee A_2)$: check whether $A_1 \to B$ and also whether $\neg A_1 \wedge A_2 \to B$, succeed if both tests succeed;
7. otherwise: give up and fail.

We try to postpone the expansion of disjunctions, because (recursively) trying all combinations of conditions in disjunctions can be rather costly: if A is a conjunction containing n disjunctions, each containing m conditions, there are m^n cases that have to be checked. This is why we check entailment of B *before* a disjunction is expanded. Conjunctions in B are dealt with in the obvious way. If B is a disjunction $B_1 \vee B_2$, we add `known`$(\neg B_2)$ to the store and test B_1. We can stop (and succeed) if B_1 is entailed, otherwise we backtrack, add `known`$(\neg B_1)$ to the store and return the result of testing entailment of B_2.

5.2   Code Details

The negation of a condition is computed in a straightforward way for host-language built-ins. For example, the negation of `X == Y` is `X \== Y`, `\+ Cond` becomes `Cond`, disjunctions become conjunctions of the negated disjuncts, and so on. For user-defined predicates `p` we simply use `(\+ p)`.

Figure 3 shows how the normalization of `known/1` and `test/1` constraints is done. Ground conditions are evaluated using rules like the following:

```
known(X=<Y) <=> number(X), number(Y), X=<Y | true.
known(X=<Y) <=> number(X), number(Y), X>Y | known(fail).
test(X=<Y) <=> number(X), number(Y), X=<Y | true.
```

In Fig. 4 some examples are given of rules that propagate entailed information. The `idempotence` rule and execution under the refined semantics is crucial for termination of this propagation phase.

A simplified version of the rest of the entailment checker is listed in Fig. 5.

Note that Prolog disjunction in the rule body is used to check disjunctions in `test/1` constraints. To deal with disjunctions in `known/1` constraints, a bit of trickery is needed. We want to avoid branching until it is needed. While the propagation rules are already applied before the `test` constraint is activated, the `disjunction` rule can only be applied when the `test` constraint has almost reached its last occurrence. Now we use a double Prolog negation to test both disjuncts. The predicate `try`(A, X) fails if $A \to X$ can be shown, so its

```
:- chr_constraint known/1, test/1.

known(G) <=> normal_form(G,N) | known(N).
test(G) <=> normal_form(G,N) | test(N).

normal_form(X>Y, (Y=<X, X=\=Y)).
normal_form(X>=Y, Y=<X).
normal_form(X<Y, (X=<Y, X=\=Y)).
normal_form(X is Y, X=:=Y).
normal_form(\+ G, NotG) :- negation(G,NotG).

negation(X = Y, X \= Y).                negation(X \= Y, X = Y).
negation(X < Y, Y =< X).                negation(X > Y, X =< Y).
negation(X =< Y, Y < X).                negation(X >= Y, X < Y).
negation(X == Y, X \== Y).              negation(X \== Y, X == Y).
negation(X =\= Y, X =:= Y).             negation(X =:= Y, X =\= Y).
negation(var(X), nonvar(X)).            negation(nonvar(X), var(X)).
negation((A;B), (\+ A, \+ B)).          negation((A,B), (\+ A; \+ B)).
negation(true,fail).                    negation(fail,true).
negation(\+ G, G).       % double negation
```

Fig. 3. Conversion to normal form

```
idempotence           @ known(G) \ known(G) <=> true.
inconsistency         @ known(X), known(\+ X) <=> known(fail).
conjunction           @ known((A,B)) <=> known(A), known(B).

eq_neq_inconsistency  @ known(X\==Y), known(X==Y) <=> known(fail).
eq_transitivity       @ known(X==Y), known(Y==Z) ==> known(X==Z).
neq_substitution      @ known(X==Y), known(Y\==Z) ==> known(X\==Z).
eq_symmetry           @ known(X==Y) ==> known(Y==X).
neq_symmetry          @ known(X\==Y) ==> known(Y\==X).
neq_inconsistency     @ known(X\==X) ==> known(fail).

leq_antisymmetry      @ known(X=<Y), known(Y=<X) <=> known(X=:=Y).
leq_transitivity      @ known(X=<Y), known(Y=<Z) ==> known(X=<Z).
leq_substitution1     @ known(X=:=Y), known(X =< Z) ==> known(Y =< Z).
leq_substitution2     @ known(X=:=Y), known(Z =< X) ==> known(Z =< Y).
strict_lt_transitivity @ known(X=<Y), known(X=\=Y), known(Y=<Z), known(Y=\=Z)
                                 ==> known(X=\=Z).

aneq_inconsistency    @ known(X=\=X) <=> known(fail).
aeq_aneq_inconsistency @ known(X=:=Y), known(X=\=Y) <=> known(fail).
aeq_transitivity      @ known(X=:=Y), known(Y=:=Z) ==> X \== Z | known(X=:=Z).
aeq_symmetry          @ known(X=:=Y) ==> known(Y=:=X).
aneq_symmetry         @ known(X=\=Y) ==> known(Y=\=X).
```

Fig. 4. Propagation of known/1 constraints

negation succeeds if $A \rightarrow X$ holds. By using a double negation, all propagated consequences of A are automatically undone.

Disjunctions in the antecedent are the main bottleneck of the entailment checker: every disjunction potentially doubles the amount of work to be done,

```
fail_implies_everything @ known(fail) \ test(X) <=> true.
trivial_entailment       @ known(G) \ test(G) <=> true.
eq_implies_leq1          @ known(X=:=Y) \ test(X=<Y) <=> true.
eq_implies_leq2          @ known(X=:=Z) \ test(X=<Y) <=> number(Y), number(Z), Z=<Y | true.
eq_implies_leq3          @ known(X=:=Z) \ test(Y=<X) <=> number(Y), number(Z), Y=<Z | true.
leq_implies_leq1         @ known(X=<Z) \ test(X=<Y) <=> number(Y), number(Z), Z=<Y | true.
leq_implies_leq2         @ known(X=<Y) \ test(Z=<Y) <=> number(X), number(Z), Z=<X | true.
leq_implies_neq1         @ known(X=<Z) \ test(X=\=Y) <=> number(Y), number(Z), Y>Z | true.
leq_implies_neq2         @ known(X=<Y) \ test(Y=\=Z) <=> number(X), number(Z), Z<X | true.
leq_implies_neq2         @ known(X=<Y) \ test(Z=\=Y) <=> number(X), number(Z), Z<X | true.
true_is_true             @ test(true) <=> true.

test_conjunction         @ test((A,B)) <=> test(A), known(A), test(B).
test_disjunction         @ test((A;B)) <=> known(\+ B),test(A) ; known(\+ A),test(B).

disjunction              @ test(X), known((A;B))
                             <=> \+ try(A,X), !, known(\+ A), \+ try(B,X).
give_up                  @ test(_) <=> fail.

try(A,X) :- known(A), (test(X) -> fail ; true).
```

Fig. 5. Part of the program to check entailments

so the checking is potentially exponential in the input size. In the case of guard
simplification, the antecedents consist of negations of guards, and guards are
typically conjunctions. As a result, after normalization the antecedent consists
of disjunctions (of negated conjuncts). Hence, for efficiency reasons it is important to avoid disjunction branching if possible. In addition to the above strategy
of delaying disjunctions, we have added rules to simplify some common cases of
redundant disjunctions. Examples of such rules are the following:

```
known((fail; B)) <=> known(B).
known((true ; A)) <=> true.
known(A) \ known((\+ A; B)) <=> known(B).
known(A) \ known((\+ A, C; B)) <=> known(B).
```

5.3   Flattening

The generic constraints known/1 and test/1 provide a conceptual simplicity
in formulating and maintaining the rules of the entailment checker. However,
this genericity incurs a runtime penalty: the CHR compiler fails to efficiently
index the constraints, and each active constraint has to consider (almost) all
occurrences.

Because the entailment checker is one of the main performance bottlenecks
in the K.U.Leuven CHR compiler, the above inefficiency is unacceptable. For-
tunately, it can be mitigated with little effort by automated rule specialization. Sarna-Starosta and Schrijvers [11] propose a technique for specializing constraints with respect to the different toplevel function symbols in their arguments
that rules try to match. In the current version of the compiler, this specialization leads to 20 versions of test/1 and 26 versions of known/1, e.g. known_==/2,
test_true/0, ...

This specialization provides indexing on the toplevel function symbol for free. The CHR compiler always allocates separate indexing datastructures for distinct constraint symbols.

Of course, the specialization of constraints leads to the specialization of rules, and, because many rules only apply to one specialized form, fewer occurrences for each specialized constraint. For instance, we obtain only two occurrences for test_true/0:

```
known_fail \ test_true <=> true.
test_true <=> true.
```

This fully automatic specialization makes the entailment checker roughly twice as fast.

6   Implementation

We have implemented guard simplification and occurrence subsumption in the K.U.Leuven CHR compiler [13], which can be found in recent releases of SWI-Prolog [21]. In this section we give a brief overview of our implementation of guard simplification and occurrence subsumption, which depends heavily on the entailment checker discussed in the previous section.

The guard simplification / occurrence subsumption compilation phase rewrites every rule in the CHR program. In the rewritten rules, the redundant parts of the guard have been removed, the head matchings (an implicit part of the guard) are made as general as possible and subsumed occurrences are declared to be passive. As a result, the generated code is more efficient because redundant checks are removed, and also the next compilation phases – like storage analysis – are more effective.

Our implementation works as follows. For every rule R_i, we first compute a conjunction of inferred information. Then we use this information to transform the rule to a simpler and more efficient form.

6.1   Inferring Information

First we make the head matchings explicit, inserting fresh variables in the arguments of head constraints as needed. For example, the rule

```
c([X|Xs],Y,Y) <=> ... | ...
```

would be rewritten to the equivalent rule in head normal form:

```
c(A,Y,B) <=> A = [X|Xs], B == Y, ... | ...
```

Next we iteratively construct a conjunction similar to $\mathsf{nesr}(R_i)$ from section 4, containing the negations of the guards of the earlier subrules $R_j \prec R_i$. All possible substitutions have to be considered. As an example, consider the program:

```
c(X) <=> p(X) | ...
c(2) <=> q | ...
c(A), c(B) <=> ... | ...
```

For the third rule, the following conjunction would be computed:

```
(A \== 2; \+ q), (B \== 2; \+ q), \+ p(A), \+ p(B)
```

Finally we add type and mode information by looking up the type and mode declarations for the head constraints of R_i, unfolding the type definitions to the nesting depth needed (see Section 4.1). We also add the relevant information from the domain knowledge declarations.

6.2   Using the Information

Now we can use the derived information to transform the rule. Schematically, our implementation works as follows:

1. for every part of the guard of R_i (the $g_{i,k}$'s from section 4): check if it is entailed by the derived information and remove it if it is (i.e. replace it with **true**); if its negation is entailed, replace it with **fail**;
2. move every entailed head matching to the body if the variables in the right hand side of the matching do not occur in the guard; if they also do not occur in the body, remove the head matching;
3. produce a warning message if the guard now entails **fail**, or if the head matchings entail **fail**. This means that rule R_i will never fire, which probably indicates a bug in the CHR program;
4. for every occurrence c_k of a constraint that occurs more than once in R_i, compute $\mathsf{neocc}(R_i, c_k)$ and do occurrence subsumption by checking whether $\neg\mathsf{fc}(R_i, c_k)$ is entailed by $\mathsf{nesr}(R_i) \wedge \mathsf{neocc}(R_i, c_k)$, i.e. check whether occurrence c_k can be safely set to 'passive'.

As an example of the second step, consider the rule

```
c([X|Xs],[],A,A,[B|Bs]) <=> B>0 | d(X,A).
```

and assume the derived information entails that the first arguments of c/5 is a non-empty list, the second argument is an empty list and the third and fourth argument are identical. The rule would be rewritten to

```
c(Z,_,A,_,[B|_]) <=> B>0 | Z=[X|_], d(X,A).
```

7   Experimental Results

In order to quantify the efficiency gain obtained by guard simplification and occurrence subsumption, we have measured the performance of several CHR benchmarks, both with and without the optimization. All benchmarks were performed in SWI-Prolog [21] Pentium 4 machine running Debian GNU/Linux with a low load. Before we discuss the benchmarks, we first take a look at the code the compiler generates for an example CHR program, and how this code is improved by guard simplification.

7.1 Generated Code Comparison

Consider this fragment from a prime number generating program from the CHR web site [19]:

```
filter([X|In],P,Out) <=> 0 =\= X mod P |
                         Out = [X|Out1],
                         filter(In,P,Out1).
filter([X|In],P,Out) <=> 0 =:= X mod P |
                         filter(In,P,Out).
filter([],P,Out) <=> Out = [].
```

The CHR compiler (without guard simplification) generates general code for the filter/3 constraint. Because no information is known about the arguments of filter/3, the compiled code has to take into account variable triggering and the possibility that none of the rules apply and the constraint has to be stored. Following the compilation scheme explained in [10], we get this generated code:

```
filter(List,P,Out) :- filter(List,P,Out, _ ).

% first occurrence
filter(List,P,Out,C) :-
        nonvar(List), List = [X|In],
        0 =\= X mod P, !,
        ... % removecode
        Out = [E|Out1], filter(In,P,Out1).

% second occurrence
filter(List,P,Out,C) :-
        nonvar(List), List = [X|In],
        0 =:= X mod P, !,
        ... % removecode
        filter(In,P,Out).

% third occurrence
filter(List, _ ,Out,C) :-
        List == [], !,
        ... % removecode
        Out = [].

% insert into store if no rule applied
filter(List,P,Out,C) :-
        ... % insertcode
```

If we enable guard simplification, the guard in the second rule is removed, but this on itself does not improve efficiency considerably. Much more efficiency improvements can be obtained by adding type and mode information.

In this example, the programmer intends to call `filter/3` with the first two arguments ground, while the third one can have any instantiation. The first and the third argument are lists of integers, while the second argument is an integer. So we add the following type and mode declaration:

```
:- constraints filter(+list(int),+int,?list(int)).
```

Using this type and mode information, guard simplification now detects that all possibilities are covered by the three rules. The guard in the second rule can be removed, so the `filter/3` constraint with the first argument being a non-empty list is always removed after the second rule. Thus in order to reach the third rule, the first argument has to be the empty list – it cannot be a variable because it is ground and it cannot be anything else because of its type. As a result, we can drop the head matching in the third rule:

```
filter([X|In],P,Out) <=> 0 =\= X mod P |
                         Out = [X|Out1],
                         filter(In,P,Out1).
filter([_|In],P,Out) <=> filter(In,P,Out).
filter(_,P,Out) <=> Out = [].
```

This transformed program is compiled to more efficient code, because never-stored analysis detects `filter/3` to be never-stored after the third rule. The generated code for the guard simplified program is considerably simpler:

```
filter([X|In],P,Out) :- 0 =\= X mod P, !,
                        Out = [X|Out1],
                        filter(In,P,Out1).
filter([_|In],P,Out) :- !, filter(In,P,Out).
filter(_,_,[]).
```

7.2 Guard Simplification Results

Figure 6 gives an overview of the results of running a set of benchmarks with and without guard simplification. The first column indicates the benchmark name and the parameters that were used. These benchmarks are available at [20]. The second and third column indicate whether mode and type declarations were provided, respectively. The fourth column indicates whether guard simplification was enabled. In all these columns, an empty cell means the choice has no influence on the resulting compiled code (so it can be "yes" or "no"). The fifth column shows the size of the resulting compiled Prolog code as a pair of the form (#Clauses ; #Lines), not including auxiliary predicates. The last column shows the runtime in seconds and a percentage comparing the runtime to that of the version with mode information but without guard simplification. If a cell contains an equality sign ("="), we could not measure any performance difference compared to the version in the row just above that cell. If a cell contains an equivalence sign ("≡"), the Prolog code for that row is identical to the one in

Benchmark	Mode	Type	Guard simplification	Program size	Runtime (%)
sum	no	no		4 ; 46	12.23 (243)
(10000,500)	yes	no		3 ; 10	5.03 (100)
	yes	yes	yes	2 ; 6	4.49 (89)
	hand-optimized code			2 ; 5	= =
Takeuchi	no		no	4 ; 50	136.11 (173)
(1000)	yes		no	3 ; 17	78.62 (100)
			yes	2 ; 12	72.88 (93)
	hand-optimized code			≡	≡ ≡
nrev	no	no		8 ; 92	47.83 (342)
(30,50000)	yes	no		6 ; 20	13.97 (100)
	yes	yes	yes	4 ; 11	8.44 (60)
	hand-optimized code			4 ; 7	= =
cprimes	no		no	14 ; 160	196.48 (245)
(100000)	no		yes	12 ; 120	= =
	yes	no	no	11 ; 42	80.20 (100)
	yes	no	yes	10 ; 35	= =
	yes	yes	yes	8 ; 25	79.25 (99)
	hand-optimized code			8 ; 23	= =
dfsearch	no		no	5 ; 67	149.02 (397)
(16,500)	no		yes	5 ; 66	141.75 (377)
	yes	no	no	4 ; 16	37.58 (100)
	yes	no	yes	4 ; 15	31.63 (84)
	yes	yes	yes	3 ; 11	29.97 (80)
	hand-optimized code			3 ; 8	= =

Fig. 6. Benchmark results for guard simplification

the row just above. For every benchmark, the results for hand-optimized Prolog code are included, representing the ideal target code.

We have measured similar results [16] in hProlog [18]. The only significant difference with the results presented here, is the amount of run time improvement caused by adding mode information. In hProlog, this improvement is typically 20 to 30 percent, while in SWI-Prolog, it can be 50 to 70 percent. The reason is that the nonvar/1-test and other redundant code – which is removed when the argument is declared to be ground – is handled much more efficiently by hProlog.

Discussion. The first benchmark, sum, computes the sum of the elements of a list of 10000 numbers (all 1), and is repeated 500 times (see example 5 page 219):

```
sum([],S) <=> S = 0.
sum([A|R],S) <=> sum(R,T), S is A+T.
```

If type and mode declarations are provided, guard simplification moves the head matching to the body, enabling never-stored analysis to remove redundant code to add sum/2 to the constraint store. As in the other benchmarks, no significant performance difference could be measured between the resulting compiled program[2]

```
sum([],S) :- !, S = 0.
sum([A|R],S) :- sum(R,T), S is A+T.
```

and the handwritten Prolog code

```
sum([],S) :- S = 0.
sum([A|R],S) :- sum(R,T), S is A+T.
```

The second benchmark is an example of how guard simplification can in some way make mode information redundant. The CHR-program looks like this:

```
tak(X,Y,Z,A) <=> X =< Y | ...
tak(X,Y,Z,A) <=> X > Y | ...
```

The first three arguments are supposed to be ground integers. If this mode information is given, the possibility of variable triggering can be excluded. However, even without mode information, guard simplification removes the guard in the second rule. As a result, the constraint is detected as being never-stored, also excluding the possibility of variable triggering. In this case, the generated code is identical to the handwritten Prolog code. The guard X > Y is removed because it is (entailed by) the negation of X =< Y. When X =< Y fails, we know X and Y are ground terms evaluating to numbers, and X > Y. If in some other host language, X =< Y would fail if its arguments are invalid – instead of resulting in some fatal error message or exception – then it would have a different negation, for instance (X > Y ; \+ number(X) ; \+ number(Y)). In that case, guard simplification would not remove the guard of the second rule, except when mode and type information is given.

In the third benchmark, nrev, a list of length 30 is reversed 50000 times using the classic naive algorithm. Except for some redundant cuts, the generated code:

```
nrev([],Ans) :- !, Ans = [].
nrev([X|Xs],Ans) :- nrev(Xs,L), app(L,[X],Ans).
app([],L,M) :- !, L = M.
app([X|L1],L2,[X|L3]) :- app(L1,L2,L3).
```

is essentially identical to the handwritten Prolog program:

```
nrev([],[]).
nrev([X|Xs],Ans):- nrev(Xs,L), app(L,[X],Ans).
app([],L,L).
app([X|L1],L2,[X|L3]):- app(L1,L2,L3).
```

---

[2] For readability, variables have been renamed in the generated code shown here. The results are similar for a tail-recursive version of sum/2.

Benchmark	Occ. subsumption	# occurrences	Runtime (%)	
a	no	3	52.8	(100)
(5000)	yes	1	17.1	(32)
b	no	3	52.1	(100)
(5000)	yes	2	34.3	(66)
c	no	6	86.5	(100)
(5000)	yes	1	17.2	(20)
d	no	6	84.7	(100)
(5000)	yes	3	50.3	(59)
e	no	6	86.4	(100)
(5000)	yes	3	49.9	(58)
f	no	4	64.4	(100)
(5000)	yes	3	47.8	(74)

Fig. 7. Benchmark results for occurrence subsumption

The example in section 7.1 is a fragment from the fourth benchmark, cprimes, which computes the first 100,000 prime numbers. The last benchmark, dfsearch, performs a depth-first search on a large tree. In both cases, the generated code for the guard simplified version with mode and type information is again essentially identical to the handwritten Prolog code.

Conclusion. Overall, for these benchmarks, the net effect of the guard simplification transformation – together with never-stored analysis and use of mode information to remove redundant variable triggering code – is cleaner generated code which is much closer to what a Prolog programmer would write. As a result, a major performance improvement is observed in these benchmarks, which are CHR programs that basically implement a deterministic algorithm.

Naive compilation causes CHR programs to have a relatively low performance compared to native host-language (Prolog) alternatives. As a result, CHR programmers usually write auxiliary predicates in Prolog instead of formulating them directly in CHR. Thanks to guard simplification and other analyses, the programmer can now simply implement everything as CHR rules, relying on the compiler to generate efficient code. Mixed-language programs often use inelegant interface constructs, like rules of the form foo(X) \ getFoo(Y) <=> Y = X, to read information from the constraint store in the host-language parts when this information is needed. Host-language interface constraints like getFoo/1 can be avoided by writing the entire program in CHR. Thanks to (amongst others) guard simplification, this can be done without performance penalty.

7.3 Occurrence Subsumption Results

Figure 7 shows the results of occurrence subsumption for four benchmarks. Symmetry and set semantics analyses were disabled in both cases because they are special cases of occurrence subsumption. The second column indicates whether occurrence subsumption was enabled. The third column indicates the number of non-passive occurrences. The runtime column is as in Fig. 6. The benchmarks correspond to the rules in Example 7 (page 222).

Occurrence subsumption seems to result in a substantial performance improvement, if there are subsumable occurrences (which is of course true for these benchmarks). Occurrence subsumption also reduces the size of the generated code, by eliminating entire clauses. Compared to guard simplification, this size reduction is more visible, unless of course – as in the case of benchmarks from the previous section – guard simplification reveals the never-stored property, which also allows substantial simplification of the generated code.

8   Guard Reasoning under ω_p Semantics

Guard reasoning can also be applied in the context of different operational semantics. In this section we consider the priority semantics ω_p introduced by De Koninck et al. [3]. The programmer assigns a priority to every rule. The ω_p semantics is an instantiation of ω_t which ensures that of all applicable rules, the one with the highest priority is applied first. Priorities are strictly positive integer numbers, where smaller numbers indicate higher priority.

Consider the gcd program of example 1, executed under ω_p semantics, and annotated with the following (dynamic) priorities:

```
1    :: gcd(N) <=> N =:= 0 | true.
N+2 :: gcd(N) \ gcd(M) <=> N =\= 0, M >= N | gcd(M-N).
```

In this case, the entire guard of the second rule is redundant. The reasoning is as follows. The first rule takes priority over the second rule, so we can derive that if the second rule is applicable, the arguments of both head constraints must be different from zero. Now suppose we have the constraints gcd(A) and gcd(B) and the second rule is applicable for some matching $\theta = \{N/A, M/B\}$, with priority $A + 2$. Suppose that M < N, so $B < A$. The matching $\theta' = \{N/B, M/A\}$ has a lower priority $B + 2 < A + 2$, so the second rule cannot be applicable with matching θ. From this contradiction we can derive that M >= N should always hold when the priority semantics allows the rule to be applicable. So under the priority semantics ω_p, the following simplified program is equivalent to the original program:

```
1    :: gcd(N) <=> N =:= 0 | true.
N+2 :: gcd(N) \ gcd(M) <=> gcd(M-N).
```

We give two more examples to illustrate how we can reason about guards under the ω_p semantics.

Example 9 (static priorities). Consider the following rules:

```
1 :: domain(A,L:U) <=> L > U | fail.
2 :: domain(A,L:U), domain(A,U:L) <=> L = U | A = U.
3 :: domain(A,L:U), domain(A,U:V) <=> L < V | A = U.
```

The first rule removes `domain/2` constraints with an empty domain (lower bound strictly larger than upper bound). When the second rule is tried, we know the first rule is not applicable because of the priorities. So for the second rule, we know that $\neg(L > U)$ and also that $\neg(U > L)$, because otherwise one of the head constraints would have been removed by the first rule. Now we have $\neg(L > U) \wedge \neg(U > L) \leftrightarrow L \leq U \wedge U \leq L \leftrightarrow L = U$, so the guard of the second rule is redundant. Now for the third rule, we know that $L \leq U$ and $U \leq V$ because of the first rule, and also that $L \neq V$ because of the second rule. Hence $L < V$ and the guard of the third rule is also redundant.   □

Example 10 (dynamic priorities). Consider the following rules:

```
X :: a(X,Y,Z) <=> Y > Z | true.
Y :: a(X,Y,Z) <=> X < Z | true.
Z :: a(X,Y,Z) <=> Z > X | true.
```

We can derive that the last rule can never fire. The reasoning is as follows. When we try the last rule for a given `a/3` constraint, the first rule was not applied earlier because it would have removed the constraint. Either the first rule was not applied because the priorities allow non-application (so $Z \leq X$), or it was not applied because the guard failed (so $\neg Y > Z$). So from inspecting the first rule, assuming the last rule can be applied, we can derive that $Z \leq X \vee Y < Z$. Similarly, from inspection of the second rule, we can derive that $Z \leq Y \vee Z < X$. Now if the last rule is applicable, its guard should hold, so $Z > X$. It is easy to see that this is inconsistent with the two derived formulae, so we can conclude that the last rule is redundant and may be removed.   □

In future work we plan to formalize and implement guard reasoning under ω_p semantics.

9 Conclusion

By reasoning about guards and the operational semantics under which the program will be executed, we can automatically identify redundant guards and redundant rules. As a result, a CHR programmer can write a correct program under the general ω_t semantics, and the compiler will convert it to a more efficient program which is only correct under a particular instance of ω_t (for example ω_r or ω_p). Type and mode declarations can also be taken into account.

In order to achieve higher efficiency, CHR programmers often write parts of their program in Prolog if they do not require the additional power of CHR. They no longer need to write mixed-language programs for efficiency: they can simply write the entire program in CHR. Non-declarative auxiliary "host-language interface" constraints like `getFoo/1` (see section 7.2) can be avoided.

9.1 Related Work

Guard simplification is somewhat similar to *switch detection* in Mercury [7]. In Mercury, disjunctions – explicit or implicit (multiple clauses) – are examined for determinism analysis. In general, disjunctions cause a predicate to have multiple solutions. However, if for any given combination of input values, only one of the disjuncts can succeed, the disjunction does not affect determinism. Because they superficially resemble switches in the C programming language, such disjunctions are called *switches*. Switch detection checks unifications involving variables that are bound on entry to the disjunction and occurring in the different branches. In a sense, this is a special case of guard simplification, since guard simplification considers other tests as well, using a more general entailment checking mechanism. Guard simplification analysis can be used to remove redundant guard conditions on the source level, because CHR rules are committed-choice. It is harder to express the switch detection optimization as a source to source transformation for Mercury programs.

Guard simplification and occurrence subsumption can be combined into one analysis. In some intermediate representation, there can be a separate copy of each rule for every constraint occurrence c, where all heads except c are passive. This representation is closer to the generated Prolog code, where each occurrence gets a separate clause in which (after matching the partner constraints) the rule guard and body are duplicated. From this angle, guard simplification is simplifying the guards of all copies of a certain rule at once, while occurrence subsumption is simplifying the guard of one specific copy to `fail`, removing that copy. A stronger and more general optimization can be obtained by simplifying the guard of each copy separately. This optimization can no longer be expressed as a pure source to source transformation. We have elaborated that approach in [15]. While reasoning on the level of constraint occurrences is stronger, it is also computationally more expensive and specific to the refined semantics, which has the concept of active occurrences.

Occurrence subsumption is essentially the same as *fail continuation optimization* [8,9], although our implementation performs much more complex implication reasoning, resulting in a stronger optimization compared to [8,9]. The related concept of *success continuation optimization* [9] was explored in [15]. The K.U.Leuven CHR system currently implements a weak form of success continuation optimization: head matchings are taken into account to skip non-matching occurrences in the continuation of propagation rules. This could be generalized by taking into account all information that can be derived by guard reasoning.

9.2   Future Work

Our current entailment checker can only deal with a limited number of Prolog built-ins. Using domain knowledge declarations, properties of user-defined Prolog predicates can be declared to enhance the capabilities of the entailment checker. The expressivity of such declarations is still fairly limited, and such declarations have to be added manually by the programmer. We see two ways for substantial further improvement. Firstly, the entailment checker could statically evaluate a call to a Prolog predicate to determine its success or failure. Here a conservative approach is essential as the pitfalls of side effects and non-termination must be avoided. Secondly, we may derive a solver for the Prolog predicate from its logic program definition with the techniques of [2]. We conjecture that the latter leads to stronger results than meta-interpretation, but at a greater computational cost.

It would be interesting to explore a generalization of guard simplification that not just removes redundant conjuncts, but also replaces computationally expensive conditions by cheaper ones. For example, consider this program:

```
p(X) <=> X >= 0, g(X) | ...
p(X) <=> X < 0, \+ g(X) | ...
p(X) <=> g(X) | ...
```

If g/1 is a predicate that takes a very long time to evaluate, we could change the guard of the last rule to X<0, because $\neg(X >= 0 \wedge g(X)) \wedge \neg(X < 0 \wedge \neg g(X))$ entails $g(X) \leftrightarrow X < 0$.

When there are many earlier subrules to consider in the guard simplification analysis, the performance of our current implementation may become an issue. Rules with many shared head constraints are an even bigger performance issue, because of the combinatorial blowup caused by constructing all possible mappings from the head of an earlier subrule to the current rule head. For example, if some constraint c occurs n times in the head of an earlier subrule, and m ($\geq n$) times in the current head, there are $\frac{m!}{(m-n)!}$ conditions to be added to the nesr conjunction. In future work we hope to further improve the scalability of our implementation.

The information entailed by the failure and success of guards, used here to eliminate redundant guards and rules, would also be useful in other program analyses and transformations. Of particular interest is the generation of specialized code for individual constraint calls in rule bodies. Taking into account the success and failure leading up to this call, stronger guard simplification may be performed than in the general case.

Finally, an interesting area for future work is the formalization and implementation guard reasoning for the priority semantics, as we mentioned in Section 8. The relation between guards and rule priorities needs further investigation: perhaps a sort of reverse reasoning can be used to simplify priorities given the guards. In this way, it could be possible to replace dynamic priorities by static priorities or to execute part of a program under the more efficient refined semantics, perhaps by adding some guards.

References

1. Abdennadher, S., Frühwirth, T.: Operational equivalence of CHR programs and constraints. In: Jaffar, J. (ed.) CP 1999. LNCS, vol. 1713, pp. 43–57. Springer, Heidelberg (1999)
2. Abdennadher, S., Rigotti, C.: Automatic generation of CHR constraint solvers. In: Abdennadher, S., Frühwirth, T., Holzbaur, C. (eds.) Special Issue on Constraint Handling Rules. TPLP, vol. 5(4–5), pp. 403–418 (2005)
3. De Koninck, L., Schrijvers, T., Demoen, B.: User-definable rule priorities for CHR. In: Leuschel, M., Podelski, A. (eds.) PPDP 2007: Proc. 9th Intl. Conf. Princ. Pract. Declarative Programming, Wroclaw, Poland, pp. 25–36 (Jully 2007)

4. Duck, G., Stuckey, P., García de la Banda, M., Holzbaur, C.: Extending arbitrary solvers with Constraint Handling Rules. In: PPDP 2003: Proc. 5th Intl. Conf. Princ. Pract. Declarative Programming, Uppsala, Sweden (2003)
5. Duck, G.J., Stuckey, P.J., García de la Banda, M., Holzbaur, C.: The refined operational semantics of Constraint Handling Rules. In: Demoen, B., Lifschitz, V. (eds.) ICLP 2004. LNCS, vol. 3132, pp. 90–104. Springer, Heidelberg (2004)
6. Frühwirth, T.: Theory and Practice of Constraint Handling Rules. In: Stuckey, P., Marriot, K. (eds.) Special Issue on Constraint Logic Programming, Journal of Logic Programming, vol. 37(1–3) (October 1998)
7. Henderson, F., Somogyi, Z., Conway, T.: Determinism analysis in the Mercury compiler. In: Proceedings of the 19th Australian Computer Science Conference, Melbourne, Australia, pp. 337–346 (January 1996)
8. Holzbaur, C., García de la Banda, M., Jeffery, D., Stuckey, P.: Optimizing compilation of Constraint Handling Rules. In: Codognet, P. (ed.) ICLP 2001. LNCS, vol. 2237, pp. 74–89. Springer, Heidelberg (2001)
9. Holzbaur, C., García de la Banda, M., Stuckey, P., Duck, G.: Optimizing compilation of Constraint Handling Rules in HAL. In: Abdennadher, S., Frühwirth, T., Holzbaur, C. (eds.) Special Issue on Constraint Handling Rules. TPLP, vol. 5(4–5), pp. 503–531 (2005)
10. Holzbaur, C., Frühwirth, T.: Compiling Constraint Handling Rules into Prolog with attributed variables. In: Nadathur, G. (ed.) PPDP 1999. LNCS, vol. 1702. Springer, Heidelberg (1999)
11. Sarna-Starosta, B., Schrijvers, T.: Indexing techniques for CHR based on program transformation. Technical Report CW 500, K.U.Leuven, Dept. Computer Science (August 2007)
12. Schrijvers, T., Demoen, B.: Antimonotony-based Delay Avoidance for CHR. Technical Report CW 385, K.U.Leuven, Department of Computer Science (July 2004)
13. Schrijvers, T., Demoen, B.: The K.U.Leuven CHR system: implementation and application. In: Frühwirth, T., Meister, M. (eds.) First Workshop on Constraint Handling Rules: Selected Contributions, vol. 2004-01 (2004)
14. Schrijvers, T., Stuckey, P., Duck, G.: Abstract Interpretation for Constraint Handling Rules. In: Proceedings of the 7th Intl. Conference on Principles and Practice of Declarative Programming (PPDP 2005), Lisbon, Portugal (July 2005)
15. Sneyers, J., Schrijvers, T., Demoen, B.: Guard and continuation optimization for occurrence representations of CHR. In: Gabbrielli, M., Gupta, G. (eds.) ICLP 2005. LNCS, vol. 3668, pp. 83–97. Springer, Heidelberg (2005)
16. Sneyers, J., Schrijvers, T., Demoen, B.: Guard simplification in CHR programs. In: Wolf, A., Frühwirth, T., Meister, M. (eds.) Proceedings of the 19th Workshop on (Constraint) Logic Programming (W(C)LP 2005), Ulm, Germany. Ulmer Informatik-Berichte, vol. 2005-01, pp. 123–134 (February 2005)
17. Sneyers, J., Van Weert, P., De Koninck, L., Schrijvers, T.: As time goes by: Constraint Handling Rules — A survey of CHR research between 1998 and 2007. In: TPLP (submitted, 2008)
18. Demoen, B.: hProlog home page, http://www.cs.kuleuven.be/~bmd/hProlog
19. Kaeser, M., et al.: WebCHR., http://chr.informatik.uni-ulm.de/~webchr/
20. Schrijvers, T.: CHR benchmarks and programs. K.U.Leuven CHR home page, http://www.cs.kuleuven.be/~toms/Research/CHR/
21. Wielemaker, J.: SWI-Prolog home page, http://www.swi-prolog.org

A   Correctness Proofs

Detailed definitions of execution state, transition and derivation can be found in [5]. The summary from section 2 should suffice to understand the theorems and proofs below.

First we prove a lemma which will be useful later. Intuitively it says that for every point in a derivation (under ω_r semantics) where a rule can directly be applied with c being the active constraint, there must be an earlier execution state in which the first occurrence of c is about to be checked and where all preconditions for that rule to fire are also fulfilled.

Lemma 1. *If in a derivation $s_0 \rightarrowtail^* s_k$ for P under ω_r semantics, the execution state s_k is of the form $s_k = \langle [c\#i : j|A_k], S_k, B_k, T_k \rangle_{n_k}$, and transitions $s_k \rightarrowtail_{simplify} s_{k+1}$ or $s_k \rightarrowtail_{propagate} s_{k+1}$ are applicable, applying rule R_x, then the derivation contains an intermediate execution state $s_l = \langle [c\#i : 1|A_l], S_l, B_l, T_l \rangle_{n_l}$, such that $s_0 \rightarrowtail^* s_l \rightarrowtail^* s_k$ and for every execution state s_m with $l \leq m \leq k$, the CHR store contains all partner constraints needed for the application of rule R_x and the built-in store entails the guard of rule R_x.*

Proof. Consider the execution state

$$s_{l'} = \langle [c\#i : 1|A_{l'}], S_{l'}, B_{l'}, T_{l'} \rangle_{n_{l'}} \quad (s_0 \rightarrowtail^* s_{l'} \rightarrowtail^* s_k)$$

just after the last **Reactivate** transition that put $c\#i : 1$ at the top of the execution stack; if there was no such transition, consider $s_{l'}$ to be the execution state just after the **Activate** transition that put $c\#i : 1$ at the top of execution stack.

Suppose at some point in the derivation $s_{l'} \rightarrowtail^* s_k$, the built-in store does not entail the guard g_x of R_x. Then the built-in store has to change between that point and s_k, so that after the change it does entail g_x. This will possibly trigger some constraints:

- If c is triggered, then c is reactivated *after* $s_{l'}$, which is a contradiction given the way we defined $s_{l'}$.
- If another constraint d from the head of R_x is triggered, it becomes the active constraint. Now there are two possibilities:
  (a) All constraints from the head of R_x are in the CHR store. This means eventually, either rule R_x will be tried with d as the active constraint, or another partner constraint gets triggered (but not c, because of how we defined $s_{l'}$), in turn maybe triggering other partner constraints, but any way R_x will be tried with one of the partner constraints as the active constraint. Because the built-in store now does entail g_x, the rule fires and a tuple is added to the propagation history. In execution state s_k, this tuple will still be in the propagation history, preventing the application of rule R_x. This is of course a contradiction.
  (b) Not all constraints from the head of R_x are in the CHR store, so some have to be added before s_k is reached, and a similar early-firing happens at the moment the last partner constraint is added, also leading to a contradiction.

– If none of the constraints from the head of R_x are triggered, some of them are not in the CHR store yet, because if they are all there, at least one of them should be triggered, otherwise the change in the built-in store would not affect the entailment of g_x. As a result, some of the constraints occurring in the head of R_x have to be added before s_k is reached so we get a similar early-firing situation as above, again leading to a contradiction.

All these cases lead to a contradiction, so our assumption was wrong. This shows that during the derivation $s_{l'} \rightarrowtail^* s_k$, the built-in store always entails the guard of R_x.

Suppose at some point in the derivation $s_{l'} \rightarrowtail^* s_k$, the CHR store does not contain all partner constraints needed for rule R_x. Then somewhere in that derivation the last of these partner constraints (d) is added to the CHR store, so all constraints needed for R_x are in the CHR store. However, the only transition that could have added d to the CHR store is **Activate**, which also makes d the active constraint. We get an early-firing situation like above because the guard of R_x is entailed and every partner constraint (including c) is now in the CHR store. So we get a contradiction, proving that during the derivation $s_{l'} \rightarrowtail^* s_k$, the CHR store always contains all constraints needed for rule R_x.

To conclude our proof: we have found an execution state s_l with the required properties, namely $s_l = s_{l'}$.   □

Using the previous lemma we now show that the "no earlier subrule fired" formula $\mathsf{nesr}(R_i)$ is logically implied by the built-in store at the moment the rule R_i is applied.

Lemma 2. *If for a given CHR program P, the rule containing the jth occurrence of the CHR predicate c is $R_{c,j}$, and if there is a derivation $s_0 \rightarrowtail^* s_k = \langle [c\#i : j|A], S, B, T\rangle_n$ for P under ω_r semantics, and rule $R_{c,j}$ can be applied in execution state s_k, then we have $\mathcal{D} \models B \rightarrow \bar{\exists}_B \mathsf{nesr}(R_{c,j})$.*

Proof. From the previous lemma follows the existence of an intermediate execution state s_l ($0 \leq l \leq k$), such that for every execution state s_m with $l \leq m \leq k$, the CHR store contains all partner constraints needed for the application of rule $R_{c,j}$ and its guard is entailed by the built-in store.

To prove $\mathcal{D} \models B \rightarrow \bar{\exists}_B \mathsf{nesr}(R_{c,j})$, we show that

$$\forall R_a \in P : (R_a \prec R_{c,j} \land H_a^r \neq \epsilon) \Rightarrow \left(\mathcal{D} \models B \rightarrow \bar{\exists}_B \neg(\theta_a \land g_a)\right)$$

Suppose this is not the case, so assume there exists a non-propagation rule R_a such that $R_a \prec R_{c,j}$ and $\mathcal{D} \models B \land \theta_a \land g_a$. Since $R_{c,j}$ can be applied in execution state s_k, there exists a matching substitution σ matching c and constraints from S to corresponding head constraints of the rule $R_{c,j}$. Because $R_a \prec R_{c,j}$, there exists a number $o_a < j$ such that the o_a^{th} occurrence of c is in rule R_a. There exists an execution state $s_m = \langle [c\#i : o_a|A_m], S_m, B_m, T_m\rangle_{n_m}$ with $l \leq m < k$. From this state, a **Simplify** or **Propagate** transition can fire, applying rule R_a, because:

- all partner constraints are present in S_m;
- there exists a matching substitution θ that matches c and partner constraints from the CHR store to the head constraints of of R_a, namely $\theta = \theta_a \wedge \sigma$;
- the guard g_a is entailed because of our assumption;
- the history does not already contain a tuple for this instance, because R_a removes some of the constraints in its head.

But this application of R_a removes constraints needed for the rule application in s_k, because every head constraint of R_a also appears in $R_{c,j}$. This results in a contradiction. So our assumption was false, and $\mathcal{D} \models B \rightarrow \bar{\exists}_B \mathsf{nesr}(R_{c,j})$.   □

Now we are ready for a theorem stating that guard simplification does not affect the applicability of transitions. Correctness of guard simplification with respect to operational equivalence [1] is a trivial corollary of this theorem.

Theorem 3 (Guard simplification & transitions). *Given a CHR program P and its guard-simplified version $P' = GS(P)$. Given an execution state $s = \langle A, S, B, T \rangle_n$ occurring in some derivation for the P program under ω_r semantics, exactly the same transitions are possible from s for P and for P'. In other words, $\rightarrowtail_P \equiv \rightarrowtail_{P'}$.*

Proof. The **Solve**, **Activate** and **Reactivate** transitions do not depend on the actual CHR program, so obviously their applicability is identical for P and P'. The applicability of **Drop** only depends on the heads of the rules in the program, so again it is identical for P and P'.

If a **Simplify** or **Propagation** transition is possible for P, this means $A = [c\#i : j|A']$ and $\mathcal{D} \models B \rightarrow \bar{\exists}_B g_k$, where k is the rule number of the jth occurrence of c. According to lemma 2, we now know that $\mathcal{D} \models B \rightarrow \bar{\exists}_B \mathsf{nesr}(R_k)$. The rule R'_k is identical to R_k except for its guard g'_k, so the same transition is possible for P' unless the guard g'_k fails (while g_k succeeds). This can only happen if for some part $g_{k,x}$ of the conjunction g_k we have $\mathcal{D} \models \bar{\exists}_B \mathsf{nesr}(R_k) \wedge \bigwedge_{m<x} g_{k,m} \rightarrow \neg g_{k,x}$. Now we can derive a contradiction: $\mathcal{D} \models B \rightarrow \bar{\exists}_B \mathsf{nesr}(R_k)$ and $\mathcal{D} \models B \rightarrow \bar{\exists}_B g_k$ combined with the previous statement gives $\mathcal{D} \models B \rightarrow \neg \bar{\exists}_B g_k$ because of course $\forall m \models g_k \rightarrow g_{k,m}$.

If a **Simplify** or **Propagation** transition is possible for P', this means $A = [c\#i : j|A']$ and $\mathcal{D} \models B \rightarrow \bar{\exists}_B \mathsf{nesr}(R_k)$. Again, assume the jth occurrence of c is in the kth rule. The same transition is also possible for P, unless for some x, $\mathcal{D} \models B \rightarrow \neg \bar{\exists}_B g_{k,x}$. If there is more than one of such x's, choose the smallest one, i.e. let $g_{k,x}$ be the first part of the guard conjunction that fails. Note that $\mathcal{D} \models B \rightarrow \bar{\exists}_B \bigwedge_{m<x} g_{k,m}$. Because $\mathcal{D} \models B \rightarrow \bar{\exists}_B g'_{k,x}$, we know that $g_{k,x} \neq g'_{k,x}$, and because of the definition of guard simplification, this can only be the case if $\mathcal{D} \models \mathsf{nesr}(R_k) \wedge \bigwedge_{m<x} g_{k,m} \rightarrow g_{k,x}$. Again, this results in a contradiction, so the applicability of **Simplify** and **Propagation** is identical for P and P'.

Since the applicability of **Default** only depends on the applicability of the other transitions, it is also identical for P and P'. We showed that the applicability of any of the seven possible transitions is unchanged by guard simplification, concluding our proof.   □

Corollary 1 (Correctness of GS). *Under the refined operational semantics, any CHR program P and its guard-simplified version P' are operationally equivalent.*

Proof. According to the previous theorem, $\rightarrowtail_P \,\equiv\, \rightarrowtail_{P'}$, so all states are trivially P, P'-joinable.   □

For definitions of operational equivalence and joinable states we refer the reader to [1]. Now we can show that subsumable occurrences may be skipped (i.e. can be made passive). More formally:

Theorem 4 (Correctness of Occ. Subsumption). *Given a CHR program P and an ω_r derivation for P in which an execution state $s = \langle [c\#i : j|A], S, B, T\rangle_n$ occurs. If c_j is occurrence subsumable, **Simplify** and **Propagate** transition cannot (directly) be applied on state s.*

Proof. Suppose the **Simplify** or **Propagate** transition can be applied, firing rule R. Using the notation from definition 10, this means that $\mathcal{D} \models B \to \bar{\exists}_B \mathsf{fc}(R, c_j)$ Also, lemma 2 tells us that $\mathcal{D} \models B \to \bar{\exists}_B \mathsf{nesr}(R)$. Because of lemma 1 we know that rule R has been tried for the earlier occurrences of c in that rule. These tries must have failed, because R is a constraint-removing rule (c_j is occurrence subsumable) which cannot be applied twice on the same constraints. So

$$\forall k : m \le k < j \Rightarrow \mathcal{D} \models B \to \neg\bar{\exists}_B \theta_k\big(\mathsf{fc}(R, c_k)\big)$$

where θ_k is a renaming such that $\theta_k(c_k) = c_j$. This is equivalent to $\mathcal{D} \models B \to \bar{\exists}_B \mathsf{neocc}(R, c_j)$. Because c_j is occurrence subsumable, we have $\mathcal{D} \models B \to \neg\bar{\exists}_B \mathsf{fc}(R, c_j)$, which results in a contradiction. So the **Simplify** and **Propagate** transitions are indeed not applicable in state s.   □

Author Index